The Puritan Gift

The first American chief executive officer
John Winthrop, governor of the Massachusetts Bay Company
(1629–1633, 1637–1639, 1642–1643, 1646–1648).

The CEO is an American invention. There is no real counterpart . . . in
the management of any country
> Peter F. Drucker, author of the bestseller,
> *The Practice of Management,* who encouraged the authors
> to write this book (see page xviii)

*To Charles Warren IV
with best regards*

February 13, 2009

THE PURITAN GIFT

Reclaiming the American Dream Amidst Global Financial Chaos

KENNETH HOPPER
AND
WILLIAM HOPPER

www.puritangift.com

Will Hopper

I.B. TAURIS

LONDON · NEW YORK

New paperback edition published in 2009 by I.B.Tauris & Co Ltd
6 Salem Road, London W2 4BU
175 Fifth Avenue, New York NY 10010
www.ibtauris.com

Distributed in the United States of America and Canada Exclusively by
Palgrave Macmillan, 175 Fifth Avenue, New York NY 10010

First published in hardback in 2007 by I.B.Tauris & Co Ltd

ISBN: 978 1 84511 986 7

A full CIP record for this book is available from the British Library
A full CIP record is available from the Library of Congress

Library of Congress Catalog Card Number: available

Typeset by JCS Publishing Services Ltd, www.jcs-publishing.co.uk
Printed and bound in Great Britain by the MPG Books Group United Kingdom

To Claire,
without whose unfailing patience, support and good humor
this book could not have been written

and to Munisha and James

One ship sails East, and another West,
By the self-same winds that blow.
'Tis the set of sails, and not the gales
That tells the way we go.

Ella Wheeler Wilcox, *Poems of Progress* (1911)

This is our time – to put our people back to work and open doors of opportunity for our kids; to restore prosperity and promote the cause of peace; to reclaim the American Dream and reaffirm that fundamental truth – that out of many, we are one.

President-elect Barack Hussein Obama, Chicago, November 5, 2008

Contents

List of Illustrations

New Foreword
by Russell Lincoln Ackoff

This is one of the best books I have ever read in my long life, and I don't just mean books on business. The brothers Hopper have written a social history of the American nation, which doubles up as a commentary on managerial culture. I am indebted to them for providing an understanding of the evolution of American society from the 1630s to the present day. *The Puritan Gift* is no dry academic text. It is also exciting. I am *excited* to learn how Puritan values shaped the development of American society – and saddened to learn how a recent retreat from them has led to the economic and social problems afflicting our nation today, including the contemporary Credit Crunch. As I write, our economy is in a mess, the worst that I have experienced. Few, if any, understand what is going on. Moreover, there is little awareness of the weaknesses that led to our current discontentment. I once heard an economist say that the proof of the superiority of the American economy lay in the fact that no other could survive as much inefficiency as it generates; even if that were true, it would provide us with little comfort today. The Hoppers tell us not only how we got into the current mess, which is interesting, but also how to escape, which is useful.

In addition, the book shines a bright light on the American Occupation of Japan. Edwin E. Reischauer, President Kennedy's Ambassador to Japan, told us long ago that this event 'will stand as one of the most ... important as well as spectacular episodes in the epochal meeting of East and West, which may become increasingly the dominant theme in the history of mankind in our age, recasting or even overshadowing the [Cold War].' That the Occupation achieved such success was attributable in large part to the excellent managerial practices associated with the name of General Douglas MacArthur, the effective ruler of Japan from 1945 to 1951. I was especially impressed by the story told by the Hoppers of how MacArthur listened to the advice of one of his most junior colleagues, the American engineer, Homer Sarasohn, before making a decision that would change the nature of the world we live in (see pages 119 to 120).

There is an old saying to the effect that if you never make a mistake, you will never make anything. Intolerance of mistakes precludes learning; we will never learn anything new by doing something right, because that merely confirms what we already know. We learn by identifying mistakes and correcting them. It is not sinful to be wrong but it is sinful to fail to learn from it. There are two kinds of error: those of *commission*, doing something that should not be done, and those of *omission*, not doing something that should be done. The latter are much more serious than the former. Most corporate failures are due to errors of omission. A firm that records only mistakes of commission (as almost all do) and punishes them (as most do) creates an environment in which the best way to retain one's job is to do as little as possible, preferably nothing. The Puritans knew that progress was not possible without change; they sought and welcomed it, despite the hardships that it entailed.

The Hoppers make a serious charge in Chapter 14. In a section called 'Capital Expenditure and the (So-called) Experts' from pages 203 to 207, they remind us that the Vietnam War caused serious inflation in the 1960s. Anxious to pursue that war to its end, the administration sought to convince the American people that the rise in prices was the result of over-investment by American manufacturers. Statistics purporting to show that existing equipment was extremely young – and that large-scale additional investment was, therefore, unnecessary and perhaps even harmful – were presented to the public with the full authority of the US Department of Commerce. In June 1970, Kenneth Hopper challenged the accuracy of these figures by means of a Special Report published in a McGraw-Hill journal. The administration stopped using them there and then, but failed to acknowledge its error. Industrial investment collapsed and did not recover until the 1980s.

Most occupations have their proud traditions, an exception being the corps of industrial managers. However, no other group of people has done more to raise the standard of living of the poorest of the world, both at home and abroad. *The Puritan Gift* is the first book to acquaint American managers with their own remarkable history. They created the most effective industrial culture in the world; we can be proud that, after World War II, they shared it with the inhabitants of Japan and other developing lands.

Above all this book is a 'very good read'. I love the many and enjoyable anecdotes – for example, the story of how the youthful Homer Sarasohn taught the founders of Sony to sweep the floor (pages 117–119). There are many managers at work today who could learn from his example.

Russell Lincoln Ackoff
Anheuser-Busch Professor Emeritus of Management Science
Wharton School, University of Pennsylvania
January 1, 2009

Authors' Introduction
to the Paperback Edition

If this financial crisis has taught us anything, it's that we cannot have a thriving Wall Street while Main Street suffers – in this country, we rise or fall as one nation, as one people.
  President-elect Barack Hussein Obama, Chicago, November 5, 2008

There is nothing wrong with America that cannot be cured with what is right with America.
        President William Jefferson Clinton, First inaugural address,
                                                            January 21, 1993

The Puritan Gift depicts how America's superb managerial culture, originating in seventeenth-century New England, evolved to make the United States the most powerful nation on earth. Chapter 10 describes in addition how America shared the secrets of its economic success with Japan after World War II, resulting in an explosion of growth in that country. Japan re-taught that same methodology to her neighbors, resulting in the various Asian Economic Miracles; it now forms part of the common heritage of mankind.

We diagnose the *proximate* cause for the current Credit Crunch as an excess of borrowing by government, businesses and individuals. Credit is to a country what steroids are to an athlete; it enhances performance but, unless used in moderation, at serious cost to economic health. Increasingly, reckless lending and borrowing – two sides of the same coin – have characterized most aspects of American society for the last thirty years. In November 2008, it resulted in the near collapse and part-nationalization of the world's largest bank by revenues, Citigroup Inc.

This abuse of credit across the whole of society coincided with, and could not have occurred without, a deterioration in corporate culture occurring in the last third of the twentieth century. In the Golden Age of Management (1920–1970), executives had learned the craft of management 'on the job' from more senior colleagues. As they progressed up the ladder of promotion, they would also absorb 'domain knowledge' about the activity for which they were responsible – to borrow a term favoured by Jeff Immelt, chairman and chief executive of General Electric. Starting in the late 1960s, however, a new concept appeared on the corporate scene: that management was a profession like medicine, dentistry or the law, which people were 'licensed' to practice at the highest level if they had studied the subject in an academic setting. Business school graduates and accountants set the pattern of behavior; others would follow in their footsteps. In 2001 a 'professional' manager entered the Oval Office of the White House to take charge of the nation.

As a result of this revolutionary change in outlook, it was no longer deemed necessary for executives to learn the craft of management as they rose through the ranks – or, for that matter, to acquire and make use of 'domain knowledge'. The new style of senior manager sought to control the organization through the medium of the finance department, while delegating the tedious task of acquiring and using 'domain knowledge' to juniors. Because the executives focused on figures, rather than on the activities that generated them, they attracted to themselves an ironic monicker: 'financial engineer'. The outcome has been managerial incompetence on a scale inconceivable in earlier generations and extending over much of society. Immelt has told us that he loathes the very notion of 'professional' management (see page 253).

Citigroup Inc. was a victim of this declension. Between 1959 and 1984, it had been run by two competent commercial bankers: George S. Moore, who became president at the beginning of this period, and Walter B. Wriston, who followed suit eight years later. Moore has been described as a 'feisty Missourian who built the biggest bank in the world'; he was well known for intuitively identifying patterns in human behavior, once observing that the most important managerial skill was an ability to 'recognize the same girl with different clothes'. One of Wriston's favorite sayings was that 'you are not a real banker until you have made a bad loan'; if *he* was alive today, he would heartily agree with Professor Ackoff's observations on the importance of learning from mistakes (see the Foreword).

Things would go tragically wrong in 1984, however, when a new-style 'professional' manager was appointed as chairman and chief executive in the person of John S. Reed. The possessor of two business school degrees, he would proudly declare himself to be 'not a banker'. On his watch, the company would suffer a near-death experience in 1991, when it lost almost $1 billion and failed to pay an annual dividend for the first time since 1818. Crude cost-cutting followed and morale dropped, as thousands were sacked in an apparently random fashion. Reed has been described as the kind of boss with whom no-one wished to share bad news;[1] this meant that the flow of accurate information up a line-of-command, which lies at the heart of all good management (see page 194), could not occur.

When Reed was ousted in 2000, an opportunity existed for a new beginning; regrettably, he would be replaced by two men cast in a similar 'professional' mold: a corporate lawyer called Charles O. Prince III, who had assisted the group with some acquisitions, and the economist, Robert E. Rubin. When the financial crisis broke in August 2007, Prince was Citigroup's chairman and chief executive, while Rubin was chairman of its executive committee. Neither had been in touch with what the Japanese call the *gemba,* the real place, the place where business was done (see page 167). Prince has since been relieved of his command but Rubin soldiers on, defending his recent conduct on the absurd grounds that he was not involved in any decision-making. A century ago, Pierre du Pont, chairman and in some senses creator of the modern chemical company of that name, defined for all time the functions of an executive committee (see pages 82–89); needless to say, they include strategic decision-making, a role properly playable only if the members of the committee are close to the *gemba.* For not making decisions over the past eight years, Rubin has been rewarded with pay of $115 million.[2]

What is to be done with Citigroup? It is important for two reasons to address this question. First, as we explained above, Citigroup is the world's largest bank by revenues, employing over 350,000 people in 12,000 offices in 107 countries. Secondly, its problems are symptomatic of a sickness that affects much of American society. If we can resolve Citigroup's problems, we can cure that sickness. Many solutions have been offered, such as better regulation. Undoubtedly, some of the major abuses affecting the financial sector in recent years would not have occurred if the federal government – with Rubin's blessing when he was Secretary of the Treasury from 1995 to 1999 – had not relaxed the laws that divide commercial from investment banking. However, there are limitations to what law-makers can achieve; one can legislate against vice but not for virtue.

American business badly needs a powerful dose of Puritan virtue, in the form of a reversion to earlier ways of thinking, talking and doing. How is this to be achieved? Chapter 10, which is entitled *Three Wise Men from the West go to Japan,* offers a precedent and a solution. When General Douglas MacArthur became the effective Ruler of the Chrysanthemum Kingdom after World War II, he arranged for 1,937 incompetent senior executives in 154 leading companies to be replaced by competent managers drawn from the ranks of middle management. MacArthur was acting on the advice of a department of his command called the Civil Communications Section (CCS). Since the first edition of our book appeared in March 2007, two independent academic studies have confirmed the importance of role played by that section in teaching the Japanese how to manage.[3]

Today the senior ranks of American business are filled with 'professional' managers like Prince and Rubin who lack 'domain knowledge' but reward themselves with annual salaries of $1 million or more. Such people contribute little to the well-being of their companies or of society. Meantime, the middle ranks of those same firms include thousands of competent men and women who, perforce, possess and use 'domain knowledge'; for many of them, an annual salary well under those now demanded for senior executives would offer a share in the American Dream. President Barack Obama should invite the pension plans, insurance companies and other institutional investors who are the owners of corporate America (and who have suffered so much from the Credit Crunch) to insist on the replacement of the current generation of senior executives with less greedy men and women. The original MacArthur by his intervention paved the way for the Japanese Economic Miracle; by reincarnating the General, Obama could promote his own, strictly American, version of that event.

There is also much to do abroad. It is abundantly clear that continuing growth in developing nations is essential for the economic health of the whole world. The current crisis restricts the amount of financial help that the United States and other developed countries can offer them. However, there is one gift that is both cheaper to give and more valuable to receive than money – namely, good advice of the sort that the CCS engineers provided for Japan. As temporary US civil servants, they were obliged to document their decisions and actions in detail on onion-skins with multiple carbon copies. Millions of these items have been preserved for posterity in the US National Archives, many now on microfiche. In this book we have re-created the essential lessons which they taught their pupils. A CCS Institute should be formed to teach them to all who are interested. Post-war Japan provides a model for today's developing countries.

Kenneth Hopper
William Hopper
January 1, 2009

Preface

The origins of this book lie in the middle of the last century.

Our father, Dr. I. Vance Hopper, was a senior lecturer at the Royal Technical College in Glasgow, an institution formed in 1796 as Anderson's College under the last will and testament of John Anderson, Professor of Natural Philosophy (or Physics) in the University of Glasgow. Anderson was one of the outstanding figures of the great Scottish Enlightenment. He wanted the new college to direct its efforts to what he called 'Useful Learning' – the application of scientific theory to the solution of practical problems. It was to be a 'polytechnic' or school of all the technologies. The great Ecole Polytechnique had been founded in Paris only two years before; Anderson's was to be the first of its kind outside France. Anderson's College is now the University of Strathclyde.

Dad was proud to be an industrial chemist. Chairman of the Scottish branch of the Society of Chemical Industry, he was also one of the authors of *Systematic Organic Chemistry: Modern Methods of Preparation and Estimation* (1923, 1931, 1937, 1950), which educated more than one generation of students and is still occasionally consulted. The names of its three authors caused some amusement when the book first appeared, since each referred to some form of motion: Cumming, Hopper and Wheeler. It was Dr. W.M. Cumming who set me off on the path that led, ultimately, to the writing of this book.

Cumming was of the opinion that the best-managed manufacturing company in Britain at that time was Thomas Hedley, a wholly-owned subsidiary of Procter & Gamble. He suggested I should work for them. After serving an engineering apprenticeship at two British companies, I joined Hedley's and was at once struck by the sophistication and efficacy of its managerial culture. I would later discover that what had impressed me there was typical of US manufacturing as a whole; American industrial companies of that period were, quite simply, better managed than others. I resolved to learn a great deal more about different national approaches. It was a project that would take me to Ireland just when the 'Celtic Miracle' was getting underway; to a continental Europe resurgent after World War II; to the United States then at the height of its economic and political power; and to a Japan well on the way to possessing the second largest economy in the world. My observations were recorded in journal and newspaper articles, some of which are listed at the end of the bibliography and feature in the website, www.puritangift.com. Later I would be able to observe the decline in the quality of American management which occurred in the last third of the twentieth century.

Some years ago I resolved to summarize my thoughts in a book but was unable to complete it owing to ill-health. Fortunately, my brother William was able to come to my assistance. The greater part of this publication has been written by him. In undertaking this task, he has also widened its scope. My principal interest has always been the management of the factory and its history. A linguist by training and an investment banker by profession, William extended the range of the subject-matter to include all aspects of business, government and even, to some extent, the structure of society itself. This book is now a history of American managerial culture in the broadest sense from 1630 to the present day: its rise, triumph, decline and partial recovery. Although it has been written in non-technical language for the general reader, we hope that it will also appeal to those who have a specialist interest in the subject.

In the course of this lengthy project, many people have helped us along the way. They include that remarkable man, the late Dr. Peter Drucker, whom I met through William when they worked together at W.R. Grace & Co. in New York in the late 1950s. When Drucker saw an early draft of this book, he wrote, 'I am tremendously interested in what you write and impressed by it. I look forward to your book on the subject. Don't forget to tell your publisher to send me an order form.' Sadly, *The Puritan Gift* has been published just too late for that.

It was Drucker who introduced us to Frank Polkinghorn, Charles Protzman and Homer Sarasohn, the 'Three Wise Men from the West' featured in Chapter 10 who had taught then contemporary American managerial practices to the Japanese in the late 1940s and in 1950. Through them, my wife, Claire, and I met their former pupil, Bunzaemon Inoue. Under the US occupation of Japan (1945–1952), Inoue had been a factory manager at Sumitomo Electric, in which capacity he co-chaired the two seminars on management which the Americans presented to the communications equipment industry in Tokyo and Osaka in 1949 and 1950. On page 92, he can be seen alongside his mentors in a photograph taken at the graduation ceremony following the second of these events. In 1962, and under the direction of Inoue as its director of technical (*sic*) and production, Sumitomo Electric would win the first Deming Prize for Quality in Manufacturing in which 'participative' practices featured as a major element. Starting in 1979, he wrote me some sixty letters describing how Japanese manufacturing evolved between 1930, the year he joined Sumitomo Electric, and 1986, the year of his last letter. This correspondence constitutes a unique source of historical information.

We also remember fondly that great, generous character, the late Dr. W. Edwards Deming, after whom Sumitomo Electric's Prize was named. Deming would fight a legendary battle with the philistines of American top management in the 1980s, during what we have called the Years that the Locust Ate. When he saw the early draft of this book referred to above, he wrote to say, 'This is just what I have been looking for'; without his generous moral and financial support, it would not have gone to press.

Encouragement also came at a critical time from another independent-minded thinker, Dr. Myron Tribus, former Undersecretary of Commerce for Science and Technology under President Nixon and later the Director of the Center for Advanced Engineering Studies at MIT – a man who now calls himself 'a recovering academic'. On reading that same early draft, he wrote: 'I felt like a small boy who went out to shoot squirrels and came back with an elephant'.

We were pleased to find our admiration for the organization of mid-twentieth-century American companies echoed in the work of Alfred D. Chandler, the distinguished Harvard Historian of Business. Having been kind enough to read our essay 'Capital Expenditure and the so-called Experts' (see pages 203 to 207), he wrote to say that 'this is a fascinating, if depressing story of a significant piece of political folly . . . it is most important that this piece be published'. It appears here for the first time.

As readers will discover (see pages 114 and 115) my presence in 1964 and 1965 at the Harvard Business School did not meet with the approval of its entire Faculty. I am grateful to Professor Glenn Varney of Ohio State University at Bowling Green and the late George Odiorne, Dean of the Division of Industrial Relations at the University of Michigan, for throwing a lifeline to me from the great manufacturing Midwest when I needed it. George invited me to be the opening speaker in his winter series of lectures for industry in 1967. Glenn arranged for me to give lecture tours across America and Britain later in that decade. I learned a great deal in this way.

Lastly, may I say how grateful I am to my brother for turning *The Puritan Gift: Reclaiming the American Dream Amidst Global Financial Chaos* into a reality. He does not shirk controversy. If we achieve nothing else, we will have recorded how important parts of American society functioned at the mid-twentieth century.

Kenneth Hopper
Hackettstown, NJ 07840
November, 2006

Acknowledgements

In addition to those mentioned in the Preface, the authors wish to thank the following for their moral support and practical assistance: Norman Stone, formerly professor of Modern History at Oxford; Robert Chote, director of the Institute for Fiscal Studies in London; Professor James R. Clauson, moderator of the Deming Electronic Network, Clemson University; Anderson Ashburn; Gloria Reo; Professor Dr. Martin Haemmig, advisor to the World Economic Forum on Chinese venture capital; Roger Schenke, executive vice president, the American College of Physician Executives; Professor Peter Kawalek, Manchester Business School; David Howard, Management-NewStyle Limited; Mark Tully, the BBC's veteran India correspondent; Rona Mosler and the Hackettstown Public Library, New Jersey; Bill Bellows of Pratt & Whitney Rocketdyne, Inc.; and Charles Protzman III, chairman of Business Improvement Group LLC. Protzman provided the personal statement which appears on page 279.

We also thank Jeremy Bramah, Lynn Brian, Walter Brinkmann, Avery Chope, Nicholas Collins, Ian Craig-Wood, Jessica Cuthbert-Smith, Kenton W. Elderkin, Bill and Victoria Ellington, Robert Fenwick Elliott, John and Anita Holochwost, Claire Hopper, Rhonda Klevansky, Rick McKillop, Ian McLeish, Munisha, Mark Nevard, Jan Nussbaum, Dee and Geza Pap, Jim and Appleseed Robinson, Edith and Edward Savage, Bonnie and Steven Scher, Gerald Shalet, Martin Shelley, Melisa Treasure, Anthony Tylecote, Glenn and Connie Varney, Pip and Keith White, and Henry Winslow; as well as the staffs of the New York Public Library, the London Library and the Harvard Baker Library for their willingness to find texts and their unfailing good nature when we failed to return them on time. Kenneth Hopper would like to make a special reference to former colleagues with whom he worked at Associated Industrial Consultants in Britain and Ireland and at Procter & Gamble in Britain, from whom he learned much. Danielle Colman kindly prepared the index and checked the endnotes.

All the research required to produce this book was undertaken by us in our spare time. If there are errors of fact or opinion, we are beyond a shadow of a doubt responsible for them.

Prologue

The Puritan Gift is a rare ability to create organizations that serve a useful purpose, and to manage them well. It was first brought to the shores of North America in the seventeenth century by the migrants who founded the Commonwealth of Massachusetts, a political institution that has survived and prospered for almost four hundred years. In the eighteenth century, it inspired the creation of a federal political structure that enabled thirteen obscure colonies situated at the very edge of the civilized world to convert themselves, with the passage of time, into a Great Power situated at its center. In the nineteenth century, it underlay a series of inland migrations and the building of a network of canals and railroads that opened up, and bound together, almost an entire continent. In the twentieth, it generated unimaginable wealth that enabled the citizens of the United States, among other things, to fight two simultaneous wars, one in the Atlantic and one in the Pacific, and to send a manned spaceship to the moon.

The mature corporate culture that emerged in this way would be successfully transplanted to Japan under the US Occupation (1945–1952), initiating, first, a managerial revolution and, then, an Economic Miracle that turned a poor country lacking natural resources into the second richest in the world. The principles and practices enshrined in this culture would then be re-exported from Japan to other parts of East Asia – in the 1960s and 1970s to the future 'Asian Tigers', and, from the 1980s onwards, to an impoverished mainland China, which now enjoys the greatest economic boom experienced anywhere in human history.

Back on the American ranch, however, all was not well. Businessmen and others abandoned the very procedures that the Occupation authorities had taught Japan's manufacturers, replacing them with the worship of the false gods of the Cult of the (so-called) Expert, which we describe in detail in the later chapters of this book. Inflation, almost unknown in the United States in the Eisenhower years (1953–1961), became the order of the day. Growth slowed and, at times, disappeared. Simultaneously, wealth was massively redistributed in relative terms from poor to rich. Since 2000, there has been a modest reversal of direction, leading one to hope that there will be a return to traditional ways of doing things.

This book describes in outline, and occasionally in some detail, all of these developments. It also draws three lessons. The first is that, if the rate of economic growth characterizing the American economy from 1870 to 1970 is to be restored, businessmen and others must re-discover the secrets of their predecessors' success as organizers. There is a surprising ignorance today about how business was done only half a century ago, totally misleading statements being routinely offered to an unsuspecting public by academics and consultants who should know better. This book attempts to set the record straight by recording how the nation's corporate culture came into being and what it was like at its zenith; and by elucidating, in the Appendix, the half-forgotten principles of good management on which it depended.

The second lesson is that, if the whoring after false managerial gods is abandoned in favor of the pursuit of true ones, the uneven redistribution of relative wealth that occurred in the United States in recent decades can be halted and perhaps even reversed. Much commercial activity in the United States since 1970 is best described as 'financial engineering', rather than true wealth creation – and the chief beneficiaries, needless to say, are the 'financial engineers'. The vogue for this kind of activity started on Wall Street in the 1960s but, as Mark Gimein told us in *BusinessWeek* in 2006, 'over the last two decades, it has migrated from Wall Street to the rest of the business world'.[1] Insofar as true wealth creation becomes once again the norm, all elements in society will benefit, as they did before.

The third lesson is to be drawn specifically from East Asia: no nation or society is condemned to poverty by its past. Until World War II, it was assumed that rapid economic growth was a characteristic only of Western societies. When General Douglas MacArthur became the ruler of Japan at the mid-twentieth century, he demonstrated that America's inherited managerial culture could be successfully introduced to a less enlightened land. There is no absolute reason why, with the right approach and the right teachers, his success cannot be replicated today throughout Asia and Africa. Humanity does not have to live perpetually in a two-speed world, in which over half the people are sunk in perpetual misery.

The lessons that America brought to Japan in the 1940s, and which the Japanese taught to the Asian Tigers and China, will continue to reverberate round the world. Capitalism, as practiced in the United States at the mid-twentieth century, is achieving what Marxism could never do; the Puritan Gift to America is also America's gift to the world.

PART I

ORIGINS

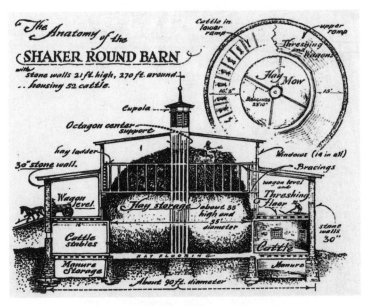

1: Round Stone Barn (1780). See page 31.

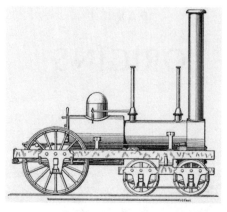

2: A locomotive called *Brother Jonathan*, originally known as
The Experiment (1832).[1] See page 65.

3: SS *Brother Jonathan* (1865). See also page 65.

1

The Puritan Origins of American Managerial Culture[1]

Traditional American society, particularly but not only in New England, possessed a quartet of characteristics, intimately bound together, that reached back to the earliest days of the Bay Colony of Massachusetts and still colors the outlook of most citizens of the United States. These were: a conviction that the purpose of life, however vaguely conceived, was to establish the Kingdom of Heaven on Earth; an aptitude for the exercise of mechanical skills; a moral outlook that subordinated the interests of the individual to the group; and an ability to assemble, galvanize and marshal financial, material and human resources to a single purpose and on a massive, or a lesser, scale. All of these elements were associated with the colony's Puritan origins.

The Puritan movement originated in the British Isles around 1560, when dissident members of the Church of England, still the mother church of the Anglican Communion today, attempted to 'purify' it by removing all trace of its Roman Catholic past. All four of the characteristics described above were already present among the founders, the Bay Colony being simply an extension of an important part of English society. Thus, for a brief period, some people on both sides of the Atlantic sought to create their ideal society on earth as a material as well as a spiritual realm – a society to be constructed by dint of hard, physical work and the application of intelligence. From the outset, there was an emphasis on the importance of both mechanical and managerial skills, as well as a willingness on the part of individuals to subordinate their personal interests to a concept of a greater good. The Puritan migration to America of the 1630s – of which much more in Chapter 2 – was a masterpiece of organization, from which many important lessons can be learned today.

The famous English essayist and jurist, Sir Francis Bacon (1561–1626), was both the philosopher of Puritanism and the prophet, at least by implication, of the Industrial Revolution to come. Bacon had studied at Cambridge University, which (unlike its more conservative rival, Oxford) was a hotbed of religious dissent. A pious Christian, he told us that: 'A little philosophy inclineth man's mind to atheism, but depth in philosophy bringeth men's minds about to religion'.[2] He also wrote, eloquently, about the importance of the 'mechanical arts' – as he called them – which, 'founded on nature and the light of experience . . . are continually thriving and growing, as having in them a breath of life, at the first rude, then convenient, afterwards adorned, and at all times advancing'.[3] For him, there were three things that made a nation great: 'a fertile soil, busy workshops [and] easy conveyance for men and goods from place to place' – all being dependent on tools devised by man and the third pointing to an increasing mastery of the technology of travel, without which the Puritan migration could not have succeeded.

Bacon particularly admired the 'recent' inventions of printing, gunpowder and the compass (the 'mariner's needle'):

> For these three have changed the whole face and state of things throughout the world; the first in literature, the second in warfare, the third in navigation; whence have followed innumerable changes, insomuch that no empire, no sect, no star seems to have exerted greater power and influence in human affairs than these mechanical discoveries.[4]

Joint-stock companies would pay a key role in the future industrialization of both Old and New England. Bacon was a pioneer in their development in his capacity as one of the seven hundred shareholders in the Virginia Company, which made the first permanent English settlement in North American in 1607. Like many future capitalists, he lost money on this venture.[5] The Baconian view of life and work was imported by the Puritans into New England, where it took deeper root than in Old England and would shape not just the economy but the very nature and structure of society. In 1865, the French author, Jules Verne, would remark in his novel *From the Earth to the Moon* that 'Yankees, who are the world's finest mechanics, are engineers in the same way as Italians are musicians and Germans are metaphysicians – they were born that way'.[6] With uncanny insight, Verne foresaw the moon shot of 1969, when human beings first set foot on the earth's largest satellite, the ultimate achievement (in both senses of that term) of America's great mechanic culture.

The desire to create the Kingdom of Heaven on Earth was famously encapsulated in a sermon delivered by John Winthrop, founding governor of the colony, to his fellow migrants in 1630 apparently before they set sail. New England was to be 'as a Citty on a Hill', a phrase he borrowed from the gospel of St. Matthew. As such, it was to be a model for succeeding American 'plantations' – the name then often given to colonies – so that men would say that the Lord had made them 'like that of New England'.

In 1835, the French writer, Alexis de Tocqueville, in *Democracy in America*, would describe the civilization of New England as 'a beacon lit upon mountain tops which, after warming all in its vicinity, casts a glow over the distant horizon', permeating the entire Union.[7] This characteristic would be partly secularized by the 1850s into a belief in 'manifest destiny', leading to the famous call to the nation's male youth to 'go West and grow up with the country', attributed to Horace Greeley, founder and first editor of the *New York Tribune*. In its original form, it finds a persisting expression in the beliefs and practices of certain Protestant sects, which believe that Christ will return again and even make his appearance in America.

More generally, it expresses itself in a spirit of unyielding optimism about the future of society – which the citizens of other countries do not share – coupled with a conviction that problems exist to be solved. One of its purest exemplars was Benjamin Franklin, of whom Stacy Schiff has said that he 'truly believed it was always morning in America'. (According to Schiff, Franklin also offered us the best one-line definition of America: 'the New World judges a man not by who he is but by what he can do'.)[8] In much the same spirit, Thomas Jefferson cunningly converted John Locke's 'life, liberty and the pursuit of estate [property]' into 'life, liberty and the pursuit of happiness'. More recently, this outlook has found a popular embodiment in the cartoon figure, Superman, who believes in 'Truth, Justice and the American Way'. Although born on the planet Krypton, Superman grew up in Smallville, USA and, therefore doubles up as an ordinary American as well as a heroic, indeed godlike, figure.[9]

There is more than a hint of Superman in the personalities and outlook of Larry Page and Sergey Brin, the two roller-skating, flower-power-inspired founders of the computer science company, Google Inc., which now dominates the world of communications. Their motto is, 'Don't be evil'. We have been told that they are motivated by 'puritanical fanaticism' and a desire to change the world, making it a better place'; a visitor to their head office is reported to have said that he felt he was in the 'company of missionaries'. Another observer says that 'Google is a religion posing as a company'.[10] What will the world resemble if they succeed in transforming it? No-one knows – not even they.

A willingness to become involved in mechanical tasks and to get one's hands dirty distinguished American society from older and more stratified nations in Europe from the outset. This was not just a matter of indentured servants and the artisan class. An anonymous source tells us that, by the time they made landfall, the settlers from the advance party had become demoralized. However, 'Now so soon as Mr Winthrop was landed, perceiving what misery was like to ensewe through theire Idleness, he presently fell to worke with his own hands & thereby soe encouradged the rest that there was not an idle person in the whole plantation'. When not involved in governing, he would be observed 'putting his hand to ordinary labor with the servants'.[11] When he died, a box of carpenter's tools was found among his effects.

The connection between craftsmanship and godliness is well illustrated in the sermons of the Rev. John Cotton. Having served as the parish priest of Boston in Old England, he was appointed to the new post of teacher in the parish of Boston, Massachusetts, the pastorate of that church being already occupied. (Puritans preferred the term pastor to priest.) So authoritative were his observations on religious and related matters that he became known as the Un-mitred Pope of New England. Handiwork and holiness, observation and action are intimately tied together in his sermons: for example, 'It is a disgrace to a good workman not to look at his work, but to slight it' and 'When a good workman seeth a man taken with his work, he is willing to show him all his Art in it'.[12]

With the coming of the machine tool in the first decades of the nineteenth century, this aptitude would translate itself into a fascination with the problems and opportunities of mass production. However, American men would retain in their bones at least some of the instincts of the craftsman. They loved to tinker, as Thomas Jefferson did in the eighteenth century; the third president of the United States wrote to a friend: 'I am so much immersed in farming and nail making (for I have set up a nailery) that politicks are entirely banished from my mind'.[13] David Freedman tells us of Tom Paine, author of *The Rights of Man* (1791), that '. . . long years as a staymaker left him with a skill that gave him great pleasure. Like his friend Franklin, he continued in many ways to be what he had been – a craftsman at heart.'[14]

Franklin had many credits to his name when he died. He had signed the Declaration of Independence on behalf of Pennsylvania. He had also invented bifocal lenses, the lightning rod and, to replace wasteful and dangerous open fires, the iron furnace stove that is still in use to this day. As a diplomat he had involved France in the war against the British, thereby turning the tide in favor of the colonists. Max Weber, sometimes described as the 'founding father' of sociology,[15] regarded him as an exemplar of the Protestant Ethic – although the progenitor of some of its less attractive aspects. However, he retained to the end of his life a profound pride in his original trade – a pride first manifested in an epitaph penned for himself in his youth:

> The body of
> Benjamin Franklin, printer
> like the cover of an old book,
> its contents worn out.
> and stripped of its lettering and gilding
> lies here, food for worms!
> yet the work itself shall not be lost,
> for it will, as he believed, appear once more
> in a new
> and more beautiful edition
> corrected and amended
> by its author.

Regrettably, this epitaph would not be used on his tomb in Christ Church, Philadelphia.

One reason why American men became obsessed with their automobiles in the early twentieth century was precisely that they could tinker with them on Saturday morning. As late as the 1960s, if a company president did his own plumbing, he would ensure that this fact appeared in his official company biography; it showed he was a 'real American'. A willingness to get their hands dirty distinguished managers from their European equivalents; this distinction reflected the relative lack of social stratification in the New World, the men at the top and bottom being considered to be made from the same common clay. Even today the ordinary house, being built of wood – unlike its European equivalent, which is of brick or stone – requires a large amount of maintenance and there is an assumption that the householder will do most of it himself or (increasingly) herself.

The third member of our quartet of traditional characteristics – the collective and co-operative nature of American Puritanism – is the one least remarked on. Many writers (like Weber) have perceived only a self-assertive and selfish individualism in the society that emerged from early colonial days but the truth is both more complex and more reassuring; while releasing the energies of the individual, the movement possessed a genius for bending them to a common purpose. In 1625, Bacon had set the tone in his essay, 'On Friendship', telling us that whoever 'delighted in solitude is either a wild beast or a god'. However, he distinguished between a community and a crowd: 'A crowd is not company, and faces are but a gallery of pictures, and talk but a tinkling cymbal, where there is no love'.[16] 'Love' was what bound a community together. Ten years later, Winthrop developed this point in his 'Citty on a Hill' sermon with particular reference to the voyage of the *Arbella*. To avoid shipwreck and to provide for our posterity, he said: 'wee must knit together in this worke as one man, wee must be willing to abridge ourselves of our superfluities for the supply of others necessities ... we must make others Conditions our own[,] rejoice together, mourne together, labour and suffer together ...'. The Rev. John Cotton would express similar sentiments soon afterwards, telling us that: 'Society in all sorts of humane affaires is better that Solitariness'.[17]

Which brings us to the fourth Puritan characteristic. In order to 'worke as one man' effectively, the Puritan migrants needed organizational ability – something they possessed in full, rare measure from the outset; indeed they could never have reached beyond that outset without it. As the historian Perry Miller would tell us in 1964:

> Puritans moved in groups and towns, settled in whole communities, and maintained firm government over all units ... The theorists of New England thought of society ... not as aggregation of individuals but as an organism, functioning for a definite purpose, with all parts subordinate to the whole, all members contributing a definite share, every person occupying a particular status.[18]

Good organization implies hierarchy, although hierarchy need not mean good organization. Two colloquial American terms, 'hands on' and 'can do', emerged from this way of life; they somehow conveyed, not just that opportunities of all kinds were there for the taking, but that the game was worth the candle. Even today, when groups of Americans settle in a foreign city, they tend to take over the running of any organization that they join. Each of our quartet of characteristics supported and enhanced the others – which is, of course, the hallmark of a system. Together they lie at the core of the inherited managerial culture which is the principal subject matter of this book.

The nexus between religious doctrine, manual skills, social outlook and organizational ability appears to have lain originally in the fact that the physical world was perceived to be evil, whereas the spiritual world was considered to be good. De-sanctified in this way, the former becomes a resource to exploit. You might disfigure it if you wished. You could use bits of it for your comfort and then discard them. You could also use them to build the physical infrastructure of the Kingdom of Heaven on Earth. Puritanism by its nature tended to be exploitative in the pejorative sense of that term, although, as will be shown by the examples of the Shakers and the Mormons (see Chapter 3), it need not be so.

For the Puritans, the Bible was the unmediated word of God. His instructions as expressed in this medium were not to be questioned:

> Be fruitful, and multiply, and replenish the earth, and subdue it: and have dominion over the fish of the sea, and over the fowl of the air, and over every living thing that moveth upon the earth. Behold, I have given thee every herb bearing seed, which is upon the face of all the earth, and every tree, in the which is the fruit of a tree yielding seed; *to you it shall be for meat.*[19]

Puritans found justification for their exploitative approach in holy writ. They believed themselves to be obligated to make the fullest use of God's works, which most of them interpreted as meaning to exploit the world around them for their own benefit and His greater glory, the two objectives being regarded as the same. To do this, they needed tools to work the material universe into useful shapes, as well as the skills required to use them. Whence the importance of craftsmanship and the veneration with which the craftsman was treated – veneration extending to the tools themselves. 'The very wheelbarrow', said one of the early migrants, 'is to be with respect looked upon'.[20]

The relationship between religion and commerce would be close but uneasy. When the late seventeenth-century Puritan divine, Cotton Mather, remarked that religion begot prosperity and the daughter had destroyed the mother, he meant that diligence and economy had created wealth – and that the newly wealthy colonists were straying from the path of virtue. However, as the twentieth-century historian, Alan Taylor, has pointed out, the extent of the 'declension' from traditional behavior patterns has been much exaggerated: '. . . the core principles persisted, especially the commitment to a moral, educated, commercial, and homogeneous people'.[21]

The first college in America (later Harvard University) was founded by the migrants in 1636 and the first factory was created by Winthrop's son in 1643, when he brought workmen over from the village of Hammersmith near London, England to Massachusetts to build and man a blast furnace. Like his father, John Jr. was a remarkable man; a governor of Connecticut for thirty years, his interest in science and its application, technology, led in 1664 to his election to the newly formed Royal Society in London, the first American to be so honored.

His membership overlapped by five years that of the great Sir Isaac Newton, president of that august body. It was of Newton that Albert Einstein would say: 'in one person he combined the experimenter, the theorist, the mechanic and, not least, the artist in exposition'.[22] John Winthrop Jr. was himself no slouch when it came to scientific observation and experimentation. Using his three-and-a-half-foot long telescope, he formed the impression that Jupiter possessed a fifth moon and reported accordingly to the Society; its existence would be confirmed by Edward Barnard in 1892.[23]

R.H. Tawney in a graphic passage of his book, *Religion and the Rise of Capitalism*, has described 'the tremendous storm of the Puritan Movement': 'The forest bent; the oaks snapped; the dry leaves were driven before a gale, neither all of winter nor all of spring, but violent and life-giving, pitiless and tender, sounding strange notes of yearning and contrition . . .'.[24] Puritanism was brought to North America by English colonists (including the later Quakers in Nantucket and Pennsylvania) but they were followed by other sets of a similar outlook, such as the French Huguenots in New Rochelle; the Dutch Reformed community elsewhere in New York State; the Moravians in New Jersey, the Mennonites in Pennsylvania, the Scots in Nova Scotia and, above all, the Scotch-Irish – that extraordinary breed (of whom the authors are humble examples) known in Britain as Ulstermen, who arrived from north-east Ireland in the eighteenth century, settled in the Appalachian mountain chain from Pennsylvania to Mississippi, and then spread slowly westwards.

The Scotch-Irish were the source of much of a popular and lively American language that lingers to this day, like 'redneck' (which meant one of them), 'young-un', 'critter', 'growed up', 'fixin' to', 'whar' (for where) and 'thar' (for there). In 1760, North Carolina would be described by one commentator on their account as a 'Macocracy'.[25] They formed the backbone of Washington's army and, after Independence, provided nearly one-third of the presidents of United States, through either the male or female line. Less happily, some of them created the nineteenth-century Ku Klux Klan, borrowing the last part of its name from the tribes of the Scottish Highlands. Today their descendants in the 'red' (or Republican) states and elsewhere are said to number thirty million and be largely responsible for electing George W. Bush as president in 1999 and 2003.[26] Why are states which support the Republican Party now called 'red', the traditional color of the left wing (as in 'reds under the bed')? The best explanation appears to be that it is derived from 'redneck'. At the time of writing, for better or worse, the Scotch-Irish rule America and, through America, the world.

All of these groupings were inspired by the great Swiss theologian, Jean Calvin – with the exception of the Moravians and the Mennonites who were followers, respectively, of his predecessor, Jan Hus and his contemporary, Menno Simons, men who held similar beliefs. Early Calvinists did not believe that good behavior would lead people to heaven but they 'hoped that a moral society would abate God's wrath in this world, sparing New England from famines, epidemics, wars, and other collective afflictions'.[27] This could be achieved only through thrift, sobriety and industriousness, which became the greatest of Puritan values. Tawney viewed the typical Puritan in this way: 'tempered by self-examination, self-discipline, self-control, he is the practical ascetic, whose victories are won not in the cloister, but on the battlefield, in the counting house and in the market'. Describing God as 'the great Taskmaster', Calvin had looked around for tasks to be performed. 'What reason is there', he wrote, 'why the income from business should not be larger than from land-owning? Whence do the merchant's profits come, except from his own diligence and industry?'[28] (Daniel Wren tells us that Calvin's ideas 'did not espouse the cause of capitalism' – a view that is difficult to reconcile with this observation.[29])

Two centuries after the Puritan migration, Starbuck, the first mate of the whaler *Pequod* in Melville's great novel *Moby Dick* – after whom the well-known chain of coffee houses would be named by its three literate and caffeine-stained founders – would remark, 'duty and profit, hand in hand' as his boat set out in search of its prey; *Moby Dick* is an allegory of Good and Evil seen through harsh New England eyes. In the next century, the aptly named Calvin Coolidge, a man who was born in Vermont and died in Massachusetts, president of the United States from 1923 to 1929, would tell us that 'America recognizes no aristocracy save those who work'. He also believed that 'the badge of service is the sole requirement for admission to the ranks of our nobility'[30] but that it is 'only when men begin to worship that they begin to grow'.[31] For 'Silent Cal' (as he was known, being a man of few words) 'the man who builds a factory builds a temple,' and 'the man who works there worships there.'[32]

Newcomers to the colonies, and later to the United States, who were not Puritans by inheritance, would become infected with a similar outlook. As the historian, William Graham Sumner, wrote in 1907:

> The mores of New England ... still show deep traces of the Puritan temper and world philosophy. Perhaps nowhere else in the world can

so strong an illustration be seen, both of the persistency of the spirit of mores, and their variability and adaptability. The mores of New England have extended to a large immigrant population, and have won control over them. They have also been carried to the new states by emigrants, and their perpetuation there is an often-noticed phenomenon.[33]

The authors, although proud of their Puritan, Scotch-Irish ancestry, totally disassociate themselves from the views of writers such as Samuel P. Huntington, who believe that traditional American culture is in some sense ethnic or racial in origin and nature.[34] Puritanism is, essentially, an attitude of mind and an associated series of practices which, in the right circumstances, can be, and have been, transferred between races, tribes, nations and even religions. Although historians rightly site the American movement's origins in sixteenth-century England, it did not suddenly materialize there and then out of nowhere – there had been a long, multi-ethnic pre-history, well beyond the scope of this book and probably dating back to the Prophet Mani in third-century Mesopotamia. If this is true, the land between the rivers Tigris and Euphrates was the cradle of modern civilization in more ways than one.

It follows that the close connection between practices that can be considered Puritan and good organization is not an exclusively or essentially a Protestant or even Christian phenomenon. In Chapter 10, we shall talk about the influence of the *bushido* code on Japanese business in the late nineteenth century, preparing the way for the creation of the company that ultimately became Toyota Motor. In India today, much of steelmaking and the tea trade is owned and controlled by members of the Marwari sect, traditionally strict vegetarians who followed the practice known as *partha*, which meant 'starting business days with Hindu prayer and ending each day with an accounting of the day's cash flow'. They used to possess a secret language known as *modi*, which enabled them to exchange business secrets with one another. The term Marwari comes from the Sanskrit word *maru*, meaning desert, referring to the Thar desert of Rajasthan in north-west India where they originated. The best known example of a Marwari company today is Mittal Steel, which has recently merged with the Luxembourg company, Arcelor, to form the largest steel company in the world; this merger also breaks an implicit rule by which the Marwari community has functioned for over a century, since it involves a surrender of control to non-members. Like late seventeenth-century American Puritans, the Marwaris have recently undergone something of a 'declension', and for the same reason; as religion begets prosperity, ostentation threatens to replace frugality.[35]

The settlers of the 1630s had modeled themselves on the people of the Old Testament, the Puritan values and practices which Tawney described so vividly being largely Jewish in inspiration. It is therefore not surprising that, when first German and then Russian Jews moved in large numbers to the New World in the nineteenth century, they should have found the established American *mores* to their liking and become successful in business. In so doing, the newcomers both per-petuated and enhanced the great tradition of good management inherited from the first settlers. (Interestingly, the prophet Mani is said to have formed his religious outlook while dwelling in an ascetic Jew-ish community called the Elkasites.)

For a century and a half, historians have been asking themselves the chicken-and-egg question: which came first: Puritanism or Capital-ism? At least four conflicting answers have been offered. For Karl Marx and his collaborator and sponsor, Friedrich Engels, in the mid-nineteenth century, Puritanism was a product of economic and social change – in other words, it came second. By way of contrast, Weber, in *The Protestant Ethic and the Spirit of Capitalism* (1904), and his disciple, R.H. Tawney, in *Religion and the Rise of Capitalism* (1926), argued that it was the other way round – Puritanism came first, inspiring and inform-ing the subsequent changes in commerce and manufacturing.

A third view was espoused by Hugh Trevor-Roper in a lecture[36] and taken up again by Diarmaid MacCulloch in his magisterial *Reformation – Europe's House Divided 1490–1700*.[37] Both these historians cast doubt on the existence of a direct causal link between the two movements but did not entirely disconnect them. They attributed the rise of Capital-ism to the impact of established state religions on disenfranchized minorities. Denied access to many public roles and activities, such as politics and the law, the members of these communities would have turned their hand to commerce and prospered. Capitalism was, there-fore, a product of what MacCulloch called 'pluralism' (meaning that a number of different sets of beliefs and practices existed within one society, some more dominant than others) and, therefore, only a by-product of religion.

More recently, Rodney Stark in his *The Victory of Reason* has argued that Capitalism long preceded Protestantism and arose out of an increasing focus on 'reason' within medieval Catholicism.[38] Where do the authors stand in this controversy? Their conclusion is that whether Puritanism caused Capitalism, or vice versa, is impossible to determine – and less important than that each fed the other in a symbiotic relationship lasting centuries; in their American manifestation, they are different facets of one and the same phenomenon. (In this book, which is a kind of American social history, Protestantism and Puritanism are assumed to be more or less the same thing.)

MacCulloch's disengagement of Puritanism from Capitalism appears to be due to his belief that the first was 'communitarian' – it reinforced a sense of community in any society – whereas the second was a 'denial or betrayal' of community. For the authors, this view demonstrates a misunderstanding of the true nature of Capitalism. It may be significant that only three out of MacCulloch's 832 pages are devoted to wealth creation. A subtle but robust blend of respect for the rights of the individual and of the group – which, in its managerial expression, may be described as *collegiality* – lay at the beating heart of America's evolving commercial and industrial life. The outcome was a new and vibrant version of civil society, known as the market economy.

2

The Great Migration
of the 1630s

The organizers of the 1630s Great Migration to New England, which began the systematic colonization of North America by English-speaking people under the leadership of Governor Winthrop, enjoyed one important advantage over the sponsors of previous migrations: they were able to study the records of the twin disasters known to history as the settlement of Jamestown and the expedition of the Pilgrim Fathers.

A party of settlers for Jamestown in Virginia had sailed from England in December 1606. This would have been a sensible time to depart if they had gone straight to their future home. Although they would have had to brave the winter storms on the North Atlantic, they would have arrived in time to plow, sow and harvest before the next winter. Instead, they took the soft option, namely the long, warm, southern route, visiting various islands. For this unpuritanical act of self-indulgence they paid a heavy price after arriving at their destination. Too late to sow, they had used up most of their provisions; of the 144 people who sailed, only thirty-eight remained alive at the end of 1607, not one leaving behind a descendant.[1] The account of their suffering on land is harrowing. Starving settlers ate books, shoes or any other leather items and licked up blood that had fallen from their weaker brethren. One demented wretch killed his wife and ate her, being burned at the stake for his crime. Captain John Smith, the future leader of the expedition, spoke of the event with sardonic Elizabethan humor: 'Whether she was better roasted, boyled, or carbonado'd, I know not . . . But such a dish as powdered wife I never heard of'.[2] Smith was allegedly saved from execution by Indians through the intervention of Pocahontas, daughter of the chief, Powhatan.[3]

Other errors contributed to the disaster, some of considerable magnitude. First of all, the choice of migrants was poor. According to the historian Alan Taylor, the party consisted of 'an unstable and fractious mix of gentlemen-adventurers in command and poor vagrants rounded up from the streets of London and forcibly sent to Virginia' –

both groups being utterly different in outlook and behavior from the future participants in the migration of the 1630s. 'Neither group had much prior experience with work'.[4] Smith later wrote to the expedition's organizers in London: 'send me thirty carpenters, husbandmen, gardiners, blacksmiths, masons and diggers-up of tree roots, well provided, then a thousand such as we have'.[5] Winthrop would call the Virginian colonists 'unfit instruments – a multitude of rude and misgoverned persons, the very scum of the land'.[6] Smith would be forced out of his position by his rebellious fellow colonists when he tried, unsuccessfully, to make them work at least six hours per day.

Moreover, the identity of the leader of the expedition was not disclosed to the colonists until after the final landfall; this implies that no-one was fully in charge during the voyage and could explain why the emigrants were allowed to consume precious provisions *en route* rather than keep them for their first winter in Virginia.[7] Finally, the colonists' masters, comfortably located in London, had given instructions to the effect that one-third of the settlers were to concentrate on looking for gold and silver and on finding a passage to the South Seas, not the best of strategies when the need was to survive in a hostile environment and to grow food to eat. This was 'top-down' management with a vengeance (see Chapter 9). Larger parties followed but, by 1622, of 10,000 souls who had sailed to Virginia, only 2,000 remained alive.[8] Such was the scale of the disaster that in 1624, the Crown revoked the Virginia Company's charter.[9]

The Pilgrim Fathers who emigrated to New England in 1620 managed their migration little better. An account of their departure for the future Plymouth Colony reads like a farce. They took no cattle or horses with them, though they were going to set up a farming community; the first horse does not appear in the records until 1644.[10] They took no 'butter, or oil, not a sole to mend a shoe, not every man a sword to his side, wanting many muskets, much armour'.[11] As with the Virginians, there were two distinct groups of participants; first of all, the Pilgrims proper, a sect within the general Puritan Movement also known as the Separationists who, as this name implies, sought a complete break from Church of England; and secondly a miscellaneous collection of people – known as 'The Strangers' – who did not belong to the Pilgrims' sect, had been chosen in an apparently random fashion and constituted a majority. This duality created long-standing tensions, not helped by the fact that the Separationists were:

> men of little or no education, and those who followed for the next
> nine years were of the same type. Only a score of university men came

to Plymouth during its first forty years, and of these only three, all ministers, settled there permanently ... During the first fifty years there was no public school, and no boy from Plymouth Colony reached Harvard College.[12]

The new age of mass migration required a mastery of the technology of transportation, which the organizers of neither this nor the previous expedition possessed. The Pilgrims had chartered two vessels, the *Mayflower* and the *Speedwell*. The first started off from Rotherhithe on the River Thames in mid-July; this was an error, since the prevailing wind in that area is westerly and a north-easter was required to turn the clumsy square-riggers of the period into the English Channel. The migrants spent three weeks idling in the sea area known as the Downs, using up scarce provisions, before a favorable wind developed. Then they made their way to Southampton on the south coast of England, where the *Speedwell* would encounter problems of a different kind. It had brought the other part of the expedition from Holland to that port, whereupon it required such extensive repairs that the expedition's funds were depleted. The departure of both ships did not take place until August 1619, far too late in the year for crops to be planted and successfully harvested before winter.

When the two ships were a few days out into the Atlantic, the *Speedwell* was found to be 'open and leakie as a sieve'. Had she 'stayed at sea but 3 or 4 howers more, she would have sunke right downe'.[13] Both ships put into Dartmouth, from which they sailed a second time, only to encounter the same problem and put into Plymouth. On September 6 the *Mayflower* sailed again and alone, the intention being to settle in Virginia. It is assumed that it also traveled to the south, although probably not as far in that direction as the Jamestown settlers. Having failed to make a satisfactory landfall in Virginia or in the future New York, it arrived by default in New England on November 10. Three days later, when the crew attempted to put their longboat in the water, they found it to be unseaworthy, the seams having opened up 'with the people's lying in her'.[14] It was not until the beginning of December that this boat was sufficiently repaired to enable them to explore Cape Cod and look for a place to settle. When the Pilgrims found Thievish Harbor, the site of the future Plymouth, the harsh New England winter was upon them. Not until Christmas Day was the construction of the first house intended for common use begun; and not until March 21, 1621 were the last of the Pilgrims able to quit their ship. They had been afloat since July of the previous year in an unhygienic cockleshell. The diary of March 24 records the grim reckoning: 'And in the three months past dies halfe our company'.[15] The toll included John Carver, their first governor.

Led by Winthrop on his flagship, the *Arbella,* the Great Puritan Migration was, by way of contrast, a brilliant exercise that established the English-speaking people permanently on North American soil. Why did it succeed when the first two expeditions had largely failed? The answer, in a nutshell, is that it exhibited to the full all four of the quartet of characteristics listed at the beginning of Chapter 1. As the historian Charles Andrews has told us, the voyage of the *Arbella* 'saw the transfer across the Atlantic of . . . a state in the making, dominated by a powerful conviction as to its place in the divine scheme . . . led by . . . men of wealth and education, of middle-class origin with a quantum of political training, hardheaded and dogmatic.'[16]

The structure and *modus operandi* of the Massachusetts Bay Company foreshadowed to a surprising extent the American corporations of the Golden Age of Management which Chapter 9 will celebrate as 'Great Engines of Growth and Prosperity', even to the extent of being a joint-stock company. It had been founded in 1628 in the City of London – already the financial as well as the political capital of England – by rich, well-established merchants of Puritan inclination or sympathy, some of them members of the City's guilds or livery companies. Careful accounts were kept. Unlike the Virginia Company or the expedition of the Pilgrims, it was not underfunded – indeed, it commanded financial resources on a scale that was, by the standards of its time, enormous. The total cost of the Massachusetts settlement over a period of thirteen years would be put at around £200,000 – say, some $40 million in today's money.

The availability of capital meant that there were ample material resources. No fewer than sixteen ships departed in 1630 for New England, which compares with the Pilgrim's single, ill-equipped vessel. The fleet brought everything that would be required: soap, candles, tools, utensils, steel, iron, clothing, shoes, house furnishings, sail cloth, cattle, horses, goats, hay for fodder, prayer books and Bibles. The *Arbella* also carried 10,000 gallons of beer, required partly because water went sour on a long voyage; 'total abstinence' was by no means a requirement among early Puritans.

The body of men and women that the Governor and Company of the Massachusetts Bay assembled for the migration was by any standard impressive for its quantity, its quality – and its homogeneity. In 1630 alone, over one thousand people were carried to the Bay Colony in the tiny ships.[17] They were but the vanguard; between 1630 and 1640, roughly two hundred ships carried no fewer than 14,000 souls.[18] And the leaders ensured that all of the necessary skills were represented. The passengers in the first ships included a tanner and a weaver; fishermen, herdsmen and masons (two of each); clothiers, chandlers, coopers, military officers, physicians and tailors (three of each); and armorers, bakers, blacksmiths, butchers, carpenters, cordwainers and merchants (five of each).

According to Loring Bigelow, a descendant of early migrants, the Winthrop Fleet consisted mostly of 'sweet ships', designed for the Mediterranean trade. In the seventeenth century, most passengers were transported in ordinary cargo ships, which squandered enough edibles to maintain a permanent population of rats, mice and lice. By selecting 'sweet ships', which normally carried wine and were therefore vermin-free, Winthrop did much to preserve the health of the migrants and to ease their discomfort. MacCulloch may therefore be wrong when he refers to 'the cramped and stinking ships' which carried the migrants across the Atlantic; cramped they undoubtedly were, but probably not stinking.[19]

If anyone had asked for the seventeenth-century equivalent of a 'mission statement', Winthrop need not have hesitated: the Puritans went to New England to create God's Kingdom on Earth. As businessmen they also had to earn a return on capital, the two objectives not being thought to be in conflict. This juxtaposition of motives would reproduce itself in varying forms and to various degrees over and over again in American society during the next four centuries. The Marxist idea that the development of American society was impelled purely by personal and collective greed is simplistic. This is not to deny the presence of greed and indeed all of the seven deadly sins. However, amongst many of the entrepreneurs and their successors – particularly in the future Great Engine companies – there has always been a concern about non-monetary objectives. An obsession with quality in manufacture, or in anything else, cannot be totally explained in terms of the profit motive; it can be explained partly in terms of creating the Kingdom of Heaven on Earth.

The governor, the treasurer, the secretary and the court of assistants of the Company had met at regular intervals and deliberated in their head office, first in London and then in the New World. Like future good corporate managers, they first undertook a 'pilot project' by sending a small expedition ahead to Salem in 1629 consisting of 300 colonists in five ships.[20] In that same year, they conducted an extensive correspondence with the ministers of the established church throughout England about the selection of emigrants and related matters. The Undertakers (the name given to the sponsors or principal investors) studied carefully the errors of the previous colonizers. Having read Smith's account of the Virginia expedition, Winthrop made a point of meeting him. Significantly, however, Winthrop turned down Smith's offer of assistance; the captain had been weighed in the balance and found wanting. Lessons learned from past experience included the desirability of sailing early in the year so as to arrive in time to sow and reap a harvest before winter set in (an objective, in the event, which was not realized). With this in mind, the migrants were required to journey to the south coast of England on the appalling roads of the time during the harsh winter of 1629/30 from as far away as Lancashire in the north – and then to face the spring gales on the Atlantic.

Another lesson was not to sail from the Thames, however convenient it would have been for the large contingent from East Anglia, so avoiding the trap of the Downs that had delayed the Pilgrims. A third was to sail directly across the Atlantic, 'tacking' (taking the nose of the vessel repeatedly through the prevailing westerly wind) as necessary, rather than to follow the slow, safe but, in the end, fatal southerly route favored by the Jamestown settlers. Unlike their predecessors, Winthrop's migrants were masters of the developing technology of travel.

The excellence of the planning permitted the project to be executed with a speed that would be remarkable even today. As the historian, Samuel Eliot Morison, has told us,

> In view of the long time that it takes nowadays to prepare even a summit conference or a tercentennial, it seems almost incredible that in the slow-moving days of horse and sail, when even good roads were wanting, when the beef for a long voyage had to be bought on the hoof, and corn on the stalk, only nine months were required to assemble sixteen vessels all found and sound, and a thousand colonists prepared in mind, body and estate for a fresh start in the New World.[21]

The main party sailed only six months after the final decision to proceed had been taken. During that brief time, migrants throughout England had been notified by means of the primitive postal service of the time of the proposed travel plans; they had to sell their houses and other properties in the primitive markets of the day and travel to their respective departure points; and the organizers had to complete arrangements for assembling, equipping and victualing the largest English colonial migration in history. Of the eleven vessels in the Winthrop fleet, five including the *Arbella* left Yarmouth on the Isle of Wight, just off the southern coast, on or soon after April 7, 1630 and made landfall on June 8. On June 12, Winthrop and some of his companions went ashore and dined on 'good venison, pasty and good beer' in Salem as guests of Governor Endicott, who had been in charge of their advance party. The contrast with the earlier arrivals could not have been greater.[22]

Winthrop and companions looked at the stony peninsula of Salem and 'liked it not'. They decided that the political and commercial center should be in the estuary of the Charles River, south of Salem, and chose as the provisional capital Charleston, where a settlement had been made in the previous year on Endicott's instructions; it was there that the first formal meeting of the court of assistants (directors) took place on American soil; at that point the Company became the Commonwealth. Before long the newcomers found Charleston to be unsatisfactory, on account of the lack of fresh water. When they finally settled into permanent quarters on the peninsula that would later become Boston, on the south side of the Charles River, it was too late in the year to plow and sow.[23] They had possessed the foresight, however, to bring with them sufficient provisions to survive the winter; this was an early example of effective 'contingency planning' – again a feature of future, good American corporate practice. They had also brought with them enough financial resources to fund the dispatch of a ship, the *Lion*, back to England for more provisions. Moreover, the settlement possessed what would now be called 'critical size', in the sense that it was large enough to attract traders from Bermuda and Virginia, who also brought supplies.

The Puritans operated *ahead* of the leading edge of contemporary medical technology: the *Lion* brought back a quantity of lime juice to cure the scurvy that was afflicting the colonists and had previously taken a toll of the Pilgrim Fathers. It was over a century later, in 1754, that James Lind, a graduate of Edinburgh University, published *A Treatise on the Scurvy* which first recommended this practice with the authority of the medical profession. Both the Puritan migrants and Lind probably learned of the cure from the Dutch, who had used it at least since the sixteenth century.

During the entire seventeenth century, New England received only 21,000 emigrants, a fraction of the 120,000 who would go to Virginia and Maryland; yet by 1700 its population at 91,000 exceeded that of the two Chesapeake colonies by 6,000. The difference was longevity: in New England anyone who survived childhood could expect to live to the age of seventy; further south, only a minority lived beyond forty-five. New Englanders were healthier, partly because they lived in a temperate climate where mosquitoes did not spread malaria and where there was little dysentery (an early migrant boasted that 'a sup of New England's air' was better than 'a whole draught of old England's ale'[24]); and partly because they were better educated and enjoyed a more even distribution of wealth than their southern counterparts.

Two critical decisions of a legal nature permanently affected the outcome. First, Winthrop and his companions had acquired all the shares in the Company, even before the expedition sailed, so that there was no body of shareholders left in England asking for dividends or interfering in other ways. Secondly, the Company's charter and its headquarters were transferred to New England with the expedition. This had an interesting side effect: no copy of the document was left behind in London. When the king's ministers in London later wanted to amend it, they were unable to do so because they did not know what it contained. When they requested a copy, we are told, none was forthcoming; eventually it would be amended. Various other chartered companies, of which the best known is the East India Company, were set up in London between the sixteenth and the nineteenth century to conduct foreign trade and effect colonization, but the Massachusetts Bay Company is the only one that moved both headquarters and charter from London.

Morison believed that it was a mystery 'why Winthrop should have been selected as the leader. He was not an original member of the Massachusetts Bay Company nor related to any member.' Nor was he a member of the upper classes or even, by the standards of his time, a wealthy man. The historian infers that the organizers had been impressed by his character and ability.[25] Francis J. Bremer, in his biography of Winthrop, offers a different explanation, arguing that a major part of the explanation for the election of 'an obscure Suffolk gentleman' to lead the venture lay 'in the perceived unimportance of the corporation';[26] it is difficult to reconcile this latter view with the extent of the financial, material and human resources committed to it. Is it just possible that the relative obscurity of Winthrop's birth was regarded as a virtue by the organizers? Only five years before the migration, the Puritan Bacon had written that 'nobility of birth commonly abateth industry'.[27]

Winthrop's colleagues had no doubt about the wisdom of the appointment: 'The principal persons who wished to emigrate with the charter agreed that the one man for that position was John Winthrop, and *that without him they would not go*' (emphasis added).[28] Winthrop's form of leadership appears to have been collegial. It is certain that he was no autocrat – indeed, he was criticized at the time for being lax. The deputy governor, an old soldier who was ten years Winthrop's senior, even took the view that he was 'soft, evasive and lenient'. It is, therefore, likely that his immediate subordinates were in day-to-day control of events. The acid test of his and their competence must lie in the amazing success of the enterprise which he led. Winthrop appears to have been selected for his position of leadership on what we would now call meritocratic grounds – increasing the resemblance of the Massachusetts Bay Company to one of America's latter-day Great Engine companies. A relative disregard for social class in the selection of the leader would be carried forward into the colony and become a characteristic of North American enterprise and society as a whole.

The egalitarian and meritocratic nature of Puritan England in the seventeenth century is well illustrated by the controversy over the 'gentlemen and the tarps'. 'Tarps' were a species of naval officer promoted from the ranks, and named after tarpaulin, the oiled canvas from which their foul-weather gear was made.[29] 'Gentlemen' were men who had acquired naval commissions on account of their social status. During the brief English Republic (1648–1660), the navy would be officered almost entirely by 'tarps'. Oliver Cromwell, who commanded the Puritan army in the English Civil War, followed a similar practice of promoting from the ranks of enlisted men. Both the republic's navy and its army were notably successful in battle.

When the English monarchy was restored in 1660, there was a lively and long-lasting debate about whether 'gentlemen' or 'tarps' should officer the king's ships, not helped by the fact that no-one quite knew how to define a 'gentleman'. In determining its outcome, a critical role would be played by a remarkable public servant whom the king had inherited from the republic – Samuel Pepys, now famous as a diarist but then secretary to the admiralty, a Member of Parliament and president of the newly formed Royal Society. Pepys argued successfully that future officers could master seamanship only 'by . . . doing and suffering all things'[30] – that is, by behaving like someone promoted from the ranks. His approach shaped the Royal Navy at least until the age of Admiral Lord Nelson, who would go to sea at the age of twelve. We return briefly to the subject of Nelson's navy in Chapter 9; business in particular and society in general have much to learn from how the military organizes itself.

Winthrop was no Separationist; on the contrary, by creating a 'purer', less liturgical version of Anglicanism in the New World, he sought to set an example for the Church of England to follow at home. His outlook on religion can be illustrated with reference to the Miracle of the Puritan Mice. His son possessed not only a Greek New Testament and a metrical Psalter (both being books favored by religious non-conformists) but also a copy of the Book of Common Prayer (which they disfavored), all bound together in one volume. John Sr.'s journal for October 15, 1640 records with approval that rodents had attacked every page of the Prayer Book but left the other two documents intact.[31]

Half a century after the colonization of Massachusetts, history would substantially repeat itself with the establishment of the new colony of Pennsylvania, mostly by English Quakers under the direction of their remarkable leader, William Penn. The original founders of Quakerism have been described as 'the extreme left wing of the 17th century English Puritan Movement'. They acquired their strange name because they called on other Christians 'to tremble at the word of God'.[32] While Winthrop's Puritans sought to purify only the Church of England, the Quakers' aim was to purify the whole of Christendom. We are told that, masterfully employing his capital:

> ... Penn organized the fastest and most efficient colonization in the seventeenth-century English Empire. During 1682, twenty-three ships from England reached the Delaware River, bearing about two thousand colonists and their tools, clothes, provisions and livestock. A year later, twenty more ships brought another two thousand immigrants. By 1686, Pennsylvania's population exceeded eight thousand.[33]

In both migrations, the desire to create a new and superior type of society was combined with a wish and need to earn a return on capital. The sponsors of the Great Migration of the 1630s had learned how to colonize effectively by studying two failed 'plantations'; Penn and his friends also learned from a successful one.

The Puritan migration of the 1630s had been the result of an exercise in planning and implementation that can be compared with any in American history, ranking alongside not just the colonization of Pennsylvania but also the very creation of the United States as an independent republic between 1776 and 1782. Collectively and individually, the founders of the republic would exhibit all four of the traditional characteristics which we have ascribed to the original Puritan migrants. As soldier and then first president, George Washington was particularly good at delegating responsibility and resolving disputes, both characteristics of a good manager. According to the historian, Ron Chernow, he was also an innovative farmer, who 'invented a plough and presided over a small industrial village at Mount Vernon that included a flour mill and a shop for manufacturing cloth ...'.[34] Chernow tells us of Alexander Hamilton that: 'No other founder articulated such a clear and prescient vision of America's future political, military, and economic strength or crafted such ingenious mechanisms to bind the nation together'.[35]

One of Hamilton's creations was the Bank of New York, which survives and flourishes to this day; in forming it, he may be said to have created the first modern American business corporation. Unlike the Constitution of the United States – which was born fully formed and in need of only minor subsequent adjustments – the corporation would have a long way to go before achieving the state of organizational excellence that characterized it by the mid-twentieth century. This book is, among other things, an account of progress along that way. Hamilton also founded the newspaper, the *New-York Evening Post,* which survives and flourishes to this day as the downmarket *New York Post.*

When one looks back at the character of, and roles played by, the Founding Fathers of the nation, one is stuck by the sheer *complementarity* of their skills and outlooks. Each man contributed something special that was essential to the success of the whole. The rationale for this approach is easy to state: since no one person ever knows all the answers or possesses all the skills, good policies are likely to emerge out of a thoughtful debate covering all relevant issues amongst competent, dedicated and knowledgeable colleagues. Complementarity and its close relative, collegiality, would be recurring features of American management teams for the next two hundred years. They would be eclipsed, in the late twentieth century, by the disastrous regime of the 'imperial' chief executive, alone deemed to know all the answers, of whom much more later.

What can be called 'integrated decision-making' was also a recurring feature of American life from the earliest days until the late twentieth century. By this expression is meant that the *same group* of people would be involved in both planning and execution, which therefore constituted a continuum; that the possibility for error was minimized by the careful study of the mistakes and successes of pioneers in the field; that 'pilot' exercises were undertaken when practicable; *that the implications of any important proposal were worked out in detail* before *a decision was taken to proceed or not*; that provision was made against the contingency that some of the original assumptions might be incorrect; and that, finally, while decision-making was often painfully slow, execution could be swift. Integrated decision-making arose out of the relatively unstratified, 'hands-on' nature of Puritan society, with its emphasis on direct, personal responsibility.

The contrasting, traditional European (which here includes British) procedure can be called 'split-level decision-making'; this means that planning and execution are functions reserved for different groups of people, often from distinct social classes; that a decision to proceed will be made 'in principle' before its implications have been worked out in detail; that little or no provision is made for contingencies; that, while decision-making can be swift, execution is likely to be deadly slow; and that the possibility of error is maximized. If there was one, central, over-riding 'secret' that accounted for the success of American business and society in general from 1630 until the 1960s, it is in the way in which decisions were made and put into effect. Some evidence of this cautious Puritan approach may be found in Bacon's essay, 'Of Despatch', written in 1625: 'I knew a wise man that had it for a by-word, when he saw men hasten to a conclusion. "Stay a little, that we may make an end the sooner" '.[36]

An important precedent would be set in 1628 and 1629, when Winthrop and his colleagues planned the Puritan migration in enormous detail, not just before they emigrated to Massachusetts, but *before they made the decision whether or not to migrate*. It was followed implicitly by Hamilton and his friends when they laid the foundations of the republic. Since 1970, by way of contrast, Americans have tended to adopt the more relaxed European approach, with unfortunate consequences for the quality of decision-making in all walks of life.

When one scans through the whole of history, it is difficult to find examples of mass migrations that were so totally successful – in political, economic and social terms – as that of the Puritans to New England or the Quakers to Pennsylvania. What about Australia? Here is a country that resembles the United States in a number of important senses – English speaking, politically stable, enjoying the rule of law, populated largely by immigrants (almost a quarter of current inhabitants having been born elsewhere), socially unstratified, providing an open, agreeable environment for its citizens and visitors, and enjoying a high and, so far, increasing standard of living. However, it was founded as a penal – not a Puritan – colony and its history has not been characterized by the frequent arrival of immigrants consciously motivated by a desire to create the Kingdom of Heaven on Earth. Do the successes achieved by the country which the British affectionately call 'Downunder' not in some sense disprove the underlying thesis of this book? An examination of the chapter entitled ' "Mining" Australia' in Jared Diamond's fascinating *Collapse: How Societies Choose to Fail or Survive* (2005) suggests otherwise. In spite of a recent wave of non-Anglo-Saxon immigration, Australia remains a profoundly British country, possessing most of the weaknesses as well as the genuine strengths of its motherland. Furthermore, its high standard of living is derived not so much from the quality of its managerial culture as from the spendthrift practice of 'blowing' its capital – coal, iron, gold, wood, fish, wool and land – with little thought to the future. That being so, 'the best estimate of a population sustainable at the present standard of living is 8 million people, less than half the current population'.[37]

A comparison can also be made with the sixteenth- and seventeenth-century Spanish and Portuguese occupations of Latin America. Of the quartet of characteristics that we have ascribed to the North American colonists, however, it is doubtful if even one could be said to apply consistently to the citizens of the Hispanic colonies. It is, therefore, not surprising that the societies which emerged from them in the nineteenth century were like Africa today, 'an economic and political basket case', to quote the Harvard economist, Jeffrey G. Williamson.[38] Not one Latin American country can be described nowadays as a prosperous, stable, long-standing democracy, with the possible exception of tiny Costa Rica. There is, however, one community in the Southern Cone which provides a textbook illustration of the thesis of this book. In the late 1920s, a group of Mennonites escaped from Stalinist Russia to establish themselves in Paraguay's empty Chaco desert. The Mennonites are a Puritan sect founded in the seventeenth century by the defrocked Catholic priest, Menno Simons.

Life was hard at first in the desert where the temperature was frequently over 45 degrees Celsius, water was scarce, crops failed and one-tenth of the original settlers perished. However, the migrants possessed to the full all four of our Puritan characteristics. By dint of hard work they have made their desert bloom like the proverbial rose, turning it into 'one of the thriving agricultural hubs of the otherwise depressed Paraguayan economy'. The Mennonite now control four-fifths of Paraguay's dairy industry and have a prosperous business exporting beef. Average wages in the community are three times the national average. And it is not just the economy that they are transforming; in a financially corrupt culture, they stand out and are valued for their honesty. Three key members of the national government are now Mennonite: the finance minister, the tax minister and the president's economic advisor. Can Puritans save Latin America from itself?[39]

In recent times, there has been just one other migration that is comparable in important senses with the original Puritan migration: the Jewish 'plantation' of Palestine, now Israel. Above we quoted Andrews' observation that the voyage of the *Arbella* 'saw the transfer across the Atlantic of a state in the making'. Much the same can be said of the foundation of the state of Israel. It is not a coincidence that the earlier migrants also believed themselves to be God's Chosen People in search of the Promised Land.

3

'Westward the Course of Empire Takes its Way'[1]

How did the outlook first brought to New England by the Puritan migrants in the 1630s spread across the continent in the subsequent two and a half centuries? The answer is: along myriad channels by a series of inland migrations undertaken by individuals and groups. Two of the group migrations, undertaken by the Shakers and the Mormons, are of particular interest to us because they show that the Puritan outlook affected not only property-owners, such as we met among the Puritan migrants and the Quakers. Although both the Shakers and the Mormons would achieve prosperity – in the case of the Mormon citizens of the future state of Utah, acquiring considerable and lasting wealth – each of these migrations was originally composed of, and led by, people from the bottom end of the social scale. Ann Lee (1736–1784), the Shaker leader, was born in Toad Lane in Manchester, England, the daughter of a blacksmith.[2] Sixty-five years later, Brigham Young (1801–1877), the leader of the Mormons, was born in a humble log cabin in Whitingham, Vermont, the son of a common soldier from the Revolutionary War.[3]

At an early age, Ann Lee went to work in the mills of Manchester as a cutter of velvet and a helper in preparing cotton for the looms. The Shaker movement had originated in the 1740s in that city as a radical sub-sect of the Quakers, themselves a radical wing of the Puritans. If it is not quite clear whether the original English Quakers really did 'quake' in a literal sense during their religious services, it is quite certain that the 'Shaking Quakers' or Shakers did – a practice that they had acquired from Huguenot preachers called *camisards* (after the *chemise* or blouse that peasants wore), who had fled to England in 1685 to escape persecution in France.

Converted to Shakerism in 1758, Ann Lee emigrated with a small and devoted band of followers to New York in 1774, where she founded a utopian movement that would last for 200 years and leave an imprint on more than one aspect of American society. A period of imprisonment in 1780, for preaching pacifism – a Quaker tenet – and openly expressing her disloyalty to the Crown, publicized her cause. When she undertook missionary journeys in New England between 1781 and 1783, such was the magnetism of her personality that many farming families joined her movement. Eleven 'communities of ownership' would be established in the north-eastern states after her death. Around the turn of the eighteenth century, missionaries set out to the Ohio–Kentucky border region, resulting, in the course of twenty years, in the creation of seven more communities.

In terms of conventional Christianity, many Shaker beliefs and practices were downright heretical. Shakers believed that Ann Lee was Christ's *alter ego* – the 'woman clothed with the Sun' described in the Book of Revelation – and that Jesus and Ann the Word or Mother Ann (two titles by which she became known), male and female, would rule side by side after the Second Coming predicted by the apostle Paul in his Letters to the Corinthians. In both this and other senses, Shakers were among America's first feminists. An early American female convert expressed this theological point with intellectual elegance: 'There are few in this day, who will pretend to deny the agency of the first woman in leading mankind into sin. Why should it be thought incredible that the agency of a woman should necessarily be first in leading the human race out of sin?'[4] Furthermore, believing literally that the Second Coming was at hand, Shakers saw no point in breeding and, therefore, forbad sexual intercourse. (That Ann's own four children had died in infancy may have affected her theological views.) How then did the movement survive and prosper without procreation for over two centuries? – the answer is, in part, by conversion and, in part, by adoption; in an age when foundling hospitals barely existed, it filled a gap in the social structure.

The Shakers' aptitude for the exercise of mechanical skills led to an amazing list of inventions. They have been credited with creating the circular saw; the screw propeller; the common clothespeg; the flat broom (still called the Shaker broom); an apple parer; a silk-reeling machine; a pea sheller; a wood-burning stove; a sash balance for ventilation; a chimney cap; a threshing machine; planing, splint-making and basketry machines; and, essential for the mail-order business referred to below, a machine that filled packets with dried herbs. A washing machine designed by Shakers would win the gold medal at the Centennial Exhibition in 1876.[5] In their designs for furniture and other goods, the Shakers anticipated, by a century or more, the principle and practice that the American architect, Louis Henry Sullivan, would encapsulate in the expression 'form follows function'.

The movement has left behind a legacy of craftsmanship and innovation out of all proportion to the number of its adherents, who never exceeded 6,000 at any one time.

However, this remarkable aptitude for invention would have achieved little if the members had not possessed unusual organizational abilities. They were rightly famous for the model farms and workshops which they created and integrated into the wider non-Shaker world. In *The Shaker Experience in America*, Dr. Stephen J. Stein, Chancellor's Professor of Religious Studies at Indiana University, has explained how:

> they took advantage of the community's ability to produce labor-intensive agricultural products and manufactured goods at lower prices than their competitors [... becoming] knowledgeable about production costs, the marketplace, distribution systems, and profit margins. They interacted regularly with suppliers, merchants, lawyers and bankers ... They were known for both honesty and shrewdness. Outsiders continued to hold many of their products in high esteem ... and frequently solicited the Shakers' judgment on business matters.

Important new marketing practices, such as establishing salesrooms to display products and distributing catalogs and products by mail, which are now in universal use, appear to have originated in the movement. Eastern Shakers were at one time the largest producers and distributors of seeds and medicinal herbs in the United States, their salesmen traveling as far south as Louisiana in the 1830s; Western communities were well regarded for the production of cattle. The Mount Lebanon community in New York State, which created a chair-making business in the 1860s, is credited with establishing a nationwide market for its products that lasted into the next century. Born in the age of handicrafts, the Shaker movement acted as a midwife for the age of mass distribution, although not of mass production.[6]

Underlying it all was their unshakeable belief that the purpose of life was to create the Kingdom of Heaven on Earth. The United Society of Believers in Christ's Second Appearing – as they were formally called – was preparing for Christ's and Ann's earthly rule. Reference has been made earlier to the general failure of Puritan society to protect the environment; like the Amish community in Pennsylvania, Shakers were to show that Puritan religious belief and practice could be combined with care for one's surroundings. Not content with being among America's first feminists, they were among its first environmentalists.

The lovingly restored Shaker village at Hancock in Massachusetts is a fascinating monument to the movement. First occupied in 1780, it functioned as a community until 1960. Its most remarkable features are the clothes washing complex and the Round Stone Barn (see page 1). Ninety-five feet in diameter and three stories high, the barn's top stories are shaped like doughnuts. Its large central well is roofed over. The barn was built into the side of a hill so that, in the autumn, hay could be brought by wagons to the top story and then tipped down into the well. During the winter, cattle were kept in manger stalls in the middle story, separated from the hay in the well by stanchions; in this way, a single farmhand could feed all the community's cattle. Cattle droppings were shoveled through trap doors into the bottom story for removal in the spring as field fertilizer. The Shakers were masters of the art of integrating systems within systems (see page 56).

Why did the Shaker movement decline after the Civil War and vanish altogether in the second half of the twentieth century? According to Stein, there were at least two reasons. First, 'the creation of orphanages' meant that there was no longer a supply of parentless children to replenish the movement. Second, the 'new economic order' arising from the Second Industrial Revolution 'altered the demand for Shaker hand products'. By inventing mass marketing, the Shakers had prepared the way for mass manufacturing, but their social structure did not allow them to take part in this new activity. The result was a 'precipitate decline in numbers and a geographical retreat from the Ohio Valley to New England and New York State'. More recently, orphanages have been replaced by a system of fostering; in a sense, society has reverted to the Shaker solution.

An obvious difference between the Shakers and Mormons was that the latter were allowed – indeed, encouraged – to procreate. Far from dying out, the Mormons would eventually form the state of Utah, which was admitted to the Union in 1896. Mormonism had been founded in Illinois around 1830 by its first prophet, Joseph Smith. It sprang out of the nationwide movement known to historians as the Second Great (religious) Awakening, which spanned the half century from 1790 to 1840, the first one having occurred on either side of 1740. The two awakenings were alike in the sense that both sought to bring errant Christians back within the fold but otherwise they were very different in character. The first had re-asserted the doctrines of predestination and original sin, being a reversion to the strict Calvinist theology of the early migrants. Jonathan Edwards, its leader, believed that Christ's Second Coming would occur in the New World but this prediction carried no explicit economic connotation. The second blended the optimistic secular outlook of the eighteenth century Enlightenment with Christian millennialism. It was decidedly pro-business in that it 'provided spiritual approbation for material success':[7] the merchants and manufacturers were preparing for the return of our Lord. Thus religion of Puritan inspiration and origin gave a new and fresh kind of impetus to the economic development of nineteenth-century America. The Mormons sought first to create a perfect Christian community and then, by example and by proselytizing, to convert the rest of society to their way of thinking and doing. They achieved the first of these ambitions, at least by their own lights, and – Mormonism being today one of the fastest growing religious movements in the world, the number of its adherents having risen from 1.1 million to 12.6 million in the last half century[8] – have gone some way to succeeding in the second.

When Smith was murdered by a mob in 1844, Brigham Young succeeded him as the second prophet. It was Young who would lead the epic Mormon migration in 1846–1847 from Nauvoo in Illinois to their Great Basin Kingdom between the Rockies and the Sierra, which was one of the great, formative movements that made modern America. As carpenter and cabinet maker, glazier and painter, he was proud of his mechanic skills; and like Governor Winthrop of Massachusetts two centuries before, he used them not just to make things but also to provide a lesson for others. As a result, idleness was scorned in the community. An old Mormon hymn encapsulated this outlook:

> The world has need of willing men,
> Who wear the worker's seal;
> Come, help the good work move along;
> Put your shoulder to the wheel.[9]

Young was by no means the only person in his community to combine an interest in things mechanic with a commitment to religion, Brothers William Clayton and Appleton Harmon being cases in point. In Iowa in 1846, Brother William wrote the much-loved Mormon hymn, 'Come, come ye saints!', in which he expressed a faith that the migrants would 'find the place which God for us prepared, / Far away in the West'. He recorded the creation of a device for measuring elapsed miles – now called an odometer – in his journal for May 12, 1847: 'About noon today Brother Appleton Harmon completed the machinery on the wagon called a "roadometer" by adding a wheel to revolve once in ten miles, showing each mile and also each quarter mile we travel, and then casing the whole over so as to secure it from the weather'.[10] Thus was launched one of the innumerable inventions with which the Latter-day Saints have endowed the world.[11] The Shakers' list is inevitably closed, since there are no more Shakers. Mormons continue to provide new developments in all spheres of life – recently, for example, Utah has been a center of innovation and excellence for the electronics industry.

Young was a superlative manager. According to Jonathan Hughes,

> ... the Mormon trek to Utah was a singular masterpiece of organization, a living mechanism, nourishing itself as it slowly moved some 20,000 souls across the long trail to Utah. Without such organization the Mormon pioneers doubtless could not have succeeded as they did in their efforts to build their Zion in the wilderness. They were too ill-equipped to have made the trek on an individual basis and to have withstood the initial rigors of life in the high deserts. Until the organization was completed, they suffered terribly.[12]

As an exercise in planning, it ranked alongside Winthrop's expedition of 1630. It was not a 'combined operation' on land and at sea in a literal sense like the earlier event but it was not so very different. The prairies and deserts that the Mormons traversed for over 1,300 miles had to be navigated like the ocean. The covered wagons in which better-off migrants of the period traveled were even referred to as 'prairie schooners'. Of the 195 ships that had brought the Puritans to Massachusetts in the 1630s, only one was lost; the overland trails of the 1840s were much more hazardous, the real killers being not the weather but diseases like diphtheria, typhoid and 'exotic complaints such as Rocky Mountain spotted fever'.[13]

Both the Massachusetts Puritans and the Saints were escaping from intolerance and persecution – the latter seeking refuge from the descendants of the former. Without the Mormons, Utah would be as sparsely populated today as are the rest of the Mountain States. Instead it is one of America's best-settled and most prosperous provinces. *Absit* Young, the major contribution that the Mormons have made to the rest of the United States – not only in the effective management of manufacturing industry but also in finance, politics and in preserving a sense of spiritual direction – would not have occurred. At the mid-twentieth century, in the Golden Age of Management, the presidents of the Fortune 500 companies, calculated as a proportion of the state's population, were more likely to come from Utah than from any other state.

Both the original Puritan migration and the Mormon trek were planned with care and imagination. In the case of the Mormons, however, persecution had been so extreme that the kind of *advanced* preparations that the Puritan migrants undertook was out of the question. The detailed work, therefore, took place in the so-called Winter

Quarters in Iowa, where Brother Clayton wrote his hymn, and after the migration had begun. Just as Winthrop had consulted Captain John Smith, Young interviewed people who had traveled to the West; he concluded from these conversations that the area of the Great Salt Lake was the place to settle. Parties of younger people were sent ahead along the chosen trail to clear the bushes and trees, build bridges and create rest camps; in Iowa crops were planted for later migrants to harvest.[14] By nightfall on the day in July 1847 when the first members in the major party arrived in the Salt Lake valley, some potatoes and corn had been planted. By the beginning of the winter of that year, 350 log cabins had been constructed. Before long, the settlers built a dam, the Mormons being the first white men to irrigate farmland in North America.[15] If anything, the planning of the settlement was an even greater act of organizational genius than the planning of the trek; Young knew how to systematize systems.[16]

In both the Shaker and the Mormon migrations, responsibility for the execution of policies was in the hands of the same people who formulated them; thus what we have called 'integrated decision-making' prevailed: responsibility could not slip down the crack between policy-making and implementation. If necessary, therefore, decisions could be rapidly reviewed and reversed or altered to meet new circumstances, the executor not having to labor hard to persuade a physically or socially remote superior that there was a need for change. As in the Puritan migration, it would have been easy to draw up a 'mission statement': the Mormons' principal purpose was to create the Kingdom of God on Earth but, once again, a subsidiary motive was to create a prosperous society.

In 1849 the Mormons established a Perpetual Emigrating Fund in Salt Lake City. Ezra Taft Benson, grandfather of the future President Eisenhower's secretary for agriculture, together with a colleague, was given the task of moving those adherents still remaining in Nauvoo; in 1852 alone, 10,000 were brought out. From 1861 to 1867 a large-scale wagon train went yearly from Utah to Missouri carrying Mormon products and returning with new migrants. And the Saints looked beyond America's shores. Missionaries traveled overseas, particularly to Lancashire and the Midlands in England and to Wales to convert and recruit textile workers, ironworkers and miners. The new migrants came by the thousand. The Mormons knew how to marshal large resources – and still do.

In selecting New England, Winthrop had chosen a place which he believed to be both accessible and fertile – and therefore likely to attract other migrants of a similar persuasion. Young's criteria were the reverse: seeking seclusion in a place where the community could be to some extent self-sufficient, he chose a valley which, although well-watered, was situated in a remote and infertile plain between the Rockies and the Sierra unlikely to attract 'gentiles', as non-adherents were called. He believed that, by hard work and superior organization, the Mormons could convert it into a new home – a refuge where they would be safe from persecution – and he was right. He called it Deseret, a word meaning honey bee, which appears in the Book of Mormon, and carrying an obvious reference to the biblical Promised Land, flowing in milk and honey.

The Mormons were unpuritanical in their attitude to the theater. In the late sixteenth century, the Puritan magistrates of the City of London – the very sort of people who would later finance the Massachusetts Bay Company – had closed all the theaters that came under their jurisdiction, which is why Shakespeare's plays had to be presented in the Globe Theatre on the south side of the Thames. Two hundred and fifty years later, Young went in the other direction, opening a theater in Salt Lake City which would become famous. We are told that he loved plays but had doubts about the value of tragedies and brought one performance to a halt saying: 'There is enough tragedy in everyday life . . . we ought to have amusement when we come here'.[17]

The London magistrates proscribed theaters not because they were against public entertainment but because these institutions were breeding grounds of crime and prostitution. That, however, was not how their actions were viewed by playwrights, whose livelihood was threatened. Shakespeare satirized Puritans in the person of Malvolio, Olivia's steward in the comedy *Twelfth Night*:

> *Maria:*   Marry, sir, sometimes he is a kind of Puritan.
> *Sir Andrew:*   If I thought that, I would beat him like a dog.[18]

The deliberate humiliation of Malvolio is the principal subplot in the play. It is clear that the playwright's sympathies lay with the established non-Puritan order – he is said to have been a closet Roman Catholic – but he was too great an artist to look at any one character from a single angle only. What starts as a farcical subplot soon acquires tragic overtones. Since tragedy is more powerful than comedy, the subplot threatens to take over the play.

In attacking Malvolio, Sir Toby Belch uttered his famous line: 'Doest thou think that because thou art virtuous, there shall be no more cakes and ale?' The Mormons showed that a Puritan outlook could be combined with 'cakes and ale'. After a hard day's trek, Young sometimes led a square dance under the stars. The relative importance of the Mormon community, both spiritually and economically, increased in the second half of the twentieth century as some other parts of American society departed from the country's religious roots. Today, Utah remains a safe and orderly place, with a violent crime rate in 2003 at 237 per 100,000 citizens, less than half the national average.[19] (Curiously enough in a state whose inhabitants frown on coffee, tea, nicotine and alcohol, Utah ranks third for the number of arrested men who test positive for the highly addictive drug, methamphetamine – also known as meth, ice, crack, crystal or glass. Crimes related to this drug are said to constitute 80 per cent of criminal activity in Utah.)[20]

More than any group in American life, it was the Mormons who took the Puritan outlook on work, life and organization to the West. It remained largely an American phenomenon until the late 1940s when, in the hands of another group of people unconnected with Mormonism – one of them a Quaker by birth and upbringing, if not by persuasion, but still strongly influenced by Quaker values – it would make a great leap across the Pacific to Japan, an event which will be briefly chronicled in Chapter 10. The US Occupation of Japan would change the way business was done in that and other countries, and much else besides.

4

The Profound Influence
of French Technology

If Puritan England was the father of America's emerging managerial culture, revolutionary France was its mother. Seventeenth-century England had endowed its colonies with the four Puritan characteristics discussed at length in the opening chapter of this book. Eighteenth-century France would embed a fifth: a very un-British interest in technology – by which we mean the application of scientific knowledge to the resolution of practical problems – coupled with a respect for the technologist on the part of laymen.

The thirteen colonies had come under strong French influence towards the end of the eighteenth century. Three of the leaders of the American Revolution – Benjamin Franklin, Thomas Jefferson and Tom Paine – spent formative years in Paris, the last only just avoiding being lynched by the mob whose rights he had espoused. France's influence was strongest in three spheres: political ideology, the military and technology. In the case of political ideology the influence was two-way – indeed, if you assume that Paine, though born and brought up in England, was for this purpose an American, America's influence on France was probably greater than France's on America: his political tract, *The Rights of Man* inspired the declaration of *Les Droits de l'Homme*. In the case of the military and technology, however, the influence was strictly from the Old World to the New.

France had secured victory for the colonists. In spite of lackluster British generalship and the extraordinary length of the lines of supply – over three thousand miles – Britain might well have retained at least the southern colonies if its navy had controlled the seas. The nascent United States would then have found itself sandwiched between a loyalist Canada to the north and an enlarged loyalist Georgia to the south. However, the French navy broke Britain's blockade of the colonial ports and disrupted its supply lines just long enough to 'allow the Americans to regroup and win their decisive victory under George Washington at Yorktown in 1781'.[1]

It was widely believed in Britain at that time that French men-of-war were technically superior to their British counterparts, a view that led to the formation of the Society for the Improvement of Naval Architecture in London in the 1790s. In support of this point of view, one can quote the fact that British naval officers loved to capture and sail French ships, which were faster and more maneuverable than their own. Indeed, the *Hebe*, captured in 1782, would provide the blueprint for the *Leda* class of British frigate, which constituted the backbone of Nelson's fleet at Trafalgar.[2] A totally contrary opinion was held and put forward by the delightfully named Gabriel Snodgrass, surveyor to the East India Company, although one suspects that he was motivated more by a spirit of patriotism – 'damn the French!' – than a quest for the truth. Recently, a third view has been persuasively argued by the historian, N.A.M. Rodger, namely that, by the late eighteenth century, the French had made genuine advances in developing the *theory* of shipbuilding but not yet succeeded in putting it usefully into *practice*. He tells us that '[t]he foundations that they laid ... were built upon over the next two centuries to develop the modern science of naval architecture ...'.[3] Whatever the truth about these matters, the young Republic severed its political link with England and came under French influence at exactly the right moment for the future of American manufacturing – just when interest in the practical uses of scientific knowledge was gaining momentum in France. Gratitude for military favors also predisposed the former colonists to look to Paris for inspiration in intellectual matters.

The esteem in which technology is held in France may go back two thousand years to the Roman Empire. Academic study began in the seventeenth century, when Louis XIV's great minister, Colbert, founded the Académie des Sciences and the Académie de l'Architecture. In 1794 the French revolutionary government would group together a number of similar institutions to establish the Ecole Polytechnique – the school of all the technologies – in Paris, to be known to future generations of its students as 'X', an algebraic term symbolizing the importance of engineering, which is dependent on mathematics. The term's very brevity also indicates an institution of such importance that it did not require a normal name. 'X' would exercise an overwhelming influence on French society, business and government, which persisted until the foundation of the *grandes écoles* of the mid-twentieth century.

'X' had been founded as a school of military engineering and to this day reports to the French Ministry of Defense, not to the Ministry of

Education. Most of the polytechnics created in other countries under its influence would not be related to the army – a grand exception being that even greater school of military engineering, the US Military Academy at West Point. A French military engineer and artillerist, Louis de Tousard, played the key role in its foundation. Having served in America under General Lafayette in the Revolutionary War, de Tousard went back to France, only to return to the United States to escape the Terror of 1793. Two years later, he joined the US Corps of Artillerists and Engineers as a major, whereupon he was able to teach his fellow officers the principles of engineering that he had learned at home. In 1798 he sent to the secretary of war, James McHenry, a proposal entitled *Formation of a School of Artillerists and Engineers*, now generally thought of as the blueprint for the future West Point; and in 1809 he published the *American Artillerist's Companion*, which became a standard textbook for military officers.[4]

The school's French character would be enhanced in 1819 when a New Englander, Sylvanus Thayer, was appointed its superintendent, a role that he occupied for twenty-four years. A man of unbending principle, he was one in the long chain of what may be called 'secular Puritans' who have played such a large part in developing America's managerial and corporate culture. An admirer of Napoleon, Thayer had been present in Paris in 1815 when the victorious Wellington occupied the former emperor's box in the Paris Opera. The audience hissed the British commander-in-chief so loudly that he was obliged to leave at the interval, which pleased Thayer no end. Thayer brought back engineering textbooks from Paris to West Point, where the language of technical instruction became French.

Although first and foremost a school of military engineering, West Point was to have a profound impact on the application of technology in the civilian world. In all, more than 120 West Pointers would work on American railroads before the Civil War in engineering, supervisory or executive capacities. One of the first of these was a Lieutenant George Washington Whistler, who graduated from the academy in 1819; thirty years later, he would die of cholera in Russia, where he was building the Moscow to St Petersburg line. (His wife survived him, to be immortalized when her portrait was painted by their son, James Abbott McNeill Whistler.) In 1824, a landmark law, the General Survey Act, authorized the president of the United States 'to assign army engineers to state-owned and privately owned transportation companies for the purpose of conducting topographical surveys, estimating costs, and supervising construction'; initially, the cost of the assignments was borne by the federal government.[5]

It was, therefore, not surprising that, when both French and American construction companies failed to complete the Panama Canal, another graduate of the academy, named like Whistler after the first president, was called upon to do so. George Washington Goethals' success was, in part, due to the extraordinarily high *esprit de corps* that he instilled into a large, disparate team operating in appalling circumstances;[6] this could have been achieved only if good managerial practices were being observed. By that time it was common for retiring military officers to take up senior positions in manufacturing industry. The same kind of problem arose in both walks of life. Scarce resources, human, financial and material, had to be marshaled on an enormous scale. Decisions had to be made, and risks incurred, often on the basis of inadequate information. Technology had to be mastered and managed.

A second American polytechnic would be founded five years after Thayer took up his charge at West Point – and this one betrayed its patrimony in its name. The Rensselaer Polytechnic Institute at Troy, New York remains to this day one of the foremost colleges of technology on the North American continent. It was followed by a series of similar bodies. Thayer had undertaken a great deal of work for the early railroads. Unlike present-day business school academics, he thought it improper to accept payment for his advisory services. When the railroads deposited money in his bank account, he refused to touch it. However, when he reached the age of ninety, Thayer was told that, if he did not spend this money, the government would get it when he died; this prompted him to found and fund the Thayer School of Engineering in 1867 at his alma mater, Dartmouth College. (Thayer is, by the way, the only engineering school in the United States that insists that its students possess a liberal arts degree on entrance.) He also founded the Thayer Academy for boys in Braintree, Massachusetts. Thayer's strict moral outlook is exemplified in the letters he wrote about how this academy was to be managed. The foundation of polytechnics and similar bodies was paralleled by the creation of mechanics' institutes designed to teach simpler skills at the foreman level. The United States, however, never systematically introduced the kind of vocational education in secondary schools – sometimes known as 'technician training' – which would be developed in continental Europe and adopted by Japan in the early twentieth century.

It is instructive to compare and contrast the status of engineers in the United States, Britain and continental Western Europe at the end of the nineteenth century. In continental Western Europe, they were accepted into the highest levels of industrial management and simultaneously achieved the highest social status. Respectable families liked to marry their daughters to engineers; this was the litmus test. In America, engineers would never achieve a comparable social status, which was reserved rather for 'old money', lawyers and descendants of the bungling Pilgrim Fathers, but they reached the highest positions in manufacturing and commerce. In Britain, broadly speaking and with important exceptions, they achieved neither authoritative positions in business nor social status; Britain's answer to the polytechnic was the 'public' (i.e. private) school, for which technology was anathema and came late. The resultant superiority of German over British engineering was illustrated in World War II when the Messerschmitt 109 and Focke-Wulf 190 proved themselves able to fly faster, higher and further, and carry a greater weight, than the equivalent British fighter planes. Such was the esteem in which the 190 was held that Winston Churchill decided to mount a commando raid on its base to seize a specimen – a raid that would be aborted when one accidentally landed in England; what Britain learned from its revolutionary technology was used in designing the subsequent Typhoon series of fighters.[7]

In the 1630s, Britain's American colonies had been an extension of English society – no more, no less. As the British historian, A.L. Rowse, has pointed out, Virginia and Massachusetts were 'extrapolations' of, respectively, 'the establishment' and of 'the opposition' – by which he meant conformist Anglicans (or Episcopalians) on the one hand and non-conformist or dissenting Puritans on the other.[8] On both sides of the Atlantic, Puritans would be (more or less) egalitarian in outlook, valued commerce and crafts (and later manufacturing), believed that political sovereignty should lie with the people and held that authority within the church should lie in the congregation. Also on both sides of the Atlantic, Anglicans would believe (more or less) in a socially stratified society, favored agriculture, distrusted the people as a source of political power and held that ecclesiastical authority should lie with bishops.

Much of the subsequent domestic histories of both countries can properly be interpreted as a series of conflicts between these opposing tendencies. The drama would be played out twice in Britain, once with sword and musket in the mid-seventeenth century, when the Puritan forces under Oliver Cromwell won the Civil War but lost the subsequent peace; and again when the Puritan industrial spirit was defeated by the Anglican forces of gentrification in the late nineteenth century. The ambition of the successful late Victorian entrepreneur was to acquire a title of nobility and an estate and pretend not to be 'in trade'.

The same drama has also been played out twice on the North American continent – once in the American Revolution, when colonial gentlemen in the King's Rangers of Carolina, the Georgia Light Dragoons and the Bucks County Light Dragoons, together with lowly Scottish and Irish immigrants,[9] fought alongside the redcoats against forces representing, among others, the commercial and industrial interests of New England; and, once again, in the American Civil War. The first St. Patrick's Day Parade in New York City took place in 1779 as an expression of loyalty to the Crown by the – Protestant – Volunteers of Ireland.

The distinguished American historian David Hacker Fischer has written of the similarities between the English and American civil wars. Of the latter, he says:

> [t]he armies of the north were at first very like those of [the Puritan General, Sir Thomas] Fairfax in the English Civil War; gradually they became [like Cromwell's] New Model Army, ruthless, methodical and efficient. The Army of Northern Virginia, important parts of it at least, consciously modeled itself upon the *beaux sabreurs* of Prince Rupert.[10]

There would be many eddies and cross-currents in both British and American history; George Washington himself, for example, was, literally, an Anglican and aristocratic Virginian who sided with the Puritan merchants of New England in the Revolution; as A.L. Rowse has told us in *The Elizabethans and America*, when Virginia 'joined with New England, against the old country, the new nation was made'.[11] The Yankee, Puritan spirit would predominate from an early date and triumph in the Civil War of the 1860s – a 'war of supply' won ultimately not so much by soldiers as by the northern businessmen who had built the railroads. Victory would result in a society dominated, to a greater or lesser extent, by a common set of commercial and industrial values. Theory and practice being in harmony, it became easy to think and act *systemically* about manufacturing, technology and their respective roles in society.

The influence of French technology was particularly important in the manufacture of arms. We spoke above about de Tousard's impact on the education of American officers, both within his regiment and at West Point. He was also a proponent of a manufacturing methodology called *le système Gribeauval*. As early as the 1765, General Jean-Baptiste de Gribeauval, inspector-general of artillery, had 'sought to rationalize the French armaments by introducing standardized weapons with standardized parts'.[12] With this in mind, he appointed a watchmaker, Honoré Le Blanc, as superintendent of three arsenals. In 1785, Le Blanc showed fifty identical musket locks to Thomas Jefferson, who was American minister in Paris from 1785 to 1789. The lock, which is so-called because of a supposed resemblance to a door lock, is the firing mechanism in a musket, the two other parts being the wooden stock or butt and the metal barrel. Since the lock, the stock and the barrel constituted the entire gun, it is easy to see how, taken together, the words came to mean 'completely'. (The first recorded metaphorical use of the expression in writing is to be found in a letter from the Scottish novelist, Sir Walter Scott, in 1817 in which he said that a Highlander's gun lacked 'lock, stock and barrel' – meaning that the unfortunate man was penniless.)

In a report to his government, Jefferson commented: 'I put several of them together myself taking pieces at hazard, as they came to hand, and they fitted in the most perfect manner. The advantages of this, when arms need repair, are evident.'[13] Jefferson tried to persuade his political masters to bring Le Blanc to Washington but failed. However, even if he had succeeded, it is by no means certain that the age of mass production of guns would have been launched there and then: Le Blanc must have achieved interchangeability by using traditional craftsmen and watchmaker's tools. The *système Gribeauval* had to be combined with the new machine tools emerging from the First (or British) Industrial Revolution to make the American System of Manufacturing possible. While in Paris, Jefferson bought a copy of Diderot's great *Encyclopédie des Arts, des Sciences et des Métiers*, for which he paid 15,068 pounds of good tobacco. This book has been described as 'one of the most ambitious attempts in early modern history to describe technological knowledge';[14] in the preface, Diderot acknowledged his intellectual debt to the Englishman, Bacon.

The outstanding example of French influence on the American world of manufacturing lay in the creation of EI du Pont de Nemours, still one of the world's leading chemical companies. It was founded in America in 1804 to produce black gunpowder by Éleuthère Irénée du Pont de Nemours, a French immigrant. DuPont[15] was the first of our Great Engine companies to be created. Its eponymous founder had been a student in Paris of the great Antoine Lavoisier (1743–1794), generally regarded as the father of modern chemistry, who formulated the First Law of Thermodynamics and is also one of the two men separately credited with discovering oxygen, the other being the English Unitarian minister, Joseph Priestley. Despite his intellectual distinction, Lavoisier was guillotined under the Terror.

There was nothing new about black gunpowder in America in the first decade of the nineteenth century. What du Pont introduced to the American explosives industry was *quality in manufacture*, a recurring theme in this book. His gunpowder was reliable: it exploded when you wanted it to and did not explode when you did not want it to. As such it was highly valued throughout the Union. Jefferson wrote to thank him for supplying the explosives used to clear land at Monticello. In 1834, the Eleutherian Mills would produce more than 1 million pounds of black gunpowder.[16] DuPont's headquarters in Wilmington became the center of a cluster of chemical companies that were attracted to it as suppliers, customers or simply imitators of the company, and which survives to this day.

Why did the United States welcome technology with open arms, whereas Britain accepted it only reluctantly or not at all? The answer almost certainly lies in the combination of the universality of public education in the north-eastern states with the pragmatic, utilitarian outlook of its Puritan citizens, which predisposed them to entertain new ways of doing things, when they were demonstrably better than what had gone before. For the early Puritan migrants, literacy had been a priority because they wished every citizen to have direct access to Holy Writ – not just to the gospels but also to the Old Testament, to which they attached so much importance. They also valued numeracy; both were important for the ordinary conduct of life – tools just like the wheelbarrow or the spade. Compulsory universal primary education was established by law in Massachusetts in 1647 and rapidly copied in most of the other New England colonies. The famous 'common schools' emerged, where the three Rs, and much else besides, were drilled into the minds of generation after generation of children. To judge by the US government's recent National Assessment of Adult Literacy (see page 201), the average citizen in the New England of the seventeenth and eighteen centuries was more literate and numerate than are his counterparts throughout the nation today; he or she was infinitely better educated than the average English person of the same period. Universal primary education would not materialize in England until around 1890, when William Gladstone's Education Act of 1870 came into effect – nearly two and a half centuries after the Puritan migrants had established it in the Bay Colony.

When the employment of children in New England textile mills became routine in the early nineteenth century, their educational needs were not overlooked. In 1836 a statute passed by the Massachusetts legislature, which was enforced, provided that no child under the age of fifteen years should be employed in any manufacturing establishment, unless he or she spent one-quarter of his or her time attending a day school: 'where instruction is given by a teacher qualified according to law to teach orthography, reading, writing, English grammar, geography, arithmetic, and good behaviour (*sic*)'.

In the previous year, Richard Cobden, the British statesman and apostle of free trade, had visited the United States and taken note of the quality of education there. Prophetically, he wrote the lines:

> If knowledge be power, and if education give knowledge, then must the Americans inevitably become the most powerful people in the world.[17]

– which is also why the Second Industrial Revolution would be primarily an American affair. In nineteenth-century Britain, the blossoming flower of technology was trampled underfoot. A century or so later, Brooke Hindle, future senior historian at the National Museum of American History, part of the Smithsonian Institution, would serve in the US army in Germany during World War II. He observed that, when an American officer had trouble with his jeep, he could usually tell his mechanic what the problem was but that, if a British officer encountered a similar problem, he would leave the diagnosis to others.[18] National cultures run deep and last long.

The following list identifies the inventors and their primary contributions in the order in which they appear in the portrait opposite, starting from the left side:

Dr. William Thomas Green Morton: surgical anesthesia
James Bogardus: cast-iron construction
Samuel Colt: revolving pistol
Cyrus Hall McCormick: mechanical reaper
Joseph Saxton: coal-burning stove, hydrometer, ever-pointed pencil
Charles Goodyear: vulcanization of rubber
Peter Cooper: railway locomotive
Jordan Lawrence Mott: coal-burning cooking stove
Joseph Henry: electromagnet design
Eliphalet Nott: efficient heat conduction for stoves and steam engines
John Ericsson: armored turret warship
Frederick Sickels: steam-engine gear and steering device for ships
Samuel F.B. Morse: electric telegraph
Henry Burden: horseshoe manufacturing machine
Richard March: rotary press
Erastus Bigelow: power loom for carpets
Isaiah Jennings: threshing machine, repeating gun, friction match
Thomas Blanchard: irregular turning lathe
Elias Howe: sewing machine

PART II
RISE

4: *Men of Progress* by Christian Schussele (1824–1879).
See key on facing page and page 63.

5: Robbins and Lawrence Armoury, Windsor, Vermont (c. 1840).[1]
See page 62.

6: 'Mr. Taylor Discusses the Principles of Scientific Management. Oh joy!'[2]
See page 129.

5

Colonel Roswell Lee Designs
the Prototype

With the impact of French technology on the traditional Puritan out-look, the way was open for the creation of an American System of Manufactures, which would be so much admired by the British public in London at the Great Exhibition in 1851 and which led to the Second (or American) Industrial Revolution. Who was the principal agent in creating it? Historians give the credit to an army officer, Col. Roswell Lee, a Connecticut man who was superintendent of the federal armory at Springfield, Massachusetts from 1815 until his death in 1833. The Springfield Armory had been established ten years before, by no less a person than President Washington, as a center for weapon-making. Lee transformed it from a workshop of skilled craftsmen into a mecha-nized manufacturing plant, the first in the country.[1]

It would be an exaggeration to say that Lee created an assembly line; at Springfield, the various manufacturing units were so far apart that the Armory had to employ a 'teamster' (a driver of a team of mules) full-time to ferry materials and parts between them. Nevertheless, the key elements of future lines were present – including specialized machine tools at a succession of distinct work stations and a flow of parts and unfinished goods towards a single destination. It was less of an assembly line than the block mill that the British admiralty had established in Portsmouth, England in 1805 but it constituted, none-theless, an enormous leap forward. If, as we are told, Hamilton conceived the role of the American chief executive in a political and banking context,[2] Lee can be regarded as its earliest manifestation in manufacturing.

The typical Great Engine company of the mid-twentieth century would contain various semi-autonomous divisions making different products. It would be 'managed by a hierarchy of salaried executives' consisting of a line-of-command and a number of 'staff' departments.[3] The line-of-command was essentially a conduit, up which informa-tion, and down which both information *and* instructions, were expected to travel expeditiously. The 'staff' departments reported to senior 'line' managers and carried out various supporting functions. There was a 'bottom-up' approach to management (see Chapter 9), although not by that name, which meant that effective responsibility for decision-making was passed down to the lowest level capable of accepting it. Finally, the company would in many cases constitute a kind of miniature 'welfare state' for its employees – in the case of enterprises in 'company towns', looking after many of them in one way or another from the cradle to the grave.

Lee's Armory exemplified all but one of these traits at least in outline, the exception being that it did not possess a multiplicity of divisions – unsurprising, since it made only guns. However, there was a clear line-of-command flowing from the superintendent down through the foremen to the leading hands. Employees who performed the 'staff' functions of purchasing, sales, accounts and transportation reported to the superintendent's deputy, the master armorer, while those who performed the role of quality inspectors reported to the assistant master armorer. The existence of this well-articulated hierarchy permitted what is now known as 'management development' to figure high on the superintendent's agenda: 'a system of internal job ladders meant that skilled mechanics could be promoted to positions of shop foreman, inspector, Assistant Master Armorer and Master Armorer. The latter were especially prestigious positions, with high salaries.'[4]

The master armorer could stand in for the superintendent when the latter was absent on business or sick, which meant that there was 'depth of management'. As evidence of the existence of some 'bottom-up' elements, one can cite the freedom given to workers in the choice of techniques (when Lehigh coal first became available for welding metal barrels, employees who preferred to continue using charcoal were permitted to do so) and the encouragement given to workers to innovate. Significantly, when new techniques were being tested, generous day rates would replace piece rates, so that the workmen did not associate the introduction of new methods with a loss of pay. The Armory became a test bed for the development of new techniques in wood and metalworking as well as in management. As gauges, machine tools and other instruments multiplied and improved, it became possible for its employees to make guns to closer tolerances, bringing manufacturing in general ever-nearer to the Holy Grail of complete interchangeability of parts.

Finally, like many a future Great Engine company, the Armory was an 'enlightened' employer. It housed its employees. Employees' children were not entitled to be educated in the local schools; Lee therefore arranged for them to be taught within the Armory precincts. (Interestingly, adult employees were also allowed to attend the lessons part time.) Lee built a church for his employees, his son, who became the incumbent, going on in time to become the episcopal bishop of Kentucky. The Armory even ran an out-placement service for ex-employees, finding them positions, first in other armories, and then, increasingly, in other kinds of manufacturing where their skills were much appreciated. In these and other ways, Lee looked after his 250 employees – as many Great Engine companies would do in the next century.

Springfield also performed another, quite distinct, role in society: it acted as a clearing house for new concepts and practices, providing leadership and a sense of direction to the whole confraternity of New England gun-makers. These men were collegial in their outlook, sharing information with each other about new opportunities and new techniques, even sharing business. Information passed by outsiders to the Armory could not, by law, be patented, which meant that it passed rapidly into general circulation. A willingness to share information on best practice (for example, on the 'best way to schedule maintenance') would also be normal among the Great Engine companies of the mid-twentieth century – something one cannot say of British and continental European companies of the same or, indeed, of any period. It survives today among better-managed American companies: recently Whirlpool Corporation has 'hosted delegations from Hewlett-Packard, Nokia, and Procter & Gamble' – all eager to learn about the appliance maker's innovative approach to the development and design of new products.[5]

Until the 1840s, the largest employers in the United States had been the textile mills. The contrast in managerial styles with Lee's Armory could not have been greater. Although some of the mills had incorporated as companies, from a managerial point of view they continued to operate like old-style partnerships. The only full-time senior executive was likely to be the treasurer, who would also be a major shareholder; the mill itself might be supervised by an agent, to whom the charge hands reported. In other words, there was no managerial hierarchy as we would understand it today. It follows that the various organizational changes introduced by Lee were completely new to the world of American business. However, the Armory and its emulators would benefit greatly from the achievement of the textile mills in creating a pool of able mechanics and in developing the basic commercial skills of buying and selling.

It would be wrong to characterize the new manufacturing regime simply as one in which interesting, skilled work was replaced by boring, unskilled labor. Much of the work of the eighteenth-century craftsmen had been dull, repetitive and inaccurate. Moreover, building the new machines required technical ingenuity and dexterity, as did maintaining them in good working order. Operating was a responsible and not always a simple task; one mistake could destroy the machine and perhaps the operative as well. As Frederick W. Taylor, would say much later:

> A lathe is not like a loom which, after it is set, can only weave the one particular pattern for which it is set. A lathe is run from morning till night by an intelligent man who is obliged to guide it, as it were, just as if it were a high spirited horse . . . He has to have a lot of brains to use his machine.[6]

The skills of the machine builder, the maintenance engineer and the operator would replace those of the craftsman – and the quality of the products would be immeasurably enhanced.

Lee had distinguished himself as a major in the war of 1812 against the British. We can assume that it was in the course of his career as a soldier that he had learned the value of hierarchy.[7] His genius, therefore, lay in being able to apply in one walk of life a lesson he had learned in another. If anyone can be credited with initiating what Alfred Chandler – the doyen of business historians – has described as 'the Managerial Revolution in American Business', it was he. Or, as that other leading business historian, Daniel Wren, has told us:

> The principles of manufacturing pioneered at the Springfield Armory provided the basis for the later manufacture of axes, shovels, sewing machines, clocks, locks, watches, steam engines, reapers, and other products. What visitors admired at the Crystal Palace exhibit of 1851 was the product of a long chain of developments – beginning with the Springfield Armory and transferring to private industry. Mass production had not yet been perfected, but its antecedents were present.[8]

He was referring, of course, to the American exhibits at the Great Exhibition held in London in 1851, of which more later in this chapter. The fact that the Armory was open to visitors meant that its message was widely spread and set a pattern for the future Great Engine companies, which would also open their doors freely to strangers. The continuation of this practice would surprise and please the Japanese, who came by the thousand between 1950 and 1970, notebooks and cameras in hand, to visit hundreds of factories and to learn about both the practice of management and the latest manufacturing techniques.

When was complete uniformity achieved in the manufacture of American machinery in general, as opposed to being merely promised or approximated? That question is difficult to answer precisely. Wren has suggested that it had already been achieved by 1851. Not only were the American products displayed there, he tells us: 'superior to those of other nations, they were all made in a unique fashion – the parts were built to such exacting standards that they were interchangeable, so a person could pick up the parts at random and assemble a complete product'.[9] This is an overstatement.

When Colt was interviewed about his methods by a committee of the British House of Commons in 1854, he was asked: 'When you made those 50,000 in a year, could any one part of one gun, for instance, be adapted to another gun; were they so accurately made that you might assemble the parts together, the locks and other parts, indiscriminately?' He replied *not* with an unambiguous 'yes' but by saying, 'I should say that they would do that a great deal better than any arms made by hand', adding that with 'a touch of a polishing machine' perhaps 95 per cent of the parts could be made to interchange.[10] If nineteen out of twenty of the parts were interchangeable with the help of an adjustment by a machine tool, what percentage could have been switched without one? The US Census of 1880 put the matter in a nutshell, comparing practices then current with those in use at the beginning of the century:

> Uniformity in gun-work was then, as now, a comparative term; but then it meant within a thirty-second of an inch or more, where now it means within half a thousandth of an inch. Then interchangeability may have signified a great deal of filing and fitting, and an uneven joint when fitted, where now it signifies slipping in a piece, turning a screw-driver, and having a close, even fit.[11]

Moreover, what was true of guns was not necessarily true of other products. We are told that the parts of Singer sewing machines were numbered until late in the century 'to show the order in which they were made and therefore which parts would fit together'.[12] The probability is that complete uniformity was not achieved across the whole of manufacturing until the early twentieth century; by 1914, when Henry Ford was successfully mass-producing the Model T, it could be taken for granted.

Perfection was not necessary for the American System to effect its transformative magic on business and society; partial interchangeability accompanied by numbering of parts as required, or by the judicious use of a hand file or polishing machine, was good enough. As first the canals in the 1820s and then the railroads in the 1830s spread across the land, goods produced according to the new methods traveled with them to meet the needs of an emerging market. Paradoxically, in the age of the factory and the machine tool, a major new cottage industry grew up as half the population learned how to make and mend clothes at home, using the new-fangled, mass-produced sewing machines. Mass production created *affordable* goods of *high quality* that could be, and increasingly were, bought by ordinary citizens.

Why did the American System of Manufactures develop and triumph in the United States and not in Britain where the Industrial Revolution had originated and which was in some ways technically more advanced than the United States, even towards the end of the nineteenth century when Andrew Carnegie would adopt from Britain the Bessemer process for steel-making? Economic historians like to reply in terms of broad statistical abstractions, the received view being that it was a question of differential wage rates. Labor was plentiful and cheap in the Old World but scarce and expensive in the New; there was therefore a powerful incentive to replace human beings with machinery. There is, however, a flaw in this argument: if labor was plentiful and cheap in Britain, why did the First Industrial Revolution take place there? L.T.C. Rolt doubts, by the way, whether there really was such a scarcity of cheap labor in America, pointing to the large numbers of immigrants employed in New England sweat shops and opining that: 'The idea that the "American System", which we now call mass production, was introduced for the purpose of saving labour is therefore fallacious'.[13]

A variant on the labor theory has been put forward by Geoffrey Owen, who argues that it was a shortage of *skilled* people that led to the development of the American System: 'Since American manufacturers did not have access to the pool of skilled workers which was available in Britain, they looked for manufacturing methods which economized on the use of craft skills'.[14] It is undeniable both that the new manufacturing methods reduced the need for skilled craftsmen and that there was a shortage of such people in the New World, particularly gun makers. However, it is doubtful if the development of the American System was due to this shortage. The new kind of entrepreneur *preferred* to hire the unskilled and to train them up for the new kinds of skill required in a machine shop, so that they did not have to 'unlearn' bad habits.

Yet others have maintained that it was the abundance of raw materials like wood, coal and iron that led to the development of the American System in America and not in Britain. According to this view, mass production was wasteful of raw material and therefore a luxury that Britain could ill afford. It is a matter of fact that such abundance did exist in America and not in Britain, and no-one will dispute that mass production was relatively wasteful. However, the availability of raw materials has to be regarded as a pre-condition for the development of the System, rather than a cause. It is more fruitful to seek for an answer to the question in the social context.

Classical economics is essentially quantitative in approach and treats labor as a more or less uniform commodity to be bought and sold, hired and fired. This book addresses primarily the *quality* of the national workforces of the period. On that subject, useful information can be gleaned from two kinds of source: reports by Britons who visited the United States either before or soon after the Great Exhibition and comparisons made by American entrepreneurs who, as a result of the exhibition, set up plants in Britain. The second kind is to be trusted more since it represents the views of practitioners with direct experience of both sides of the Atlantic. Both, however, point in the same direction.

At a meeting at the Society of Arts in London in 1857, the lock maker, Alfred C. Hobbs, presented an extreme version of a typical view arising from his own experience. If a manufacturer tried to 'invent a machine' in America, he said:

> ... all the workmen in the establishment would, if possible, lend a helping hand. If they saw an error, they would mention it, and in every possible way they would aid in carrying out the idea. But in England it was quite the reverse. If the workmen could do anything to make a machine go wrong they would do it . . .[15]

Colt would in the end shut down his British gun factories for a similar reason; Hobbs kept his open.

Most commentators agree in attributing the supportive attitude of the American workforce to better education. Education in the common schools had all kinds of consequences and implications. For one thing, it facilitated the practice of thinking and behaving rationally, abstract thought not coming easily to an illiterate and innumerate population. Since it applied to both sexes, it tended to equalize them. It created a more open and receptive mind on the part of workmen. It also served to eliminate social barriers, never very strong in any case in the north-eastern colonies or states. The ordinary workman, who could talk, write and count as easily as his bosses, was a natural candidate for promotion to the new junior, middle and senior management positions that the American System was throwing up. This aspect was much remarked on by visitors from the Old World at that time. For example, the British engineer, Sir Joseph Whitworth (1803–1887), wrote in 1854:

> It rarely happens that an [American] workman who possesses peculiar skill in his craft is disqualified to take the responsible position of superintendent, by want of education and general knowledge, as is frequently the case in this country. In every State in the Union, and

particularly in the north, education is, by means of the common schools, placed within the reach of each individual, and all classes avail themselves of the opportunities afforded.[16]

A similar point of view would be expressed eleven years later in evidence to a House of Commons committee by a British hardware manufacturer, A. Field, who had spent fourteen years in the United States: 'An American [workman] readily produces a new article; he understands everything you say to him *as well as a man from a college in England* would; he helps the employer by his own acuteness and intelligence . . .' (emphasis added).[17]

If the attitude of what we now call the American 'blue-collar' workforce was positive to the new methodology, what can one say about the attitude of the emerging American managerial class – some of whom would have risen from its ranks? A clue is to be found in the very name that the British gave to the new methodology: it was a *System*. Systems existed in Britain too – her water mills, steam engines and machine tools were so every bit as much as their equivalents in America and were even referred to as such. It was in the *systematizing,* or integration, of systems that the Americans scored. Colt, Hobbs and McCormick were all in that sense archetypical figures because they each combined in one person the skills of invention, entrepreneurship, supervision and marketing.

According to the dictionary, a system is 'a set of connected things or parts', bound together to a purpose. If ever a society deserved to be called a System with a capital S, it was that of the Bay Colony of Massachusetts. It had been planned and created according to a 'blueprint' by its Puritan founders. It was set in a new, empty site so that there was no legacy of dissident citizens whose views might call into question the principles on which it was based. Every aspect of its life and work was bent to a single purpose: the creation of a New Jerusalem, Governor Winthrop's 'Citty on the Hill'. (Jeru)Salem was the name of the place where they settled first; it had been named by an earlier settler. With the passage of time, the harsh Puritan outlook would soften but the systemic approach incorporating the ethic of work and the habit of thrift generated by Calvinism would extend across the entire nation. It underlay the creation of the typical manufacturing and other companies of the Golden Age of Management, which we will describe as Great Engines of Growth and Prosperity, as well as the organization of much else besides.

The academic, Merritt Roe Smith, attributes the success of Springfield to a variety of causes including its location, willing workers and excellent managers. Behind all these, however, he saw the Puritan influence which:

> ... steeped in religion and accentuated by social control, extended back to the mid-seventeenth century. While the underpinnings of Congregational orthodoxy had been diluted by continuous infusions of new people and secular ideas, many distinct shades of the Puritan ethic could still be seen in widely shared norms that encouraged industriousness, sanctioned discipline, and viewed change as a positive force for social betterment. Such deeply internalized values provided excellent incentives at Springfield, and invariably visitors noted them while commenting upon the community's vitality and flair for innovation.[18]

The great, indeed unique, American tradition of salesmanship had started in the First Great Awakening of the mid-eighteenth century as Puritan divines 'packaged' and 'sold' their religious beliefs to their often backsliding congregations. It was reinforced during the Second Great Awakening in the early nineteenth century when spiritual and material concerns became intertwined in the minds of Protestant divines and their flocks.

It was in the mid-nineteenth century that the British (into whom the English had metamorphosed a century and a half before) became aware that they were being overtaken by their American cousins in the exercise of Bacon's 'mechanical arts'. The occasion was the Great Exhibition referred to above and held in London in 1851 with the purpose of celebrating the successes of Britain's own manufacturing and of providing a showcase for her products. It was housed in a specially constructed glass building, soon nicknamed 'the Crystal Palace' by thousands of enthusiastic visitors. There was much for the locals to celebrate. The wealth generated by the First Industrial Revolution had allowed, first, Admiral Nelson to defeat Napoleon's navy at Trafalgar in 1805 and, then, the Duke of Wellington to defeat Napoleon's army at Waterloo in 1815. In the brief thirty-six years since the end of the French wars, Britain had become 'the workshop of the world'. Her Majesty's ships ruled the seven seas and ensured freedom for everyone's commerce. A combination of industrial might and martial skill had turned a medium-sized country into a Great Power in a few brief decades.

There was, however, a second reason motivating the sponsors of the exhibition: the early 1850s were a period of great social optimism in Britain, accompanied by a belief that free trade benefited all nations. This view was strongly held by Queen Victoria's German husband and

cousin, Prince Albert of Saxe-Coburg-Gotha, who was one of its principal sponsors. The mid-Victorians believed in the value of competition.
There were over 100,000 entries submitted by 13,937 exhibitors, almost
half of the latter foreign.[19]

The American exhibits arrived late, occasioning derision, the area
allotted to them being labeled the Prairie Ground on account of its vast
emptiness. A large, threatening double-headed eagle erected above it
caused irritation. However, when the exhibits did arrive, derision and
irritation turned first to curiosity and then to amazement. In addition
to many new versions of old products, there were new types of product
like Samuel Colt's revolving pistols, Isaac Singer's sewing machines
and Cyrus McCormick's mechanical reapers. The Great Exhibition
marked a watershed in the history of both countries. It was in these
exhibits that the roots of America's future rise as an industrial, economic and, ultimately, political power, as well as Britain's future
decline, were first made manifest to the general public.

In 1835, Cobden had observed that, in matters of manufacture, the
former colonists were pulling ahead of their motherland, as the British
had earlier pulled ahead of the Dutch:

> The Americans possess a quicker mechanical genius than even our-
> selves . . . as witness their patents, and the improvements for which
> we are indebted to individuals of that country in mechanics – such as
> spinning, engraving &c. We gave additional speed to our ships, by
> improving upon the naval architecture of the Dutch; and the simili-
> tude again applies to the superiority which, in comparison with the
> British models, the Americans have . . . imparted to their vessels.[20]

In the First Industrial Revolution, machinery had been constructed
using traditional hand-operated tools, which lacked power and precision. The Americans had replaced them with machine tools –
sometimes described as 'machines for making machines' – powered by
water or, later, steam and had also made extensive use of accurate
gauges for measurement. These developments would allow manufacturing to be undertaken with sufficient precision for guns, and then
other articles, to be made with interchangeable parts. It was at the
Great Exhibition that the British dubbed the new methodology 'the
American System of Manufactures'.

Achieving interchangeability would have three spectacular consequences for manufacturing – and ultimately for mankind as a whole. It
became possible to create inventories of spare parts, which meant that
the new machinery coming into use everywhere could be repaired
without the intervention of a craftsman – sometimes thousands of
miles from the place where it had been made. Moreover, the door was

opened for what would later be called 'mass production', which depended on the manufacture of thousands of identical parts and their subsequent assembly into complete machines or consumer goods, whether or not on a formal 'assembly line'. Finally, mass production would permit the creation of a mass market, which in turn necessitated, and depended on, distribution and advertising on a large scale. The decades immediately after 1880, when the System was in full swing, are referred to as the Second (or American) Industrial Revolution.[21]

Sam Colt typified that great stock figure of early American life and comedy, the traveling showman-cum-salesman. As a young man, he had sailed before the mast. Later, as 'Dr Coult (*sic*) of London, New York and Calcutta', he peddled laughing gas; patrons paid 25 cents to watch other patrons make fools of themselves under the influence of nitrous oxide. Before going to London for the Great Exhibition, he had persuaded Governor Horatio Seymour of Connecticut to bestow on him a rank in the state's militia in exchange for services rendered during a recent election campaign – his job as aide-de-camp appears to have been to get the candidate home from meetings before he became drunk. He knew that as Col. Samuel Colt (actually he was a lieutenant colonel) he was more likely to impress the British military than as plain old Sam. Whatever the reason, Wellington is said to have paid over fifty visits to his site.

However, Colt was also a visionary and a man with a good business sense. Although he had conceived and patented the revolving pistol, he was aware of his own deficiencies as a mechanic and had entered into a partnership with an Elisha K. Root. In his authoritative book, *Tools for the Job: A Short History of Machine Tools*, L.T.C. Rolt has described Root as 'a Massachusetts farmer's son who was then considered the best mechanic in New England';[22] Root's technical and managerial skills, coupled with Colt's vision and salesmanship, were responsible for the success of their products. They provided another example of the application of the doctrine of complementarity, which would become an indispensable element in the success of the large companies of the mid-twentieth century. This doctrine means that, within any team, the strengths and weakness of individual members complement one another; it works only when there is a sufficient degree of humility on the part of each person for him to admit to his own deficiencies and acknowledge the strengths of another or others.

McCormick's mowing machine, the Virginia reaper, provided even more excitement at the Great Exhibition than did the Colt revolver. A Virginian by birth and domicile, as the name he gave to his invention implies, he was among the first of the great American mechanics *not* to have been born in New England; of Scotch-Irish stock, he was, correspondingly, a Presbyterian and, therefore, a Calvinist by religion or, at least, by origin.[23] His father, a blacksmith, had spent twenty years trying to invent a mechanical reaper and failed; the son successfully demonstrated his own version in 1831. Doggedness, combined with a high degree of irascibility, seems to have been a family trait; Cyrus famously sued the Pennsylvania Railroad for twenty-one years over one damaged piece of baggage. A century later his great-nephew, Col. Robert R. McCormick, the legendary editor of the *Chicago Tribune*, would pursue political vendettas for decades; an arch-conservative, he regarded the Republican President Herbert Hoover as 'the greatest state socialist in history' and the Democratic President Franklin D. Roosevelt quite simply as 'a Communist'. A man who detested both Britain and America's anglicized eastern seaboard, he believed that, if the country was ever invaded from the east, it should be defended only along a line that ran from Albany south to Pittsburgh, Atlanta and Houston.[24] When he visited General Douglas MacArthur in Tokyo during the US Occupation of Japan (see page 108), McCormick would be horrified to discover that Japan's effective ruler had been applying New Deal-style social policies in that country.

When Cyrus displayed a model of his reaper in London in 1851, he found himself in competition with another American manufacturer called Hussey. Both men were invited to a trial on a model farm near London. The wheat was still green and, predictably, it rained all day, not unusual in a British summer. The Hussey machine slid over the wet grain without catching. McCormick's cut the soggy stalks with dispatch, at a pace estimated to be the equivalent of twenty acres a day. When the Virginia reaper was re-assembled in the Crystal Palace a few days later, the Prairie Ground filled up with people enquiring about it. The American commissioner to the exhibition reported that it probably received even more visitors than the Queen Victoria's Koh-i-noor diamond, which was also on display.

The most excitement of all to be generated by any American visitor, however, arose from the activities of the locksmith, Hobbs. In 1784, Joseph Bramah, a London toolmaker, had applied for a patent for a new and complicated padlock, which was granted in 1787. He placed the invention in his shop window, offering a prize of 200 guineas (equivalent to something like $15,000 today) to anyone who could pick it.[25] Many attempts were made in the next half century, all of which failed. Hobbs asked if he could have a go. The lock was moved for the purpose to the Crystal Palace. Challenges of this kind were not uncommon in the mid-Victorian era and the curiosity of the public was aroused, particularly as Hobbs had just successfully picked another British lock made by a firm called Chubb. (Chubb effected a kind of revenge a century later when it bought out the successor firm of Hobbs, Hart & Co.)

It took Hobbs fifty-one hours of work, spread over sixteen days, to discover how to pick the Bramah lock, after which he could open it in just twenty-five minutes.[26] He was awarded a medal by the exhibition jurors. He then put one of his own locks on display, alongside the Bramah padlock, and challenged anyone to open it. No-one could. (Five years later, even his lock would be picked by another American, Linus Yale.) The Bramah padlock now sits in the Science Museum in London; so far as the current members of the Bramah family are aware, no-one has been able to open it since, except with a key.[27]

By a coincidence that is happy or not, depending on one's nationality, on August 22, 1851, the day before Hobbs finally picked the Bramah lock,[28] a schooner called simply and patriotically *America*, entered by the New York Yacht Club, won a race around the Isle of Wight. It was not just any old race. In 1848, Queen Victoria had authorized the creation of a One Hundred Guinea Cup of solid silver for an event 'open to all nations' – the same kind of idealism that had led to the invitation to other countries to participate in the exhibition. The host was the Royal Yacht Squadron, the premier private yacht club. *America*'s designer, W.H. Brown, had been so confident of the quality of his design that he offered to take the yacht back and repay the purchase price if it did not win. It did – by a huge margin.

According to legend, when Queen Victoria was informed of the result, she asked who was second, to which the reply was: 'Your Majesty, there is no second'. This outcome of this race established an American supremacy in yachtsmanship and design that lasted until 1983, when an Australian yacht would capture what had become known as the America's Cup. Curiously enough, both these American victories were controversial. We are told that the *America* sailed a shorter course than the other yachts and that she would, in any case, have lost if she had been properly handicapped. Hobbs declined to allow the Bramah family to open the lock with a key immediately after he had picked it, creating a suspicion that he had deliberately broken it and effected a repair. In any case, as many people pointed out at the time, if it took one of the world's greatest experts, operating in the most favorable of circumstances conceivable, fifty-one hours to pick a lock, it was for practical purposes burglar-proof. Both the *America* and Hobbs were formally adjudged to have won.

Parliament was so shocked by what it had learned about the Americans' ability to manufacture machines with (more or less) interchangeable parts that it sent a commission to the United States in 1853 to learn more. The occasion was a second Great Exhibition, held in New York and modeled on the London event. The same system of classification was used for the items on display, which were housed in another Crystal Palace. The importance attached by the authorities in London to this visit is indicated by the fact that the commissioners included not only Whitworth, the greatest British toolmaker of his day, but also George Wallis, headmaster of the Birmingham School of Art, Charles Dilke, who had been one of the most zealous promoters of the first Great Exhibition and a member of its executive committee as well as the distinguished Scottish geologist Charles Lyell, who would take a special interest in the availability of raw materials. (Charles Darwin relied on Lyell's studies of fossils in developing his theory of evolution.[29]) Whitworth had a second reason for wishing to attend: a selection of his excellent machine tools were on display.

Fortunately for posterity, the New York exhibition opened late. So that his time would not be wasted, Whitworth set off on a tour of manufacturing and other establishments in the north-eastern states, using the extensive railroad network that had been created in the two previous decades and now reached as far as Pittsburgh. Other commissioners did likewise. As a result, they were able to obtain a deeper understanding of the American System of Manufactures than they could have by visiting only the show.

Under the influence of their highly favorable reports, the British Board of Ordnance decided to create a new armory at Enfield near London, equipped with American machine tools, to make small arms with interchangeable parts. To achieve this end, they set up a Committee on the Machinery of the United States, some of whose members would go to the small hill town of Windsor, Vermont the following year, where they purchased machine tools from the firm of Robbins and Lawrence, which had exhibited at the first Great Exhibition. London was in those days at the center of the civilized world, the United States at its periphery – and Vermont at the northern edge of the United States. Something seismic was afoot; the center of industrial and, ultimately, of economic and political, power was beginning to shift.

In the new armory, muskets were 'assembled' from parts already made. As Nathan Rosenberg has pointed out his *The American System of Manufactures*, it is significant that John Anderson, the Scottish civil servant and engineer who wrote the committee's report, felt it necessary to surround this verb with inverted commas.[30] It was a neologism that, like all good ones, had been devised to describe a new article or practice. The word was pregnant with meaning. Traditional craftsmen did not 'assemble' muskets in a few minutes, they *fitted* them – which could take hours, or even a day, for one gun. Fitting (which meant mostly hand filing) had been the most skilled part of musket-making; creating parts for guns using machine tools required a different skill set; the actual act of 'assembling' them required no skill at all. Henry Ford would say the final word on this matter: 'in mass production, there are no fitters'.[31]

The American System's popular heroes would be inventors *and* their artifacts. Christian Schussele's portrait of *Men of Progress* painted in 1863 (see page 47) celebrated the role of both in American society and sought to place them in a national pantheon.[32] Those portrayed include: Cyrus McCormick (whom we have already met in London) standing beside a model of his reaper; Charles Goodyear, with a pair of rubber boots under his chair; Elias Howe seated behind his patented sewing machine, which would soon be overtaken by the Singer model; and Samuel Morse, seated beside a transmission key. Hanging on the wall is a picture of Benjamin Franklin, an important precursor of Morse in electrical experimentation. While it is right to admire these men and their creations, however, we should not overlook Rolt's stricture: 'The whole history of technology proves that major technical revolutions of this order [e.g. achieving interchangeability] are never brought about by one individual.'[33]

In 1851, the London *Daily News* would refer to the American site at the Great Exhibition as 'the domain of Brother Jonathan', that being the name for the archetypal American of the period. As John Russell Bartlett wrote in his *Dictionary of Americanisms* published in 1848, the term 'Yankee' was applied to a portion of the United States but '"*Brother Jonathan*" has now become a designation for the whole country, as John Bull has for England'. How did the expression originate? The most likely origin is the Biblical saying, 'I am distressed for thee, my brother Jonathan'. Used as a term of abuse for their Bible-thumping Puritan opponents by Royalists during the English Civil War (1642–1651), it was applied by British officers to the rebellious colonists during the American Revolution. The last-named must have adopted it as a badge of honor, something which has happened in history to a number of terms of abuse, whereupon it became a name for a typical citizen.[34] A novel by John Neal with this name had been published in 1825.

Winifred Morgan in her delightful monograph *An American Icon: Brother Jonathan and American Identity*, points to the use of the word 'brother' as an honorific which reflected usage in small New England communities, where neighbors would greet each other in this way in the morning on their way to work.[35] She adds that:

Jonathan's fullest development occurred roughly between ... 1800 and ... 1840. At no time since in peacetime history, except perhaps the 1930s, have the popular media in the United States so exalted the strength, courage, and wisdom of the common man. For these forty years Jonathan was the pre-eminent representative of the American everyman.[36]

It is curious, however, that Morgan makes no reference to the association of the name with manufactures. The American System was an expression and outcome of the inherited, highly integrated and systematized Puritan culture that Jonathan, in at least one of his persona, symbolized. It was used twice to name artifacts that would become famous in their time – first, for a railroad locomotive and, then, for a steamship.

Railroads had been invented and developed in Britain. However, on early American railroads, the tracks were not laid as pedantically straight as on their British counterparts, with the unfortunate result that early locomotives of British origin or design tended to leap off, sometimes taking the carriages and passengers or goods with them. In theory, there were two possible solutions: either the existing tracks could be re-laid, and new tracks put down, to more exacting specifications, which would have been vastly expensive given the millions of miles to be covered; or the design of locomotives could be altered to suit the existing style of track. Sensibly, American engineers chose the simpler and cheaper course.

The problem was first addressed in August 1831, soon after the Camden and Amboy Railroad (later part of the Pennsylvania Railroad) took delivery of a shiny new locomotive built by Stephenson & Company of Newcastle-on-Tyne in Britain. In honor of its country of origin, it was named the *John Bull* and entered in the company's books as engine 'No. 1'. The reception party included the last-surviving signatory of the Declaration of Independence; it is an indication of the importance that the citizens of the young republic attached to technical innovation that he declared the arrival of the *John Bull* to be the most important event in his life! In Britain, by way of contrast, the railways would be greeted with fear, contempt and derision – evidence of a popular distrust of technology that lasts to this day. However, the *John Bull*'s framework proved to be too inflexible for the local roadbed; something had to give. 'As the railroad curves were very sharp, the coupling rods and cranks were removed and a lateral play of 1½ in. given to the leading axle, to which a cowcatcher was connected'.[37] The *John Bull* was being naturalized.

An even bigger step in the same direction would be taken in the next year when John B. Jervis, the chief engineer of the Mohawk and Hudson Railroad (later part of the New York Central), created an all-American locomotive at his West Point foundry, in which the rigid front axle with its single pair of wheels was replaced with a flexible 'leading truck' consisting of two axles and two pairs of wheels. The function of the truck's small front wheels was to guide the locomotive along uneven tracks. The engine was christened the *Brother Jonathan* – no doubt with the *John Bull* in mind; capable of traveling at sixty miles an hour, it would become the fastest locomotive in the world and provide a model for most of its successors. In 1987, it would feature on a US postage stamp.[38] Pragmatism was not only an academic philosophy later espoused and developed by American thinkers like William James; in the sense of securing the maximum return for effort expended or, vulgarly, 'more bang for your buck', it was and would remain until the late 1960s an essential part of the American outlook.

Just over three decades after the locomotive of that name was built, in 1865, a paddle steamer called the *S.S. Brother Jonathan* struck the Saint George Reef near San Francisco and carried most of its 200 passengers and a treasure trove of gold coins, arising from the recent California Gold Rush, to the bottom;[39] for no obvious reason, the archetypal Jonathan disappeared from American public consciousness around the same time. (It is sometimes said that Uncle Sam replaced him, but that is a half truth; although represented by the same cartoon figure, Uncle Sam is a personification of the federal government, not of the average citizen.) However, Jonathan's Puritan spirit did not die with his name. It lived on and flourished for another hundred years, driving forward, first, the Second Industrial Revolution in the United States; and then a Third Industrial Revolution in Japan, East Asia and China.

Of the youthful United States in the 1830s, de Tocqueville had said: '. . . the human mind there is . . . constantly active, but it is much more involved in the infinite variations that flow from well-known principles and in the discovery of new variations than in seeking new principles themselves'.[40] His description of society would remain broadly correct until the last third of the twentieth century. It was then that 'new principles' derived ultimately from the writings of the management consultant, Frederick Winslow Taylor – see, in particular, Chapter 11 – would be applied in the form of the Cult of the (so-called) Expert, with disastrous results for business and society. The first three Parts of this book describe some of 'the infinite variations' that flowed between 1630 and 1970 from de Tocqueville's original 'well-known principles'; the fourth recounts the consequences of their abandonment after 1970; while the fifth looks at recent developments giving grounds for hope of recovery.

6

Dan McCallum Creates the
Multidivisional Corporation

As we have seen, the Springfield Armory offered us a miniature version
of the future American Great Engine companies in all respects except
one: it consisted of one operating unit only. It was the ante-bellum railroads that would provide the missing piece of the jigsaw by creating
the multidivisional or M-form pattern,[1] completing the template for
the future DuPonts, General Motors, General Electrics, Procter & Gam-
bles and, in the end, Toyotas. Creating the first M-form companies
posed numerous practical problems, to which obvious answers were
not readily available but with which the prevailing American management culture between 1830 and 1860 was well able to cope. A talent for
organization was one of the four enduring characteristics that American society had derived from its Puritan origins; all of these would be
tested to the full and not found wanting as the railroads set forth on
their adventurous journey across the continent.

The small, local, early railroads that came into existence in the 1830s
were easy to manage, being not very different in structure from some
family businesses of the period. There would be a single boss, the general superintendent, who knew the names of all his employees and told
them what to do; if they did not obey instructions, he admonished or
dismissed them. If they performed well, he promoted them as opportunities opened up. Reporting lines were simple and direct. However,
when the railroads extended outwards for first hundreds and then for
thousands of miles, and when they hired first hundreds and then
thousands of people, the structure came under strain. The general
superintendent became remote from most of his employees, whose
names he could not possibly know. How was a man sitting in Maryland, for example, to ensure that trains in Ohio ran on time, that
revenues were properly collected and that safety precautions were
observed?

Plugging that gap was accomplished by dividing the railroads into geographical sections under divisional superintendents, who would seek to replicate in their bailiwicks the direct relationships between management and labor that had existed on the earlier, smaller entities. Formally creating the divisions was the easy part of this reform; the difficult part was devising and introducing the many underlying routines that would enable the entire network to operate smoothly, safely and profitably as one system. This task fell originally to one Scottish-born immigrant, Daniel Craig McCallum (1815–1878).

McCallum's career is a classic, Horatio Alger-type story – although his *douce* Scottish mother would have objected strongly to the first word in the expression 'rags to riches' that usually accompanies that phrase.[2] Alger, a Unitarian minister, wrote improving tales about his fictional hero, Ragged Dick, who went from poverty to wealth through virtuous behavior. His books were to be found in most American households towards the end of the nineteenth century. Easy to sneer at today (and even then – Mark Twain satirized them), they embodied an important part of the Puritan conscience. Alger's own life was less successful than that of his hero; he found wealth but not happiness, ending up with a serious mental illness, possibly due to the suppression of homosexuality.

Arriving in the United States at the age of seven in 1822, McCallum had obtained some elementary schooling in Rochester, New York. Thereafter he became an accomplished carpenter, a successful architect and finally a civil engineer. In this last capacity he joined the New York and Erie Railroad (always known as 'the Erie') in 1848, soon becoming superintendent of its Susquehanna Division. (The Susquehanna River had formed the western frontier of Penn's Pennsylvania.) It was there that he first conceived, developed and successfully applied the practices and principles that would be identified with him. Six years later, the Erie Board, faced with an unacceptably high accident rate, appointed him to the post of general superintendent, with the brief of applying his approach to the whole network.

McCallum wrote in the Erie's annual report for 1855 that 'the larger roads were losing money because they lacked 'a system perfect in its details, properly adapted and vigilantly enforced'.[3] He sought 'a proper division of responsibilities', wishing to confer 'sufficient authority' on each divisional superintendent for them to be discharged. With that in mind, he laid down formal lines of authority and provided the means for measuring the performance of individuals, devised methods of cost accounting and improved the flow of information. Most of the managerial questions that would later have to be answered by the Great

Engine companies were first addressed by McCallum, both in theory and practice.

McCallum's great contribution was to discover how to combine a divisional structure with Lee's line-and-staff system; he did this by creating non-geographic, functional or 'staff' divisions, that overlay the geographic ones, and determining the precise relationship between the two. His line-of-command proceeded from the general superintendent down through the superintendents of the geographic divisions and then out to those directly in charge of traffic. In a well-run organization, a properly functioning line-of-command enables the most senior executive to take charge of a far-flung empire, while delegating operating responsibilities to the appropriate level. Meantime, the 'staff' divisions undertake a variety of supporting functions – in a railroad, for example, the construction of the track, the maintenance of the rolling stock, the accounts and personnel. Each 'staff' division would be endowed with its own miniature line-of-command. Whereas the principal line led directly from and to the general superintendent, these more modest lines would report to him through one of his deputies, a formula we first met at Lee's Armory.

There was just one serious flaw in McCallum's general approach to corporate control: he overlooked the human factor – in which respect he stood at the opposite end of the scale from the soldier, Lee. Believing that 'the enforcement of a rigid system of discipline' was indispensable to success, the Scots-American sought to eliminate any element of discretion at lower levels of management. This authoritarian outlook was manifest in his Six Principles of Management. Two of them sounded like something from the Shorter Catechism of the Calvinist Church of Scotland: '(4) Great promptness in the report of all derelictions of duty, so that evils may be corrected quickly', and '(6) The adoption of a system, as whole, which will not only enable the general superintendent to detect errors immediately, but to point to the delinquent'. In one's mind's eye, one sees an unfortunate *delinquent* employee, the *evil* of his *derelictions of duty* duly exposed, standing penitent before the elders of the railroad Kirk, from which he is about to be excommunicated.

It was McCallum who was excommunicated. The railroad's engineers resented the discipline that he imposed on them so much that they went on a strike that lasted for six months, resulting in his resignation in 1857. It was the end of his career as an executive of a railroad company but not as a businessman. In that same year, he founded the McCallum Bridge Company to market and install a kind of bridge that he had himself designed and patented, and which would earn him a small fortune. During the later years of the Civil War, he returned briefly to his earlier love, taking charge of the railroads on behalf of President Lincoln when, with the military rank of major general, he would organize the provision of supplies for General Sherman's famous (or infamous, if one is a Southerner) March through Georgia. He was one of the railroad men who were ultimately responsible for the Northern victory in the Civil War.

Later in life, McCallum retired to Brooklyn where, as Wren has wryly observed, he did not get involved in the bridge-building business but wrote and published poetry. The kindest thing that can be said of his verse is that it did not attain the high standards of his other work. In it self-abnegation ('thyself consider last') and exaltation of the work ethic ('work on while yet the sun doth shine, thou man of strength and will') is combined with a general pessimism about this world and optimism about the next:

> Soon will this fight of life be o'er, and earth recede from view,
> And Heaven in all its glory shine, where all is pure and true
> Ah! then thou'lt see more clearly still, the proverb deep and vast,
> The mill will never grind with water that is past.

He was a dour Calvinist to the end.[4]

Did McCallum simply invent the divisional structure, combining it with Lee's line-and-staff system, or did he derive it from some other source, for example the military or the churches? No-one really knows. Many of the civil engineers who were at that time building or running railroads were graduates of the United States Military Academy at West Point, the nation's first polytechnic; it is therefore tempting to derive the railroads' new structure from the hierarchical structure of the military. However, McCallum had no experience of the military way of life until Lincoln made him a major general. The word 'staff' makes one think of the Prussian General Staff, parts of which performed functions similar to (but not identical with) those performed by McCallum's staff departments. On the other hand, there is little evidence of German influence on the US military or on society until long after McCallum had resigned from the Erie. Karl von Clausewitz's famous treatise *On War*, although published in German between 1832 and 1837, would not be available in an English translation until 1873.[5] The probability is that McCallum developed his combination of a divisional structure with line-and-staff as a commonsense response to the discipline of the technical and commercial tasks facing him.

That McCallum's reformist influence on railroads in general did not cease on his resignation from the Erie was due in large measure to his friend and admirer, Henry Varnum Poor (1812–1905), editor of the *American Railroad Journal*, the leading business periodical of ante-bellum America and ancestor of one of the founders of Standard & Poor's, today a leading credit-rating agency much critcized because of its contribution to the current financial crisis. The nation's first great business journalist, Poor had been highly critical of the Erie in its earlier days but, on the appointment of McCallum, he became its 'big-gest booster'[6] as an example of proper management. He particularly admired the way in which: 'By an arrangement now perfected, the superintendent can tell at any hour in the day, the precise location of every car and engine on the line of the road, and the duty it is per-forming. Formerly, the utmost confusion prevailed in this department . . .'.[7]

From McCallum's Erie, Poor derived his principles of management, which he summed up in three words: *organization* (meaning the proper division of labor among employees), *communication* (meaning an accu-rate system of reporting) and *information* (meaning a data bank of useful information on which sensible decisions can be based). McCal-lum had drawn up what was probably the world's first corporate organization chart to illustrate the structure of the Erie. His model was a 'family tree' in which ancestors were represented by roots, the line of descent by the upward-thrusting branches and descendants by leaves. McCallum's chart equated the roots of the tree with the Erie's directors and president; its branches with the five operating and 'staff' divisions; and its leaves with the people at the sharp end of the business – in other words, it was upside down compared to future charts of this kind. Poor was so impressed that he lithographed it, selling copies to the public for $1.00 each.

Poor's editorials, taken together, constitute one of the most impor-tant treatises on management ever published in America – or indeed anywhere. (Their substance is readily accessible in A.D. Chandler's *Henry Poor: Business Editor, Analyst and Reformer*.) The strength and importance of its contents derives from the fact that they were drawn largely from the views of a real-life practitioner (McCallum); and medi-ated by an able journalist who was a close observer of the relevant industry over several decades. Unlike many management writers in the late twentieth century, Poor did not sit remotely in an academic ivory tower. Well aware of the critical weakness in McCallum's approach, his solution was for top management to become '. . . the soul of the enter-prise, reaching and infusing life, intelligence and obedience into every portion of it'. In a telling phrase, he told his readers that '. . . duties can-not always be prescribed and the most valuable are often *voluntary* ones' (emphasis added).[8] Obedience there had to be, but it was not to be blind. This theme would be taken up in greater detail a century later by William B. Given, president of American Brake Shoe, in his book *Bottom-Up Management: People Working Together* (see Chapter 9).

Because McCallum was forced to resign as its chief superintendent, the Erie would not benefit to the full from his reforms. Another railroad would: the Pennsylvania (always know as 'the Pennsy'), whose president, J. Edgar Thomson, had long been an admirer of McCallum and his works. Thomson adopted the latter's principles and introduced his practices, subject to some important variations. The new organization manual, which was issued in December 1857, would contain many of the Scots-American's words and phrases. In December 1859 the Pennsylvania would formally promulgate the doctrine of 'line-and-staff', which we have observed implicitly and in embryo at Lee's Armory, explicitly and fully developed in McCallum's Erie. Since Thomson's reforms at the Pennsylvania were highly successful, one must assume that he took greater account of the human factor than his mentor had done.

Meantime, the Erie fell under the control of unscrupulous investors like Daniel Drew, who cared little for efficient administration and less for the other shareholders. It was Thomson's Pennsylvania and not McCallum's Erie that became a shining model of good corporate administration. In 1894, a foreign visitor would observe that: 'The Pennsylvania is in every respect the standard railroad of America . . . Its rails and rolling stock, its ballast and bridges, its stations and service are regarded as embodying a state of perfection to equal which should be the highest ambition of every railroad company in the country'.[9]

What was the impact of the railroads on American manufacturing in particular and society in general? The answer is twofold. First, they enabled the mass distribution of goods to take place. The American System of Manufactures had made large-scale *production* possible but for the Second (or American) Industrial Revolution to occur, it was necessary to supplement manufacturing with swift, safe and cheap methods of distribution; this was achieved by the iron horse, assisted by the newly invented electric telegraph. Secondly, the railroads – as America's first Big Businesses – provided a model for the future manufacturing companies, that would replace geographical divisions with product-centered ones. Among the earliest to make that organizational leap were two other Horatio Alger characters, Gustavus Swift (1839–1903), a 'tight-lipped' farmer's son from Massachusetts, and Andrew Carnegie (1835–1919), the son of yet another Scottish immigrant, who would create respectively the meatpacking and steel companies that were to bear their names. Swift & Co. was America's first 'vertically integrated' company, which means that it controlled:

> ... each step in the process of bringing meat products to the consumer. Although Swift did not raise cattle, the company took over at the point of sale and conducted each step thereafter: buying, packing, shipping, and marketing. Furthermore, each of these steps was the province of a different division of the company. That is, rather than creating geographic divisions, as the railroads had done, Swift based divisions on different functions.[10]

Before going into the steel business, Carnegie had been a young telegrapher working for the Pennsy. He would make his mark there one day when he 'untangled a traffic tie-up after a derailment'[11] by signing an instruction with his boss's initials – a clear breach of the rules. At the absolutist Erie this example of 'the Nelson touch' (see page 107) might have led to his dismissal; at the more tolerant Pennsylvania, it resulted in a change of the rules and, eventually, promotion for the rule-breaker. In 1859, at the age of twenty-one, remarkably, Carnegie attained the position of superintendent of the western division, where business would quickly quadruple. In 1865, he was offered the position of general superintendent of the whole network; he declined because he had decided to set up in business for himself. A brilliant new career lay ahead of him in the steel industry that would turn the son of a radical Scottish weaver into the richest man in the world. In his new occupation, he would apply the operational procedures – including, for example, detailed cost accounting – that he had absorbed at the Pennsy, and which the Pennsy had in turn learned through Poor from the Erie. Memorably, he summed up his entire steel operations in fewer than a hundred words:

> Two pounds of iron-stone purchased on the shores of Lake Superior and transported to Pittsburgh. Two pounds of coal mined in Connellsville and manufactured into coke and brought to Pittsburgh. One-half pound of limestone mined east of the Alleghenies and brought to Pittsburgh. A little manganese ore mined in Virginia and brought to Pittsburgh. And these four and one half pounds of material manufactured into one pound of solid steel and sold for one cent. That's all that need be said about the steel business.[12]

He would also carry into steel-making a Puritan belief that 'he was one of Calvin's blessed, a sanctified trustee for all of civilisation'. He was not so keen on listening to preachers, however, paying for 7,689 church organs 'to lessen the pain of the sermons'.[13]

The mighty Pennsy, a company noted for its magnificent locomotives, would prosper for a hundred years. During the Great Depression of the 1930s, it never failed to pay a dividend. When peace came, the advent of the airlines created a wonderful new opportunity. The long-distance railroads had never really wanted to carry passengers in the first place. Unlike freight, passengers were ornery creatures; they complained if trains did not depart and arrive at precisely pre-determined times. Unlike goods, they had to be watered and fed with alarming frequency and they liked to go to bed at night between clean sheets. As one famous railroad man said in the mid-nineteenth century, 'passengers are as much good to a railroad as teats to a bull'. What the railroads did best, from the day of their inception, was to carry freight for long distances and commuters for short ones. The coming of the age of the airlines resolved this problem, at least in theory. Instead, faced with the finest opportunity offered to them in their entire history, a large part of the railroad system quite simply collapsed, led by the Pennsy which declared itself bankrupt in 1970 – of which much more in Chapter 13. The reason for this collapse would be a rejection, which occurred across much of the national economy, of the principles and practices of managerial culture derived from the nation's Puritan past and developed by Lee, McCallum, Poor, Thomson, Carnegie and many others.

7

Frederick W. Taylor Reorganizes the Factory Floor

Frederick Winslow Taylor (1856–1915) was America's – and the world's – first management consultant. When he set up in business on his own in 1880, his stationery bore the title 'consultant engineer in management', an expression that his successors would shorten to the present tag. He was also one of the great formative figures of the twentieth century. The impact of his work was worldwide, affecting profoundly – in differing ways and at different times – capitalist America, Stalinist Russia, Nazi Germany and Thatcherite Britain. Taylor called the movement that he founded Scientific Management; others would call it Taylorism. The application of his methods was known as Taylorization. The attempt to apply his principles across the whole of society (including manufacturing, commerce, the domestic household, education, the churches, the law and the military) became known as the Efficiency Movement. In the second half of the twentieth century, it would enjoy a new, highly damaging lease of life in the form of the Cult of the (so-called) Expert, which we also refer to as neo-Taylorism. The definitive work on Taylorism's impact on business and society remains to be written; this chapter, together with Chapters 11 to 14, may be regarded as a first sketch.

To what extent did Taylor's life and work exemplify the quartet of enduring Puritan characteristics that we have listed in earlier chapters as defining much of American society from the Puritan Migration until 1970? The answer is: fully in respect only of the second – to the end of his life, he would be intensely proud of his aptitude for mechanical skills and of the engineering apprenticeship he had served in a machine shop. As far as the first was concerned – 'a desire to in some sense to create the Kingdom of Heaven on Earth' – he could be said to exemplify it only in a somewhat odd fashion. His father had been a 'fairly prosperous lawyer of Quaker stock' and his mother 'traced her Puritan roots to a Plymouth, Massachusetts, ancestor who arrived in America in 1629'.[1] (By the time Taylor was born, his family, like many

Quakers, had become Unitarians.) It is therefore not surprising that, in the words of Glen Porter's multi-volume *History of Technology*, Taylorism 'took on some of the trappings of a secular religion'; Taylor was 'the messiah', and his followers, who spread the word, were (and still are) commonly referred to as 'disciples'. '[R]arely', says Taylor's most recent biographer, Robert Kanigel, 'has an ostensibly secular movement so embraced religious language and imagery . . . Taylorism grew out of Frederick Winslow Taylor's attempt to reclaim a lost Eden'.[2] A contemporary Swedish visitor compared Taylor not with Calvin, but with Luther, that other great founder of Protestantism.[3] Consciously or not – probably more the latter than the former – Taylor used religion to advance his ideas and interests.

As for the other two early Puritan characteristics, Taylor scored zero. An utter egomaniac, he cannot in any sense be said to have been moved by 'a specific moral outlook which subordinated the interests of the individual to the group'. He most certainly did not possess 'an ability to assemble, galvanize and marshal financial, material and human resources to a single purpose and on a massive (or lesser) scale'. The ultimate paradox about Taylor, the great reorganizer of the factory floor, is that he was an incompetent manager of men, a point to which we return in Chapter 11. This is a weakness that is shared by many who followed in his footsteps as industrial consultants.

The First Industrial Revolution had introduced the principle and practice known as the division of labor, which led to significant economies of scale. In his famous description of the manufacture of pins, the Scottish economist, Adam Smith, recorded, by way of example, how the different parts of the process were allocated to different workers. However, the application of this principle was by no means uniform or complete in practice across the whole of manufacturing by Smith's time; as late as the 1880s, each worker, or group of workers, in many American factories was still responsible for the production of entire articles. Taylor would bring nineteenth-century American practice into line with eighteenth-century Scottish economic theory. In doing so, he anticipated, and undoubtedly influenced, the work of Henry Ford.

Taylor sought to measure the human inputs and outputs in manufacturing – an objective that presented serious problems, both practical and moral. In this respect, he may be regarded as having invented, and certainly promoted, 'time-and-motion study'. Like all who seek to rule by the use of a measuring rod, he required 'numerators'. Workers were evaluated and rewarded in terms of the 'work units' they produced. This was a sophisticated form of piecework that meant that changes in the cost of labor did not have to be factored into the calculation of efficiency. The regime was maintained by a new class of employee: the so-called 'efficiency experts' or 'work-study men' who are still to be found, white-coated and carrying stopwatches, in some factories. Needless to say, these men were disliked and distrusted by the operatives, particularly when they first made an appearance.

Taylor maintained that the benefits of higher productivity achieved by means of greater efficiency would be shared with the workforce. However, workers were not deceived and soon recognized that, although they had been promised more, they were being paid less. If care was not taken to ensure an adequate flow of work, dissatisfaction could spread, followed by a strike. In its early, crude form, the application of work study led to the alienation of the workforce, the dehumanization of the factory floor, hostility between employee and employer and an increase in the power of labor unions. In Ford's plant at Dearborn, in one single year, the staff turnover actually reached 900 per cent; it is no wonder that Chaplin satirized it in his film *Modern Times*. Before long, Congress would legislate to restrict the use of 'work study' in contracts where government money was involved.

At the heart of Taylor's personal approach to the organization of the factory floor lay contempt for the ordinary working man. The factory operative was to be treated as a 'grown-up child' and was 'not supposed to think'. (One fault Taylor did not possess was hypocrisy.) In a famous passage he described the selection of a 'first-class man' for the job of hauling pig iron, referring to him as Schmidt, 'a little Pennsylvania Dutchman': 'Now one of the very first requirements for a man who is fit to handle pig-iron as a regular occupation is that he shall be so stupid and so phlegmatic that he more nearly resembles in his mental make-up the ox than any other type'.[4] Taylor came to regret the use of Schmidt as an illustration. Concern was publicly expressed by labor leaders about the latter's welfare and then a rumor spread that he had died – presumably because he was expected to carry forty-seven tons of pig-iron for a distance of thirty to forty feet each day. (He was a 130-pound weakling.) Taylor felt obliged to hire a man to locate Schmidt, who was then examined by a doctor and pronounced to be alive and well.[5]

The high noon of early Taylorism on the factory floor coincided with what is known as the Progressive Era in American society, usually defined as from 1900 to 1915 but actually extending by a decade or more on either side. Progressives were mostly high-minded, well-educated Americans of English stock who crusaded against corruption in public life and business and in favor of all kinds of reforms. This was when Upton Sinclair's great novel, *The Jungle* (1906), exposed the insanitary conditions prevailing in the great Chicago meatpacking houses. Sinclair was a socialist for whom the American Dream was an illusion, 'nothing but one gigantic lie', and the slaughter-houses were, 'the [evil] spirit of capitalism made flesh' – places in which 'a hundred human lives did not balance a penny of profit'.[6] Described as 'fiercely puritanical and judgemental', he wanted his book to do for his *bête noire* what *Uncle Tom's Cabin* had done for slavery.[7] The effect of his work was not, however, to overthrow the system but to reform it; it led to the first federal food-safety laws.[8]

This was also the era of the 'muckraking journalist'. Teddy Roosevelt (president from 1901 to 1909) had acknowledged the need for crusading journalists to publicize the need for reform, but only as long as they knew when to 'stop raking the muck' and so avoid stirring up radical unrest. He had borrowed the term from one of the sacred texts of Puritanism, John Bunyan's *Pilgrim's Progress*, which spoke of a man who, 'muck-rake in his hand', raked filth rather than raise his eyes to nobler things. Under progressive influence, legislation would be introduced in various states to protect factory workers and the general public from abusive employers. Congress created the Department of Commerce and Labor with much the same objective in mind. Anti-trust laws (preventing companies in the same industry from conspiring against the interests of their customers or suppliers) were enforced. As a result of the Progressive Movement, American society became generally more just.[9]

In time, Taylor's 'time-and-motion study' would be absorbed into the inherited managerial culture and become less crude in its impact. After his death, two famous efficiency experts, Frank and Lillian Gilbreth, modified it to create 'method study'. They re-labeled Taylor's 'work units' by almost reversing their own name, so that they became *therbligs*. From that time on, the emphasis would be more on improving working methods and less on making people work harder. Allowances would also be made for fatigue and other contingencies. This softer approach being more acceptable to the workforce, relations between the efficiency experts and the shop-floor became warmer. It was then that, to mark the shift, the 'efficiency experts' adopted for themselves the less aggressive title: 'industrial engineers'. Very much later, under Japanese influence, groups of workers would be trained to analyze their own movements, using a stopwatch.

Ordinary Americans who did not work in factories learned about time-and-motion study from the humorous book and film, *Cheaper by the*

Dozen. The book appeared in 1948 at the very height of the Golden Age of Management. Written by two of the Gilbreths' twelve children, it gave a touching and entertaining account of family life, describing how their parents had 'mass-produced' them by organizing their home life into a human 'assembly line'. When Dad whistled, they moved:

> Dad installed process and work charts in the bathrooms. Every child old enough to write – and Dad expected his offspring to start writing at a tender age – was required to initial the charts in the morning after he had brushed his teeth, taken a bath, combed his hair, and made his bed. At night, each child had to weigh himself, plot the figure on a graph, and initial the process charts again after he had done his homework, washed his hands and face and brushed his teeth. Mother wanted to have a place on the charts for saying prayers, but Dad said that as far as he was concerned prayers were voluntary.[10]

Since all fourteen Gilbreths drove around Montclair, New Jersey in a huge Pierce Arrow convertible, the whole town was entertained by their activities – including a girl called Priscilla Douglas. She attended school with the Gilbreth children and would later become the wife of Frank Polkinghorn, an engineer and one of the Three Wise Men from the West would teach modern American management methods to the Japanese after World War II (see Chapter 10).

The Gilbreths were not the only industrial engineers to humanize Taylorism. Another was Allan H. Mogensen, always known as Mogy, who taught his methodology in seminars at Lake Placid in the Adirondacks. He had developed his ideas in the late 1920s while working as an engineer at Eastman Kodak and later as a teacher at the University of Rochester. As his nickname suggests, he was one of the few members of his trade to have been loved by those who met him. Mogy replaced cruder forms of Taylorite work study with a procedure which became known as 'work simplification', a name suggested by his devoted colleague, Erwin Schell, in 1932. Mogy's principles were simply stated, for example: 'The person doing the job knows far more than anyone else about the best way of doing that job, and therefore is the one person best fitted to improve it'. And, 'Recognition of individual contributions stimulates further action'.[11]

Taylorism evolved after Taylor's death, never becoming a fixed body of principles and practices. By the 1930s, many shop-floor disciplines sheltered under its umbrella in addition to time-and-motion study – for example: production control, which organized the flow of material through the factory from the raw material to the final product; quality control (including statistical quality control), which maintained high standards by means of inspection; and scheduled maintenance. Furthermore, in the form of cost accounting, the preparation of job descriptions, the systematization of salary scales and the like, its influence extended far beyond the factory, the office and indeed beyond business.

Taylor's single most important disciple was not Frank or Lillian Gilbreth or Mogy but an extraordinary man called Charles Eugene Bedaux (1886–1944). Since he did more than anyone else to advance the cause of Taylorism in the United States and elsewhere in the first half of the twentieth century, he deserves a place in this book. His life story is also worth briefly retelling because it adds color and spice to what could otherwise be a dull part of our tale; it is not easy to write compellingly for the lay reader about the reorganization of the factory floor.

The authors would have liked to record that Bedaux's life was one of puritanical simplicity but that would be far from the truth. He had started work in Paris as an assistant to a pimp,[12] a job which came to an end when his employer was shot dead by a prostitute on the rue Pigalle. He arrived in New York during World War I at the age of nineteen, allegedly with one dollar in his pocket. Discovering the importance of work study, he set up a management consultancy in Cleveland, Ohio in 1918, publishing tables of efficiency that would pass into general use throughout the world. (These would be used by Kenneth Hopper when he worked for the successor to Bedaux's company in London from 1957 to 1965.) He conferred his own name on his version of Taylor's work units but, unlike the Gilbreths, he did not all-but reverse it – so that they became 'Bedaux units'. About two hundred American companies would adopt his system by the 1930s, including General Electric, Campbell Soup and Goodrich Rubber.

In 1927, Bedaux moved to London, establishing a company called British Bedaux which would also enjoy success in attracting leading manufacturing companies as clients; eventually, it changed its name to Associated Industrial Consultants. There Bedaux flirted with royalty. The Duke of Windsor and Wallis Warfield Simpson were married in his French chateau in 1937, quite a coup for someone of such lowly origins. After the fall of France, Bedaux – whose ideas appealed to the fascist state – persuaded the collaborating French leader, Marshal Pétain, to set up an experimental economy in the town of Roquefort where a new improved Bedaux unit, the Bex, was to replace the franc as a currency; this ambitious project failed.

Bedaux also obtained the approval of the Nazi authorities for the construction of a trans-Saharan railroad and, running alongside it, a pipeline to carry water in one direction and peanut oil in the other. This idea was in itself quite sensible – what was absurd was that the Axis powers should have devoted massive amounts of scarce wartime resources on a project that could not possibly contribute to their victory. The Allied invasion of North Africa put paid to it. Bedaux was arrested in Algiers and extradited to the United States, where he was charged with treason. Confined to a prison cell in Miami, he apparently committed suicide in 1944 by taking an overdose of sleeping pills – we say 'apparently' because there has been a suggestion that he was murdered to prevent him revealing the names of prominent Americans who had traded with the enemy. His very important legacy, however, lives on in workplaces throughout the world and in the fact that he made a modest, if unintended, contribution to the defeat of the Axis powers.

There was nothing really scientific about Scientific Management. Apart from statistical quality control, which was a much later development, the nearest that Taylorism's practitioners ever came to scientific method was the use of elementary arithmetic. It was, instead, the systematic application of common sense that characterized this movement in its mature phase at the mid-twentieth century. Although methods of measurement might be used in forming judgments, there was nothing robotic or impersonal about the procedure at its best – rather, it brought the whole human personality into play.

Kanigel quotes Taylor's famous dictum: 'In the past the man has been first. In the future the System must be first' – on which he comments: 'And it is'.[13] To which one may reasonably respond: 'but is it?' The answer to this question will depend, in large part, on what one means by 'the System' and to which epoch one is referring. In this book, the word 'system' is often used, uncapitalized, to imply that a group of human beings work *systemically*, consensually and fruitfully together to a common purpose. For Taylor, however, it appears to have meant something like a superior pattern of behavior (also called the 'One Best Way') imposed from above by one group of human beings upon another without the latter's consent and with little regard to its interests or feelings. In this sense, as far as the Great Engine companies of the Golden Age of Management and their lesser siblings at the mid-twentieth century were concerned, Kanigel was wrong; in them 'the man' would on the whole predominate, thanks to the humanizing of Taylorism by people like the Gilbreths and Mogy as well as to the commonsense approach adopted by American managers in general. After 1970, on the other hand, 'the man' (or 'the woman') would become a poor second to something resembling Taylor's capitalized 'System'. In this later, degenerate phase, neo-Taylorism in the shape of the Cult of the (so-called) Expert would do much to damage or destroy the great Puritan tradition of 'hands-on', 'can-do' management – a matter to which we shall return at length and in detail in later chapters.

8

Pierre du Pont Invents the Modern Manufacturing Company

EI du Pont de Nemours was among the first of what we will call the Great Engine manufacturing companies to emerge between 1890 and 1930. For nearly half a century, it had been run in an idiosyncratic fashion by General Henry du Pont. The void that he left behind when he departed in the 1880s would be filled by Hamilton MacFarlane Barksdale, a civil engineer from the Baltimore and Ohio Railroad; it was while the railroad was being built through Wilmington, Delaware, that Barksdale had met members of the du Pont family. Aware of the gaping managerial hole in the center of their company, and that the railroads were at that time the best-managed large businesses in the United States, they appointed him to the vacancy. It was Barksdale who initiated the reorganization of Dupont on systemic lines, dividing activities between 'line' and 'staff' departments, a pattern that he had learned as a railroad engineer.

The man who perfected the model, however, was Pierre Samuel du Pont (1870–1954). A great-grandson of the founder, he had inherited a large, but not controlling, stake in the company. Between 1902 and 1919, but particularly after 1904 when he became president, he would be responsible for completing the conversion of the loose association of businesses patched together by his uncle, General Henry, into the first 'modern business enterprise' – to borrow an expression from Alfred D. Chandler's and Stephen Salsbury's book, *Pierre S. du Pont and the Making of the Modern Corporation*: 'Pierre, his cousin Coleman and their associates brought the ways of both Carnegie and Taylor to the Du Pont Company, modifying them to meet the special needs of the explosives industry'.[1]

The lifestyle of Pierre's parents had been unostentatious. They lived in a mansion situated on company ground adjacent to the mill – the rich man's equivalent of 'living above the shop'. Although they lacked nothing of importance, there were few luxuries in the house. In later life Pierre would recall how, when the oilcloth that covered the floor of the entrance hall had to be replaced because it was badly worn, a part of it was re-used in the side hall. He also recalled that ice cream was served only once a week, on a Thursday, when the ice cream van called. One is reminded of Mrs. Henry Ford's darning her husband's socks[2] when he was already the richest man on earth. Not all du Ponts conducted their private lives with such restraint. Pierre's bachelor uncle, Alfred, for example, died memorably in a brothel. The family reacted prudishly to this episode, attempting unsuccessfully to keep it out of the newspapers. Although Pierre wrote a great deal in later life about Alfred's work, he would never refer to his uncle's demise as having been anything but 'sudden' or 'unexpected'.

Although French by origin, correspondingly named and sentimentally attached to France, the du Pont family fitted easily into the great American Puritan managerial culture, the evolution of which is chronicled in this book. Whereas Taylor had fully exemplified only one of the four characteristics that we have described as defining American society from the early seventeenth century to the late 1960s, Pierre scored well on all four counts. He was an active Episcopal churchman possessing 'a profound respect for the ethical values of orthodox Protestant Christianity'.[3] Early Puritan migrants and their successors had sought to prepare the world, quite literally, for Christ's Second Coming. This was certainly not Pierre's approach: his earthly kingdom was to be built on Christian values rather than on a supernatural event. If monetary greed ever played an important part of his motivation, it was contained by other powerful, balancing factors. Moreover, the traditional Puritan 'aptitude for mechanical skills' was transmuted in Pierre's case into a fascination with chemical processes, both in the laboratory and on the shop-floor. Being 'hands-on' was an inherited family trait. He had started his working life in the very same Upper Powder Yard on the Brandywine River where his father, grandfather and great-grandfather had begun theirs – and where his father had ended his in an explosion. Dying as a result of an industrial accident is, undoubtedly, 'hands-on' although it may not be particularly 'can-do'.

Pierre also possessed to the full that particular Puritan outlook on life that subordinated personal interests to those of the group – in his case, to those of the family and the family firm; then to his church; then to his state (he devoted much of his free time to attempting to improve public education in Delaware, being effectively the founder of its state university); and, finally, to his country and society in general. Unlike Taylor, he was gifted with organizational skills of the highest possible order. A shy man and a good listener, Pierre would hear out every opinion before reaching a conclusion; when he made a decision, it was likely to reflect the collective views of the entire senior management team, including his own. Today we tend to think of collegiate decision-making (wrongly) as something invented by the Japanese after World War II; it was certainly a feature of Dupont (and, later, General Motors) under Pierre in the 1920s and would also be observable in most of the Great Engine companies that emerged in emulation.

Finally (and not surprisingly, in view of his inheritance), Pierre possessed to the full the profound interest in technology and respect for the technologist that the United States had derived from France after the Revolution and which we refer to as a fifth characteristic of American business until 1970. Dupont had – and still has – a close link with MIT, that ultimate flowering of the polytechnic movement, Pierre and many of colleagues and close relations having studied there. A diligent student, he had spent as much time as he could in the laboratories, even at weekends, looking down on 'Old Ivy' (Harvard College) as a kind of country club. When an undergraduate, he had been horrified when a rumor spread to the effect that the two institutions might merge.

Pierre reorganized Dupont into autonomous and largely self-sufficient functional divisions, each headed by its own president. Central control was achieved by creating a powerful executive committee, chaired by himself, which was responsible for group strategy. An elaborate financial reporting system was brought into being to keep this body informed about what was going on, in cost and revenue terms, throughout the group. This committee was forbidden to meddle directly in the details of divisional work but that did not mean it was remote from the factory floor; on the contrary, most of its members were, simultaneously, divisional presidents or had been so in the recent past. The executive committee's outlook and *modus operandi* was therefore quite different from that of a present-day corporate Board composed, mostly, of financially-oriented directors who identify themselves with the shareholders rather than other employees and who buy and sell divisions, some of which they might never have visited, as if they were commodities.

Pierre addressed and solved the twin problems that faced all the great family firms at the turn of the nineteenth century: reconciling ownership and control by the founders' heirs with the need for new capital which the family could not, or would not, supply; and recruiting and promoting new talent from outside the family to work alongside, or in place of, family members. The dilemma was an acute one: if controlling shareholders did not admit new investors as shareholders and also new non-family members as executives, a company could go into decline and, possibly, out of business. Pierre resolved both problems at Dupont by a mixture of diplomacy and boldness, issuing new shares on the stock exchange and insisting that the performance of family and non-family managers be judged according to identical criteria. To non-family members of the executive committee, he awarded substantial stock options, turning them into quasi-relatives. (The sensible Barksdale had actually married into the family.) The du Ponts would continue to play an important role as managers in the chemical company for some decades after Pierre retired, but they had to earn their keep. Today, the founding family is no longer active, although one member sits on the main Board in a non-executive capacity. Meanwhile, in faraway India, the family companies belonging to the Marwari sect (see page 12) face exactly the same kind of problem as Pierre addressed a century ago, and are adopting the same kind of solution.

Pierre also adopted from Gustavus Swift and others (see pages 71 and 72) a policy of 'vertical integration', which would become the norm for Great Engine companies. General Henry had purchased supplies where he could; on behalf of the new and transformed Dupont, Pierre liked to acquire ownership of the suppliers, thus protecting the company from scarcities and adverse price movements and ensuring that raw materials were of adequate and consistent quality. Equally, Dupont ceased to rely on independent dealers to market its products, building up its own nationwide network of sales offices. Meanwhile, the product line was widened. Since the day of its foundation, Dupont had manufactured chiefly explosives; as a chemist and engineer, Pierre could perceive the many opportunities that would arise from the expansion of the chemical industry and sought to exploit them. It was under his leadership that the company became a leading producer of paints and varnishes, which it supplied, for example, to General Motors. At the same time, to avoid being pursued by the federal government under newly enacted anti-trust legislation, he disposed of much of the traditional explosives business.

Having saved Dupont from implosion, Pierre would go on to save General Motors from extinction – and, in so doing, create a second Great Engine company. In 1920, the automobile manufacturer was teetering on the point of collapse. Using the vast profits Dupont had generated in World War I, Pierre du Pont recapitalized and decentralized it, becoming president in 1920, a position he retained until he was replaced by the famous Alfred Sloan, subsequently the founder of the Sloan School of Management at MIT. By January 1921, all but two of the senior positions at General Motors had been filled by former

Dupont employees. Most of these were also graduates of MIT, where some had been Pierre's classmates.

It was Pierre who created Dupont's new research laboratory in Wilmington with the object of improving existing products and developing new ones; by the end of 1904 it housed over 100 technicians, including several graduate scientists, in its gleaming new buildings. In so doing, Pierre provided an important precedent for other Great Engine companies. It is customary to divide research activities into two categories: 'pure', which is supposed to advance human knowledge about the physical world; and 'applied', which exploits such knowledge by creating new products and services. The reality is, of course, that it has never been possible to effect an absolute separation. At the beginning of the nineteenth century, the British chemist, Humphry Davy, discovered seven of the chemical elements – and applied his knowledge to invent the safety lamp, which would save thousands of miners' lives. At the end of that century in France, the Curies uncovered the nature of radioactivity – and applied their knowledge to develop X-rays for medical and other purposes. Somewhere in between, their fellow countryman, Louis Pasteur, investigated the properties of molecules – and worked out how to stop milk spoiling.[4]

The Dupont laboratory was encouraged to pursue a kind of research activity, difficult to define in theory, that encompassed both 'pure' and 'applied'. While its ultimate aim was to produce new or improved products, no auditor stood over the researchers, saying that they must achieve results within a given period of time. As a result, projects could be carried on for years, and perhaps even decades, before they achieved a return – and always with the risk that they might not do so. In 1928, for example, Wallace Hume Carothers was appointed head of organic chemistry. His brief was to investigate the structure of substances of high molecular weight and their formation by polymerization. These inquiries into the basic nature of matter led to two discoveries that would transform much of our world: nylon, an artificial fiber with properties similar, but in many ways superior, to wool, cotton and silk; and neoprene, a synthetic rubber. Neoprene became commercially available only three years after Carothers' appointment, meeting a timetable that would have satisfied the most exigent auditor, but nylon took a decade to appear on the scene. Pierre lived long enough to savor the latter triumph but Carothers did not; a sufferer from depression, he killed himself in 1937.

Just as the structure of Dupont became the model for other Great Engines, so did its research laboratory provide a model for the large establishments maintained by such as General Electric, Hewlett Packard, Hughes Aircraft, Westinghouse and General Motors. General Electric's 'House of Magic' at Schenectady, New York, was the brainchild of Charles Proteus Steinmetz a 'gnarled mathematical genius' who had 'ignited the popular imagination with his man-made electrical storms'. Given a free rein to develop his ideas, Steinmetz became a magnet for other creative spirits. Einstein and Kelvin (the Scottish physicist after whom the unit of temperature was named) were among those who visited him. It was there that William Coolidge would invent the X-ray tube and Irving Langmuir win a Nobel Prize for Chemistry. When another employee, Ernst Alexanderson, invented the high-frequency alternator, making commercial broadcasting possible, General Electric would form both the Radio Corporation of America and the National Broadcasting Corporation to exploit the discovery.[5]

The greatest of all the corporate research establishments, however, was undoubtedly the Bell Laboratories, the research arm of the Western Electric Division of AT&T, initially situated in an undistinguished set of buildings in Basking Ridge, New Jersey. The Bell Labs (as they were always known) employed 'a remarkable collection of really outstanding people who were pretty well paid to do whatever they wanted . . .'. One outcome was sixteen Nobel Prizes in the course of half a century. The theory behind the revolution in information technology originated there in the form of a paper published by Claude Elwood Shannon in 1948, *A Mathematical Theory of Communications*. A distant relative of Thomas Edison – the ultimate progenitor, although not the founder, of General Electric – Shannon was born in 1916 in Gaylord, Michigan, the son of a judge and the principal of a local high school. Of his paper, which described the similarity of patterns in Boolean logic and in the design of electronic circuits, Robert Lucky, a later director of research at the Bell Labs, would say: 'I know of no greater work of genius in the annals of technological thought'. Personally an eccentric, Shannon would bounce along the corridors of the Labs on his pogo stick, or ride through them on a unicycle which he had specially designed with an off-center wheel to enable him to juggle balls whilst in motion.[6] One wonders what today's management theorists like Michael Jensen (see page 179) or Michael Porter (see pages 168 and 169) would have made of him. Were his interests and objectives always strictly aligned with those of AT&T's shareholders?

Much of modern computer hardware and software originated in the Labs. In the late 1940s John Bardeen, Walter H. Brattain and William B. Shockley created the transistor, making possible solid-state computing and paving the way for the invention of the microchip; for this they were awarded a Nobel Prize in 1956. The birth of Silicon Valley and the start of the Digital Age can reasonably be dated to September 18, 1957, when a group of Shockley's colleagues – ever after known as the 'traitorous eight' – walked out on him to found Intel and other companies; without the work of the Bell Labs, there might be no Silicon Valley today.[7] It was in the Labs again in 1971 that Dennis Ritchie and Ken Thomson invented the UNIX operating system, which (evolved by others) still powers much of the world's corporate computers[8] and has recently been transmuted into Linux, increasingly the operating system of choice for governments and many other users. (The word, 'Linux', was derived by telescoping the first name of its inventor of the system, Linus Torvalds, with 'Unix'.)

On any narrow definition of commercial interest, the research laboratories of the Great Engine companies should not have existed. Alec Broers – who worked in IBM's research laboratory at that time and is immediate past president of the Royal Academy of Engineering in London – has sought to resolve this paradox by drawing attention to the fact that Great Engine companies were monopolies and, therefore, not subject to the discipline of the free market.[9] This argument is flawed for two reasons. First, as Louis Galambos has told us: '. . . lacking the pressure of competition, monopolists should be slow to explore and even slower to introduce new technologies; they should sit back on their haunches and enjoy the fruits of the market power'.[10] Secondly, most of the Great Engine companies were not monopolies, AT&T being an exception.

At this point, a metaphor from biology may be helpful – and perhaps it is not entirely a metaphor, since companies consist mostly of living beings: in their heyday, Dupont, General Electric, AT&T and the like were autonomous organisms that had achieved a delicate state of balance between the interests and objectives of shareholders, employees, managers, suppliers, customers – and researchers. For the organism to flourish, the needs of each of these demanding elements had to be met. If the best scientists were to be attracted into employment, they had to be allowed a great deal of latitude in deciding which projects to undertake. Nobel Prize-winners did not just invent fascinating new products, they attracted the brightest of aspiring young scientists to work under them. The name 'stakeholder' had not come into general use but each of these elements was just that.

The Rev. John Cotton, the 'Un-mitred Pope' of early New England (see page 6), once observed that 'knowledge of all things under heaven' was to be pursued *both* for its own sake *and* for its usefulness. There can be no better description of the work of the research laboratories of the Great Engine companies at the mid-twentieth century.

England expects every Man to do his duty

LORD NELSON *explaining to the Officers the* PLAN of ATTACK *previous to the* BATTLE of TRAFALGAR.

NAMES of the GALLANT HEROES who Commanded on the 21 Oct. 1805

POSITION of the COMBINED FORCES of FRANCE & SPAIN,

at the commencement of the Action 21 Oct 1805 with LORD NELSON, Cape Trafalgar bearing E.S.E 4 Leagues

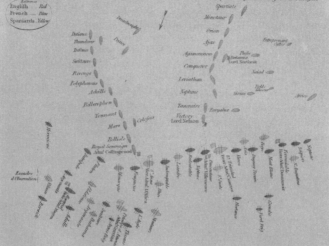

The above plan has been Certified as to its correctness by the Flag Officers of the Gibraltar & Adm Collingwood.

SUBSCRIPTIONS for a SPLENDID ENGRAVING of the DEATH of NELSON, SIZE 25 by 17 are RECEIVED at 59 BOND STREET.

PART III

TRIUMPH

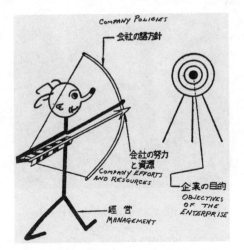

(above) 8: The Fundamental Objectives of the Enterprise: Homer Sarasohn's Diagram about the Purpose of Business. See page 117.

(facing page) 7: The 'Nelson Touch' or the 'total indoctrination' that precedes 'near-absolute initiative'. *Lord Nelson Explaining to the Officers the Plan of Attack Previous to the Battle of Trafalgar,* by W.M. Craig. See page 107.

9: Three Wise Men from the West with pupils at the second CCS Seminar, Osaka (1950):
First row (from left): Bunzaemon Inoue (plant manager, Sumitomo Electric; chairman, Top Management Study Group for the Kansai; later chairman, Sumitomo Rubber); Y. Horiuchi (translator); Homer M. Sarasohn (industry division, CCS); Frank A. Polkinghorn (director, research and industry divisions, CCS); Charles W. Protzman (industry division, CCS).
Second row (first from left): Masaharu Matsushita (now honorary chairman, Matsushita Electric).
See page 121.

9

The Golden Age of American Management (1920–1970)

The Golden Age of American Management[1] lasted, approximately, from 1920 to 1970, marking the climax of a journey that had started with the appointment of Lee as superintendent of the Springfield Armory in 1815. The national economy of this age was dominated by large, highly competent, manufacturing and service companies, which we shall call Great Engines of Growth and Prosperity, which not only generated wealth for themselves and their shareholders but also permitted a host of lesser companies to prosper under their wings. While each Great Engine company possessed its own distinctive character, those few employees who moved from one to another would have recognized a large number of familiar features in their new place of employment – an experience they would not have encountered by joining a foreign company. These familiar features constituted the common culture that gave its golden sheen to the quality of management at the mid-twentieth century.

Each of the four Puritan characteristics that we named at the start of Chapter 1 was mirrored in the structures that emerged. There can be no doubt at all about the last three: an aptitude for the exercise of mechanical skills; a moral outlook that subordinated the interests of the individual to the group; and exceptional organizing ability. What about the first: a conviction that the purpose of life, however vaguely conceived, was to establish the Kingdom of Heaven on Earth? It was in these companies that the American Dream – a belief that a shining future lay before all of the nation's citizens – found one of its fullest expressions. Add to all that the fifth cultural characteristic that America learned from the French at the turn of the eighteenth century, a respect for technology and the technologist, simmer for a century, leavening with the managerial innovations introduced by Lee, McCallum, du Pont, Sloan and many others; and the outcome was the Great Engine companies.

Professor Edgar Schein has told us that an organization's culture is 'a pattern of basic assumptions' that develops as it strives to deal with internal divisions and external threats. This approach is valid as far as it goes but it overlooks the historical and social context. Cultures do not just 'develop' within organizations – they have points of departure that precede the creation of those organizations. Andrew Carnegie did not just 'invent' the *modus operandi* of Carnegie Steel – he borrowed much of it from the Pennsy, which had learned from the Erie, which had benefited from Springfield's 'Armory practice'. Schein also argues that companies have not one but three distinct cultures: an 'operational culture' of day-to-day management; an 'executive culture' whose priorities revolve round capital and cash flow; and an 'engineering culture' dominated by technical specialists.[2] There is nothing wrong with this view as long as one recognizes that he is speaking of the decadent corporate culture of the period from 1970 to 1995, which we will describe in Part IV of this book. In the Golden Age of Management, by way of contrast, Great Engine companies possessed and enjoyed one common corporate culture embracing all divisions and disciplines.

Collectively, the Great Engine companies represented one of mankind's greatest achievements. Most of them had come into being and grown to maturity in the fifty years after 1870. More than anything or anyone else, it was they who were responsible for the amazing average annual increase of 2.2 per cent in productivity per man-hour that characterized the US economy in the 100 years starting from then – a rate that would actually accelerate to just under 3.0 per cent during the 1950s and 1960s. (After 1970, it would plummet disastrously, for reasons to be examined later). The best description of America's corporate chief executives in the Golden Age was provided by a Vassar professor, Mabel Newcomer, in *The Big Business Executive: The Factors that Made Him* (1950). The eponymous hero of her book was:

> . . . a native[-born] American, the son of a small, independent businessman. His family income was moderate. And such small jobs as he pursued during his boyhood were for extra spending rather than to help support his family. His parents managed to put him through college, with such contributions as he himself made to his own expenses through part-time employment. Upon graduation he obtained a full-time job, with no assistance from his family. Thenceforth he was on his own. While still relatively young and inexperienced, he obtained a minor position with the corporation that he eventually headed, and he gradually worked up, through operations or production, to a vice-presidency, from which he was promoted to the presidency at the age of fifty-two.[3]

In other words, there was something of a Ragged Dick in him, a person who made his way from near the bottom to the top by dint of dedication to the task in hand. Newcomer, by the way, did not like the typical career pattern that she described so well but, in disapproving, she defined it for us for all time. An advocate of business school education, she was one of those who can be held accountable for the subsequent deterioration in the general quality of management.

In most Great Engine companies, the supreme burden was shared between two full-time executives, a chairman and a president; the Japanese have a name for it: 'two men in a box'. Either could additionally perform the role, and carry the title of, chief executive officer or CEO. When, in the normal course of events, a president/CEO became chairman, he was likely to retain the title of CEO for a period of years until the new president had played himself in; at which point it would be passed down. It followed that one and the same manager might be, successively, president, president/CEO, chairman/CEO, then just plain chairman. The senior executives reported to the CEO. The most famous American example of 'two men in a box', though not one that followed this pattern exactly, undoubtedly consisted of Dave Packard and Bill Hewlett, founders of the electronics company that still bears their names. The former was an organizer of talent, the latter an inventor of originality. Packard became chairman/CEO but Hewlett never rose above president, not surprising in view of their different roles.

This discussion illustrates a more general point: in Great Engine companies, managers were motivated to perform well by the prospect of promotion more than by the hope of financial reward. Providing a recruit had (or acquired) a basic academic qualification, he could hope to rise from any part of his company to the presidency or chairmanship. No-one raised an eyebrow in 1969 when Louis K. Eilers, who started off as a foreman in Eastman Kodak's acetate making unit, became chairman; or when a former maintenance supervisor, Kenneth Jamieson, from the Moose Jaw refinery in Saskatchewan became Chairman of Standard Oil of New Jersey, the largest company in the world. This factor, which can be called 'universal promotability,' had huge consequences for every aspect of corporate life: it incentivized all ranks; it also meant that the heads of a company were likely to possess an extensive knowledge of its affairs. It used to be said of Napoleon's army that every private soldier carried a field marshal's baton in his knapsack; much the same could be said of America's Great Engine companies.[4]

A contrasting view from Newcomer's was provided by the sociologist, William H. Whyte, in his book, *The Organization Man*, published in 1956. The essential nature of Whyte's anti-hero was his identification with the third of our four Puritan characteristics, an outlook that subordinated the interests of the individual to the group. Whyte even described this phenomenon in quasi-religious terms. For him, Organization Men had: '. . . left home, spiritually as well as physically, to take the vows of organization life, and it is they who are the mind and soul of our great self-perpetuating institutions . . . [I]t is their values which will set the American temper'.[5] Regrettably, from the present authors' point of view, this prophecy would not be borne out by events, as will be explained in later chapters.

The best description of the Great Engine companies is still to be found in Alfred D. Chandler Jr.'s *The Visible Hand: The Managerial Revolution in American Business*, published in 1977 just after the end of our Golden Age. Chandler's middle initial stands for du Pont; and Alfred, as we have seen in the case of wicked 'Uncle Alfred' (see page 83), was a du Pont family name. As an adoptive member of one of the founding families of the Golden Age, Chandler was in a position to observe it from inside and out. The title that he chose for his book was particularly significant: in simple economies, the allocation of resources is made by the operation of what Adam Smith called an 'invisible hand' – more prosaically, the interaction of demand and supply operating through a system of prices. According to Chandler, a 'visible hand' replaced an 'invisible' one within mid-twentieth-century industrial enterprises. Externally, the new corporations remained fully and actively part of a market economy; internally, 'administrative co-ordination' replaced 'market co-ordination'. The typical organization that emerged was not a group of competing individuals but a hierarchy bearing some resemblance to a military regiment (our expression, not his). As the historian has told us, 'Although administrative coordination has been a basic function in the modernization of the American economy, economists have given it little attention. Many have remained satisfied with Adam Smith's dictum that the division of labor reflects the extent of the market . . . Such an analysis has historical validity for the years before 1850 but has little relevance to much of the economy [thereafter].'[6]

Whence the ultimate paradox of the Great Engine companies and one of the most significant lessons contained in this book – the triumph of market economics was based in part on its rejection, or at least its severe attenuation, within the confines of the industrial corporation. The introduction to Chandler's book lays out on twelve pages and in eight propositions the essential character of the new age. For example, Proposition Seven tells us that, 'in making administrative decisions, career managers preferred policies that favored the long-term stability and growth of their enterprises to those that maximized short-term profits'.[7] In the last third of the twentieth century, a new generation of foolish theorists and practitioners would attempt to restore the *status quo ante Chandler* by both highlighting the importance of 'short-term profits' and re-establishing 'market coordination' in place of its administrative cousin at the heart of the Great Engine companies. All economists should be forced to learn his eight propositions by heart.

It may seem odd to some to include the troubled decade of the 1930s in any Golden Age but there are two good reasons for doing so, one positive and one negative. The positive one is that many of our Great Engine companies belonged to the 'New Economy' of the period, which included electricity generation and distribution, radio manufacture and broadcasting, telephony, commercial flying and aircraft manufacture; expanding fast, even in troubled times, these industries made an impact on the standard of living of all who were in employment, which was the majority of citizens. In terms of creature comforts and general efficiency, America would be a far better place in which to live in 1940 than in 1930.

The negative reason why our Great Engine companies were able to survive the Great Depression was the absence of debt in their balance sheets. A disinclination to borrow is a Puritan trait with a history stretching back to the biblical Ecclesiasticus, who told us: 'Be not made a beggar by banqueting upon borrowing'. On page 35, we met Malvolio, one of Shakespeare's two great Puritan characters; the other was Polonius, father of Ophelia in *Hamlet*. Polonius' address to his son Laertes included a line that has passed into the English language, 'Neither a borrower, nor a lender be'. Polonius explained why: 'For loan oft loses both itself and friend, / And borrowing dulls the edge of husbandry'.[8]

The outlook on life that Polonius exemplified would pass down the centuries through the Puritan migrants and their successors to the young Republic and beyond. In 1739, Benjamin Franklin had told us in *Poor Richard's Almanac*, that he would 'Rather go to bed supperless, than run in debt for a Breakfast'. George Washington would tell his fellow countrymen that 'there is no practice more dangerous than that of borrowing money'[9] – a caution that was still well heeded until the 1960s by so-called 'New England Companies' and their imitators in other parts of the country. Custom permitted utilities and railroads to borrow as long as they subjected themselves to the discipline of securing their obligations on real property, but large-scale manufacturers, by and large, did not indulge themselves in this way. IBM's first major long-term borrowing did not take place until the 1970s, when it was sub-underwritten by, among many others, William Hopper. This particular fund-raising was regarded by the company as an exceptional event, occasioned by the fact that raising capital in Europe carried certain benefits not available in the United States, owing to different forms of regulation.

Avoiding debt is a practice that has been carried forward into today's leading Japanese company, which is in part modeled on America's Great Engines. Toyota's Financial Rule 1 is: 'No enemy is more terrible than money, and no friend is more trustworthy. Other people's money – borrowed money – quickly turns into an enemy. Money is a trustworthy ally only when it is your own; only when you earn it yourself'.[10] In one's mind's eye, one can see the founder, Sakichi Toyoda, sitting in his peasant hut a century and a half ago, a copy of Samuel Smiles' *Self-Help* in his hand: chapter 12 of that book compares a debtor with 'an empty bag [that] cannot stand upright'[11] – a phrase that Smiles borrowed from *Poor Richard's Almanac*. An excess of borrowing, based on inflated property prices, would put an end to Japan's great Economic Miracle, just a year after the event that symbolized its peak: the purchase of New York's Rockefeller Center by Mitsubishi Estate Co. in 1989.[12] Toyota neither needed nor wanted to raise substantial capital in this way.

Had the Board of the Enron Corporation heeded the advice of Ecclesiasticus, Polonius, Franklin, Washington, Smiles and Toyota Motor, their company would not have gone bankrupt in the year 2002; some of its executives would not have lost their liberty as well as their loans and friends; and thousands of others would not have lost their life savings. And it was not just the avoidance of debt that characterized New England companies; there was also a puritanical dislike of ostentation. William Hopper well recalls calling on the treasurer of Gillette in Boston in 1964; he was courteously received in a pleasant but plainly furnished office framed by bare brick walls situated in a former factory building. By his behavior, this man set an example for all the company's staff.

The twenty years from 1950 to 1970 could also be called a Golden Age of American Society, as far as the majority of white citizens were concerned.[13] There had been much social deprivation during the 1930s but the approach of World War II brought the nation's great industrial machine into play, creating full employment. When peace came, the need to supply not only the general public, but also the rest of the world, with the goods denied to them during the years of depression and war would keep prosperity in being for another generation. The war had also engendered a strong spirit of national solidarity, which would survive for a similar length of time.

Huge housing developments, often called Levittowns, after William Levitt who had taken the lead in creating them, were built to accommodate the booming middle class. The Interstate Highway System, unparalleled anywhere in the world (though inferior in significant ways to the comparable European railroad network– see page 181) would bind the nation together and open up large new areas for development. Ethnic minorities were still subjected to discrimination throughout the country; for example, residents of the first Levittown had to be 'of the Caucasian race' although they could employ non-Caucasian servants.[14] However, for blacks and others, the Civil Rights Movement of the 1960s was not so much a revolt against the established order as an attempt to join it; they too were better off than they had been before.

Post-war society would bear little outward resemblance to the 'Citty on a Hill' envisaged by Winthrop, but it had been shaped in part by the Puritan migrants' theological outlook, important traces of which lurked just below the surface of public consciousness. Americans believed that they deserved their good fortune, not for what they did, but for what they were; this was an echo, sounding down the centuries, of the Puritan doctrine of justification by faith and not by works. For them the land they lived in was 'God's Own Country' – a phrase common then but which has since passed right out of the vocabulary. (Ask a young American today if she or he lives in God's Own Country and you will receive a blank stare.) They believed that what they had was owed to them. They also owned a shining future, conceived as a kind of extrapolation of the recent past. 'Onwards and upwards' was not just the unofficial motto of the Boy Scout movement – it was the badge of a generation.

In later decades, management theorists would speak eloquently about the need for adaptability in the making and execution of corporate policy, as if this was something new and different from what had gone before. In fact, an amazing operational flexibility was the one of the most obvious characteristics of the Great Engine companies at the mid-century. As late as 1940, the US economy had been dedicated almost exclusively to the arts of peace; only 3.0 per cent of gross national product was devoted to defense. In less than two years, the nation would be able to equip herself so well with military hardware that she could fight and win two simultaneous wars to the death – one in the Pacific and one in the Atlantic.

Aircraft manufacture provides a case in point. When the Japanese attacked Pearl Harbor in December 1941, the United States had nothing to match Japan's Mitsubishi A6M fighter, also known as the Zero.

(The name Zero was taken from the last digit of the Japanese year 2600 – our year 1940 – the year in which the first production model was received by the Japanese navy.) Its extraordinary powers of maneuver and ability to traverse vast stretches of water, together with the willingness of the Japanese to accept apparently unlimited losses in both aircraft and men, would create an illusion of invincibility. Yet just two years after Pearl Harbor, the Zero had been out-flown and out-fought. The arrival of Grumman Hellcats in 1943 on aircraft carriers of the USS Essex class changed the balance of power in the Pacific War overnight. Before another year was out, American industry had thrown into the fray the North American Mustang, the Chance Vought Corsair and the Lockheed Lightning, as well as other aircraft that Japan could simply not match. Delivery of Hellcats to active service began just seven months after the initial flight of the first prototype. North American Aviation, with only limited experience in fighter production, turned out a prototype of the immensely important Mustang in six months and encountered few snags during flight-testing.

One of the best descriptions of the Great Engine companies in their Golden Age has been provided by the French critic, Michel Crozier:

> America's business superiority lies not in the resources of its firms, however immense those may be, but in the capacities of its corporations to create and develop efficient organizations rapidly, to recruit and employ able people anywhere, competing among themselves to maintain the necessary pressure and at the same time cooperating so that each organization can utilize its talents constructively.[15]

Crozier believed that the success of the Great Engine companies was due not so much to the resources that they controlled as 'in the capacities of its corporations to create and develop efficient organizations'. A French academic and sociologist, he has made the same kind of adverse criticism of the influence of the *grandes écoles* on French business and society as the authors have made of the impact of business schools in America. It is regrettable that, having offered the tantalizing statement quoted above, he did not go on to explain *how* the major American corporations of the period achieved this remarkable feat – presumably because he did not know.

The culture of which Crozier wrote was largely implicit in nature. However, it had not started that way. As we have seen, the advent of the railroads had provoked an intensive discussion in the third quarter of the nineteenth century, chiefly in journals or railroad manuals rather than in books, about the nature, structure and purpose of business organization. These writings are as relevant today as they were then. Around the turn of the century, the proponents of so-called Scientific Management also wrote extensively, again mostly in journals. (Frederick Taylor's *The Principles of Scientific Management* is so short and badly written that it barely counts as a book.) By the mid-twentieth century, however, the new methodology was so well established that it could be taken for granted. Americans, then as now, were not much interested in their own – or indeed anyone's – history, apart from their Civil War. If they thought about it at all, most successful practicing businessmen of the Golden Age viewed such features of their companies as 'divisional structure' and 'line-and-staff' simply as 'the way business is done'. They were largely unaware that the principles they followed and the practices they observed had been laboriously hammered out, a hundred years before, in both theory and practice, by practitioners like McCallum and Thomson, who enjoyed the assistance of the journalist Poor.

In *The Practice of Management* (1954), Drucker commented on the paucity of contemporary writing and thinking at that time: 'Everywhere I found the same situation: a near-total absence of study, thought and knowledge regarding the job, function and challenges of management – nothing but fragments and specialized monographs'. For him, the subject was then a 'dark continent'.[16] To this day no completely satisfactory description has been put into print of the managerial culture of the Golden Age and, as a result, many serious misconceptions abound, often in places where they should not. One of the principal motives of the authors in writing this book has been to fill that gap.

The main characteristics of the managerial culture of the Golden Age are set out in the form of Twenty-five Principles underlying Good Practice from the Golden Age of Management (all with Puritan overtones) in the Appendix to this book. These principles are inter-related in the sense that each depends on, and buttresses, the others. For example, if you violate Principle Seven ('One man, one boss'), you destroy the main channel of communication in the company, which is the line-of-command. You therefore make it difficult for information to travel upwards to decision makers, the principal objective enshrined in Principle Twelve. If you eliminate the supervisory role of the middle manager, as defined in Principle Six ('The middle manager is the keystone of the managerial arch'), you make it impossible for full 'bottom-up' management to function as required under Principle Four; senior executives on their own cannot possibly supervise, and assist, hundreds of first-level managers. If you disregard Principle Twenty-two ('Employment should in general be for the long term . . .'), you endanger the application of Principle Nineteen ('The training and testing of managers should be

pragmatic and continuous'). And so on. The principles therefore constitute a kind of managerial house of cards: if you withdraw one, you risk
bringing down the entire structure. Management as practiced by the
Great Engine companies was a difficult and delicate business precisely
because it entailed balancing all these requirements, one against
another.

The authors have derived their information about the nature of
American management in the mid-twentieth century from a small
number of sources. The first and most important of these is their own
personal, unmediated experience as managers and consultants on the
factory floor and in financial institutions in the United States, Britain
and other countries, soon after the mid-point of the twentieth century. Their second source is information that they have collected about
the origins of the Japanese Economic Miracle, which is summarized in
the next chapter. These origins lay in the aftermath of World War II,
when the United States occupied Japan and a group of American communications engineers under instructions from Washington set out to
teach executives in the Japanese communications equipment industry
how to manage their factories. What these engineers taught was best
contemporary practice as they had themselves observed it at home. In
order to teach, you have to be explicit; and since the teaching occurred
under the auspices of the US government, everything that was said and
done was recorded on paper. It is for these reasons that the written
records of the Occupation, which sit in the National Archives in Washington DC, shed light on how business in general and manufacturing
in particular were organized in the United States at that time.

Other useful sources include Alfred D. Chandler's classic business
history. *The Visible Hand*; Professor Newcomer's *The Big Business Executive* and Drucker's *The Practice of Management* – from all of which we
have quoted above – as well as a small number of books by practicing
American managers of the period, among them: *Functions of the Executive* (1938) by Chester Bernard, president of New Jersey Bell; *Bottom-up
Management: People Working Together* (1949) by William B. Given; and
David Packard's *The HP Way* (1995). Packard wrote long after the
Golden Age, but he described it accurately as it had been in its (and his)
heyday. Andrew Grove's *High Output Management* (1985) is another valuable source, although Grove's company, Intel, was founded only in
1968, in the closing years of our Golden Age.

If there is one phrase that conveys the essence of American corporate
and non-corporate management at its best in the mid-twentieth century, it is 'bottom-up'. It appears to have been first used in print in 1949
by Given, a graduate of the Sheffield Scientific School at Yale and of

MIT and president of American Brake Shoe. The second part of his book's title is almost as significant as the first: according to Given, the good manager had to be a team player; like the captain of an athletic team, he did not need to be the best player but he must be a leader.[17] Furthermore, he had to exert a moral influence

Given had served in the army during World War I and, on returning to the company, been asked to take charge of a group of plants. He soon realized that he had been advanced to a 'position of responsibility beyond his experience':

> To succeed, it was necessary for me to try to develop the individuals at the heads of the divisions and to give them as free a rein as possible. This meant that more and more the initiative flowed up, less and less from the top down . . . More and more the seniors put pressure on the bosses under them to grant greater authority to the men in the ranks below them and to invite their fullest freedom of expression and initiative.[18]

One day, a student of business management called to discuss the degree of decentralization that American Brake Shoe was trying to achieve and christened it 'bottom-up management'. This was one of the earliest examples of a business school alumnus making an impact on the big world.

Given exercised less influence than du Pont or Taylor. These were men of great originality who, in their different ways, stamped not only their ideas but also their personalities on their companies, on society and on posterity. Given is to be valued, in the first place, as a representative figure who brought his company into line with an evolution that was affecting the whole country, while helping to push it forward; and, in the second place, as a man who could describe in homely, pungent prose what his contemporaries and he were seeking to achieve. Had he not existed, however, the world today would not be a radically different place from what it is – something that one would hesitate to say of the other two.

As we have seen, the growing complexity of business had led to the creation of divisional structures within companies, resulting in a transfer of responsibility to their respective heads; within the divisions, delegation also occurred. However, 'bottom-up' management went far beyond the systematic delegation of authority that was normal and, indeed, inevitable in any well-run hierarchy; it implied that each manager was in the habit of passing some of his *own* responsibility for decision-making down the chain of command to the lowest level ready, willing and able to accept it. Given called this 'progressive decentralization', using 'progressive' in the 'pathological' (his word) sense of 'spreading from one part to others'. Bottom-up, he said, gave a stimulating feeling of personal freedom to superintendents (factory managers), foremen, chief clerks – 'freedom to venture along new and untried paths; freedom to fight back if their ideas or plans are attacked by superiors; freedom to take calculated risks; freedom to fail'.[19]

At first blush, there is something quite elusive about this concept; it entailed the imposition of a highly informal type of organization on top of a totally formal one, but in a manner which was seamless and frictionless. How was this miracle of coincidence and compression to be achieved? The answer is best conveyed in metaphorical terms. Imagine an automobile with dual controls. The manager sits at one set and his subordinate at the other. The manager has the final responsibility for deciding where the car is going and by what route but, since he trusts his assistant, he shuts his eyes and reflects on other matters while the other person drives. However, if a change of plan is required, the manager can take over the controls at the drop of a hat. More usually, he will simply offer advice – and his advice will be heeded because he is respected for what he is and knows. The informal structure does not in any sense supersede or replace the formal one; they co-exist and feed on each other. At the heart of the system lies mutual trust.

How far down the hierarchy of American Brake Shoe did bottom-up practices penetrate? Given believed that it was the job of top management 'to create a sense of independence and freedom of initiative down through the middle management levels'. However, for him that was simply the first step: 'if that is done successfully, the feeling spreads and the least important workers share in it'. Even the blue-collar workforce below the rank of foreman was, therefore, expected to become involved in decision-making. Given was describing what would later become known as 'participatory' managerial practices:

> The chief executive makes clear the objectives, charts the course and holds the organization to it. Naturally, he makes many suggestions, *but he seldom gives orders* ... It is his responsibility to see that the heads of all divisions and departments are encouraged to follow a similar policy at their respective levels – or, if necessary, are even instructed to follow it, for this is one point on which the chief executive is justified in exerting authority ...[20]

In this way, the manager (any manager) multiplied his effectiveness and value by the number of people under him whom he had encouraged and persuaded to think and act for themselves. Given was offering a prime example of what Andrew Grove would later call 'managerial leverage'.[21]

Given's approach was avowedly descriptive rather than prescriptive, the author telling us that he had set out not to promote the methodology but to explain why it had been introduced and how it worked. However, his enthusiasm for it was so overwhelming that it is difficult not to treat his book as a manifesto. Since it probably, more than any other single factor, accounted for the success of some of the country's large corporations, he laid no personal claim to it. He was also in no doubt about the applicability of the methodology to the charitable and government sectors,[22] characteristically comparing a meeting of his divisional presidents with a New England town meeting.[23]

Given's book has long been out of print. It would almost certainly have been 'lost in the literature', to the use a scholars' expression, if its title, and some of its ideas, had not been picked up, with attribution, by Drucker in *The Practice of Management*.[24] Drucker objected on what he calls 'aesthetic' grounds to the term 'bottom-up'. It is a recurring theme of our book that the good managerial practices that characterized mid-twentieth-century America were inspired by Puritanism; it is perhaps not totally surprising therefore that some of its practitioners and theorists should also have been guilty of prudery about bodily parts. Fortunately, Drucker's 'aesthetic' reservations did not prevent him from discussing and promoting Given's approach – otherwise we would never have heard of it.

Given had expressed all his ideas in homespun language: Drucker enunciated them precisely and unemotionally – for him, Given's approach meant that decisions had to 'be taken as close as possible to the action to which they apply'. He referred to the chief recipient of responsibility as 'the firing-line manager' – which would normally have been at the first or foreman level in a manufacturing context:

> The managers on the firing line have the basic management jobs – the ones on whose performance everything else ultimately rests. Seen this way, the jobs of higher management are derivative, are, in the last analysis, aimed at helping the firing-line manager do his job. Viewed structurally and organically, it is the firing line manager in whom all authority and responsibility center; only what he cannot do himself passes up to higher management. He is, so to speak, the gene of organization in which all higher organs are prefigured and out of which they are developed.[25]

In support of these views, Drucker tells us that successful companies such as IBM had defined the role of the manager as one of 'assistant' to his subordinates. He also quoted the 'management charter' of General Electric's Lamp Division which was, as he pointed out, based on the US

Constitution: 'All authority not expressly and in writing reserved to higher management is granted to lower management'.[26]

Where did General Motors stand in the bottom-up stakes? It introduced decentralized decision-making under Pierre du Pont – being a much-respected model for other companies in this respect – but had it then gone the whole nine yards and pushed decision-making down to the first level of management or below? Drucker appears to think so; in his earlier book, *Concept of the Corporation* (1946), he told us that in that company: 'Every executive down to the lowliest assistant foreman makes policy decisions . . .'.[27] The vice-president in charge of a group of divisions had very real power but it was rarely, if ever, exercised in the form of giving orders. 'Rather it makes itself felt through suggestions . . . as a result of the respect the divisional manager has for a man who, as is usually the case, has successfully been a divisional manager himself'.[28]

In large companies, as Drucker has explained:

> There is usually someone called a 'chief executive officer' . . . [b]ut actually the job is discharged by a group working as a team . . . This trend has gone furthest at Standard Oil of New Jersey where the chief executive consists of a fourteen-man Board of Directors composed entirely of full-time officers of the company. More common is the General Electric pattern of an Executive Committee composed of a president, a number of group executives who are, so to speak deputy presidents, and a number of vice-presidents charged with responsibilities for objectives and policy-making.[29]

Bottom-up management also flourished at Hewlett-Packard in its glory days. As Dave Packard told us, 'our success depends in large part on giving the responsibility to the level where it can be exercised effectively, usually on the lowest possible level of the organization, the level nearest the customer'.[30]

Given provided a clear and accurate account of the nature of bottom-up management as it functioned in many, and probably most, leading American companies in the second and third quarters of the twentieth century. However, his account of the preceding regime was less satisfactory – so much so that he can be held responsible for launching what would become a remarkably tenacious and damaging corporate myth – the belief that, at some not very clearly specified time between 1630 and the present day, American business management was essentially 'dictatorial' in character. Other terms that would be used by later commentators with more or less the same intent include 'feudal', 'autocratic', 'military', 'military-style', 'command-and-control' and 'hierarchical'.

Two of these terms – 'hierarchical' and 'command and control' – are particularly objectionable, the first because hierarchies are not necessarily dictatorial in character – indeed, the best are the reverse, some form of hierarchy being inevitable in every organization. 'Command and control' is to be avoided for a quite different reason: if the scores of management writers who routinely misuse it were to consult a military manual, they will discover that it meant precisely the opposite of what they think. The US Department of the Navy's *Naval Doctrine Publication 6, Command and Control*, illustrates the concept with a description of Nelson's style of command: 'The key to the "Nelson touch" was neither his tactics nor his understanding of his enemies, but his belief that the best way to achieve a decisive victory was to give his subordinates a thorough indoctrination before the engagement and near-absolute initiative once it had begun'.[31] The manner of Nelson's death at Trafalgar in 1805 illustrates the success of his approach; mortally wounded at the start of the action, he was unable to give further orders but that did not affect the outcome. Happily, he lived just long enough to hear that his strategy had won the day. 'Thorough indoctrination', 'near-absolute initiative' – it all sounds remarkably like what Bill Given would have called 'bottom-up' management and reminds us of how much businessmen can learn from the military. In spite of appearances, good decision-making is essentially the same in all walks of life.

The Golden Age of American Management came to an end in the late 1960s under the influence of the neo-Taylorite Cult of the (so-called) Expert as propagated by business schools and others, a subject to which we return in detail in Chapters 11 to 14. However, its Japanese offspring would inspire an East Asian Golden Age, which began in the 1960s in the Chrysanthemum Kingdom and spread to the 'Tiger Economies' of South Korea, Taiwan, Malaysia, Singapore and Hong Kong, enlivening China in the present century; since 2000, digitalization has given parts of Japanese manufacturing a new lease of life.[32] A managerial culture with deep roots in Puritan New England today enjoys its fullest and finest flowering on distant, alien soil, of which more in the next chapter and Chapter 17.

10

Three Wise Men from the West Go to Japan

... that things are not so ill with you and me as they might have been, is half owing to the number who lived faithfully a hidden life, and rest in unvisited tombs.

George Eliot, *Middlemarch*

In the aftermath of World War II, from 1945 to 1952, the victorious United States set out to turn Japan into a Western-style democracy. Considering the obstacles in the way, it enjoyed remarkable success. Almost every aspect of Japanese life would be transformed; the rule of law was restored, farmland given to the peasants, wealth in general redistributed, human rights such as freedom of speech and of the press guaranteed, women's suffrage introduced, and a divine ruler converted into a constitutional monarch. Roosevelt's New Deal would have a profound effect on the social order that emerged; indeed, some have argued that it had an even greater impact on post-war Japanese society than it ever had in the United States.

The American Supreme Commander, General Douglas MacArthur, was not only a successful military commander – he was also a great populist reformer whose footprints, metaphorically speaking, can be found all over Japan to this day. His activities were governed by a Secret Directive, numbered JCS 1380/15 and issued by the US Joint Chiefs of Staff, paragraph 25 of which prescribed that he was to 'show favor to policies that permit a wide distribution of income and ownership of the means of production and trade'. That chief executives of large Japanese companies are today paid only eleven times the wages of an ordinary worker is in part due to him; the comparable American figure is 475 (Germany enjoys the next lowest multiple: twelve).[1] Col. Robert McCormick, the right-wing editor of the *Chicago Tribune*, whom we met briefly in Chapter 5 and who had been one of MacArthur's greatest admirers, was so shocked when he heard about the general's 'socialist' reforms[2] that he flew to Japan to discover for himself what was going on. His worst fears confirmed, he abandoned his campaign to make

MacArthur president of the United States; Japan's gain would be America's loss.

Anyone who wishes to understand how the New Deal's social policies shaped post-war Japan should read two important books, Edwin O. Reischauer's *Japan: The Story of a Nation*.[3] and Ted Cohen's *Remaking Japan: The American Occupation as New Deal*. Reischauer, after whom the Edwin O. Reischauer Institute of Japanese Studies at Harvard is named, was born in Japan and would become President Kennedy's ambassador to that country. For six years, Cohen was an active participant in the Occupation and its scholarly witness: his book is enlivened by a robust sense of humor. He tells us, for example, what happened when Ralph Young, Deputy Director of Research at the Federal Reserve, ventured to issue a report of which MacArthur did not approve, recommending the institution of a single international exchange rate for the yen. Ever a master tactician, the General classified it as Top Secret, removing it from circulation.[4] Or take the story of the three geishas who tottered through MacArthur's headquarters in full regalia to inform the authorities that geishas as a whole had decided to form a labor union. (As New Dealers, the Occupation authorities favored such bodies.) According to Cohen, the women 'accomplished in five minutes what four years of Japanese military attacks had failed to do – put a good part of General MacArthur's headquarters out of action'.[5]

In addition, a managerial revolution was initiated by the Occupation authorities that would in time transform the balance of economic – and, prospectively, of political – power not just in East Asia but throughout the world. It was led by three civilian communications engineers who were part of MacArthur's command: Homer M. Sarasohn, Charles W. Protzman and Frank A. Polkinghorn.[6] The subsequent Economic Miracle – really an Industrial Miracle – turned a war-torn, poverty-stricken, underdeveloped land into the second largest economy in the world in the course of three decades. This transformation could not have been accomplished without both the New Deal-like revolution which preceded it (which alleviated social tensions) and the change in the way companies were managed introduced under the influence of our Three Wise Men. One of their pupils, Bunzaemon Inoue, who went on to become president and chairman of Sumitomo Rubber, would tell Kenneth Hopper in 1979 that the lessons taught by the engineers were 'the light that illuminated everything'. Inspired by it, Inoue had 'wanted to set the Kansai on fire'[7] – the Kansai being, of course, Japan's equivalent of America's industrial Mid West. The enthusiasm generated in this way spread to the whole population, the most popular Japanese radio program of the 1950s being *Quality for Foremen*.

Paragraph 13 of the Secret Directive stipulated that: 'You will not assume any responsibility for the economic rehabilitation of Japan or the strengthening of the Japanese economy . . .'. America did not want to recreate Japan's capacity for waging war. However, an exception was made where the interests of the Occupation forces were concerned. An example was provided by the various public communications systems which, when the Occupation began, were 'in a shambles';[8] telephones, telegraphs and radio stations scarcely functioned. There were very few radio sets in the hands of the public. Most central and switching telephone and telegraph systems, as well as the interconnecting lines, had been destroyed by bombing; what remained was mostly unusable, due to neglect both before and during the war. Few technicians were available to effect repairs and, for those still there, travel was almost impossible.

The small military advance party which landed at Atsugi Airport near Tokyo on August 28, 1945, two days before MacArthur, had consisted mostly of members of the US Army Signal Corps. After completing its work in connection with the surrender, the corps' principal task would be to create a Civil Communications Section (or CCS) within the Supreme Commander's headquarters. CCS was formally established on October 2, 1945. Its senior staff were civilian engineers on loan mostly from 'Ma Bell', its manufacturing arm, Western Electric (including the famous Laboratories) and the 'Baby Bells' or regional affiliates. Sarasohn was an exception: a radio engineer, he had previously worked at the 'Rad Lab' – the world-famous Radiation Laboratory at MIT.

The civil communications systems were reconnected with commendable speed but were frequently out of action for the lack of reliable equipment. Congress had refused to meet the cost of buying and exporting American-made goods; for the CCS, consequently, the most intractable problem was the lack of local manufacturing capacity capable of producing equipment of adequate quality. Its industry division, where our engineers worked, became in effect a management consultancy whose principal occupation was teaching contemporary American management methods to the Japanese communications equipment manufacturers. A number of unusual factors operated in favor of the rapid adoption of good American practices by that industry. First, there was the personal authority that the CCS engineers enjoyed; as a result of the Allies' overwhelming victory; they did not need to give orders – according to Protzman, their slightest wish was taken to be a command. This authority was reinforced by the fact that the engineers also operated, *de facto*, as procurement agents for the communications companies; money spoke. Then again, there was a widespread realization on the part of Japanese managers that their industry had to be modernized if it was to compete in the post-war world – and that the engineers held the key to that future.

There is one other factor that cannot be left out of account in explaining the extraordinary impact of the Civil Communications Section on Japan: a strain of old-fashioned Puritan zeal in the characters of our Three Wise Men. Sarasohn, Protzman and Polkinghorn could have treated their sojourn in Japan as an extended vacation, as many of their compatriots did. Instead they devoted themselves to the task in hand with a dedication that went beyond the call of duty and was certainly not reflected in the money which they earned while there or the rewards they would receive on their return home. Each was motivated by a disinterested desire to create a better Japan. They wanted to do good. Sensing this motivation, their pupils responded with enthusiasm.

The Japanese have long possessed their own equivalent of the Western Puritan creed. Originating in the thirteenth century as an aspect of Zen Buddhism, *bushido* – the code of conduct of the *samurai* or warrior class – had over time influenced all classes of Japanese society with its call for honesty, austerity and devotion to duty. At least two of the quartet of lasting characteristics of American society which we listed at the beginning of Chapter 1 found a reflection in it, in the sense that its adherents sought to create an ideal society on earth, which was to be achieved by subordinating the interests of the individual to those of the group. Cross-pollination had occurred between these two traditions before when Samuel Smiles' book, *Self-Help, with Illustrations of Character and Conduct*, published in London in 1859, appeared in a Japanese translation. A best-seller in its new home, it would become one of the formative texts of the Meiji Era (1868–1912).[9] *Self-Help* was able to exert a profound influence on its Japanese readers because they were more than half converted before they turned the first page. One of those affected in this way by this book was a peasant farmer, Sakichi Toyoda, who founded a small company to make textile machinery in 1866. Its direct, linear descendant is today the most successful manufacturing company, with a *modus operandi* (the Toyota Production System) that sets a model of practice and a standard of excellence for manufacturers, and indeed for organizations of all kinds, throughout the world.

The impact of *Self-Help* on its American readers was every bit as great, and for the same reason – they were more than half converted before they opened it up. In addition, its Scottish authorship made a particular appeal to the large number of Scotch-Irish settlers who were then pushing westwards from the Appalachians. Smiles drew both from the circumstances of his birth (he was one of eleven children left fatherless in 1832) and from the Calvinism of his native surroundings a belief that life was not merely best understood, but also best experienced, as a struggle. His book's motto was, 'Heaven helps those who help themselves'.[10] However, his outlook was remote from the self-centeredness of an Ayn Rand (see page 211); for Smiles, self-help was indissolubly bound up with obligation. As he said in the third, revised, edition of 1867, 'The duty of helping one's self in the highest sense involves the helping of one's neighbours.'[11] In many American households, *Self-Help* sat beside – and ranked just after – the Bible.

The reforms promoted by the CCS would have been ineffective without the so-called Economic Purges that MacArthur imposed in 1947 on all of Japanese manufacturing – not just on the makers of communication equipment. A total of 1,937 company executives at the level of managing director and above in 154 large companies were affected. No compensation was offered – some of the men dismissed ended up driving taxis. These purges were undertaken primarily for political reasons – to discourage Japan from becoming a warlike nation again – but the Occupation forces were not unaware of their purely economic implications. According to Col. Charles L. Kades, who has been called the second most important member of the Occupation staff, the Americans thought that putting new blood into top executive positions would be good for Japanese industry.[12] In Germany, under its simultaneous Occupation, the proportion of senior managers purged on account of their past affiliations was even higher than in Japan. However, many were promptly re-appointed by the Allies because it was thought that no-one else could do their jobs. In Japan the Supreme Commander faced the same dilemma. He was personally unsympathetic to the former senior executives, saying they were – the ultimate insult in his vocabulary – 'like New York clubmen'. However, always a believer in good managerial practices, such as consulting his staff before making up his mind, he sought the advice of Sarasohn in his capacity as head of the CCS's industry division.

It was unusual for the Supreme Commander to consult such a junior person – Sarasohn was only twenty-nine years old. He had, however, by then become acquainted with the old top executives and found them to be seriously lacking by American standards. He told MacArthur so, arguing earnestly that their replacements could cope. Many years later, when we asked him to comment on the advice he had given on this occasion, he replied: '*that is what America is all about*'.[13] There is a great deal of wisdom tied up in that simple phrase; in writing this book one of our objects has been to untie it for the benefit of a wider public. Sarasohn had another reason for wanting them out of the way: many were 'horrible men' who had been in charge of the Japanese occupation of Manchuria.

Japanese industry, founded on a British model in the late nineteenth century, inherited two weaknesses from which Britain suffers to this day. First, it was stratified, resulting in poor communications and worse decision-making; and, secondly, both management and work-force lacked technical qualifications. In the first quarter of the twentieth century, Japan would come under strong German influence. This corrected the second of the weaknesses: henceforth there was a strong emphasis on technological education for Japanese managers (although of a somewhat theoretical kind). By the beginning of World War II, the engineer had become almost as important a figure in Japa-nese industry (although not in society) as his German counterpart. However, German influence did not correct the other inherited weak-ness: stratification. The economic purges may not have provided a solution to this problem but they removed a barrier to finding one; if the old guard had remained in place, it is doubtful if a new methodol-ogy and structure could have been introduced.

What lessons did the CCS engineers teach to their pupils? First of all, they described good Scientific Management practices (the kind we will refer to as 'procedural' on page 129), particularly on the factory floor.[14] The Japanese had been attempting to introduce them, and had failed, ever since 1913. This failure was one of the numerous reasons why Japan lost World War II. That was put bluntly in the following passage, which appeared in *Engineers Club*, the journal of the Union of Japanese Scientists and Engineers, soon after World War II:

> ... every Japanese will remember the fact that during the war our industry produced innumerable planes which couldn't keep aloft long enough to meet any enemy plane to fight with. Many promising youths were doomed to die in the Pacific Ocean because our produc-tion control, so formidably imposed, lacked the least bit of scientific spirit.[15]

Secondly, the CCS engineers taught the Japanese how to organize the structure of management – a subject on which Taylor had either been silent or had even given thoroughly misleading advice, as we shall see in the next chapter. The lessons that Pierre du Pont, Alfred Sloan, William Given and many others had learned and applied to American industry in the first quarter of the twentieth century would now be conveyed by the CCS engineers to their Japanese pupils – and, even more important, absorbed by the latter. According to Bunzaemon Inoue, Japanese management had been 'all line, no staff' until the time of the Occupation. It was from the Americans that the Japanese would learn how to lighten the load on 'line' managers by entrusting functions like accounting and personnel to specialized 'staff' departments.

The engineers also promoted 'bottom-up management', although not by name; the expression would not enter the Japanese lexicon until Drucker's book, *The Practice of Management*, appeared in translation in 1955, but the practice itself features large in the CCS Manual (see page 120). Here is a description of 'the first class executive leader':

> ... he leads by letting others take part in the leadership. He takes people into his confidence, shows them where he is going and why, then gives them responsibility and authority so they can help him reach the goals. He passes down the line the power to make plans and decisions in order to develop a sense of participation among his followers.[16]

'Bottom-up management' is an example of a non-Scientific Management practice introduced by our engineers that would be adapted to meet local needs. Readers will recall from the last chapter that, in the United States, the heaviest burden of responsibility had been thrown informally onto the lowest possible level: the departmental managers or foremen. Major postwar Japanese companies studied the American system but ended up with something significantly different: the *kacho* system, which we describe below.

In the typical British company of the period, foremen were almost entirely recruited from the shop floor, having left school at fourteen. On the other side of the Atlantic, their equivalents could have a wide range of educational backgrounds reflecting the work which they did – some were blue-collar workers, some had doctorates. At Procter & Gamble, when Kenneth Hopper joined its British subsidiary, half of the first-level supervisors had honors degrees, mostly in science or engineering. They were not called foremen but department managers or section engineers, the title which he bore.

So far as the authors know, the only research on the use of graduates in the 'mixed' American foreman force was that undertaken by Kenneth Hopper, when he attended the Harvard Business School in 1965–1966, under the sponsorship of the International Teachers Program and the British Foundation for Management Education. While he was there, he felt that his material was sufficiently important for it to be offered for a doctorate – a proposal that upset the faculty so much that his intiative was stopped in its tracks by one of the most important figures in academia. The verdict and sentence were delivered by Professor Felix Roethlisberger, leader in the Human Relations Movement (who will re-appear in Chapter 13) with the memorable words: 'Mr. Hopper, you do not belong here. You must leave this place. You belong in the medium [i.e. industry]. You must return there. Tell us what you observe and we will write about it'.[17] Kenneth's findings, written by himself, would be published in the respected *Management of Personnel Quarterly* of the Division of Industrial Relations of the University of Michigan and in the British journal, *Management Today*.[18]

In the early twentieth century, German influence had led not just to the teaching of technology in Japanese universities but also to the introduction of technical training in high schools. Japan might have developed its own equivalent of the German *Werkmeister*, a highly qualified super-foreman possessing both a practical and a theoretical grasp of his trade, which would have endowed the country with an even more formidable foreman force than America possessed. Regrettably, technical classes were discontinued in high schools under the occupation; Japan was being re-created on an American model. Manufacturers responded by intensifying in-company training; the authors possess a copy of the test in calculus that Sumitomo Metal foremen took in 1979.

After a period of trial and error, the Japanese would throw the principal burden of responsibility for decision-making not on the foreman or *honcho* but on the middle manager or *kacho*, where it remains to this day. *Ka* means section and *cho* means head, the literal translation of *ka-cho* being, therefore, section head. The *kacho* system would become the heart and soul of Japanese management. However, confusingly, the Japanese borrowed the English-language term 'bottom-up', learned from Drucker in 1955, to describe it. This semantic inaccuracy caused confusion when Japanese-style management arrived in the United States in the 1980s in the baggage train of the Quality Movement; nobody quite knew what the term meant. Essentially, a *kacho* is responsible for an area of activity. In a large factory making electrical consumer goods, for example, he might be in charge of 'white goods' (i.e. cookers, washing machines, and so on) production in all its aspects. He has no real equivalent in the US company. An American assistant plant manager occupies a similar place in the organization chart (i.e. somewhere between top and bottom) but his role lacks the status, responsibility and influence of his Japanese opposite number.

The strength of the *kacho* system is that all information regarding a group of products is concentrated in one person. The *kacho* knows, or should know, everything that goes on beneath, alongside and above him, with regard to his own product area: company policy, research, relations with customers and suppliers, information about the competition, and all activities on the shop-floor. We are grateful to

S. Nagasaki, president of Sumitomo Electric, USA for putting the matter in a nutshell: 'All information should be concentrated in the *kacho*'.[19] The weakness of the system is that it throws an enormous burden onto one person, the relative inactivity of the senior manager, or *bucho*, contrasting with the continuous activity of his subordinate. In American-style bottom-up management, responsibility was (and is, to the extent that it still exists) spread more evenly across the senior, middle and junior ranks. According to Inoue (in letter number 31 to Kenneth Hopper – see page xii), the *kacho*s were a reincarnation in an industrial setting of the classic Japanese *samurai*, the highly competent warriors who administered much of Japan on behalf of their incompetent feudal overlords, the *daimyo,* during the Tokugawa shogunate (1608–1868). If this is so, which seems likely, the underemployed *bucho*s were (and are) in some sense the heirs of the *daimyo*.

A number of Japanese companies would try to vary the formula to meet changing conditions – for example, giving the *bucho* a more active role, particularly in coordinating complex 'high-tech' operations. However, in the end they found it difficult to abandon *kacho* management. In the early 1980s, Toyota Motor attempted to de-layer itself in accordance with the prevailing American re-engineering fad (see page 239) by removing the *kacho* layer altogether. The attempt was unsuccessful; as Maryann Keller reported: 'Even though the *kacho* title was gone, it still appears on name cards so that counterparts in other companies can understand the rank of the person with whom they are dealing. Inside the company, everyone knows who is the section chief or *kacho*, even though he is no longer being referred to by that title.'[20] Non-Japanese executives who visit Japanese companies today should be aware that, if they make a proposal and fail to secure the approval of the relevant person, they are unlikely to succeed in what they are trying to do.

Along with 'bottom-up management', our Three Wise Men taught the need to specify the objectives of the organization. These were not simply 'to make a profit':

> The business enterprise must be founded on a sense of responsibility to the public and to its employees. Service to its customers, the wellbeing of its employees, good citizenship in the communities in which it operates – these are cardinal principles fundamental to any business. They provide the platform upon which a profitable company is built.

In support of this view, the engineers quoted a well-known motto that had been placed on a wall in a shipyard in Newport News, Virginia on January 1, 1917: 'We shall build good ships here; at a profit if we can – at a loss if we must – but always good ships'; the curious, subsequent history of this plaque is told on page 152; an illustration of the plaque appears on page 254. Sarasohn illustrated this 'first lesson' with the diagram that features on page 91 entitled 'The Fundamental Objectives of the Enterprise'.

The engineers also called for flexibility and decentralization. According to the CCS Manual: 'Flexibility usually calls for decentralization of authority – putting authority as far down the line and as close to the scene of action as circumstances and the abilities of subordinates allow'.[21] The manual underlined the need for flexibility by quoting an observation of George S. Dively, president of Harris-Seybold Co:

> I have never felt I knew enough about any man's job or his potentialities to put a frame around him. We leave a twilight zone around every (supervisory) job definition to give the more competent man room to expand and the less competent to shrink, without stumbling over each other.[22]

There was an emphasis on the value of cross-departmental teams: 'In a flexible organization, men and functions from different areas can be welded into an efficient team on short notice. Flow of ideas and information across formal lines is continual.'[23] Such teams were compared in the manual with a naval taskforce:

> During the war, the Navy detached specialized units from their regular departments – the battle fleet, the air arm, and the submarine service – and organized them into a combined fighting force to carry out certain special assignments ... We need to do more of this in business ... Advertising agencies do this frequently.[24]

And there are several references to the interaction between formal and informal structures, for example:

> If formal and informal organizations didn't match, the formal organization would mean little because people would tend to ignore it. But if the right men are chosen for leadership jobs, and if the formal organization is fitted to the work to be done, the two organizations will [work in] parallel as a matter of course.[25]

In other words, many of the remedies to be advanced in the 1980s by proponents of the Quality Movement and their successors had actually been the commonplaces of good American management thirty years before.

In the early days of the Occupation, the communications equipment manufacturers had to be taught the virtue of cleanliness. Sarasohn visited a small company with a large name situated in the Shinagawa section of Tokyo: Tokyo Tsushin Kogyo Kabushiki Kaisha (or TTK, the Tokyo Telecommunications Engineering Company). Its listed capital was under $600. The minuscule staff was housed in a few dilapidated army huts, where in a rainstorm the executives had to work with umbrellas over their desks. To reach it, visitors ducked under clotheslines, on which neighbors hung their children's diapers. Bomb damage was everywhere.

Thinking that this little company had potential, Sarasohn approved the award of an order for a sophisticated audio-mixing console on behalf of NHK (Nihon Hoso Kyokai), the Japanese national broadcasting company, an organization modeled on the British Broadcasting Corporation. Hearing nothing for some time, he paid a surprise visit. The workplace was dirty. The components lay about covered in dust. The design was crude and incomplete. Neither the president of the company nor the chief engineer was present. He called the staff together to discuss what should be done, but they were unresponsive. To make his displeasure clear, he did something that would be rude in any country but especially so in Japan: he stood up in the middle of the meeting and walked out without saying a word.

Shortly afterwards, the president and the chief engineer arrived in his office, full of apologies. They wanted to know what specifically they should do. Sarasohn told them what was expected. The company responded well to the challenge and produced an excellent mixer console. And it was on time. As a result, the company received many more orders under CCS's auspices. The small company with a large name in time became a large company with a small name: Sony. The change to the new title took place in 1958. The president and the chief engineer who called on Sarasohn were its founders, Masaru Ibuka and Akio Morita. Sony would become famous for technical innovation and quality in the consumer electronics market. It adapted the newly invented transistor for radios and other small household appliances, making possible our modern electronic world; set new standards for color television; and invented and popularized the Walkman. Later it was foolish enough to acquire Columbia Pictures and CBS Records.

Two different books based on Sony material, one by Morita[26] himself and the other by Nick Lyons,[27] recount this incident. Both correctly point out that the production of the mixer was a milestone in the company's history. However, Morita's account contains a serious inaccuracy; it tells us that it was an American brigadier general who visited to the plant. According to Sarasohn, it was absurd to suggest that the senior military officer to whom the CCS reported would have called to inspect a console for NHK when he had a department of highly qualified specialists to deal with such matters. (MacArthur was 'death' on intervention by the military in the work of the civilian specialists – 'you do not own a dog and bark'.) Furthermore, in Morita's account, the visitor, far from objecting to the dirty working conditions, the crudity of the drawings and the fact that the design was incomplete, had marveled at the quality of the design and the fact 'that a small, new company in a make-shift factory could produce such a high-technology product'. When he read Morita's account of this encounter, Sarasohn wrote to him to object but there was no reply.[28] Sarasohn contrasts Morita's ungracious behavior with that of two other former pupils: Koji Kobayashi and Masaharu Matsushita, who became, respectively, chairmen of NEC and of Matsushita Electric. The former would embrace him 'like a long lost brother' when they met years after the Occupation. As explained below, the latter would visit him in his retirement home in Phoenix, Arizona in 1993 to thank him for all he had done.

When the Cold War reached a peak of intensity in the late 1940s, Washington instructed the Allied Command to do what it could to stimulate Japanese industry in general. According to Sarasohn, when the news of this change of policy arrived, it 'rang down the corridors of MacArthur's headquarters'. Sarasohn and Protzman proposed that CCS should present a course of lectures on contemporary American management methods to the communications equipment manufacturers. There was opposition to this idea from elsewhere within the Allied Command, on the grounds that this would be a step too far; America, it was argued, should not give away *all* her industrial secrets to a former enemy which could, after all, become a future competitor.

Only the Supreme Commander could decide between these competing points of view on this new and important subject. It fell to Sarasohn with his long experience of Japanese industry to make the pitch on behalf of his section. It took place in the meeting room outside the general's penthouse office on the sixth floor of the headquarters building. There was a formal presentation of opposing arguments, each side having twenty minutes to make its case. This procedure, known as a 'floor show', was standard practice when there was disagreement at a high level about an important matter. Sarasohn explained that CCS had done a great deal for the communications equipment manufacturers but not enough. This industry should be a model for the whole of manufacturing; if that did not begin to generate wealth on a large scale, society could revert to its former fascist state. Many of the former senior executives in manufacturing industry had found the earlier close relationship with the military only too comfortable – profits had been guaranteed and labor unions suppressed. If the new generation of managers, whose aim was to produce goods that the mass of the population wanted and could afford, was to survive and prosper, they required guidance while settling in.

Behind Sarasohn's presentation lay a belief that leaving enemies in destitution had been tried after World War I and had led to totalitarianism, militarism and fascism. The Japanese people were still not far from destitution. The average annual income per head was still under $132 – or $2.50 a week – even in 1950 when the economy was already on the mend. There was no doubt that the ordinary people were delighted with the experience of living in a democracy where individual rights were respected and where the secret police were only a memory. Nevertheless, if there was not a return to at least the modest standard of living of pre-war years, there was a probability that that the old political and economic systems would be restored. Something had to be done to prevent a collapse of this emerging Asian democracy.

'No-one ever accused MacArthur of being open-minded', Sarasohn would later say jokingly, 'but you could reach him with reason'. The general sat at his desk listening intently, smoking his corncob pipe, uttering not a word and without changing his expression. When the presentations were over, he sat for a minute or so in further silence and then walked towards the door. Sarasohn thought to himself, 'I've blown it'. However, just as he reached the exit, the general turned round, glared at Sarasohn and said 'Go do it!' The two engineers retreated for two and a half months to a quiet and rundown hotel in Osaka that had been taken over by the US Army for officers' rest and recreation. No noisy parties were permitted and female guests were excluded – even wives. A period of intensive work followed while the men wrote the series of lectures they would present. The typed copies when assembled became the 'CCS Manual'. (The authors possess Protzman's personal copy of what can be called the 1950 first edition.) There was a rather grand title page. Like a normal book, the manual had a publisher: Civil Communications Section, General Headquarters, Supreme Commander for the Allied Powers and even a publication date and place: Tokyo, Japan, January, 1950. The text was preceded by Polkinghorn's crisp foreword, which argued that, in the long term, industry could be efficient only in a democratic environment.

The Civil Communications Section of the Allied Command was the principal but not the only gateway through which contemporary American 'top management' principles and practices entered Japan. Its pupils absorbed what they were taught into their own traditional ways of managing to create a new and distinctively Japanese-American way of doing business. Within fifteen years the communications equipment industry would evolve into the world-beating Japanese consumer electronics industry. After the Americans left, Inoue created and chaired the Top Management Study Group for the Kansai, a body set up under the auspices of Nikkeiren, the federation of Japanese employers' associations; his object was to share the best management practices with the whole of Japanese industry. According to Protzman, 'without him the seminars would not have been a success. He worked and he worked and he worked'.

The CCS Seminar was presented by the engineers only twice – in Tokyo in 1949 and in Osaka in 1950. However, after the Occupation it was taken over by the training arm of Nikkeiren, which continued to present it regularly as a top management training course until 1974. Its contents never varied. By that time all the objectives of CCS engineers had been achieved. However, that was not quite the end of the matter: the course continued to feature in a place of honor in the training arm's syllabus until 1982, thirty-three years after the first seminar, even though it was no longer being presented.[29]

Since the late 1980s, Japan has suffered from deflation and rising unemployment. However, the best Japanese companies continue to be world-beaters; in spite of the precipitous decline in Tokyo stock exchange prices after 1990, the market capitalization of Toyota Motor is today many times that of General Motors and Ford together. Japan's economy may have ceased to expand dramatically, but it is still the second largest in the world at current exchange rates. The average wage in Japan remains higher than in the United States. In spite of recent setbacks, most of the achievements of the Economic Miracle are still with us, and starting in 2005, Japanese manufacturing entered on a new period of economic expansion due to the impact of digitalization.

D. W. Brogan, a distinguished Scottish professor of American history, used to refer to the legends of the American West as the *matière d'Amérique*, an expression derived from the name given to the body of French medieval myth called the *matière de Bretagne*. One of the most persistent tells of strangers who arrive in a troubled town, set the place to rights and, having neither sought nor obtained a reward for themselves, ride off into the sunset. It reflects the quality of moral life on the frontier, the emphasis on service to one's neighbor, the Puritan belief that wrong has to be countered. The CCS engineers were strangers not only to the Japanese but to each other. They arrived in a troubled town; if they did not sort it out, they at least showed others how to do so; there was even a shoot-out, albeit a verbal one, in the form of the 'floor show' described above; and they disappeared quite suddenly without reward to themselves other than the knowledge of a job well done. A re-enactment of a great American legend lay at the root of Japan's Economic Miracle.

Some years after he left Japan, Sarasohn would involve himself in another verbal shoot-out, also with dramatic consequences – in this case, for the development of mainframe computers. It is told in an entertaining book called *Accidental Empires* by the columnist Robert X. Cringely:

> Here's a scene that happened in the early 1960s at IBM headquarters in Armonk, New York. IBM chairman Tom Watson, Jr, and president Al Williams were being briefed on the concept of computing with video display terminals and time sharing, rather than with batches of punch cards. They didn't understand the idea. They were intelligent men, but they had a fairly fixed concept of what computing was supposed to be, and it didn't include video display terminals. They started over a second time, and finally a light bulb went off in Al Williams's head. 'So what you are talking about is data-processing but not in the same room!' he exclaimed.[30]

The expression *data-processing but not in the same room* defined the modern computer in seven words; the company would later name this activity 'teleprocessing'. What Cringely did not tell his readers, and may not have known, was that the presentation in question was made by Sarasohn, who had joined IBM in 1957 and later became its director of engineering information. Once again, the engineer would win his point. Cringely, however, made an error in his brief account. He says, 'they started over a second time'. In fact it was only at the third attempt that the metaphorical light bulb went off in the president's mind. Sarasohn's proposal had been turned down twice on the grounds that IBM would in no circumstances wish to compete with its biggest client, AT&T. On the second occasion Sarasohn had even been ordered out of the room. It required considerable courage for him to return yet again to make the same pitch. At that time IBM was already a manufacturer of mainframe computers using software called Fortran. However, pioneers often abandon the field when the going gets difficult; had Sarasohn not made his stand, Big Blue might well have gone down the plughole of history as a company that made punch cards in an electronic age.[31]

We have credited the CCS engineers with initiating the managerial revolution that led to the Economic Miracle. Success having many fathers, others have also laid claim to the title. In an atypical moment of immodesty, Drucker recorded that the Japanese attribute their achievement to reading *The Practice of Management*: '. . . the book was an immediate success, not only in the United States but worldwide, in Latin America and, especially, in Japan. Indeed, the Japanese consider it the foundation of their economic success and industrial performance.'[32] Others have asserted that the Miracle all started with a series of lectures on Statistical Quality Control delivered in Japan in June, 1950 by the statistician, Dr. W. Edwards Deming, of whom much more in Chapter 16, which led to the establishment of the highly influential Deming Prize for Quality. Yet others attribute it to the work of a distinguished American consultant, Dr. J.J. Juran. Influential as Drucker's book undoubtedly was, it cannot be credited with a revolution that had been initiated before it was published. Regarding the contributions of Deming and Juran, Juran himself said the last word: 'Had Deming and I stayed at home, the Japanese would have achieved world quality leadership all the same'.

At 9.30 am on July 18, 1962 (his sixty-second birthday), Protzman and his wife, Aileen, were returning home along a highway in North Carolina in their 1961 Nash Rambler when a 1959 Ford driven in the opposite direction by two young men veered across the divide and collided with them.[33] Protzman heard an ambulance man say: 'He's dead – let's take the woman'. Some minutes later, Protzman startled a policeman by sitting up in his body bag; it would be Mrs Protzman who died. Her husband lay unconscious in hospital for several weeks until, one day, the surgeons called in his son to say the older man would not last until the morning. The son went to his motel room and prayed. On returning to the hospital in the morning, however, he was astonished to discover his father conscious and awake. Protzman described how he had traveled out of his body and watched surgeons extracting broken glass from his flesh. There had been the same, powerful white light that others have described in similar circumstances. He understood that he could follow the light or return to earth. He had decided to go back because he had a mission to perform. He recalled waking up briefly at that point, giving the hospital staff his name and address, and falling unconscious again.

Protzman revisited Japan in 1967, where he was honored at formal dinners in Tokyo and Osaka by top executives of the evolving electronics industry; it had not yet acquired its trendy new name. The English-language *Mainichi Daily News* for May 13, carried the following report:

JAPANESE TELECOM INDUSTRY WELCOMES POST-WAR ADVISOR:
The man responsible for improving management and control in the Japanese telecommunications industry during the Occupation days is back in Japan – and being welcomed heartily by his former students. He is C. W. Protzman and both in Tokyo and Osaka, welcome

receptions in his honor have been given by the men he helped train in 1948–50. Now they are company presidents and managing directors. Among them are Yoshikazu Inoue, Managing Director of the Osaka Management Association; President Hanzo Omi of Fujitsu; President Tsunatoshi Nabeshima of Sumitomo Electric Industries; Managing Director Kitae Ogawa of Matsushita Electric Industries Co., and a long and impressive list of company presidents, managing directors and other directors.

When Kenneth and Claire Hopper met Protzman for the first time in 1979, he was living with his son's family. A striking figure, slender and erect, who hobbled on one real and one artificial leg, he took his visitors to his study where he had filed the papers from his Tokyo years. When they asked why he had preserved them with such care, his answer was simple: 'What we did was very important. I hope that the spirit of CCS will never die.' He wondered if he had been spared to tell the story. Without him and his records, the CCS story would have vanished from human recollection.

In 1993, two events occurred which would further demonstrate how much the work of our Three Wise Men had meant to the Japanese. First, Masaharu Matsushita, adoptive son of the great Konosuke Matsushita – founder of the company which bears their name – visited Sarasohn in Phoenix, Arizona, to thank him for what he and his colleagues had done for the company and for Japan. It was a touching moment. At the second CCS Seminar in Osaka in 1950, they had been pupil and teacher (see picture on page 92). And shortly after this visit, Matsushita Electric republished the CCS Manual in an elegant Japanese-language version for distribution to all its senior executives. We were given a copy, which is before us as we write. At the front appears a photograph of Sarasohn and Masaharu Matsushita. There are prefaces in English by the former and in Japanese by the latter. Matsushita-san had kept a copy of the original version in his office since it was first issued and had frequently thumbed through it looking for inspiration. Although re-publication was a compliment to the work of the CCS engineers, that is not why it had been undertaken. The chairman's motive was that he wished to re-introduce his staff to the pure milk of the CCS gospel.

PART IV

COLLAPSE – The Cult of the (So-called) Expert

Statistics are a wonderful servant and an appaling master.

The authors

10: Ralph Bradley (HBS, 1910)
See page 172.

(below left) 11: Dr. W. Edwards Deming (1900–1993). See Chapter 16.
(below right) 12: *America's Hopeful Future* by Erika Rothenberg (1990),
Museum of Contemporary Art, Chicago. See page 229.

11

Origins and Nature of the Cult

Frederick Taylor transformed procedures on the factory shop-floor and, to a lesser extent, in the office, as explained in Chapter 7, but his ambition went beyond that – he wanted to revolutionize the whole of society. According to him, the principles of Scientific Management were applicable not just to 'our great corporations' but also: '. . . with equal force to all social activities: to the management of our homes; the management of our farms; the management of the business of our tradesmen, large and small; of our churches, our philanthropic institutions, our universities, and our governmental departments'.[1]

'There is a need', said Taylor, 'for a complete mental revolution'. Rarely has an ambition been so boundless, so completely achieved and so disastrous. During its later phase, neo-Taylorism in the shape of what we call the Cult of the (so-called) Expert would severely damage the great tradition of 'generalist', 'hands-on' management that underlay the creation of the Great Engines of Growth and Prosperity. The Cult would thus be responsible for bringing to an end our Golden Age of American Management. A good society being among other things well-ordered, it would also destroy America's Golden Age of Society.

Why did Taylor, a failed manager, become a management consultant and then set out on a third career as a social engineer? His biographers tell us that the explanation lies in the intricacies of his character and in his intellectual arrogance. Of these intricacies there can be no doubt. According to Kanigel, his 'rigidities, excesses and idiosyncrasies were enough to drive anyone a little crazy'.[2] For example, he suffered from nightmares in which he found himself trapped within 'a maze of machinery' from which he could not escape and which he could not make to work.[3] He also had 'a genius for making enemies': 'As time went on, he exhibited a fighting spirit of an intensity almost pathological. Men in his own little group were shocked by some of his outbursts. "If I know that a man is going to stab me," he said, "I'll stab him first, and if he hits me, I'll hit him twice." '[4] Taylor was mildly insane; and his madness would infect the whole of society.

His career as a manager, we are told, had been 'riddled with failure, disappointment, and rejections'.[5] If a brilliant man like him – and he was, by any standard, brilliant – could not create and run successful, profitable businesses using traditional methods, there must have been something wrong with those methods, not with him. He would therefore create a new methodology of management under the banner of 'Science' (although cloaked in the language of religion) which he would not apply himself – that would be tempting providence – but which he would teach to others.

By its very nature, the Cult which he launched constituted an attack on the four abiding Puritan characteristics of American society that we identified in Chapter 1. All of these hinged upon an acceptance of personal responsibility – whether by a community trying in some sense to create the Kingdom of God on Earth, by the craftsman who undertook to create goods of quality, by an individual who dedicated himself to working towards some common good, or by a manager directing some difficult enterprise. By diffusing responsibility among his so-called Experts, Taylorism in this degenerate phase created a state of affairs in which no-one could be properly called to account. It also constituted an attack on the fifth abiding American characteristic, identified in Chapter 4 as the respect for technology and the technologist, which America had learned from France; this development may seem odd since Taylor was himself a technologist and not just any – he was a man who helped to change the way metals were made. We shall explain how that happened in Chapter 13.

Taylor's work and ideas were first brought to the attention of the general public in 1910 through the activities of a future justice of the Supreme Court, Louis Brandeis, who was representing the interests of Eastern railroad users before the Interstate Commerce Commission in Washington. The railroads had asked permission to raise their rates in order, so they said, to be able to maintain the standard of service and improve the infrastructure. According to one of their representatives, their claim was based on 'practice, contact and experience'. Brandeis had come across Taylor's book, *On Shop Management*[6] (meaning on the management of the factory shop-floor), which argued that it was possible to improve the productivity of the workforce by up to nine times by redesigning the tasks that they performed. At the time of its publication in 1903, the book had not been widely noticed. Brandeis quoted it in support of his pleadings; it demonstrated, said he, that there was no need for the railroads to raise rates. The next day's edition of the *New York Times* carried the headline:

ROADS COULD SAVE
$1,000,000 A DAY.
Brandeis Says Scientific Management
Would Do It – Calls Rate Increases Unnecessary.[7]

This marked the first appearance in the public prints of the expression 'Scientific Management', which Brandeis had coined and Taylor would adopt – Brandeis' justification being that Taylor had frequently used the word 'scientific' to describe his methodology.

The Railroad Commission was unimpressed and devoted only two paragraphs of its report to this part of the argument. Although Brandeis won his case, it would be for other reasons. However, the publicity for Taylor and Taylorism was immense; all over the country, businessmen called for copies of *On Shop Management*. To cash in, Taylor reissued this book and also published his *magnum opus, The Principles of Scientific Management* in 1911. This slim volume was badly written, dishonestly argued and poorly printed but what did that matter? – the title was magnificent and the timing brilliant. Something called 'Science' had contributed so much to the material well-being of mankind in the previous century; was it not time to apply its methods to the organization of society itself? President Theodore Roosevelt publicly endorsed it. Popular magazines took up the theme, which was regarded as a panacea for all social ills. Attempts would be made to apply it to the military, the law, medicine and even the home. *The Principles* launched Taylor on his third career (largely posthumous, since he died four years later) as a social engineer.

The kind of Taylorism which we described in Chapter 7 can be described as 'procedural' since it dealt with routines undertaken on the shop-floor and in the office. Neo-Taylorism focused on the structure of management; its origins also go right back to the 1880s, when the line-and-staff revolution (see page 71) was spreading slowly through the economy. Most manufacturing companies were 'all line, no staff', as they would be in Japan until the US Occupation of the late 1940s. An entire plant could be managed by a general foreman, who was directly responsible to the general manager of the company not only for the physical production of goods but also, for example, for accounting and personnel matters; the general foreman's clerk carried out such book-keeping as was necessary. Broadly speaking, what would later become known as the 'staff' functions was then the responsibility of the 'line' managers, who thus bore a harsh double burden.

In typical companies of the period, the senior executives were expected to be 'generalists', which we define as meaning, first, that they were endowed with the kind of good interpersonal skills required for success in all organizations, whether in business or not; and, secondly, that they possessed what a future chief executive of General Electric would characterize as 'domain knowledge' – see page 266 – information that could be gained only by spending a lifetime in an organization or industry, or by working closely with people who have done so. Taylor correctly perceived, however, that technology was achieving a complexity that made it difficult for 'generalists' of this kind to run factories and businesses efficiently on their own. For him, the solution lay in breaking down managerial responsibilities into separate functions; he was seeking to apply to management the same specialization of function that Adam Smith had described in principle as applying to labor and which Taylor had himself applied in practice to humble factory operatives.

In a famous passage in *On Shop Management*, Taylor presented his so-called 'Fourth Element': the general foreman would be replaced by eight 'functional foremen or bosses', namely: the route clerks; the instruction card clerks; the cost and time clerks; the gang bosses; the speed boss; the repair boss; the inspector; and the shop disciplinarian.[8] Observe, by the way, that some of these names are in the plural – so he was really talking about many more than eight men replacing one. Taylor also sought to abolish the general manager (roughly today's chief executive); he was to be replaced by 'a planning department' consisting of the first four *kinds* of functional foremen listed above, acting collectively, the actual number of persons again not being specified. So an unspecified number of people in excess of eight were being asked to report to an unspecified number in excess of four! And to whom did the planning department report? To itself, as far as one can judge – the text is ambiguous. While highlighting a real problem, Taylor was producing an absurd solution. The more one divides up the functions of the operatives on the factory floor or in the office, the greater is the need for 'generalist' managers to pull the threads back together again – a fact that Taylor seemed not to appreciate. As that paragon of managerial common sense, Florence Nightingale, would have said in her blunt way, (see page 164) *someone has to be in charge.* The business historian, Alfred Chandler, has pointed out that in a fully neo-Taylorized company it was no longer possible to 'pinpoint authority'.[9] Unsurprisingly, we are told that a number of early attempts to run businesses on these lines resulted in commercial failure.

One of those who stood out against Taylor's functional foremen was another management consultant, Harrington Emerson (1853–1931). The son of a Presbyterian minister, he 'believed in the Protestant virtues of thrift and the economical use of resources'.[10] Having started his career by working for the Burlington and Santa Fe railroads, he would transfer his attention to manufacturing. Emerson saw 'waste and inefficiency' as the evils that beset the land. An admirer of the Prussian military, he published his own highly articulated version of the doctrine of line-and-staff.

We have already seen how the Gilbreths and others transformed early 'procedural' Taylorism on the factory floor and in the office by developing new practices that were both more acceptable to the work force and beneficial to the company and to society. 'Structural' Taylorism (as we may call it) would undergo a comparable process of adaptation; around the turn of the nineteenth century, the traditional managers would re-assert themselves, kenneling Taylor's functional foremen or functional bosses into new 'staff' departments within the evolving 'line-and-staff' system. This solution had an almost mathematical elegance: senior managers retained their traditional 'line' responsibilities, while being able to rely on the support of new and specialized accounting, personnel and technical departments. The future Great Engine companies of the mid-twentieth century and their smaller siblings were taking shape. The history of American business in the first half of that century is an account of the successful application of the doctrine of 'line-and-staff', as adapted in this way to include Taylor's specialists.

In the second half of the century, however, some of the 'staffers' would escape from their kennels and wreak havoc on the very concept and nature of 'line-and-staff'. The 'line' would not be abolished; Taylor had tried that and, patently, it did not work. The result was, rather, a mish-mash. In some cases, former 'staffers' would take over the control of the 'line', while possessing neither the skills of people management nor the profound knowledge of the business as a whole that had characterized their predecessors. In others, managerial control was divided awkwardly between 'line' and the 'staff' departments. In yet others, some 'staff' functions were 'out-sourced' to external experts. The outcome in all these cases was the same: *no-one was truly in charge*. The management guru, Rosabeth Moss Kanter, has described the new arrangement as one in which no person has 'sufficient span of control to manage at the required level of complexity'.[11] One cannot possibly disagree with this analysis; Kanter, however, then confuses the descriptive with the prescriptive, a common failing in business school professors, accepting the absence of a 'sufficient span of control' as an inevitable fact of life and arguing that, to make up for the deficiency, everyone should learn to co-operate as never before.

As a piece of advice, this is about as useful as saying that everyone ought to be nice. If everyone was really, *really* nice, we could dispense not only with managers but also with police forces and armies. Kanter's brief and controversial editorship of the *Harvard Business Review* (1989–1992) raises serious questions about her right to lecture others on her subject of choice. According to former editors of the *Review*, difficulties arose there because of her 'hit-and-run management style'; it seems that, although relieved of teaching duties so that she could edit the magazine, she was often absent on speaking or consulting engagements. In defense of his colleague, William Sahlman, an associate dean, and another prominent consultant, tells us that members of the business school faculty are good 'at a variety of different things, not many of which have to do with the day-to-day management of people'. He adds that he himself would never succeed as a manager.[12]

Why an elegant solution – 'line-and-staff' – was partially discarded in favor of a mishmash is not entirely clear but the explanation must surely lie in the general brainwashing of society with Taylor's ideas that had occurred in the years just before World War I. Ideas have legs and they walk. Let us pause for a moment to consider how they do so and where they end up. Typically they start off as explicit beliefs or observations originating from one person or in one group; if they are widely and favorably enough received, they may sink unobtrusively into the human unconscious where they acquire even more potency than before because, being now implicit, they stand beyond examination and criticism. The British prime minister, Stanley Baldwin, once described power without responsibility as the prerogative of the harlot in every age. (He was referring to the owners of newspapers.) Implicit ideas are the ultimate harlots of history – even more so than Shelley's 'unacknowledged' legislator, the poet. They determine the pattern of human behavior, while their carriers may remain in ignorance of their very existence. To borrow the language of electronic software, they are like the 'cookies' implanted in the hard drive of a computer by third parties, with the object of determining how it will interact with a website. It is only by becoming aware of the metaphorical 'cookies' implanted in our brains by our ancestors *and turning them off* or, if we prefer, *not turning them off*, that we become fully and truly human.

The economist John Maynard Keynes has described, in an over-quoted but succinct passage, the anonymous role that such ideas play:

> The ideas of economists and political philosophers, both when they are right and when they are wrong, are more powerful than is commonly understood. Indeed the world is ruled by little else. Practical men who believe themselves to be quite exempt from any intellectual influence are usually the slaves of some defunct economist.[13]

One may reasonably ask, however, why Keynes limited his observation to economists and political philosophers – there are many other serious candidates for the role, one undoubtedly being the originator of Scientific Management, who determines much of what we think and do today. To the extent that this is so, we are all slaves to a defunct management consultant. The author, Alfie Kohn, draws attention to the wider dangers that we face in this way:

> There is a time to admire the *grace and persuasive power of an influential idea*, and there is a time to fear its hold over us. The time to worry is when the idea is so widely shared that we no longer even notice it, when it is so deeply rooted that it feels to us like plain common sense. At the point when objections are not answered any more because they are not longer even raised, we are not in control; we do not have the idea; it has us.[14]

What were the attributes of organizations affected by neo-Taylorism? They were five in number. First and most important, they could be administered only by men who had been 'scientifically' taught *how to measure*. The Cult of the Expert, which we refer to as the Cult of the (so-called) Expert, was born; this ironic, capitalized phrase originating in the early part of the last century, suggested a widespread appreciation, even then, that its practitioners had feet of clay. It led to an extreme, and in some cases exclusive, reliance on the use of quantitative 'benchmarks' as a method of control – information not capable of being expressed in numbers being at a heavy discount. Some practitioners went so far as to assert, absurdly, 'if it can't be measured, it does not exist'. Others, more modestly, said that 'If can't be measured, it can't be managed.' The best comment on this kind of approach was contained in a punning notice which hung in Albert Einstein's office at Princeton: 'Not everything that counts can be counted, and not everything that can be counted counts'. Our (so-called) Experts were, mostly, pseudo-scientists.

Neo-Taylorism weakened the traditional line-of-command, which relied primarily on trusting human relationships for the transmission of information, most of which was of a qualitative nature. The (so-called) Expert, in the form of the 'professional' manager, would live in a world of semi-fantasy, making life-and-death decisions about organizations that he saw only through a statistical glass darkly. Since his success or failure, and his rewards, would be judged primarily against 'benchmarks', there was also a permanent incentive either to falsify data, or to manipulate events underlying them, so as to produce apparently favorable outcomes. Those who successfully played this game could make vast fortunes; those who were perceived to have 'missed their targets' could become of the victims of a procedure summed up in three rhyming words: name, blame and shame. This obsession with dubious statistics disguised an absence of 'domain knowledge'.

Secondly, the only sure way of telling an Expert apart from a non-Expert was by calling for his credentials; this led to 'credentialism', defined by the economist, Samuel Brittan, as 'the multiplication of paper certificates and qualifications as a condition for more and more kinds of professional and other employment'.[15] Thirdly, the *modus operandi* became 'top-down'; other than raw information, what has a non-Expert to communicate to an Expert that can be of any significance? In any case, is not an Expert someone who already knows the answers? Fourthly, since responsibility under the new regime was inevitably diffused among a number of Experts (accountants, salesmen, personnel officers, consultants of all kinds), it became difficult to 'pinpoint responsibility' – to borrow Chandler's comment on early neo-Taylorized companies – which meant that it was no longer possible to call individuals properly to account for their actions. Everyone would be willing to share in the credit for a success, no-one wanted to accept blame for a failure.

Fifthly, it was widely believed that major problems could be solved by formally declaring certain Experts to be 'responsible' for them, at least on paper; divorced from the line-of-command – to the extent that it survived – the newly appointed 'czars', 'overlords' or 'co-ordinators' became the late twentieth century's answer to the magic wand. This general approach was often accompanied by the announcement of major 'Initiatives', often capitalized for effect, which were attempts to procure the consequences of a policy while avoiding the need to define exactly what it was; to determine how it was to be put into effect; and to allocate the resources necessary for this purpose. On page 25, we ascribed the success of America as a society to the practice of what we called 'integrated decision-making'; the appointment of 'czars' to undertake 'Initiatives' was the supreme example of its opposite.

The federal government would be even more deeply afflicted with this kind of approach than the corporate sector. By announcing an 'Initiative', and appointing a (so-called) Expert, to deal with a vexatious problem, a president could at least pretend that he was 'doing something about it'. George W. Bush's creation of a 'toothless and wasteful'[16] Directorate of Homeland Security in 2001 was a case in point. His appointment of a director of national intelligence to co-ordinate all fifteen federal intelligence agencies was another. Unsurprisingly, Porter Goss, the then head of the Central Intelligence Agency, told the world that there was 'a lot of ambiguity' in the new arrangements and that he did not know what his relationship was supposed to be with the new director. For good measure, Goss added that the five hats that he himself wore were 'too much for this mortal' and that he was amazed at his own workload, which suggests that he was himself something of a 'czar'.[17] NASA's promulgation of its Moon, Mars and Beyond Initiative, also in 2005, of which the object is to put man on the red planet, was a third example – and one likely to cost the United States dear in money and even lives.[18] As the American Physical Society has told us, 'The scope of the Moon-Mars initiative has not been well-defined, its long-term cost has not been adequately addressed, and no budgetary mechanisms have been established to avoid causing major, irreparable damage to the agency's scientific program'.[19]

In Chapter 9, we drew attention to the paradox that the culminating triumph of America's market economy – the creation of the Great Engine companies – had been achieved by abolishing the price mechanism, or at least attenuating its impact, within the confines of those companies. The nation's greatest business historian, Alfred Chandler, identified this development as the substitution of 'administrative co-ordination' for 'market co-ordination', a 'visible hand' replacing Smith's 'invisible' one. The decline of the Great Engine companies after 1970 can be attributed to a reversal of this evolution as attempts were made to convert corporations back into 'internal markets' consisting allegedly of independent agents competing against one another, as in a *souk*. At the mid-century, remuneration had been determined primarily by rank, managers being assumed to be fully capable of performing the task assigned to them. For them, reward took the form of promotion, if, as and when a suitable opening occurred; failure resulted in demotion or dismissal. Under the new regime, an effort would be made to evaluate and reward executives in terms of the *personal* contribution they had made to the success of their organization, disregarding the fact that each functioned as part of a system within a system. In any well-run organization, an individual's achievements were likely to be due as much to the wisdom with which he was directed from above, and to the support of his equals and subordinates, as to his own efforts. If you attempt the impossible, you will achieve a mess; hence the general decline in corporate and other productivity to be discussed in the next chapter.

Neo-Taylorism in this form has led to the apotheosis of the accountant. In the 1960s, he stuck his snout out of the kennel where he had been tethered for half a century by the doctrine of line-and-staff, liked the smell and, as often as not, was able to leap with a loud bark onto his former master's chair. *He* was now, in many cases, the head of the 'line', but its nature was affected. The new boss saw the company not as a traditional, 'generalist' manager would have done (i.e. from all relevant angles, including finance and accounting, and with the benefit of a profound knowledge of the business) but strictly or largely through the prism of profit and loss; he was a 'bottom-line' (and therefore, by definition, a 'top-down') man. In accountants' jargon, the 'bottom line' is the profit, a figure which appears conventionally on the last line of an income statement. A 'bottom-line' man is someone who looks at some event or happening only or primarily from the point of view of the financial return that it generates, or appears to generate, in the short term.

There was a perverse logic to this development. By definition, a Scientific Manager sought to rule by measuring. What was the one quantitative approach that enabled you to peer into every nook and cranny of an organization, to study its past and even to project the future – a technique that enabled you to relate current to capital expenditure and both to revenues? The answer was: the accounts. Except, of course, that the prism distorted, taking little or no account of the all-important *qualitative* factors that actually determined success or failure of any venture and which could not be measured precisely or at all. How did you put a value on the accumulated knowledge and experience of the employees of a well-run, long-established company? How did you put a figure on morale, honesty or dedication?

Intra-company accounting also made its appearance. Divisions of companies would be classified as autonomous profit or cost centers. The former were expected to earn a financial return as if they were independent entities, a dangerous fiction since a decision that generated a book-keeping 'profit' in one division might well produce a larger 'loss' in others – and, even more serious, a catastrophe in the organization as a whole. The latter were there to be 'squeezed', whatever the effect on the health of the company as a whole. Profit and cost centers promoted intra-company competition, which – since knowledge is power – encouraged the hoarding of information within departments and was therefore retrograde from the point of view of the profitability of the organization as a whole. Organizations flourish only when information flows freely in all directions, upwards, downwards and sdieways, but, above all, upwards.

Accountants were not the only 'staffers' to effect an escape from their kennel; salesmen also stumbled out, conferring on themselves the more dignified title of 'marketing men'. Like their financial cousins, the marketers were able to seize partial or complete control of the 'line-of-command' in some companies; when they did, they too saw the world through a distorting prism of their own – the brand. A pseudo-science grew up known as 'marketing metrics', or, less kindly, as 'brandolatry', which treated the brand as an asset with a value independent of the goods that bore its name. Recently, some of the more extreme exponents of this outlook have sought to brand even events such as wars and battles. According to the New York brand consultants, T.G. Riese & Associates, 'every war needs a compelling brand proposition, whether or not it is publicly acknowledged'.[20] In Britain, the Labour government has discussed the 'branding' of ethnic minorities, an unfortunate metaphor.

One of America's greatest salesman-managers, the inventor of 'shoppertainment',[21] Stanley Marcus, chairman of the department store company, Nieman Marcus, supplied a corrective view in 1995: 'It is not the name than makes or breaks a new business. It is the quality and value of the product and the integrity of its service, plus its financial strength to hang on during the first few years of growth.'[22] Stanley Marcus had two British equivalents. In 1924, Jack Cohen founded what became, and is still, one of the world's most successful retailers, Tesco plc; his motto – and the title of his autobiography – was 'Pile it High and Sell it Cheap'[23] – not the sort of thing a *bien pensant* brand manager would say or think. Simon Marks, a director of the retail chain, Marks and Spencer, used even pithier language: 'good goods will sell ass upwards'[24] – that is, irrespective of what you call them. Marks and Spencer had a brand name (St Michael – a curious choice for a company of Jewish origin, and perhaps chosen for that reason) but Simon Marks was well aware that the value of that brand arose from the quality and price of the products, not the other way round. Since the 1970s, brand managers in Britain and America have turned commercial reality 'ass upwards'. Intel Corporation, the world's largest computer-chip maker, has suffered in the marketplace because it 'famously relied on branding to woo customers', while its competitor, AMD, offered its product on the basis of simple energy efficiency.[25]

Recently, major brands have been considered to be of global significance; the ultimate in 'globaloney', as it is called, is represented by two publications. Theodore Levitt's 'The globalization of markets', a seminal paper published by *Harvard Business Review* in May 1993, argued that, as new media and technology shrank the world, people's tastes would converge, creating a single global market that would be dominated by the world's most successful brands.[26] Naomi Klein's anti-globalization manifesto *No Logo: Taking Aim at the Brand Bullies,* published in 1999, accepted the Levitt thesis but lamented it. Levitt is a professor at Harvard Business School; contrary to what he foresaw and Klein regretted, global brands are now failing all over the world. Wal-Mart is struggling to establish itself in Germany and Japan;[27] France's Carrefour failed in Japan. Coca-Cola's best-selling soft drink in Japan today is called Georgia coffee – 'a local brand that outsells all Coca-Cola's carbonate drinks put together'. Starbucks' overseas outlets account for only 9 per cent of sales and lose money.[28] In Japan today powerful new anti-brands are emerging such as Muji, short for Muji-rushi Ryohin or 'no-brand quality goods', and Uniqlo, the cut-price clothes chain.[29] (Defenders of brands would argue that Muji and Uniqlo have become brands in their own right.)

The unspoken assumption underlying the roles of both types of ex-'staffer' was identical – if you understood and used your prism properly, a thorough knowledge of the actual business for which you were responsible was of secondary, and perhaps even of no, importance. On these grounds, (so-called) Experts in this field were deemed to be inter-changeable not only between companies but also between industries. The result was frequently disappointment. By way of example, in the 1990s Ronald L. Zarrella, who had marketed spectacles at Bausch and Lomb, and James C. Schroer, who had marketed tobacco at RJ Reynolds, would be appointed to develop new automobile products at General Motors and Ford respectively. Both men set out to 'build brands' in their new positions.[30] When Zarrella was replaced in 2001, *BusinessWeek* welcomed the event as 'another blow against brand management', telling us that during his stay he championed a philosophy which had 'largely failed'.[31] Schroer's appointment at Ford was equally short and inglorious, as was his subsequent period at Chrysler.[32] Coca-Cola, one of the best-managed of all the Great Engine companies at the mid-twentieth century, fell into the trap in its subsequent years of decline; in June 2003, it appointed Daniel Palumbo, formerly in charge of a 'core photographic unit' at Eastman Kodak, as its chief marketing officer.[33] In their own 'staff' kennels, the brand managers had performed a useful role but as 'line' executives they were likely to fail, unless they had also absorbed a 'generalist' training of the old-fashioned kind – whereupon they were no longer to be regarded, primarily, as brand managers.

The personnel managers also attempted to flee from their 'staff' kennels. If they have been less successful than accountants and salesmen in capturing, or interfering with, the commanding heights of 'line' management, it is not for lack of trying. To advance their case, they too changed their name – to Human Resource Managers, usually capitalized to convey a sense of their importance. Another pseudo-science called psychometrics emerged to enable them to determine which candidates were suitable for appointment or promotion as managers and which were not. Note the suffix '-metrics' which directs our attention once again to the neo-Taylorite world of the bogusly quantitative. Note also the large number of websites now on offer teaching candidates how to cheat – an indicator of an approach lacking intellectual rigor.

Under the new dispensation, those candidates who did well in psychometric tests could expect to be 'fast-tracked' to positions over the heads of their contemporaries. It is axiomatic that there were no 'fast tracks' in Great Engine companies in the mid-twentieth century. Drucker explained why:

> I have yet to see any method which can predict a man's development more than a short time ahead. And even if we could predict human growth, we should have no right to play providence. However 'scientific' the method, it would still at best work with 60% or 70% of accuracy; and no man has a right to dispose of other people's lives and careers on probability.[34]

Nor are there any 'fast tracks' in the well-run Japanese companies that would emerge after World War II; in both cases, satisfactory performance in a specific job was the sole criterion for advancement. As a general rule, the initial appointment of young men and women from college will always be a gamble on the part of any employer, a careful interview offered only to those with reasonable degrees from a good university being as good a way as any of separating wheat from chaff. Thereafter, the only proper grounds for promotion can be performance – and the only person capable of making a proper assessment of the performance of a 'line' manager is a boss, who has observed him or her in action over a period of at least a year. In a well-run organization, important decisions about appointments and promotion are strictly a 'line', not a 'staff', responsibility (except, of course, in the 'staff' departments which will possess their own miniature 'lines').

'Out-sourcing' also became prevalent under the impact of the Cult, the justification being that the organization to which the responsibility for a task had been transferred was more 'Expert' than the 'outsourcing' party and could therefore discharge it better or cheaper or both. This approach led, as often as not, to failure. Michael Dell, one of the computer industry's great innovators, has explained why; in 1998, he told the *Harvard Business Review* that 'outsourcing is usually a way of getting rid of a problem a company cannot solve itself'; by 'getting rid of it', of course, he meant not so much providing a solution as transfer-ring responsibility to a third party and hoping against hope:

> the classic case is the company with 2,000 people in the IT depart-ment. Nobody knows what they do, and nobody knows what to do with them. The solution: outsource IT to a service provider, and hopefully they'll fix it. But if you look at what happens five years later, it's not necessarily a pretty picture.[35]

In 2003, it was reported that two-thirds of 'out-sourcing' companies were dissatisfied with the performance of the organization to which the activity in question had been transferred and that over one-third would not renew the appointment when the contracts ended. One-sixth of the companies surveyed went so far as to say that they intended to bring the activity back into the fold. At Electronic Data Services, which was one of the principal recipients of 'out-sourcing' mandates, this practice was cynically referred to 'your mess for less' – in other words, the recipient did the work almost as badly but more cheaply.[36] This company would lose a contract with the British Inland Revenue worth $5.4 billion on grounds of incompetence; as a consequence, its own corporate debt would be reclassified as 'junk' in 2004 by the credit-rating agency, Moody's. Meantime, the company to which the Revenue contract was transferred, Cap Gemini, made such heavy losses that its debt would be reclassified downwards to only one notch above 'junk'.[37]

In September 2004, the bank, JP Morgan Chase & Co., announced that it was terminating a seven-year, $5 billion technology 'out-sourcing' deal with IBM on the grounds that having the work done by its own employees 'boosts reliability and efficiency'.[38] These are not happy times for either 'out-sourcers' or 'out-sourcees'. What kinds of activities could or should a company 'out-source'? The answer is a matter of simple com-mon sense: only those which do not have the capacity to inflict serious damage on its business if they go wrong. Thus it is safe (but not necessar-ily wise) for a manufacturing company to entrust the operation of its canteen to a restaurant chain or of its car pool to a taxi firm, but unwise to ask someone else to design or maintain its manufacturing plant. In 2005 and 2006, a former Great Engine company, Boeing, would sell 350 of its Dreamliner aircraft straight off the drawing board, with the inten-tion of 'out-sourcing' the manufacture of 80 per cent of its structure and components to forty-three suppliers on three continents. We await the outcome with unease. Until then, the company had always made the fuselage and wings for its planes; that is what Boeing was all about.[39]

In the heavily Taylorized Britain of the 1980s, 'out-sourcing' cost lives when the National Health Service decided to farm out the cleaning of hospitals. This reduced its expenditure on cleaning, as intended, but it also reduced cleanliness. The country's National Audit Office tells us that 9 per cent of patients pick up an infection in hospital today, resulting in at least 5,000 deaths per year, or more than are killed in road accidents.[40] While common dirt is not the sole cause of this high mortality, it is acknowledged to be a major contributor. As a consequence, the government has recently made the farming-out of cleaning voluntary. There is a certain unconscious humor in the new instructions issued to hospitals: in reviewing existing 'out-sourcing' contracts, they were told that they could employ *an in-house person whose job is to keep the place clean*[41] – or, as we used to say, a cleaner. Meanwhile, every hospital in England is to appoint a 'czar' whose job will be 'to crack down on super-bugs'!

'Out-sourcing' in one form or another had been the normal way of doing business before the modern American corporation came into being. It was Lee at his federal armory who systematized the 'in-sourcing' of activities so as to bring them under the direct control of 'line' or 'staff' managers – the only way in which standards could be maintained, costs properly controlled, flexibility achieved and innovation encouraged. How can you properly develop new products or techniques in an activity that is being undertaken by another, quite separate, entity? In behaving as they did, the new-style managers of the late twentieth century were reversing one of Lee's achievements.

12

Impact of the Cult on the Great Engine Companies

The impact of the Cult of the (so-called) Expert on our Great Engines of Growth and Prosperity was twofold. First, the collegiate style of leadership described so eloquently and accurately by Drucker and Given was replaced by the rule of the 'imperial' (which really means 'imperious') chief executive officer. Nature as ever hating a vacuum, he or she stepped into the void created at the heart of organizations by the dissolution of the 'college' of senior executives and fractionalization of the line-of-command described in the last chapter. Collegiality vanished. Well-known examples of the new breed were: Maurice ('Hammerin' Hank') Greenberg of the insurance company, AIG; the 'brusque' and 'caustic' Lee Raymond at Exxon Mobil; the 'charismatic' Jack Welch at General Electric; the 'financial engineer', Roberto Goizueta at Coca-Cola; the 'Prince of Darkness', Ed Artzt, at Procter & Gamble;[1] the 'overpaid, abrasive and aloof' Hank McKinnell at Pfizer;[2] the 'former strategic consultant', Louis V. Gerstner at IBM; and the 'difficult and controversial' Carly Fiorina at Hewlett-Packard – not to speak of the pioneers of the breed, Frederick G. Donner at General Motors and Ralph J. Cordiner at General Electric. The ideal Golden Age chief executive had been a thoughtful listener and *primus inter pares* who shared responsibility with his entire top team and was paid only modestly more than they; most conformed recognizably to pattern. The new men or women were charged with the entire responsibility for the success of the operation and their remuneration was correspondingly stratospheric.

Secondly, the entire organization would be biased less to the provision of goods or services of quality than to the generation of satisfactory financial statistics; anyone who doubts this proposition is urged to read Maryann Keller's *Rude Awakening: The Rise, Fall and Struggle for Recovery of GM* (1989). Kellerdoes not even mention the term Scientific Management. However, her book amounts to a clinical analysis of the impact of the Cult of the (so-called) Expert on America's largest industrial organization. She quotes a retired General Motors executive as saying that 'the tyranny of the number crunchers began to

take root in the 1960s'. Before that, things had been differently and better organized: 'At one time . . . the general managers of car divisions
were *well-rounded* executives who had some responsibility for design,
styling, engineering, manufacturing, and marketing the cars they
sold'.[3] Starting with the appointment of Donner as chairman and chief
executive in 1958, the line-of-command would be usurped by the
'finance guys' – among the first of the (so-called) Experts or 'professional' managers to arrive on the American corporate scene. From that
time on, General Motors was increasingly ruled by statistical yardsticks. At the very top, 'finance guys' would alternate with 'car guys',
another version of the non-'generalist', 'professional' manager.

Keller quotes two examples to show 'how ineffective managing by
numbers' would become. One concerned a 'quality index' which the
company introduced around 1960 to enable it to compare the performance of different plants. The original system was simple: a score of 100
meant that a car had no defects per 100 cars, 95 meant it had five – and
so on, the 'pass mark' being set at 60. (Keller's text seems to suggest
that the reference was to defects *per car* but that would not make sense;
even General Motors at its worst would not have 'passed' a car as satisfactory with forty defects.) It was soon discovered, however, that some
plants were struggling to make a score of 60. The maximum score
(meaning no defects) was, therefore, arbitrarily re-named '145' in 1968,
allowing the pass mark to become '100'; 100 looked better than 60 and
was within the reach of most plants. The spin doctors had begun their
work. This revised system remained in force for twenty years, accompanied by much haggling over spots of paint and specks of dust. She
concludes: 'In all those years, the focus never wavered. The goal
remained to improve the numbers, not to improve the cars. By setting
arbitrary standards that looked good on the books, the value of the
standards became meaningless.'[4]

The other example is that in 1986 the word came down from the
holy of holies, the fourteenth floor of the head office building in
Detroit, to the effect that staff costs had to be cut. Employees were dutifully laid off, but in some cases they were at once re-hired as
contractors at higher rates. This did not seem to matter, Keller comments, since they were re-hired under different budgets. The statistical
'target' had been met, irrespective of the consequences for the organization as a whole. In the first case, the data was being 'massaged'; in the
second, the events underlying the data were being manipulated to produce the desired effect. In these ways, General Motors set a standard of
behavior on its factory floor that would be replicated or copied
throughout the land and not only on the factory floor. Fifteen years
later, the senior accounting officers of the communications company,

WorldCom, would be instructed by their bosses to 're-engineer the company's earnings, working backwards from the targets that had been supplied to Wall Street and then falsifying the underlying figures accordingly', resulting in the biggest fraud ever recorded at that time.[5] Similar events would happen elsewhere. Companies like WorldCom and Enron were not simply 'a few bad apples in a barrel', if we are to believe the respected consultancy, Stern Stewart, which informed us in 2002 that 'The real accounting scandal is not that a handful of companies like Enron and WorldCom broke accounting rules to inflate their earnings but that almost every company is bending the rules to smooth earnings and meet investor expectations'[6] – a matter to which we return later in more detail.

At General Motors, the Cult of the (so-called) Expert evolved into a way of insulating senior management from bad news and advancing the interests of the purveyors of data. According to Keller, 'If the finance guys can present the right numbers, everyone breathes a sigh of relief and the finance people look like heroes'.[7] When she re-issued her book in 1990, she asked herself whether the company was putting its house in order and concluded that the answer was 'no'. The new chairman, Roger Smith (a 'finance guy'), had proved himself to be 'a master of the happy spin'. During his reign, the company's share of the US automobile market fell from 47 per cent in 1979 to 35 per cent in 1989.[8] In 1992 it almost went bankrupt and by 2004 its market share stood at 'barely 25 per cent'. The reason was simple: a failure to produce good enough cars at low enough prices. The quality of General Motors cars has recently been improving but a generation too late. One (reliable) statistic says it all: today it takes the American company thirty-four man-hours to build a car, compared with twenty-eight for Toyota. That the fault lies with management is amply demonstrated by the fact that many cheap but excellent cars are manufactured in foreign-owned but US-based 'transplants' – using US labor.[9]

The case of the NUMMI (or New United Motor Manufacturing, Inc.) plant in Freemont, California is poignant.[10] Aware of the gap between the quality of Japanese and American cars and to provide a model for the future, General Motors had opened it in 1984 as a fifty-fifty joint venture with Toyota Motor. Today, this fully integrated factory is one of the best managed in the United States, with a capacity of 235,000 cars and 150,000 trucks per annum, producing both General Motors Chevvies and Toyota Coronas. However, as Keller has told us, General Motors never learned the true lesson from this joint venture, namely:

> . . . that management must change along with everyone else. It wasn't enough to simply put the workers in teams and expect automatic

results. In some ways the company only paid lip service to the experience, perhaps being embarrassed to learn its lessons at the knee of the Japanese competition. Full implementation of Japanese methodology necessitated a behavior change by everyone in the company, not just the people on the factory floor.[11]

An important milestone for the whole industry was passed in March 2006 when the non-profit advocacy group, Consumer Union, published its annual ranking of motor vehicles in the US market according to the number of faults recorded per 100 cars. For the first time ever, a Japanese car performed best in every one of its ten categories – two of them being Hondas and two Toyotas. On average, American brands scored eighteen faults for every 100 cars, against twelve for Japanese. On a comparable list published by the Union ranking used cars, General Motors vehicles scored high among the 'lemons';[12] Pierre du Pont and Alfred Sloan would have been horrified.

Kaizen or 'continuous improvement' lies at the heart of the Toyota Production System. A recent innovation is called 'kitting'. On a modern assembly line, cars are not identical since they have to be 'customized' to meet customers' wishes, which means that different cars require different components. The previous practice had been to stack large numbers of components at critical points along the line; under 'kitting', the relevant parts are placed in each car at the start of the line. Thus the need for shelf space is reduced, the possibility of error minimized and the cost of each car reduced. Capitalism is made to work.[13]

Today Toyota is a truly transnational company. By manufacturing cars in many different places – for example, in Britain and China as well as in the United States – it has made itself largely independent of economic conditions in any one of them. When the pound sterling rises in the exchanges, for example, thus inhibiting the export of the company's British-manufactured vehicles, Toyota can benefit by importing cheap spare parts into Britain from subsidiaries located in countries with weaker currencies; when the pound falls, this procedure can be reversed. Today Toyota's small amount of debt is rated 'AAA' by the principal rating agencies, next only to that of the US government, while the formerly 'AAA' debts of General Motors and Ford have been reclassified as at or near 'junk'.[14] Chrysler's debt has not been downgraded to this extent and it is the only one of the former 'Big Three' US automobile companies to have increased its sales in early 2005; it is by no means irrelevant that, in 1998, it had become part of the German company, Daimler-Benz.[15] Toyota is expected to take over from General Motors in 2007 as the largest manufacturer of automobiles in the world.

The appointment of Donner at General Motors in 1958 was paralleled in the same year by the appointment as chairman of General Electric of Ralph J. Cordiner – that company's equivalent of a 'finance guy'. Previously, Cordiner had scoured the business schools for ideas, founding his own 'in-house' school at Crotonville, New York;[16] the Cult of the (so-called) Expert ruled in the company from that time on, although the outcome would differ markedly from that at General Motors. A book that he had published in 1956, called – significantly – *New Frontiers in Professional Management*, was an early manifesto for the Business School Counter-Culture. The disastrous concept of the wonderfully mobile 'professional' manager – the person trained in a classroom who by definition could manage any kind of business (or indeed non-business) without knowing anything or much about it – had arrived in a second major American corporate boardroom.

General Electric would soon acquire a French computer company in a bid to rival IBM in the emerging field of electronics, placing it in the care of a man who spoke no French and knew nothing about computers; the resultant debacle would cost it $200 million – now the sort of figure that corporations write off almost without noticing but then a very substantial amount. Much more serious, the company's great research center at Schenectady would be allowed to wither away, Crotonville taking over from the 'House of Magic' (see page 87) for half a century as the spiritual center of the company. By the year 2000, only seven engineers remained among the company's 175 most senior officers.[17] In that same year, when drawing up its list of the top 500 US companies, *Fortune* discovered that less than half of the company's profits came from manufacturing and reclassified it under 'financial services' over loud but unavailing protests from its then 'celebrity CEO', Jack Welch. This change of status did not prevent the magazine, in that very same year, from declaring it to be the single, most admired American company.[18] It would also declare Welch to be the 'Manager of the Century' because of the colossal influence that he had exercised on business throughout the world.[19]

One can endlessly debate why General Electric was supremely successful in the stock market, when most conglomerates failed. Today it is one of the largest US company in terms of market capitalization; many others, for example Boeing and Home Depot fell flat on their faces when they tried to follow its example. The answer seems to be twofold. First, the pre-Cordiner culture survived in the company's manufacturing divisions; otherwise, they could not have built consistently good aero-engines and locomotives. Secondly, the company traded off the superb ('AAA') creditworthiness of those divisions to fund profitable exercises in the capital markets that would otherwise have been cata-strophic.[20] This enabled it to engage in the kind of financial wizardry that appeals to parts of Wall Street (see Chapter 19).[21] In his book, *At Any Cost: Jack Welch, General Electric and the Pursuit of Profit*, Thomas O'Boyle tells us that future historians:

> ... will wonder why GE was hailed as such a success [in the 1990s], when it was unable to grow anything new, other than financial ser-vices, and while growth in its core manufacturing business was at best anemic. They will wonder why a company that owed its very existence to technology [should have] lowered its research and devel-opment spending 19 percent, in real terms, in the 1990s, even while it continued to post record profits.[22]

During the 1960s, General Electric had annually registered more US patents than any other company; by 1999, it was twentieth on the list, the top three names being Japanese.[23] We are here speaking of an entity which, in its heyday, invented or developed many of the most important devices in common use today, from electric bulbs and refrig-erators to jet engines.

At Donner's General Motors, as we have seen, the goal had been to 'improve the numbers, not the cars'; much the same could be said of Welch's General Electric. Under the leadership of these two 'blue-chip' companies, a subtle but radical change began to overtake Big Business in general. Previously, the purchasers of automobiles, locomotives and other goods or services had been the customers of the Great Engine companies; under the new regime, institutional investors would increasingly step into that role. For them, companies would 'manufac-ture' financial statistics that did not always bear a close relationship to economic reality – or that reality would be cosmetically altered to pro-duce a desirable statistical outcome, without regard to the well-being of the entities in question in the long term or to the general public interest. Whereas the traditional customer had paid in cash or by credit for goods or services, his institutional successor would settle his account by purchasing (or failing to sell) the shares in question, confer-ring all kinds of benefits upon the companies and their executives. According to Adam Smith (see page 178), the object of economic activ-ity had been to benefit the consumer, not the producer. (It is a point that would be re-stated by Drucker in the last radio interview that he gave, three centuries after Smith, when he observed that 'the first con-stituent is the customer. If you don't satisfy the customer, there is nothing else you can do.')[24] In the last third of the twentieth century, capitalism, at least insofar as large companies were concerned, was turned on its head, as the means became the end.

It was at General Electric after 1995 that the Cult of the (so-called) Expert would enjoy its *ne plus ultra* in the form of a procedure called Six Sigma. (We will respond in Latin if we are addressed in Greek.) This was the bastardization of an earlier procedure, 3sigma (always written in lower case), developed in the 1920s by Walter Shewhart at the Bell Labs and described in his book, *The Economic Control of Quality of Manufactured Product* (1931). Shewhart was one of America's greatest statisticians. He developed 3sigma to guide manufacturers 'to the type of action which is appropriate for trying to improve the functioning of a process'[25] – in his case, to enhance the quality of telephone equipment manufactured in the Western Electric plants of AT&T. As a result of observation – which he described eloquently and precisely as 'listening to the voice of the process' – Shewhart had concluded that, if manufacturing processes could be made to run as to '93.0% error-free',[26] the quality of the resultant goods would be satisfactory. In the language which he created, one 'sigma' (the Greek letter for 's') was one 'standard deviation', a concept that measured variation from a norm. Shewhart was a supreme pragmatist. Properly and consistently applied within AT&T, 3sigma endowed that company in its heyday with a procedure similar to the future Japanese *kaizen*.

Although inspired by 3sigma, Six Sigma was really a horse of a different color. Shewhart's procedures had been directed at improving manufacturing processes and applied without fuss by engineers working quietly at their benches or desks; its successor would be the subject of a major and long-lasting public relations campaign waged by General Electric, designed to enhance its chairman's reputation and drive up its share price. 'Credentialism' ruled, those members of staff who taught or applied the procedure being awarded a fancy capitalized title ('Black Belt' or 'Green Belt'), as if their function in life was to deliver karate chops – which, in a metaphorical sense, it was. For example, SWAT-like teams of 'professional' managers who knew nothing about insurance would descend on an insurance division, allegedly to enhance its performance but in fact to engage in financial cosmetics. Whereas Shewhart's engineers had 'listened to the voice of the process'[27] in seeking to improve the quality of telephones, their more glamorous successors would hear only the sound of institutional shareholders encouraging them to work backwards from a projected rate of return on capital. W. Edwards Deming, Shewhart's friend and disciple and the future sponsor of Japanese-style management in the United

States (see Chapter 16), 'always bridled at the financial goal-oriented – as opposed to process-oriented – approach implicit in the monicker Six Sigma'.[28]

Shewhart had been content with a maximum of seven errors per *hundred manufacturing processes*; the new men and women would announce an utterly amazing goal of no more than 3.4 defects per *million products,* which raises all kinds of interesting questions. Is it possible to work to that degree of inaccuracy? And why not go the whole nine yards and ask for 'zero defects'? – is not perfection desirable in all human affairs? On this aspect, Donald J. Wheeler Jr., a specialist in statistical quality control, has offered the best comment: '. . . the arguments commonly used to explain the economics of [Six Sigma] can only be described as statistical snake oil – a blend of tortured computations and incompatible, highly questionable assumptions, having a hypnotic effect and often resulting in a suspension of critical thinking'.[29]

3sigma had been directed at operational functions on the factory floor but Six Sigma would be applied to the whole field of human endeavor. It promoted the neo-Taylorite principle that 'you cannot manage what you cannot measure' – an absurd view also put forward by Robert Kaplan and David Norton in their book *The Balanced Scorecard,* published in 1996.[30] Six Sigma's 'Belts' of different hues are the most extreme expression that the world has yet seen not just of 'credentialism' but also of the concept of the 'professional' manager: an Expert who need know nothing about the domains in which he operates and who can sort out problems because he has been trained to sort out problems. Its practitioners function in the fantasy world of 'physics envy' (see page 168) – a profitable place to be, by the way, since consultancies can charge a million dollars to install their versions of the procedure, even as they promise several times that amount in savings. Marc Hersch, another genuine specialist in quality control, has unkindly suggested that Six Sigma is promoted by people holding the naive view that, 'if 3 is good, then 6 must be better'.[31]

Xerox Corporation went wrong in 1968, just before the end of our Golden Age, when Peter McColough replaced Joe Wilson as head of the company. Wilson had converted a small manufacturer of photographic paper in Rochester, New York into one of the mightiest of the Great Engine companies. A self-effacing man who has been described as a 'latter-day saint among businessmen', he was concerned about his workers' welfare, valued his customers, worried about the position of women and ethnic minorities in the workforce, and spread credit around rather than taking it for himself. He was also responsible, against all the odds, for the development over a period of fourteen years of the Xerox 914, a copying machine which has been described as 'one of the most successful products of all time'. His successor would plunge the company into 'a series of ill-judged acquisitions and other adventures' which cost it its sense of direction, its reputation and a fortune.[32] If Wilson had been the very model of a Golden Age chief executive, McColough (Harvard Business School, HBS, 1949) was its antithesis.

AT&T's fall from corporate grace occurred in the 1970s. Until then, that company had been run mostly by engineers of 'generalist' outlook, who placed a heavy emphasis on the need for technical innovation. The first obvious deviation occurred in 1973, when a formal Marketing Department was established. Previously, marketing had been a function of the entire organization, in the manner succinctly described by Drucker in his *The Practice of Management*;[33] at that moment, it became a specialist function. This development led to a power struggle between the engineers and their new rivals, which would be resolved in favor of the latter as a result of organizational changes in 1978. From that point on, the company would be run by its marketers and its accountants, who would view its operations primarily through the twin prisms of brand and profitability in the short term. According to Peter Temin, in his authoritative *The Fall of the Bell System:* 'Planning in Bell's traditional regulatory environment had been mostly bottom-up and construction oriented. In AT&T's new competitive mode, authority would ... be exercised top-down and would emphasize the company's cash flow'.[34] As Al Gore and David Blood have recently reminded us, short-termism of this kind stifles innovation, damages the economy, further impairs the value of pensions and, ultimately, erodes the national standard of living.[35]

The formula that had made AT&T great was an intimate alliance between leading-edge technology and superb management, both deriving ultimately from Theodore N. Vail, its president from 1878 to 1887 and again from 1907 to 1919. Vail was a descendant of John Vail, a Quaker preacher who settled in New Jersey in 1710 and spawned a family of scientists and technologists. Theo's grandfather, Lewis, was a civil engineer who built canals in Ohio. His uncle, Stephen, founded an iron works in New Jersey, which built the engine for the first steamboat to cross the Atlantic. His cousin Alfred invented the Morse code (for which Samuel Morse had the idea) and was a co-inventor (with Morse) of the electric telegraph. Technology was in Theodore's blood. Interestingly, his middle initial stood for Newton; since, according to the genealogical records, no member of his family bore that name (his mother was a Quincy), one has to assume that his parents chose it out of respect for Isaac Newton, the founder of modern science – himself in every spiritual and practical sense a successor to Francis Bacon, who had also been a Fellow of Trinity College, Cambridge University in England.[36] (Although a Fellow of Trinity, Newton was a 'closet' Unitarian in his theology.)

As a result of the changes in its management structure mentioned above, AT&T lost the ability to manage technology, which would lead it to make several errors of judgment. For example, it totally failed to appreciate the future importance of wireless technology. Part of the blame for this mistake lies with a major consultancy company, McKinsey. Retained by AT&T in 1984 to report on the prospects of wireless communications, the Firm (as it is always known) famously estimated that there would be fewer than 1 million cellular phones in use by the year 2000; in the event, there were 741 million. Futurology is, of course, a difficult art and not too much blame should be attached to the authors of this report. It is, however, relevant to ask why a company like AT&T, whose employees knew more about the technology of communications than any other organization in the world, should have felt obliged to seek the advice of a firm of consultants not known for a depth of knowledge in this field. The answer is twofold: first, the company's new masters were personally ignorant of technology; and, second, they were indulging in the latest managerial fad: the 'outsourcing' of strategic decision-making (see page 158).

In 1916, the youthful and exuberant Ma Bell had placed a statue by the artist, Evelyn Beatrice Longman Batch the elder, on top of its historic building at 195 Broadway, New York City. Originally christened the Genius of Electricity and then re-named the Spirit of Communication, it has always been popularly known by its nickname, the Golden Boy, which it acquired on account of its gilded exterior. The statue symbolized all that the company stood for in its heyday. As AT&T lost its sense of direction, however, the statue would set off on a picaresque journey of its own that may still not be complete. It was taken from its original home in 1984 – an act of desecration reminiscent of the removal of August Saint-Gaudens' great statue of Diana from the old Madison Square Garden building as part of the redevelopment of Pennsylvania Station. Installed in the lobby of a new AT&T headquarters building at 550 Madison Avenue, the Golden Boy would be subjected to a second humiliation: during re-gilding, its conspicuous genitals were puritanically excised. It would be moved a second time in

1992, when that building was sold to Sony. Today, the Golden Boy sits, neutered and unloved, in front of the rambling offices in the successor company to AT&T (also called AT&T) in New Jersey, not far from the buildings of the Bell Labs. The City of New York would like to restore it to its former glory atop 195 Broadway but its offer has so far not been accepted.[37] Meantime, the ownership of the Labs, once the glory of corporate America, passed into French hands when the proposed acquisition (misleadingly described as a 'merger of equals') of Lucent by Alcatel was approved – an apt outcome, some might argue, since the respect for technology and the technologist which inspired their creation derived ultimately from America's oldest ally.[38]

In the year after the Golden Boy appeared on Broadway, another corporate icon was created at Newport News shipyard in Virginia in the form of a plaque dedicated to quality in manufacture. This plaque has already featured in the narrative of this book, having been used by our Three Wise Men as a teaching aid when they instructed the Japanese in good management practices during the US Occupation of their country (see pages 117 and 118). Its message was stark: quality came before profit. The plaque would set off on a picaresque journey of its own in subsequent years, reflecting changes in US corporate culture.

In 1969, the shipyard would be acquired by Tenneco, then one of the new-style 'conglomerates' more interested in artificially boosting reported earnings by procedures such as arbitrary cost-cutting than in creating genuine wealth for its shareholders, its employees and the community at large. With unconscious irony, Tenneco consigned the plaque to the Mariners' Museum in Newport, even as its senior managers were discarding the values for which it stood. We are pleased to report, however, that history has since reversed itself to some extent. In 1986, the shipyard was spun off by Tenneco; it now forms part of Northrop Grumman Newport News. The plaque stands once again in front of the company's head office, next to another proud monument: the yard's Hull Number 1, the tugboat *Dorothy,* launched in 1891. Pictures of both the Golden Boy and the plaque will be found on page 254.

For Coca-Cola, one of the bluest of the mid-century 'blue chips', the loss of a sense of direction did not occur until 1981, when a new chief executive, Roberto Goizueta took over. His principal contribution was to incorporate the company's US bottling operations as a separate legal entity, Coca-Cola Enterprises Inc., which he floated on the stock exchange, disposing of 51 per cent of its shares to the general public, while maintaining effective control through the balance. This successful piece of 'financial engineering' enabled him to spirit billions of dollars of debt off the parent company's balance sheet, anticipating a not-dissimilar machination at Enron a generation later. As Dean Frost has told us, in the escalating price wars that ensued between the company and Pepsi, just over half of the cost would be borne by the unfortunate shareholders of Coca-Cola's new affiliate, while the totality of the benefit flowed to the parent.

At the same time, Coca-Cola bought up large numbers of small, family-owned bottling companies and re-sold them profitably either to the new affiliate or to other so-called 'anchor bottlers'. Since Coca-Cola exercised effective managerial control over all these buyers, it could determine its own profit margin; indulgent accountants allowed the profits to be shown as normal income in its own accounts. Furthermore, between 1997 and 1999, the company engaged in 'gallon pushing', offering specially attractive terms to Japanese bottlers to persuade them to buy more concentrate than they needed; this practice, which would be subject to a cease-and-desist order from the Securities and Exchange Commission, brought earnings forward from future years and 'was the difference in eight out of 12 quarters between Coke's meeting and missing analysts' estimates'.[39]

As intended, Coca-Cola's published earnings soared and, with them, the price of the company's shares and the senior executives' remuneration. The 1960s had been marked by the arrival of the first million-dollar-a-year chief executive (see page 227); in the 1990s, Goizueta became the first of his breed to earn a billion dollars in one year. Nemesis struck around the time of his death in 1997, not because of his enforced departure but because the 'anchor' bottlers 'began to sink fast under the debt-financed acquisitions they had made at Coke's behest'. Meantime, the parent company ran out of small bottlers to buy and sell. Coca-Cola's published earnings fell sharply, and, with them, its share price. The great increase in the corporate income of the previous sixteen years had been largely (not entirely) 'smoke and mirrors'.[40]

Goizueta was a chemist by training, not an MBA, but the business school of Emory University in Atlanta has been re-named in his honor The school's website tells us that his vision provides the inspiration and momentum behind its overarching goal, the education of 'Principled Leaders'.[41] On December 12, 2005, the total market capitalization of Coca-Cola's rival, PepsiCo, which had not systematically whored after false managerial gods, overtook Coca-Cola's 'for the first time in 112 years of fierce competition'.[42] PepsiCo is today a well-run company, thanks in large part to its ex-Marine chief executive, Steve Reinmund, who brings a military precision to everything he does; a devout Presbyterian, he tells us that his primary goal is: '. . . to glorify God and to serve him in the way I am called to do. I think in the business world the manifestation of that is in actions, not in preaching.'[43] Meantime, Goizueta runs Coca-Cola from beyond the grave; in 2006, the owner of America's most valuable brand name announced that 'its directors 'would be paid only if the company met a target of 8 percent compounded annual earnings growth over three years'[44] and that it would repurchase 13 per cent of it own shares, a device that artificially raised earnings per share while usefully minimizing the payment of tax. Statistics rule. The share price stands at one-half of it 1998 peak.[45]

IBM is another company that lost its way in the 1980s, to such an extent that in 1990 the loquacious Bill Gates would predict its demise by 1996. Leading rather than following the dictates of fashion, it decided in 1981 to 'out-source' the supply of the software (specifically, the key 'operating system') for its new personal computer, the Acorn. It did this for internal political reasons and in spite of the fact that IBM had invented a large part of the field of computer science. For this departure from the traditional practices of the Great Engine companies, it would pay a terrible price. The recipient of the mandate was Microsoft, then a small, unknown company. Not possessing a suitable operating system of its own at that time, Microsoft acquired one called 'QDOS' for $50,000 from its maker, Seattle Computer Products. 'QDOS', an obvious homophone of kudos, was also short for 'Quick and Dirty Operating System', a name that reflected the casual way in which it had been cobbled together. Microsoft renamed its acquisition with the more dignified title, MS-DOS – meaning Microsoft Disk Operating System – and licensed it to IBM. As Cringely has told us: 'Never before had IBM allowed itself to be so dependent on a single supplier, much less one run by a 25-year-old who ought to wash his hair more often'.[46] The problem from IBM's point of view was that its license for MS-DOS was not exclusive. For almost twenty years, most personal computers in the world – whether made by IBM or someone else – would rely on one or other of its versions.

Launched in 1981, the Acorn was the first commercially successful personal computer in the world. For IBM, however, this was a pyrrhic victory; being first in the field was the only 'competitive advantage' that the Acorn now possessed. Compaq, Apple, Dell and Packard Bell soon entered the fray and, by 1996, IBM had fallen from being market leader to supplying only one-tenth of the demand. In 2005, it would dispose of its personal computer division to the Chinese company, Lenovo. Meantime, Big Blue had got into trouble in other divisions as well, reporting such huge losses to shareholders that it was threatened with bankruptcy. It sought salvation in the person of Lou Gerstner, chairman from 1992 until 2003.

Gerstner was an engineer by education but otherwise conformed to the stereotype of the 'professional' manager. An alumnus of the B-School as well (HBS, 1965), he had joined a management consultancy upon graduation, rising to the rank of boardroom director. Thereafter he served as president of the banking company, American Express and then chairman and chief executive of RJR Nabisco, the cigarette and food-stuffs company. During its Gerstner years, IBM's revenues increased no faster than the general economy but its published earnings per share – the key figure which investment analysts always look at – forged ahead, enhanced by such devices as buying shares from the public (which, by reducing the number of shares in circulation, increased the reported earning per share, even if earnings as a whole did not rise); well-timed sales of assets (on which the capital appreciation would be treated, mis-leadingly, as current income); and taking credit in the company's accounts for increases in the value of the pension fund (which were due to rising share prices and beyond the company's control) – not to speak of declining tax rates, which also helped. As the journalist Simon London has told us, Gerstner's success was due 'as much to financial . . . as to electrical engineering'.[47] As at General Motors and General Electric (and, indeed, most other large companies of the period), the principal goal was to improve the numbers, not the products.

During the Great Depression of the 1930s, IBM had actually invented new product lines just to keep its existing employees at work;[48] under Gerstner's rule, it would dismiss them by the thousand; today the average tenure of 60 per cent of IBM employees is five years, a fraction of what it was half a century ago. Cost-cutting also affected the company's research expenditures, which were halved after 1990.[49] The consequent decline in the quality and nature of its basic research is reflected in the tally of the awards it has earned. Between 1973 and 1987, its employees had been awarded three Nobel and four Alan Tur-ing prizes, the latter being the most prestigious honor conferred by the Association for Computing Machinery; since then, there have been no major awards.[50]

According to Drucker (see page 106), Standard Oil of New Jersey, was a model of collective management at the mid-twentieth century. Of all the former Great Engine companies, it is today probably the one least affected by our Cult of the (so-called) Expert, a fact which may be attributed to its strong engineering culture and its location in the South-West, far from the influence of New York's financial markets.

However, under Lee Raymond, its chief executive from 1993 until 2005, the company bent to the wind. The executive wing of its headquarters building in Dallas became known as the 'God Pod'. When the journalist, Nelson D. Schwartz, first called on Raymond, he felt as if he as if he was being 'ushered into an audience with the Pope'. Furthermore, Raymond undertook a number of corporate acts that belong more to the world of 'financial' rather than mechanical or civil engineering, such as buying back common stock to enhance earnings per share. As at other major oil companies, production has recently been 'sagging', output being 2 per cent less in the first quarter of 2006 than a year before.[51]

It will be clear from this account that there was no moment in time when the traditional 'bottom-up' approach of the American Great Engine companies was universally abandoned in favor of its opposite, or when the entire cast of players changed at the drop of a hat. The transformation occurred over thirty years and, in most cases, the new paradigm was simply laid on top of the old. The outcome was an unstable amalgam of styles, which survives to this day – the ratio of old to new varying from company to company and from time to time. However, it was the new, upper, 'top-down' layer that would in most cases determine policy and inhibit execution. The persistence of traditional values, if not always of the practices closely associated with them, is illustrated in Jim Collins' books *Built to Last* (1994) and *Good to Great* (2001). The first of these, written with Jerry Porras, has sold 1.5 million copies and been translated into thirteen languages. The second was on the *New York Times* best-seller list for many years after it was published.[52] Both identified characteristics of successful companies, which – like humility in chief executives and a collegiate approach to decision-making – correspond to some of the Principles underlying good managerial practice which appear in the Appendix to this book. Time has, however, tarnished a number of their idols.

For example, *Built to Last* expressed admiration for Boeing as a 'visionary' company, vision being defined as using 'bold missions' as a 'particularly powerful mechanism to stimulate progress'. It referred to such missions as 'BHAGS' (pronounced 'bee-hags', short for 'Big Hairy Audacious Goals');[53] nine years later, and for the first time ever, the company made fewer sales of civilian aircraft than its aggressive European competitor, Airbus, a company that has been 'consistently ahead of Boeing in fly-by-wire technology and computer-aided design'.[54] Meantime, Boeing was not doing so well on the defense front either, that other pillar of its business. In February 2004, the US air force conducted exercises over India in which the Boeing F-15 Eagle engaged in mock combat with the Indian air force's Russian-built Sukhoi Su-30

Flanker. In more than 90 per cent of simulated dogfights, the F-15 was out-flown and out-fought by the Russian machine.[55] Boeing's commercial ethics have also been found wanting in connection with the award of a major contract for air-to-air refueling tankers to the US air force.

The *Washington Post* columnist, Robert J. Samuelson, tells us that the story of the company's decline comes in three chapters: 'bad luck, bad management and bad government policy'.[56] The company had been a 'BHAG' in 1969 – the penultimate year of what we call America's Golden Age of Management – when it launched a flying machine that would revolutionize the world of transport: the 747. *Built to Last's* analysis was, however, several decades out of date when it was written. We are told that the company had to bring aircraft production to a complete halt in the second half of the 1990s, 'as it had lost control of the assembly system'.[57] Boeing did not introduce a full moving line to its plants until 2003 – almost a century after Ford. Fortunately for the aircraft manufacturer, its principal European competitor has recently run into serious managerial problems of its own.

Another fallen star from the same book is Fannie Mae (formerly the Federal National Mortgage Association), a company described by Collins and his twenty-strong team of researchers as 'terrifically motivated by the whole idea of helping people of all classes, backgrounds, and races realize the American dream of owning their home'.[58] The company's official regulator, Armando Falcom Jr., recently testified to Congress that the company had engaged in a 'pervasive and willful misapplication of generally accepted accounting principles'.[59] In February 2006, Randy Quarles, undersecretary for finance at the US Treasury, declared that that the company posed a 'systemic risk' to financial markets – than which there can be no greater condemnation.[60]

Merck & Company was a star of both *Built to Last* and *Good to Great*. Perhaps the greatest of the Great Engine companies in the mid-twentieth century, it succeeded against the odds in retaining most of its positive characteristics until the last decade of that century. Its subsequent fall from corporate grace cannot be disassociated from the appointment in 1994 of a new chairman and chief executive, Ray Gilmartin, the first 'non-scientist ever to run Merck'. As with non-engineers running engineering companies, there is nothing intrinsically right or wrong about appointing non-scientists to run pharmaceutical companies, provided they observe the principles of good management. Inauspiciously, Gilmartin arrived 'with a reputation as both a turnaround artist and a wizard at efficiency', not a bad description of one of the new 'professional' managers. As a company which prided itself on its scientific mission, Merck had faced little in the way of litigation over product liability; upon his arrival that was to change with a vengeance.[61]

Merck is now under a federal criminal investigation. A study by the US Food and Drug Administration estimates that its anti-arthritis drug, Vioxx, withdrawn from the market in 2004, could have caused 27,785 heart attacks or deaths since it was approved in 1999.[62] According to Eric J. Topol, chairman of cardiology at the Cleveland Clinic, in an article in the authoritative *New England Journal of Medicine*: 'had the company not valued sales over safety, a suitable trial could have been initiated rapidly at a fraction of the cost of Merck's direct-to-consumer advertising campaign'. In the 1980s, Merck had been ranked for seven consecutive years by *Fortune* as America's most admired company; today it is in trouble from massive law suits,[63] which may bankrupt it. Its recent flirtation with Six Sigma (see page 148) and heavy cost-cutting do not bode well for the future.[64]

In Great Engine companies, the three principal functions of a chief executive had been: to determine the strategy of the company; to appoint the divisional heads responsible for putting it into effect; and to supervise their work as they did so. He could perform these roles well because he had grown up in the business and knew more about its problems, opportunities and people than anyone else. He had *lived* it – to the point where he would often know almost intuitively what decisions to make. The new finance- or marketing-oriented senior executives who appeared on the scene after World War II, and particularly after 1980, inevitably lacked the knowledge and experience to behave in this way. Accountancy offered no guidance to the future – indeed, insofar as it attempted to project past trends into the future, it could be downright misleading. An understanding of finance told people how to fund activities, not which activities to fund. Brand-worship misled.

Nature once more disliking a vacuum, a new kind of (so-called) Expert and a new kind of service industry sprang into being: incredibly, the making of strategy – one of the three principal functions of the traditional chief executive – was 'out-sourced'. Taylor's humble 'efficiency experts' had worked among ordinary workmen and women and earned only a little more than they did. Their ultimate successors, the strategic consultants, would talk to no-one below the rank of chief executive – and earned as much as he did, if not more. Theoretically speaking, they were only advisors but no company was going to pay millions of dollars for advice and then lightly disregard it. There used to be a common saying in business that consultants should be 'on tap, not on top'. The older style of consultant had been 'on tap'; the new would be decidedly 'on top'.[65]

An accountant, James McKinsey, had founded the first of the strategic advisory firms as early as 1925. The Glass-Steagall Banking Act of 1932 boosted this kind of activity by making it impossible for lawyers, engineers and accountants to offer advice outside the area of their professional competence. McKinsey responded by altering his letterhead from 'certified public accountants' to 'accountants and engineers', a title which harked back to the one adopted by Taylor half a century before ('consultant engineer in management') and forward to the 're-engineering' craze of the 1990s. Taylor had employed only engineers in his company but there were none in the literal sense in McKinsey's. The consultancy 'profession' would come into its own in the decades after World War II; before long, there was hardly a major company on the North American continent, or elsewhere, that was not making extensive use of its services. In the last quarter of the twentieth century, after legal restraints on their conduct had been eased, established firms of accountants leapt back on the bandwagon, involving themselves in highly profitable conflicts of interest that would again draw the attention of regulators.[66] By 2000, half a dozen consultancy firms had become household names, their combined annual fees running into billions of dollars. McKinsey would count among its clients companies involved in most of the great corporate scandals and bankruptcies of the earliest years of the current century: Enron, World-Com, Kmart, Swissair, Global Crossing, for example – and those, as *The Business* would remind us, were just the big ones.[67]

One of McKinsey's senior consultants, Jeffrey Skilling, who had advised Enron on its disastrous corporate strategy, became that company's chief executive and has been found guilty on a criminal charge for his part in the debacle, along with Enron's chairman, the late Kenneth Lay and its chief financial officer, Richard Causey. Each faced more than three dozen accusations of insider trading, fraud and lying.[68] WorldCom's chief executive, Bernie Ebbers, was also found guilty on a criminal charge of securities fraud in March 2005 and will spend the rest of his life in jail, if he does not live beyond eighty-eight. The accounts of WorldCom had been audited by Anderson, then the largest accounting firm in the world; Anderson was found guilty of the obstruction of justice in June 2003, by which time it had, for practical purposes, ceased to exist.[69] McKinsey, however, continues to thrive; in 2005 alone, it hired 600 MBAs fresh from business school, making it one of the biggest consumers of alumni and alumnae.[70]

It is when one examines the use of strategic consultants that one appreciates to the full that the Cult of the Expert was really the Cult of the (so-called) Expert. In his *The Canterbury Tales*, the fourteenth-century English poet Chaucer offered an admiring portrait of a Poor Priest, in which the wonderful phrase appeared: 'First he wrought, then he taught' (wrought being the obsolete past tense of 'to work'). No such thing could be said about strategic consultants. Bright young men and women were recruited straight from college or business school and expected to offer instant advice on matters which, half a century before, would had been the province and preserve of experienced senior executives. They were in many cases less expert than the people who retained them. It was like consulting a doctor or a dentist who had never practiced medicine or dentistry. That guardian of traditional American values, H. Ross Perot, unerringly put his finger on the weak point. Having sold a company to General Motors, he joined that company's Board, encountered the Cult in its full flowering and resigned in frustration. As he put it:

> I come from an environment where, if you see a snake, you kill it. At GM, if you see a snake, the first thing you do is organize a committee on snakes. Then you go hire a consultant who knows a lot about snakes. Then you talk about it for a year.[71]

This is an accurate analogy, except that there has to be some doubt about the depth of the consultant's knowledge about snakes. When describing certain doctrines underlying personnel administration in the mid-twentieth century, Drucker used a delightful metaphor. He told us that nearly everything that was being written about management at that time had been better expressed in the works of an earlier author, Thomas Spates, and added: 'We have only poured on a heavy dressing of humanitarian rhetoric – the way a poor cook pours a brown starchy sauce on overcooked brussels sprouts'.[72] Drucker was referring to the malign impact of the Human Relations Movement, of which more in Chapter 13, on the whole of business and manufacturing and on much else besides in the mid-twentieth century. Here is another culinary metaphor to describe the impact of the Cult of the (so-called) Expert, in the persons of the new class of financially-oriented consultants and managers, on the established structure and methodology of American business in the last third of the twentieth century: *it was like depositing a thick layer of deep-frozen ice cream on a bed of hot, succulent apple pie.* The treatment did not totally destroy the fruit but it would profoundly affect both its taste and texture. A trend that had originated in Puritan England and survived for 350 years was being subjected to a reversal which, although spread over several decades, would be traumatic, meaning deeply wounding, in its impact.

It was not just the Great Engine companies that were damaged by the Cult. Civil government was also affected, the National Aeronautics and Space Administration (NASA) being a case in point. No critical history exists of that body in its 'glory' years; one can, however, infer that the success of the moon shot on July 20, 1969 was due, above all, to an exercise in co-operation and complementarity between three remarkable men: James Webb, ('a canny bulldog of a politician') who served as NASA's second administrator from 1961 until 1968;[73] his youthful deputy, Thomas Paine, ('a bright young engineer with a penchant for the visionary'); and the remarkable German rocket scientist, Wernher von Braun, director from 1960 to 1970 of the Marshall Space Flight Center, where the moon rocket was designed and built.[74] One is reminded of the brilliant exercises in managerial teamwork between Maudslay, Bentham and Brunel that led to the creation of the famous Admiralty block mill in England a century and a half before (see page 49); and between our Three Wise Men from the West in Japan as recorded in Chapter 10.

Saturn V was the most powerful vehicle ever created; sixty feet taller than the Statue of Liberty and weighing thirteen times more, it generated as much energy at lift-off as eighty-five Hoover Dams. The moon shot was the biggest project ever mounted by human beings[75] anywhere in peace time, at its peak employing, either directly or through subcontractors, over 400,000 people.[76] Occupying the greater part of the decade of the 1960s, the project represented the culminating triumph both of America's Golden Age of Management and of its great mechanic culture – one, as in many of the nation's earlier achievements, in which both the public and private sectors played important roles.

Webb exemplified in many ways the good American manager of the mid-twentieth century. Unlike Professor Mabel Newcomer's typical chief executives of the period (see pages 94 and 95), he had not spent his entire working life in the organization of which he became head or in the industry of which it formed a part – but then NASA had been formed only three years before, when there was no space industry. However, he otherwise conformed to type by coming from a family of modest means – his father had been superintendent of schools in Granville County, North Carolina – and by making his way right to the top of society by dint of intelligence and hard work, becoming undersecretary of state under Truman. He was able to spend long enough in his subsequent position as administrator both to shape NASA's policies and to direct their execution. In this book we have referred to 'a specific moral outlook which subordinated the interests of the individual to the group' as one of the Puritan characteristics which America inherited from its early colonists: Webb carried self-abnegation to the nth degree, taking early retirement as administrator on his sixty-second birthday in 1968, four days before the first flight by Apollo and a year before the successful moon shot, so that his successor could play himself in before the new president took office in 1969. He will receive posthumous recognition when the James Webb space telescope is named and launched in 2011.[77]

After 1970, something went seriously wrong both at NASA and in its subcontractors, resulting in various mishaps, chief of which were the losses with all hands of the space shuttles *Challenger* in 1986 and *Columbia* in 2003, in each of which seven crew members or passengers died. The existence of good management does not guarantee that mistakes will not be made; astronauts had also died on Webb's watch. The difference between him and his successors was that he learned from his own and others' mistakes, just as Governor Winthrop had done, three and a half centuries before, when planning the 'plantation' of Massachusetts. The first disaster occurred because of: '... the failure of the pressure seal in the aft field joint of the right Solid Rocket Booster. The failure was due to a faulty design unacceptably sensitive to a number of factors.'[78] Why was it allowed to happen? A NASA scientist, Roger Boisjoly had been among those who drew the attention of his superiors to this particular fault before the event but no-one listened; for his heroic but unavailing efforts, he would be awarded a prize by the American Association for the Advancement of Science.[79]

History repeated itself with disturbing exactitude in the case of *Columbia*, when the fault lay with a piece of insulating foam which broke off the main fuel tank and damaged the thermal tiles that protected the shuttle. Once again, the fault had been known to engineers in the agency but either not properly conveyed to the decision-makers or disregarded by them. If communications in an upward direction were poor at NASA, they were also deficient sideways, as is evidenced by another mishap which was less serious only because no lives were lost: in 1999, a NASA spacecraft missed the planet Mars because one group of NASA engineers had been working in metric units while another was working in imperial measure.[80] This episode cost the taxpayer millions of dollars. The weaknesses at the space agency appear to have extended to its accounting system; when some employees were accused of taking kickbacks at the Johnson Space Center in Texas in 1994, an unnamed scientist was quoted in the *New York Times* as saying, curiously, that that it was 'a lot easier to knock off a mom-and-pop than an armored car'.[81]

Why are communications now so poor? Two interviews recorded in the *New York Times* on March 3 and 29, 2003 point to an explanation. In the first, a former quality controller for a NASA contractor, Lockheed Martin, is quoted as saying that supervisors at that plant were systematically discouraged from submitting 'error reports', which would have reflected badly on their superiors.[82] In the second, a former accident investigator for NASA's chief contractor, United Space Alliance, described an occasion when a toxic gas was released from a rocket's fuel tank and was not reported as a serious accident, as it should have been. If these two accounts are correct and typical, we are in My Lai country (see page 192); as in Vietnam the people who tell the best statistical lies, or cause other people to tell them, get promoted – from which a whole series of adverse consequences may flow, including the deaths of innocents.

If an organization has a flawed culture, there is one person who is to blame, namely the chief executive (or administrator) who either allowed that culture to come into existence or tolerated its continuance. What was missing at the later NASA, as at General Motors and many other organizations in the new era, was an old-fashioned, 'hands-on', 'generalist' and 'rounded' chief executive who had spent a long time in the business, set the tone, learned from his own and others' errors, made the big decisions – after collegially consulting his subordinates – and accepted responsibility for the final outcome. The administrator of NASA at the time of the *Columbia* accident, Sean O'Keefe, was an accountant, former business school professor and 'management expert' who preferred 'to let professionals at lower levels take responsibility for evaluating engineering risks and for making decisions'.[83] This can only mean that the traditional line-of-command no longer existed. The Cult of the (so-called) Expert ruled. Donald R. Keough, a former chairman of Coca-Cola and a man famous for his Irish wit, likes to deliver a 'sermon' entitled 'Ten Commandments for Losing', in which he satirizes current management foibles. His Tenth, final and most important Commandment – 'T.N.M.J. or "that's not my job"' – was particularly relevant to NASA in 1986 and in 2003.[84] (His Fourth Commandment is: 'Make sure you do not make a move until you have consulted half a dozen business school professors'; in his view, this *guarantees* failure.)

NASA appeared to take an important step in the right direction when a highly qualified space engineer, Michael Griffin, was appointed as its eleventh administrator in April 2005.[85] However, the shuttle program was allowed to continue, although the insulation remained defective. When the *Discovery* flew in July 2005, 'a greatly reduced but still hazardous amount of foam fell from its tank'. When a second flight was proposed in 2006, both NASA's chief engineer, Christopher Scolese, and its lead safety officer, Brian O'Connor, voted against but were overruled. Believing that the foam endangered the vehicle but not its occupants, the powers-that-be argued that *another* shuttle could rescue the crew from the International Space Station if *Discovery*'s heat shield failed. No-one explained how the replacement would survive *its* defective insulation.[86] Fortunately, the flight passed off without a fatality, although part of the foam came away again.

The last word on NASA's problems was said nearly a century and a half ago by the nurse, Florence Nightingale, when she commented on an incident similar, *mutatis mutandi*, to the *Challenger* and *Columbia* disasters. An explosion had occurred on a new, state-of-the-art American steamship that killed several passengers on its trial run. A jury ruled that it was an accident. In her seminal work, *Notes on Nursing: What it is and What it is Not,* published in 1860. The Lady with the Lamp used the occasion to convey an ironic thought on the meaning of the expression *to be in charge*: 'From the most colossal calamities, down to the most trifling accidents, results are often traced (or rather *not* traced) to such want of some one "in charge" or of his knowing how to be "in charge" '.

> A short time ago the bursting of a funnel-casing on board the finest and strongest ship that ever was built, on her trial trip, destroyed several lives and put several hundreds in jeopardy – not from any undetected flaw in her new and untried works – but from a tap being closed which ought not to have been closed – from what every child knows would make its mother's tea-kettle burst. And this simply because no one seemed to know what it is to be 'in charge', or *who* was in charge. Nay more, the jury at the inquest actually altogether ignored the same, and apparently considered the tap 'in charge', for they gave as a verdict 'accidental death'.[87]

For 'tap', read 'pressure seal' in the case of *Challenger* and 'foam covering the main fuel tank' in the case of *Columbia*. All of the heroes mentioned in this book – including James Webb, his deputy, Thomas Paine, and their colleague, Wernher von Braun – and its only heroine knew full well the meaning of the expression *to be in charge*.

13

The Business Schools as Temples of the Cult

> No greater damage could be done to our economy or to our society than to attempt to 'professionalize' management by 'licensing' managers, for example, or by limiting access to management to people with a special academic degree.
>
> Peter F. Drucker, 1954[1]

Around the turn of the nineteenth century, American universities began to take an interest in something called 'management' as a subject in its own right for the purpose of both research and teaching. In 1908, the Corporation of Harvard University voted to create a Graduate School of Business Administration, now often referred to as the 'B-School', which was the first of its kind.[2] The degree that it offered, Master in Business Administration (or MBA) was also the first Harvard degree not to be conferred in Latin. A large number of similar schools would be founded in imitation across the United States in the next seventy years. They became the temples of the neo-Taylorite Cult of the (so-called) Expert that was to dominate American business and society from 1970 to the present day. Their function was to produce 'Experts' in management.

This book sites the Golden Age of Management in the period between 1920 and 1970. What contribution did the alumni of America's emerging business schools make in shaping the Great Engine companies of that period? The answer has to be: precious little. An important exception was Stanley Marcus (HBS, 1926),[3] whom we met in the last chapter. Marcus has been described as the epitome of the 'hands-on' shopkeeper, a man who missed no opportunity for making a sale. He belonged to that great American tradition of salesmanship, which we encountered earlier in people like Colt. When he gave a dinner for General Dwight D. Eisenhower in Paris in 1946, for example, he voiced the hope that the soldier would run for the presidency one day and would then allow Neiman Marcus to provide the inaugural gown for the First Lady. The future president took up the offer, providing the

store with priceless publicity on Inauguration Day, 1953.[4] Marcus'
pithy, down-home sayings have become proverbial in the world of
retailing, like: 'You achieve customer satisfaction when you sell mer-
chandise that doesn't come back to a customer that does',[5] and 'Learn
to complain, politely but firmly, when you receive what you believe to
be inferior goods or services. Don't register your complaint with the
salesperson or the waiter, but with the owner.'[6] Like Nightingale, he
liked to know who was 'in charge'. As we shall see, however, it is doubtful if his achievements had much to do with his business school
education.

Why did the business school movement exercise so little influence
on the culture of major corporations before 1970? The answer is that,
until 1930, the schools were few in number and small in size. Furthermore, during the depression years of the 1930s, business as a career
enjoyed low esteem and attendance fell off. It was only after World War
II, when the culture of the Great Engine companies was already at its
peak, that returning veterans entered the schools, creating a new generation of aspiring managers. The annual output of the schools rose
from 6,000 in the early 1960s to 77,000 in 1990. According to *Fortune*,
which reported these figures in March, 1993, many of them were
'dreadful managers' and plenty were 'greedy, lazy or incompetent'.[7] By
the turn of the twentieth century, one half of the largest corporations
would be led by someone holding an MBA or its equivalent.[8] When
George W. Bush was sworn in as president on January 20, 2001, an
MBA from Harvard became chief executive of the nation.

How did the impact of the business schools affect our Great Engine
companies? First, the social composition of the senior management
team changed. The chief executives of the previous generation had
emerged (as Newcomer put it delicately) from families of 'moderate'
means. Most of them had 'worked their way' through college; few
could have afforded the luxury of a second degree. The loss of talent to
the companies and to the nation would be real; the ladder was removed
by which an earlier generation of able men (there were few women)
had climbed to the top. Under the new dispensation, there were to be
two classes of manager, those with and those without an MBA. The
former were likely to be 'fast-tracked' to the top, creating resentment
among, and demoralizing, the latter. Engineers in particular, who had
been the cocks of the corporate walk in earlier decades, tended to lose
self-confidence and to think of themselves as mere mechanics. Secondly, those who were 'fast-tracked' in this way would miss out on the
vital experience that came from working one's way slowly and systematically up through the ranks, while spending some time in every

division. They could never therefore become truly 'generalist', and therefore 'rounded', managers like their predecessors. Thirdly, 'bottom-up' tended to become 'top-down'; what had one of the new-fangled Experts in management to learn from a blue-collar worker whom he had never met – or, for that matter, from a middle manager with a 'technical' qualification from a Middle Western college?

Fourthly, and most important, the business schools taught America's future leaders to think quantitavely as money managers, not qualitatively *and* quantitavely as managers of human and material, as well as financial, resources. Over a period of years (principally in the decade of the 1980s), this resulted in a profound shift in the general attitude of senior executives. The new men and women would conform to the neo-Taylorite stereotype as described in the last chapter, in the sense that they saw the company primarily through the prism of either the profit and loss account or of the brand name or both – but mostly the former. This narrowness of outlook created enormous difficulties; as the sociologist, Abraham Maslow, famously observed in another context, 'It is tempting, if your only tool is a hammer, to treat everything as if it were a nail'.[9] The new generation of senior managers had little knowledge of, or interest in, what was going on at 'the coal face' or, as the Japanese say, at the *gemba* – 'the real place', the point where value was created. For the Japanese, the key to successful *kaizen* (or continuous improvement) is to go to the *gemba*, work with the *gembutsu* (the actual thing, i.e. the relevant tools, materials, machines, parts and fixtures) and assemble the *genjitsu* (all the relevant facts). This is, for example, the basis of the Toyota Production System.[10] The business school graduates had little interest in any of these three. This very point would be made by Stanley Marcus in 1986:

> Thousands of aspiring executives will be graduating from the business schools in which the management of money has been the central thrust of their education ... Their perspective is such that they don't want to get behind a sales counter to learn about customers or behind a machine to learn about products ... Too many young executives know something about many things, but not a lot about anything. In their race to the presidency, [they] lose sight of the fact that some jobs within a company take years to master.[11]

Whence the Business School Counter-Culture, the academic embodiment of neo-Taylorism, at the heart of which lay the concept of the so-called 'professional' manager, possessor of a degree which would enable him to turn his hand at once to any activity in any company in any trade. Or as Graham Muggeridge has said, 'Business schools thrive on the principle that there is a body of management theory that, once absorbed, will guarantee a student's success in the business world'.[12] This concept is faulty in two respects: first, management is neither an art nor a science, but a craft that can be properly learned only 'on the job' and not in an academic setting (except possibly as a minor subject); and, secondly, no-one can usefully direct a business activity with which he or she is not thoroughly familiar. Neo-Taylorism led to the dissolution or fractionalization of the line-of-command, to which we referred in Chapter 12, as different specialists, some worthy of respect for their professional skills, others to be classed as bogus, took charge of different aspects of the business, with no one senior, 'generalist' manager being properly in charge of everything. It was a recipe for failure.

Recently, even some leading business school professors have begun to offer similar critiques of the system. For example, Leonard R. Sayles, Professor Emeritus of Management at Columbia Business School, has written a book, *The Working Leader: The Triumph of High Performance over Conventional Management*, to expose various 'MBA myths' taught at business schools; one of these is the belief that 'the best managers manage by financial results and do not get involved in work or technology'. Henry Mintzberg, Cleghorn Professor of Management Studies at McGill University in Canada, has published a book called *Developing Managers, not MBAs* which tells us that the case-study method which lies at the heart of the Harvard approach, 'trains people to provide the most superficial responses to problems' and also that 'it encourages managers to be disconnected with the people they are managing'.[13] He believes that all MBA graduates 'should have skulls and crossbones stamped on their foreheads, along with warnings that they are not fit to manage'.[14]

Professor Warren Bennis, the Distinguished Professor of Business Administration at the University of Southern California, in an article written with his colleague Professor Jim O'Toole in no less august an organ than the *Harvard Business Review* itself, tells us that 'business schools are locked in a fruitless quest for academic respectability' and suffer from 'physics envy' (i.e. they equate management with measurement), which is almost a definition of our Cult.[15] He added that 'MBA programs face intense criticism for failing to impart useful skills, . . . to prepare leaders, . . . to instill norms of ethical behavior, . . . even to lead graduates into good jobs'.[16]

The late Sumantra Ghoshal, Professor of Strategy and International Management at the London Business School and founding dean of the Indian School of Management[17] has even attacked a number of his leading fellow professors by name, including the 'ubiquitous' Michael Porter:

And wherever in the world one studies management, there is Michael Porter's theory of strategy. This asserts that to make good profits, a company must actively compete not only with its competitors but also with its suppliers, customers, regulators and employees. Profits come from restricting or distorting competition, bad though this may be for society. It is one of the most important tasks that managers are paid to do.

Ghoshal pointed out that it is not only business school graduates who have been subjected to these doctrines:

Even those who never attended a business school learnt to think this way because these theories were in the air . . . shaping the intellectual background against which day-to-day decisions were made. Is it any surprise, then, that executives in Enron, Global Crossing and scores of other companies granted themselves excessive stock options, treated their employees badly and took their customers for a ride when they could?[18]

Ghoshal concluded that pseudo-scientific theories of management had done much to reinforce, if not create, pathological behavior on the part of managers. A weakness in his approach, however, and one which he acknowledged, was that he offered no real alternative;[19] this book seeks to fill that gap.

Other business school academics who have called into doubt the benefits of business school education include Jeffrey Pfeffer of Stanford's Graduate School of Business;[20] Richard West, dean of New York University's Business School;[21] and Russell L. Ackoff, himself a pioneer of management education and formerly Professor of Management Science at Wharton, generally regarded as the second-ranking business school after Harvard. When he retired, Ackoff was asked what the 'principal achievements of a business school education' were. He replied that they were three in number:

The first was to equip students with a vocabulary that enabled them to talk authoritatively about subjects they did not understand. The second was to give students principles that would demonstrate their ability to withstand any amount of disconfirming evidence. The third was to give students a ticket of admission to a job where they could learn something about management.[22]

He recalls that these answers 'hugely endeared him to the Wharton faculty'.

When and where did it all go wrong? The answer is: right at the outset in 1908 and in Cambridge, Massachusetts. The original proposal had been to form a graduate school of administration for the American public sector – in particular, the colonial service. The principal degree awarded to alumni today – Master in Business Administration – reflects this approach, insofar as the word 'administration' is more usually associated with government than with business.

Once the idea of training colonial servants had been rejected in favor of training businessmen, the founders had to decide just what the curriculum should consist of. There were, broadly speaking, two views on the subject. The first was that the B-School should offer a general business course run by academics to train the nation's future business leaders. The second was that the school should offer a group of specialized courses taught largely by practitioners drawn from different industries and designed to train men for careers in each of those industries. The future great president of Harvard, A. Lawrence Lowell, at that time a lecturer in government, was of the latter persuasion. 'I do not believe much in the value of any special training for general business', he said presciently, adding, 'I should like very much to see training for particular branches of business which could be developed into professions'.[23] Half a century later some of Lowell's views would find an echo in two exhaustive reports by the Carnegie and Ford Foundations, one of which described business administration, as taught in universities, as a 'vague, shifting, rather formless subject'.[24] It was around this time that Drucker adopted the negative stance towards business school education in general that is illustrated by the quotation at the head of this chapter. He made an exception for the work of the Claremont Graduate School in California, which would be renamed after him.[25]

Lowell had taken Harvard Law School as his model, admiring the way it had 'jealously kept itself free from contact with academic students and professors'.[26] Accordingly, he favored the appointment of 'men from active life'[27] among its instructors and indeed thought that the dean should be drawn from them. If he had had his way, there would also have been few, if any, PhDs on its faculty; Lowell, who did not possess a doctorate, believed that the award of such degrees led to the 'mass production of mediocrity'. Together with William James, he founded the Society of Fellows at Harvard to fight what the latter called 'the Ph.D. octopus'.[28] (Needless to say, the authors are not of the opinion that mass production as such leads to the creation of second-rate goods, but that is another subject.) The profusion of doctorates existing today offers an extreme example of credentialism, one of the worst intellectual vices of our age (see page 134). This book may be regarded, among other things, as an anti-doctoral thesis.

Had Lowell had his way, and had such a Dean been appointed, the B-School might have been launched on the world as a kind of collective of colleges providing specialized training for different industries, run primarily by ex-practitioners for future practitioners. In subsequent Japanese terms, its alumni would have spent a lot of time at the *gemba*, working with the *gembutsu* and assembling the *genjitsu*. Furthermore, the kind of adverse criticism of the role of business schools in general offered by this book, as well as from within the movement by Ackoff, Mintzberg, Ghoshal, West, Bennis, Pfeffer, Sayles and others, could not have been made. The alumni would have learned a great deal about railroads, or insurance, or banking or whatever other 'branch of business' the college chose to teach and they to study. One can speculate, for example, that, had a special college been created at Harvard capable of taking a long view of the place of railroads in society, the spectacular and unnecessary collapse of that industry after World War II, as described below, might not have occurred.

It was not to be. Instead, the B-School set out on the road to which Lowell was opposed. Uncertainty about its purpose has dogged it ever since. How do you provide a 'special training for general business' when there isn't one? One of the school's historians, Melvin T. Copeland put the matter in a nutshell: 'for fifty years the *major problem* of the School has been to define and interpret the concept of administration and to apply the concept effectively in instruction'.[29] Copeland could speak with authority: he was the George Baker Emeritus Professor of Administration and had been a member of the school's faculty for all but one of its first fifty years. There is a curious irony about the title he gave to his book: *And Mark an Era: The Story of the Harvard Business School*. The first part is taken from the letter by Lowell quoted above, but Lowell had used it to support his view that a different kind of school should be created. Was Copeland trying to say to his readers, subtly, that the Lowell had been right?

Lowell's efforts would be frustrated in another closely related but more practical way. Throughout its long history, America's success in business and in other walks of life, starting with the Massachusetts Bay Company itself in the 1630s, relied on what this book calls 'integrated decision-making'. This means, among other things, that the same group of people is involved in both making and executing decisions, not to speak of follow-up, which can therefore to be viewed as a continuum. It is clear from his letters that Lowell approached decision-making in precisely this way 'We are trying a great, but, I fear, delicate experiment; and I feel that it would be wise to leave the framing of the plan in the hands of those who originated it and see clearly what they want'.[30]

By 'framing the plan' he meant, of course, taking the first step towards execution. Alas, the originators lost control. One group of people was responsible for making the original decision 'in principle' while another (the unfortunate, successive deans) would be landed with the awful task of working out what it meant in practice. This was a formula that almost guaranteed failure for someone or something. If a member of the faculty of the B-School today set out to prepare a 'case study' about its foundation, he or she would have to conclude that it offered an egregious example of how not to do it. A succession of stopgaps has plugged the hole at the ideological heart of the B-School for the past century. There have been three Big Ideas: Scientific Management, Human Relations and Stockholder Value, together with a host of fads.

Scientific Management came in the form of a course on the supervision of the factory shop-floor. It was the baby of the first dean, Edwin Gay, for whom it was a godsend – otherwise he would not have known what to offer. He invited Taylor to teach it. Taylor declined on the grounds that this particular subject should be taught on the shop-floor, not in a classroom. As Wren tells us, 'Taylor was not against business education but felt that experience was the only way to learn his particular system'.[31] However, when Gay told Taylor that the school was going to teach the course in any case, the latter gave way and lectured there every winter from 1909 until his death in 1915. In sponsoring these lectures, Gay was implicitly (perhaps even explicitly) acknowledging the importance of manufacturing. The picture on page 126 of Ralph Bradley (HBS, 1910) in the overalls of a fireman polishing the pistons of a locomotive belonging to the Wabash Railroad symbolizes this brief flirtation with the real world of business. The management of the factory shop-floor as a subject for study would pass out of favor soon after World War I.

When Wallace Brett Donham succeeded Gay as dean in 1919, he drafted a memorandum in an attempt to give meaning to the expression 'business administration' and circulated it to his colleagues in order to stimulate discussion. This document consisted of a series of questions accompanied by tentative answers. There being no response, presumably because no-one knew what to say, the memorandum became policy by default. Henceforth, the content of each course was to be divided between: 'a. Routine work. Such work is largely repetitive and ordinarily presents few problems requiring the individual judgment of those engaging upon it'; and 'b. Problem work. Generally speaking all business not of a routine nature presents itself in the form of problems.'[32]

This statement requires decoding. For 'routine work' which is 'largely repetitive', it is not difficult to read nearly all of the business of a manufacturing company. What could be more 'routine' or 'ordinarily

repetitive' than mass production? Like Marxists and indeed many others (for example, the economist, Keynes), Donham was assuming that
the problems of manufacturing had been long solved and therefore did
not deserve serious attention. As a point of view, this was, and is, quite
simply wrong. In Great Engine companies of the Golden Age, an
extraordinary amount of attention at all levels of management would
be given to 'routine work which is ordinarily repetitive'. This is because
routines were being continuously revised. It is not surprising that the
B-School's manufacturing department would be allowed to wither
away between the wars. By the 1960s it barely existed, except as an
optional subject – this was precisely when the manufacturing revolution initiated by American engineers in Japan was beginning to make
an impact on the world scene. Japanese managers would become
vitally interested in what Donham described as 'the detailed technique
of particular industries'[33] – as the B-School would also have been if
Lowell had had his way at the outset. The doctrine which underlay
Donham's memorandum ticked away like a time bomb under America's manufacturing base for fifty years. If the nation was able to
become the Arsenal of Democracy in World War II, it was because its
industry and economy was still guided by men possessed of an older
and wiser outlook.

What did Donham put in place of the management of the shop-floor?
The Big Idea that would dominate the school's work between the two
World Wars was an exercise in sociology. In 1926 an Australian, Dr.
Elton Mayo, had joined its faculty with the object of undertaking clinical research into problems of human behavior in industry.[34] In April
1927, together with his academic colleagues, he launched an exercise
aimed at testing the effects of fatigue and monotony on workers' productivity. This became known as the Hawthorne Experiment, after the
name of the Western Electric plant near Chicago where it took place.
The outcome was the vastly over-rated and hugely damaging Human
Relations Movement.

The experiment consisted of four successive studies involving test
groups, each consisting of five or six women. Three of these groups
assembled electric relays, while the fourth split mica. Each group was
segregated in separate 'experimental rooms'. Over a period of time,
alterations were made in working conditions: for example, methods of
wage payment, duration of pauses and the serving of refreshments. As
each change was made, the observers were surprised to find that productivity increased. After eighteen months the original conditions
were restored and productivity increased once more. Copeland tells us

that the experiment was to have 'many ramifying effects on the School's works'. 'From it came new evidence that desire for economic gain is not the only important factor motivating workers and that human relations often outweigh material conditions in problems of administration'.[35] The B-School may have been losing interest in manufacturing in general but it made an exception for human relations on the factory shop-floor. The impact of the movement on business, as well as on society in general, was quite the reverse of early Taylorism. Henceforth it would be assumed that management had to be 'nice' to the workforce in order to make them more productive – did not Hawthorne prove it?

Many aspects of the Hawthorne Experiment have since occasioned disquiet among scholars and others. For example, the credit went to the academics, Mayo, Roethlisberger, W.J. Dickson and H.A. Wright – Mayo for being the senior person involved and the other three for writing the most widely read account – but none of them appears to have been closely involved in its conduct. More serious, we are told that, if the experiment had been written up by Homer Hibarger and George Pennock – the Western Electric executives who did the bulk of the work including the variations in experimental designs and the data gathering – the conclusions would have been significantly different; in particular, the role of monetary incentives would not have been dismissed out of hand as inconsequential in causing increased output.

There is also doubt about the scientific rigor with which the experiment was conducted. For example, the membership of the groups was not constant. In one of the rooms, two indifferent employees were dismissed for talking while working and replaced by two outstandingly good workers, specially selected by the foreman in charge.[36] We are told (but not in the published report) that the new women 'continued to outproduce the rest of the group throughout the remaining 18 months of the study'.[37] Like was not being compared with like. Furthermore, even if the membership of each group had remained the same, was the sample large enough to be scientifically valid? The answer has to be 'no'. It is also doubtful whether the conclusion that 'material gain was not the only factor motivating workers' would have been worth publishing, even if it had been reached by an intellectually rigorous means. We all know that man does not live by bread alone; it appears three times in the Bible. Charles Protzman – one of the three American communications engineers who worked in Japan under General MacArthur and whom we met briefly in Chapter 10 – had worked as a manager at the Hawthorne Works during the experiment; when asked by the authors what he thought of it, he replied 'not much', adding that, if he had been influenced at all by academic work in the field at that time, he would have regarded it as an example of how not to do it.[38] The Hawthorne Experiment was at best pseudo-science and at worst an academic fraud. At its heart lay an abuse of statistics. As Richard Gillespie has told us in his careful analysis of the event and its aftermath: '. . . for all the emphasis on providing a realistic account of the research, [the official account of the Experiment] is a highly stylized rendering of the Hawthorne Experiment and one that has misled generations of social scientists'.[39] The (so-called) Experts were at work.

The movement had two major adverse impacts on the management of American industry. First, as a result of the much-trumpeted need to be 'nice' to the workforce, there was a deterioration in shop-floor discipline. The traditional American line manager had been 'fair' rather than 'nice'. Kenneth Hopper recalls being shown round a General Motors plant in Dayton, Ohio in 1968 by an elderly Scottish foreman with whom he had much in common by way of early industrial experience. The foreman drew his attention to some youthful machine operators who were engaged in conversation while others worked. Of those working he said: 'That is the old school. They have the protestant ethic. There's nothing I can do with the others.' The chatterboxes belonged to the Human Relations generation. Secondly, and even more serious, after World War II, the Human Relations gurus acquired such status and authority that serious debate about management–labor relations was stifled. As Drucker told us, writing in the mid-1950s, 'there is a tendency for [it] to degenerate into mere slogans which become an alibi for having no management policy in respect to the human organization'; worse still, he saw it as a means by which management could try to manipulate the workforce.[40] This hiatus lasted until the late 1970s, when senior Japanese businessmen began to visit America and talk about what they had achieved. It was only then that business academics acknowledged new developments in the field and started to explore and exploit them for their fee-earning capacity.

In fact, academia did not have to look that far. Starting in the late 1920s, a number of leading US companies such as Procter & Gamble, Maytag and Texas Instruments had begun to experiment with practices that would later come to be regarded as 'Japanese' and 'participative'. By 1950, for example, the first of these companies had introduced a procedure called Group Methods Meetings, which would foreshadow the future Japanese Quality Circles. In 1957 a well-known authority from the Human Relations Movement, Professor Frederick Herzberg of Case Western Reserve University, Ohio, called on Arthur Spinanger, co-ordinator of the Group Methods Meetings scheme, at the company's head office in Cincinnati. Spinanger attempted to tell Herzberg what the company was doing in this field but was unable to do so because (in Spinanger's own words) Herzberg was 'too busy giving out to take anything in'. Had academia made itself aware of the pioneering work being done by companies like these and propagated it to the rest of industry (and had presidents Johnson and Nixon not chosen to mount an attack on business capital expenditures – see Chapter 14), America might have enjoyed an Economic Miracle of her own, a generation before the Japanese. By not listening, Herzberg missed a golden opportunity, and not just for himself. Kenneth Hopper would be responsible for introducing the Group Methods Scheme to Procter & Gamble's British plants; Spinanger would later tell him that 'the people in the factories were my teachers' and that the scheme had been 'developed without any input from academics'.[41]

The Human Relations Movement became a vast inverted pyramid sitting on a microscopic and perhaps non-existent pin-head. However, its defects were invisible at that time. It was the Hawthorne Experiment more than anything else that established the reputation of the B-School as an academic institution, enabling it to stand tall alongside Harvard's great graduate schools, Law and Medicine, and preparing the way for the dominant role that business schools in general would play in business and society in the last third of the twentieth century. Andrea Gabor in her *The Capitalist Philosophers: The Geniuses of Modern Times – Their Lives, Times, and Ideas*, tells us that, in this way, the B-School elevated other 'backwater trade schools' offering MBAs to 'academic institutions of international prestige'.[42]

Earl Sasser, the B-School's chair of executive education, told us in 1996 that the mission of the school was 'to research and disseminate new ideas on management'.[43] The trouble with this approach is that there is no particular or lasting merit in being new, if new is not also better. Sadly, one outcome was an unending stream of passing fads; had the faculty members been true academics, they would have spent their time 'puncturing', not sponsoring or perpetuating, them. It was not simply a question of reinventing the wheel; scores of new kinds of wheels were invented and promoted, which worked rather less well than the old and well-tried models, and which were then discarded in favor of the next lot. These fads came from men or women who had never managed anything. They graduated from business schools, became faculty members or joined leading firms of strategic consultants and then wrote books or articles. Amazingly, they were listened to. Let us look briefly at two of their inventions, neither of which qualifies as a Big Idea.

The Boston Matrix was the slick title given to a form of financial analysis developed by a group of graduates of the B-School in the 1960s. It classified companies into four groups: 'Stars', which were companies having a large share of a fast-growing market; 'Cash Cows', or companies having a large share of a slow-growing market; 'Question Marks', being companies having a small share of a fast-growing market; and, finally, 'Dogs' – companies having a small share of a slow-growing market. 'Stars' were there to be sold because they had achieved their potential. 'Cash Cows' existed to be 'milked' and the surplus invested in 'Question Marks', so that these could become 'Stars'. 'Dogs' were there to be liquidated and the proceeds also invested in 'Question Marks'. Not only was this form of analysis simplistic – its very language was deeply offensive. Would you like to be described as a 'Cash Cow', a 'Question Mark' or a 'Dog' – or, for that matter, as a 'Star' if it meant you were going to be disposed of? The worse impact was on the 'Cash Cows'; the 1960s were a time when US industrial equipment was old and required renewal and when competition from imports was increasing. To the extent that it was applied, the Matrix deprived companies of funds that should have been reinvested in new machinery. More generally, it turned companies into commodities to be bought, sold or liquidated – not to be loved and cared for.[44] Mintzberg may have had the Boston Matrix in mind when he asked for 'skulls and crossbones' to be stamped on the forehead of every MBA.

Or take Sensitivity Training. This was fashionable at the B-School in that same decade. An adaptation of group therapy, it had been first developed by Chris Argyris (1923–) at the National Training Laboratories in Bethel, Maine. Group therapy had originated as a psychotherapeutic technique in the Tavistock Institute in London, where it brought comfort to thousands of people who lacked self-confidence. By making participants sensitive to the needs and fears of others, it bonded them together. Argyris is to this day a gently spoken man who simply wished to apply it within a business context. If he did little good, he also did little harm. In the hands of younger members of the faculty at the B-School, however, Sensitivity Training was turned on its head. The future leaders of the world's largest enterprises were encouraged to become 'sensitive' by insulting each other. If you did not like the cut of another man's jib, you told him so, pointedly. This resulted in dramatic classroom sessions. Those who knew how to play the game came out on top; those who did not were humiliated in public. George Odiorne, the highly respected director of the Bureau of Industrial Relations in the University of Michigan, would refer to it as Hostility Training. On one occasion, he made himself highly unpopular at a public meeting by asking questions of representatives of the National Training Laboratories about reports of suicide after – and even during – sessions. Sensitivity Training as practiced at the B-School in this perverted form was the complete opposite of what is required in good management practice. In order to draw the best out of men or women, you have to build their self-confidence, not destroy it. Sadly entertaining accounts of other fads are to be found in *The Witch Doctors* by the editor of the *Economist*, John Micklethwait and Adrian Wooldridge; and also in *The Gold and the Garbage of Management Theories and Prescriptions* by James A. Lee.

Underlying most of the fads and going back to the earliest days of the school was one consistent, unvarying theme, to which we have already referred: that businessmen were essentially money managers and that the primary, and probably the only, purpose of business was the pursuit of profit on behalf of shareholders, among whom senior managers would eventually feature through the grant and exercise of stock options. The importance of this theme to the B-School was symbolized by a glass case standing in the entrance hall to its Baker Library and containing an original copy of Adam Smith's *An Inquiry into the Nature and Cause of the Wealth of Nations*. A notice beside it stated that this was one of the most important books ever written and quoted a well-worn passage: 'It is not from the benevolence of the butcher, the brewer or the baker that we expect our dinner but from their regard to their own interest. We address ourselves not to their humanity but to their self-love.'

This sentence was not balanced by any of Smith's comments about the failings of market economics, such as: 'People of the same trade seldom meet together, even for merriment and diversion, but the conversation ends in a conspiracy against the public . . .', or the even more damning: 'Commerce sinks the courage of mankind. The minds of men are contracted and incapable of elevation.'[45] Adam Smith well understood the importance of self-love as a motivating force for businessmen but, clearly, he did not think that the primary purpose of business activity was to earn a profit for the shareholder – rather he believed that its *only* purpose was to satisfy the consumer. As he put it: 'Consumption is the sole end and purpose of production; and the interest of the producer ought to be attended to only so far as it may be necessary for promoting that of the consumer . . .'. The exhibit, by its selective use of a quotation, constituted a misrepresentation of the views of the great Scottish founder of market economics. It proffered, however, an exact representation of the attitude that was being inculcated into the school's alumni.

Harvard's Puritan founders would have been horrified to discover that the university was being used to promote 'self-love'.

The success of the Great Engine companies in the Golden Age of Management had depended on an unspoken social contract between the various 'stakeholders'. A simple but useful comparison is with the human body; if one member was diseased, the whole could not be well. This outlook would be well expressed in a Statement of Social Responsibility issued as late as 1981 by the Business Roundtable, a group of chief executives of America's 200 largest companies.

> Balancing the shareholders' expectations of maximum return against other priorities is one of the fundamental problems confronting corporate management. The shareholder must receive a good return but the legitimate concerns of other constituencies (customers, employees, communities, suppliers and society at large) also must have the appropriate attention ... [Leading managers believe] that by giving enlightened consideration to balancing the legitimate claims of all its constituents, a corporation will best serve the interest of its shareholders.

As the influence of the graduate business schools permeated the community, however, the doctrine of the primacy of shareholders' interests would come to the fore. By the 1990s, it had acquired a name and a body of theory: Stockholder Value was to be the B-School's third (and last so far) Big Idea. The pioneer was one of its professors, Michael Jensen, the creator of 'agency theory'. In view of the nature of man, he had argued as early as 1976, promoting a kind of economic version of the theological doctrine of original sin, managers could not be trusted to perform their sole function, which was to look after the interests of the shareholders, unless their remuneration was tied to reported corporate income.[46] The approach gathered momentum in the 1980s. A book, *Economic Structure of Corporate Law* written by two University of Chicago lawyers, Frank Easterhouse and Daniel Fischel, and published by Harvard University Press (not the B-School) in 1991, would become its Bible.[47]

The new doctrine became received wisdom in the American financial and business communities, leading the Roundtable to change its tune in 1997 when it announced that:

> [t]he notion that the board must somehow balance the interests of stockholders against the interests of other stakeholders fundamentally misconstrues the role of directors. It is, moreover, an unworkable notion because it would leave the board with no criteria for resolving

conflicts between the interest[s] of stockholders and of other stake-holders or among different groups of stakeholders.[48]

Thus did white become black in less than two decades, without an apology or excuse.

As Ghoshal has pointed out:

> The problem [with management studies] is that, unlike theories in the physical sciences, theories in the social sciences tend to be self-fulfilling. A theory of sub-atomic particles does not change the behaviour of those particles. A management theory, if it gains enough currency, changes the behaviour of managers. Whether right or wrong to begin with, the theory becomes 'true' as the world comes to conform with its doctrine.[49]

If Stockholder Value offered a legal, economic and, by implication, ethical justification for the belief in the primacy of profit, it also provided the intellectual backdrop to the Bubble Economy of the late 1990s, when it would be used to justify personal greed and corporate rapine on a scale not experienced since the late nineteenth century. The Business School Counter-Culture was in full fig.

Needless to say, the doctrine of Stockholder Value is both unsound and pernicious, unless it is watered down (as many writers have done) to a point where it means almost nothing. A shareholder's profit can never be more than a residual – that which is left after *all* other claims on a company have been met. In most jurisdictions the payment of tax comes first, followed by wages, then by the secured debts, then by the unsecured debts – all standing far ahead of the stockholder. By law and custom, therefore, he or she comes last, not first – and that is how it must be if an enterprise is to flourish. Generally speaking, courts of law do not strongly disagree with this point of view; as Professor Lynn Stout has told us 'corporate law has never embraced shareholder primacy with enthusiasm'.[50]

We have already met (see page 73) an early and extreme example of the folly of putting profits first, and one that pre-dated the formal promulgation of the doctrine of Stockholder Value, in the collapse of Penn Central. With the coming of the airlines, the railroads could have phased out the bulk of their unwanted, long-distance passenger business, to concentrate on the two things they did best: the carriage of freight and of commuters. The development of piggy-backing and roll-on/roll-off vehicles opened up the possibility of integrating freight transportation by rail, road, sea and (eventually) air into one system, all the units being owned in a lightly regulated private sector and with prices set by supply and demand. An outcome of this kind would also have been an environmentalists' dream, the massive discharge of noxious elements into the atmosphere that results from long-distance freight haulage by road being avoided since fuel accounts for only 9 per cent of rail transport costs, as against 40 per cent for trucks. Today only 16 per cent of US freight is carried by rail.[51]

Meantime, the railroads could have continued to carry passengers for short distances, only cheaper, faster and better. Indeed, if trains traveled smoothly at speeds approaching 200 miles an hour, as they do in Europe[52] and Japan, it would even make sense for Americans to travel up to 1,000 miles at a time by rail. Lunch or dinner on a train can be a pleasant experience, unlike eating on a plane. Furthermore, when flying is unavoidable, fast trains are often the best way of traveling from city centers to airports. Today, the inhabitants of Shanghai can cover the twenty-one miles to Pudong International Airport[53] in eight minutes in a super-clean, magnetic levitation train straight out of *Star Trek*;[54] by way of contrast, it can take up to an hour for a New Yorker to cover the fifteen miles to Kennedy Airport in a ramshackle cab. China plans to build nearly 20,000 miles of new railroad track before 2020.[55] The completion of the Qinghai-Tibet railway in 2006 is an engineering feat comparable with that of the US transcontinental route in 1869 or of Isambard Kingdom Brunel's London to Bristol line in 1849 – the last still known as 'Brunel's billiard table' because of its smooth gradients.

Faced with these outstanding opportunities, as fine as any that existed a hundred years before, the American railroad industry quite simply crumbled. Why? Historians lay the blame on over-regulation, government interference and the power of the labor unions. There is justification for all three of these explanations. There was, however, a fourth element that cannot be overlooked: the failure of management to spot the opportunity open to it, let alone to grasp it. In the 1950s, the bigger railroads were in tolerable financial condition, as a result of the heavy traffic they had carried during war-time; their leaders enjoyed high public esteem; they could have co-operated with the airlines to present their vision for the future of transport to Congress and backed it with money as other lobbies did. As a result of this lapse, both highways and railroads are today severely congested, wasting everyone's time and impeding the 'just-in-time' revolution by obliging manufacturers to maintain far larger inventories than would otherwise be necessary.

Why did this failure of management occur? Part of the blame must lie with the new and heretical ideas about the nature and purpose of management, which are one of the subject matters of this book. Until then, companies had been run essentially by practitioners who knew their businesses inside out, most of whom had spent their entire lives in one industry and, as often as not, in one company. They had a high respect for technology as a tool, even if they were not themselves technologists. They were 'company men' who regarded the stock market with suspicion, or even hostility, as little more than a gambling den. They saw themselves as playing roles integral to the successful functioning of continuing enterprises, which were in turn essential to the well-being of society.

By way of contrast, the new generation of senior managers that came to power, in a very few companies as early as in the late 1950s, took a quite different view of things. Often accountants or business school graduates, they looked at the companies that they ran primarily in financial terms. As such, they identified themselves with the shareholders rather than with the other employees, regarding the companies' divisions, and even the company itself, as commodities to be bought and sold like a pound of sugar or a loaf of bread. Far from regarding the stock market as a gambling den, they saw it as the supreme arbiter of value. The typical, trendy new organization of the period was called the 'conglomerate' – a holding company that bought and 're-structured' other companies (which usually meant firing a quarter of the staff) then reselling them, if possible at a profit. Not all senior managers followed this line; if they had, economic activity would have ground to a halt; someone has to create the wealth that others exchange. However, enough followed it to give the epoch its characteristic flavor. Typical early conglomerates were Litton Industries, Gulf & Western and WR Grace & Co., in the last of which William Hopper worked as a financial analyst in Hanover Square, New York, from 1957 until 1959.

The mighty Pennsylvania Railroad, the first in time of our Great Engine companies, fell victim to this new fashion. In the 1960s, it was run by two men: a lawyer, Stuart Saunders, who was chief executive, and David Bevan (HBS, 1931), who was chief financial officer. Bevan was only the second officer of that rank to have been appointed from outside the company; he was also among the earliest of the business school alumni to make a distinctive mark on the way business was done. Neither of these men being interested in running a railroad, they valued the Pennsy only as a vehicle for obtaining credit for the purpose of diversification into other businesses, particularly speculation in real estate in the Sun Belt. Thus they disposed of the profitable Norfolk & Western and the unprofitable Long Island lines. Saunders never concealed his scorn for railroads – Milton Sharp, a future governor of Pennsylvania, tells us:

I've been to several parties with him where he had a few drinks, and he was always talking about Litton Industries and how Litton and other conglomerates had cash and were putting it to good use, getting good returns. He said he wanted to keep the money for real estate investments instead of putting it in the f—g railroad.[56]

In the 1960s, Saunders acquired the New York Central, bringing together two companies which controlled most of the rail traffic between New York, Pittsburgh and Chicago. This may seem an odd move for someone who wanted to get out of the railroad business but there was a perverse logic to it: he thought he was acquiring additional borrowing power to fund his diversification into property. However, the outcome of the merger was disaster. Although it had been under consideration for over a decade, neither side had properly planned for it. The differing cultures of the two companies clashed. Saunders fell out with Bevan and both with their opposite numbers from the former New York Central. Trains would be misplaced for days in a manner that would have driven Daniel McCallum to distraction (see page 70). Major customers were upset, Allied Chemical moving its freight traffic onto the highways.[57] Eventually, the money ran out and the dividend was cut.

At 5.35 p.m. on Sunday, June 21, 1970, the Penn Central filed for bankruptcy before US District Judge William Kraft Jr., in the City of Brotherly Love that William Penn had founded three centuries before. It was the biggest financial failure in American history; Penn Central was not even a good conglomerate.[58] Other American railroads went into a decline, if not quite so dramatically. In the autumn of 2004, the industry would have difficulty coping with a bumper grain harvest, owing to decades of neglect of its rolling stock and infrastructure. This was when Roger Nober, chairman of the industry's regulatory body, the Surface Transportation Board, told us that '21st century freight flows' were being fitted into 'a 19th century rail network'. He explained how an employee in a wooden shack at the Brighton Park intersection, a few miles south of central Chicago, shifted levers by hand, using flaps on three wooden poles to give the all-clear to trains that linked the nation from coast to coast, adding: 'This is hardly what you would expect of the world's mightiest rail network'.[59] Or take the case of BNSF, one of the largest railroad operators in the USA today: 4 per cent of its 'flagship line' between Chicago and Los Angeles is single-tracked![60] Imagine the problems that would arise for road traffic if 4 per cent of the Interstate Highway System was constricted in this way.

It was not only old industries which were affected. By the 1950s the Radio Corporation of America had come to dominate video and audio markets worldwide. In the 1960s, however, it succumbed to fashion by making acquisitions in various unrelated industries, including rental cars and hotels. By 1970, this strategy of conglomeration had destroyed the enterprise and, with it, the entire American electronics industry, creating a void which the ever nimble Japanese would fill. As Chandler has told us in his book, Inventing the Electronic Century, *'[s]uch a swift creation and destruction of one national industry... in markets worldwide is unparalleled in world history.'[61]*

The triumph of the Business School Counter-Culture led to the rejection of all of our Principles underlying Good Managerial Practice, either directly or – because of the 'house of cards effect' (see page 102) – indirectly across almost the whole of business. Classic 'integrated decision-making', as practiced since the 'plantation' of Massachusetts, disintegrated into reaching conclusions 'in principle' before all the implications had been worked out in detail. Collegiality was succeeded by the worship of the all-powerful or 'imperial' chief executive. Remuneration ceased to reward group effort, as highly subjective 'performance-related pay' took over. Fear replaced trust. The literate, numerate, 'rounded' and 'generalist' manager of the Great Engine companies was replaced by one who saw himself or herself, primarily, to quote Stanley Marcus, as a money manager. 'Bottom-up' became 'top-down'. Consultants were no longer 'on tap' – they were 'on top'. Senior managers no longer started near the bottom and worked their way up; they started half-way up. The traditional middle manager was no longer 'the keystone to the managerial arch' (see page 101) – he became disposable. Vulgar ostentation replaced the quiet understatedness of the old-fashioned, Puritan 'New England Company' and its imitators throughout the land. The company, and much else besides, became dysfunctional.

It is important to have a clear understanding of what the authors mean by certain terms. In this book the expression 'generalist' (always in quotation marks) is used to designate a person who genuinely possesses those skills of general management (chiefly but not only to do with handling people) that are required in any organization whatsoever, whether it be a manufacturing or service company, a government department or a charity. 'Rounded' means that the person has worked in many or most of the departments or activities of the organization in question or in another one in a similar sector; in becoming 'rounded', such people acquire a profound understanding of the sector in which they work – now known in the current jargon as 'domain knowledge'. Taken together, these terms go a long way towards describing the typical chief executive of a Great Engine company of the mid-twentieth century – and, by extension, all good managers everywhere. In contrast, the term 'professional' (also always in quotation marks) designates a manager – often, but not necessarily, a business school graduate or accountant – who is neither 'rounded' nor 'generalist', lacks 'domain knowledge' and sees the world of business, or indeed any world, essentially in statistical and financial terms.

The business schools had to fail in their original, ostensible and honorable purpose, which was to create competent and honest managers. Managing can be learned only by working under a skilled practitioner in a non-academic setting and by observing and copying what he or she does. This view is not unique to the authors. Half a century ago, it was implied by the word 'practice' in the title of Drucker's book, *The Practice of Management*. Today, it is expounded by many percipient observers, including an ever-increasing number of dissident business school professors. Russell L. Ackoff, for example, tells us that the best way to learn is 'on the job, preferably in an apprenticeship relationship'.[62] While there is a certain amount of theory associated with any craft, it is infinitesimal compared with the theory (not to speak of the body of knowledge) underlying, say, medicine, law or physics. One can usefully spend years or even decades studying properly academic subjects; all the theory and knowledge underlying the craft of management can be taught in a few days and compressed into a dozen pages – as we have done in the Appendix. Furthermore, it is not necessary to learn the theory in order to master the practice, although it may help if someone has to be persuaded to 'unlearn' bad habits or if a set of practices is being 'transplanted' from one country to another.

In the last chapter we explained how the Cult of the (so-called) Expert undermined the first four of our enduring characteristics of American society: a desire in some sense to create the Kingdom of Heaven on Earth, an aptitude for the exercise of mechanical skills, a specific moral outlook on life subordinating the interests of the individual to the group, and organizational ability. The fifth enduring characteristic of American managerial culture, which we defined in Chapter 4 as an interest in technology and a respect for technologist, would also be affected. We added that this outcome was paradoxical since Taylor, ultimately the founder of the Cult, was a distinguished technologist.

To understand how American businessmen fell out of love with technology, we have to take a step back and look at the subject in a wider context. Broadly speaking, the world divides itself into two blocs from this point of view. On the one hand, there is a group of countries that were heavily influenced by the political and ideological earthquake known as the French Revolution; they comprise most of continental Europe and the former Communist Bloc including Russia and China. In these, interest in technology and respect for the technologist became deeply engrained in society long ago and remains so to this day, to the extent that the ex-communist states are now largely run by engineers. On the other hand, there is the 'Anglosphere' – chiefly Britain, the United States, and the old 'dominions' of the Commonwealth, on which the shattering events of 1789 made a fairly light impact – thanks in large part to Admiral Nelson and his enlightened approach to the management of the British fleet (see page 107). In the early nineteenth century, however, businessmen in the young Republic took an interest in technology not so much for ideological reasons as because it played to their pragmatic, Puritan hands-on approach – it provided them with additional tools. It follows that, in the United States, it lacked the deep intellectual and social roots that it possessed, for example, in France; and that it was therefore vulnerable to an assault.

The survival of 'imperial measure' 300 years after America was decolonized symbolizes the failure of technology to penetrate the fabric of society. Countries which came directly under the influence of the French Revolution decimalized their weights and measures long ago. Like Britain and Canada, most of the countries of the Anglosphere have done so recently, if sometimes in a half-hearted fashion. Today the United States stands alone in seeking to measure everyday objects and events in quasi-medieval terms of miles, yards, feet and inches, pounds and ounces, gallons and pints, not to speak of degrees Fahrenheit. This presents no great problem (and some comfort) for the ordinary citizen but sets difficulties for the nation's scientists and engineers, who cannot avoid using the decimal system in their calculations. It is at the point where 'imperial' meets 'metric' that inefficiencies arise, as in the incident already reported on page 162, when a NASA spacecraft missed Mars because some of its engineers worked in one, and some in the other, measure. When part of the foam covering of the fuel tank of the space shuttle *Discovery* broke off in 2005, the space agency made the curious announcement that the offending item 'weighed 0.9 pounds'. Are ounces about to go out of fashion?

The assault on technology and the technologist came from the business schools after World War II and took three forms. The first was social; an MBA from a top business school was believed to, and did, confer on young men and women a short cut to wealth, prestige and influence. Who would want to be a graduate engineer on call for twenty-four hours a day, seven days a week, in a factory in a remote town in Ohio, if he or she could attend a business school, join a consultancy firm in Boston or an investment bank in New York and earn ten times as much? The second attack was intellectual in nature. In any battle between explicit and implicit concepts and practices, the former will tend to drive out the latter. The managerial culture of the mid-twentieth century had been consciously and deliberately created by the business leaders whom we have met in this book. However, by the end of World War II, its origins had long been lost in the mists of time and even the best practitioners regarded its methodology as 'just how things are done'. As Drucker remarked, there was little writing on the subject and no understanding of its importance. Into this intellectual void, the professors and alumni of the business schools could pour their nostrums. In an ideological equivalent of Gresham's Law, the currency of managerial thought became debased as bad information drove out good. This book has been written, among other things, to give a voice to the men who, over the period of a century and a half, created and ran America's Great Engines of Growth and Prosperity, in the belief and expectation that good principles and practices, made explicit, will drive out bad.

The third attack was academic; the new approach carried with it the stamp of Harvard, the most famous university in the world. It appeared to many people – wrongly, of course – that the B-School was serving up the secrets of America's *past* industrial success. This illusion was particularly strong in Britain which, conscious of the failings of its own industrial economy, would embrace the new Counter-Culture with a kind of haphazard fervor, founding both the London and Manchester Business Schools in 1965, and then many others of lesser standing, more or less on the model of Harvard. This development was sustained by the illusion that, as Mitchell J. Larson has explained, management schools could do for Britain what American business schools were believed to have done for the United States.[63] Needless to say, none of these new institutions did anything to enhance Britain's economic performance. There is a sad irony in the fact that, after World War II, America offered her loyal ally an academic wooden spoon, while she conveyed to her defeated enemy, the Japanese, a thorough indoctrination in the traditional practices of good management that would allow them to initiate a third Industrial Revolution.

There has, however, been a delayed impact on Japan. Although business schools have played no significant role *within* that country, the malign Cult of the (so-called) Expert would spread there – in part, because of globalization and, in part, because so many of the brightest young Japanese men and women would enrol in American schools. Even before the 1990s, there was a loss of interest on the part of many senior Japanese managers in what Donham called 'the detailed technique of various industries'. Today some of the best-known names in Japanese manufacturing – Sony, Hitachi, Mitsubishi, Matsushita, Paloma (a maker of water heaters), even the great Toyota itself – are in trouble with customers or regulators because of a decline in the quality of the goods that they make. In the turbine of one nuclear plant built by Hitachi, 146 out of 840 blades would be found to be defective.[64] All of which explains why Masaharu Matsushita decided to republish Sarasohn's and Protzman's CCS Manual in 1993 (see page 124) and send a copy to every one of his managers.

What should America do with her business schools? It is important that someone ask again the kind of question that was debated a century ago, when the first ones were being founded, and, again, fifty years ago by the Carnegie and Ford Foundations. What is their purpose? How is it to be achieved? Who is to achieve it? One possibility would be to revert to Lowell's concept of the 'trade' school, like law and medicine. In a limited sense, this has already occurred, but for one industry only, namely: investment banking including money management. Today's leading business schools are, *de facto,* places where young men and women go to learn these skills. The dean of the B-School who was appointed in April 2006, Jay Light, although a physicist by training, is described as 'an expert in investment management'.[65] As Glenn Hubbard, current dean of Columbia Business School has told us, 'Wall Street would not exist as it does today but for the pioneering work of business schools in financial economics'.[66] Another, and perhaps more realistic, option is for the schools to act more like military staff colleges, providing a general course of learning for thirty-year-olds who have worked their way up from the junior to the middle ranks and are thought to have potential for further advancement; candidates would be referred, and paid for, by their employers and enjoy an academic 'career break'. The attention of such people will have been narrowly focused on their companies' business; they would undoubtedly perform better if their outlook was broadened and if they also had an opportunity to meet their opposite numbers from other companies, industries and countries.

If the business schools do not sort themselves out soon, the iron law of the market-place will do it for them. All over America, employers are asking themselves if a thorough in-house training is not both a cheaper and a better preparation for their aspiring managers than a business school degree. According to Edward A. Snyder, dean of the University of Chicago's Graduate School of Business, '[t]his [shift] is fundamental, not cyclical – hiring non-MBAs is something companies have become more comfortable with'. Even the leading investment bank, Goldman Sachs, has changed course; in 2000, it altered the ratio of MBAs to non-MBAs among new hires from 75/25 to 25/75.[67] If employers are unwilling to reward alumni and alumnae for the extra-ordinary amount of money and time they have to spend on procuring their qualification, the schools will wither away.

14

Impact of the Cult on Society

As we have seen, neo-Taylorism, in the form of the Cult of the (so-called) Expert, exercised a powerful, *direct* and negative effect on America's Great Engines of Growth and Prosperity in the second half of the twentieth century, the year 1958 marking a watershed, since that was when two of the largest 'blue-chip' companies, General Electric and General Motors, appointed chairmen belonging to the new breed of 'professional' managers – 'finance guys', as they were known in Detroit. The Golden Age of American Management was by no means over, but decay was in the air. Simultaneously, the Cult exercised a powerful, *indirect* and negative effect on corporate behavior through its impact on the social and economic environment in which the Great Engines had their being – for example, on education, health, the military and on the administration of the monetary and fiscal systems. The influence of the Cult on society in general was of long standing, being traceable back to Taylor's own lifetime; it is impossible to do justice to it in one short chapter. Let us, however, like Little Jack Horner, pull a few plums out of this pie, in the hope that others will be tempted to expand on the themes that emerge.

The First Plum – War and the (So-called) Experts

Anyone who doubts whether the Cult of the (so-called) Expert really affected the nature of American society is urged to read General Colin Powell's fascinating autobiography, *My American Journey* (1995). Like Maryann Keller's *Rude Awakening: The Rise, Fall and Struggle for Recovery of GM* (1989), from which we quote at length in Chapter 12, Powell's book provides an almost clinical examination of its impact on a major section of national life. Curiously, neither even mentions Taylorism.

When he was a young officer in Germany in the 1950s, Powell was subjected to rule by number. He tells us in graphic detail how he bettered every benchmark by which his brigade was judged – and then went on to do 'the things that I thought counted', which by implication had little or nothing to do with statistics:

If for example you are going to judge me on AWOL rates, I'm going to send a sergeant out by 6.30 a.m. to bloodhound the kid who failed to show up for 6.00 a.m. reveille. The guy's not considered to be AWOL until midnight. So drag him back before then and keep the AWOL rate down.[1]

As a result: 'Like the children of Lake Wobegon, everybody came out "above average". The powers that be seemed to believe that by manipulating words, we could change the truth. We had lost touch with reality.'[2] Powell was referring to Garrison Keillor's famous satirical remark, about the children in the imaginary Minnesota town of Lake Wobegon, which highlights the intellectually most absurd aspect of the age of our (so-called) Experts: everyone was expected to be, statistically, above average.

With the appointment of Robert McNamara as secretary of defense in 1961, even the making of strategy became neo-Taylorized. McNamara was an HBS graduate and had been a junior member of the school's faculty. During World War II, an extension of Scientific Management known as Operations Research or OR had been developed by the British to assist with the detection of enemy aircraft by radar. It would be adopted by the American military and used for the same purpose. McNamara was a member of the American OR team. When the war was over, he accepted an invitation to join others of the 'Whiz Kids' (as the team was called) at the Ford Motor Company. It is sometimes said that the Kids introduced OR to Ford but this is doubtful; OR is a highly sophisticated mathematical technique of limited applicability in manufacturing.

McNamara stayed at Ford for just short of fifteen years, becoming president or number two to the chairman, Henry Ford II, in November 1960. Different sources give wildly differing accounts of his performance there. At the one extreme, Jean-Jacques Servan-Schreiber tells us that he 'revolutionized the automobile industry'.[3] Others attribute Ford's post-war revival to him, drawing attention, in particular, to the success of the compact Falcon, which procured him the presidency and which later became the basis for the sporty Mustang, the original version of which is still driven by thousands of enthusiasts. Yet others in a position to know say that he 'destroyed' the company. Since he was president for less than two months, both extreme views are probably wrong – he did not have the opportunity to make his mark. The same cannot be said of his next appointment.

Appointed secretary of defense on January 3, 1961, McNamara ran the Vietnam War according to the quantitative precepts of Scientific Management. Like Taylor, he needed input and output numerators, a military equivalent of work units. What did he use? Powell provides the answer: 'The Army, under Pentagon pressure to justify the country's invest- ment in lives and billions (*sic*), desperately needed something to measure. What military objectives could we claim in this week's situa- tion report? A hill? A valley? A hamlet? Rarely. Consequently bodies became the measure.'[4] 'Our' dead was the input, 'theirs' was the output. Thus was Scientific Management reduced to both inanity and inhuman- ity – the 'body count' may convey something about the relative costs of war but, as Powell reminds us, it tells us nothing about strategic or tacti- cal advantages gained or lost as a result of incurring them. Another absurd yardstick was the number of 'secure hamlets' in existence – a hamlet being rated as 'secure' when it had a 'certain number of feet of fencing around it, a militia to guard it, and a militia chief who had not been killed by the Viet Cong in the last three weeks'.[5]

It was the doctrine of the body count that led to the appalling massacre of 128 peasants at My Lai on March 16, 1968.[6] Professional solders left to their own devices have no interest in killing for its own sake; indeed, they seek to minimize casualities on both sides; McNamara's 'grisly yard- stick' had turned both tactics and ethics on their head, at terrible cost to both America and her enemies. Competition for bodies among compa- nies, battalions and brigades became the norm. 'Good' commanders scored high – and got promoted. There may have been scores of My Lais – this one came to light owing to the moral courage of one US soldier, Hugh Thompson Jnr, and the determination of a single investigative journalist, Seymour M. Hersh, who won a Pulitzer Prize for his efforts.[7] Fortunately, some of the dafter yardsticks were never utilized – for exam- ple, the urine count. McNamara's new team of Whiz Kids had conceived of a device called the 'people sniffer', which was intended to identify the units of the enemy army by detecting concentrations of urine on the ground from an airplane. If it had been adopted, it is not difficult to visu- alize an artillery barrage killing another 128 unfortunate villagers whose only fault had been to urinate in a common latrine.[8]

Powell recalls how, on one occasion, McNamara – after a stay of only forty-eight hours in Vietnam – had concluded that 'every quantitative measure that we have shows that we are winning the war'. The ex- general comments drily: 'Measure it and it has meaning. Measure it and it is real. Yet nothing I had witnessed in the A Shau Valley indicated we were beating the Viet Cong. Beating them? Most of the time we could not even find them. McNamara's slide-rule commandos had devised precise indices to measure the unmeasurable.'[9]

The Special Commendation to the 11th Infantry Brigade under Lt. William L. Calley Jr. for the My Lai massacre on March 16, 1968 exemplified another aspect of military life under the influence of the Cult of the (so-called) Expert: a military equivalent of credentialism ruled.[10] 'Awards were piled on to a point where writing the justifying citations became a minor art form.' People got new titles for no reason at all: 'Shake-and-bake sergeants we called them. Take a private, give him a little training, shake him once or twice and pronounce him an NCO.'[11]

In Vietnam, as elsewhere, quantification was damaging for two reasons. First, there was the '(missed) opportunity cost': millions of hours of valuable managerial and non-managerial time were wasted. Secondly, and far more important, it led to deeply wrong decisions of all kinds. The wrong people were promoted. Wrong conclusions were reached. The wrong outcome was achieved. Vast numbers of lives (over 50,000 of them American) were squandered and Vietnam's movement to democracy and capitalism delayed by thirty years. Eventually, as David Halberstam tells us in *The Best and the Brightest*, even President Johnson realized that 'slide rules and the computers did not work'.[12] He kicked Secretary McNamara upstairs, making him president of the World Bank, a position which he held from 1968 to 1981.

The principal originator of the Vietnam War had been McGeorge Bundy, head of John Kennedy's and then Lyndon Johnson's National Security Council from 1961 to 1966. An intellectually brilliant man who had the ear of both presidents, he suffered from one major defect: he lacked 'domain knowledge' (see page 266) of South-East Asia. There was only one organization in the federal government that could be said to possess that kind of knowledge: the State Department. By drawing power away from Foggy Bottom to the White House, Bundy prevented the diplomats from playing their proper role in the determination, or moderation, of foreign policy and launched the United States on one of the biggest disasters in its history. An absence of 'domain knowledge' among decision makers would be one of the more obvious attributes of our (so-called) Experts; this applied every bit as much in government as in the corporate sector.[13]

Economic data published by the US government may sometimes be of dubious value but it is usually streets ahead of similar data produced by the governments of developing nations. Discovering that McNamara treated the latter as 'gospel',[14] his new subordinates at the bank quickly learned to play to his weakness, securing approval for their favorite projects with the help of specious statistics. In this way the upward flow of accurate information was impeded, exactly as it had been in Vietnam. McNamara's major contribution to the elimination of poverty worldwide was supposed to be his 'integrated rural development project'; by the end of the 1970s, this had ended in failure.[15] The

Cult of the (so-called) Expert had notched up another victim – or perhaps we should say, billions of victims. It is hardly surprising that,
today, of the sixty-six less-developed nations that have received money
from the Bank for more than twenty-five years, thirty-seven are said to
be no better off in economic terms than they were at the outset, twenty
are worse off and eight have economies that have shrunk by more than
a quarter.[16]

In World War II, the armed forces had been run by General George C.
Marshall in a quite different manner. It is of the essence of good management in any organization at any time that accurate information is
encouraged to flow rapidly upwards, sideways and downwards *but above
all upwards*. Marshall always insisted that his subordinates give him bad
news as soon as it arrived; he would not be upset, he said – he reserved
his feelings for Mrs. Marshall. Marshall was the archetypal Puritan –
austere in his private morals, deeply religious, never swearing or allowing dirty stories to be told in his presence, hard working – and a superb
organizer and leader of men. President Roosevelt once addressed him
by his first name; Marshall allowed his displeasure to be known and the
president did not try again. It was Marshall who told us that 'military
power wins battles but spiritual power wins wars'.[17] His principles were
reversed in Vietnam where the structure of the armed forces was geared
to passing statistical *dis*information up the line of command, as a result
of tacit collusion between originators and recipients. Neo-Taylorism was
one of the principal reasons for America's defeat in Vietnam; it also
explains partly why the World Bank failed to alleviate poverty in the
Third World in the 1970s and after.

McNamara possessed a soul-mate in Sherman Kent (1903–1985), the
'Father' of the present-day US intelligence community, who argued
that intelligence analysis needed an approach 'much like the method
of the physical sciences'. It was because of Kent and people like him
that the Central Intelligence Agency came to rely on computer-
tapping statisticians sitting at desks in Washington, DC who spoke no
foreign languages, rather than on agents in the field.[18] Kent is best
known today for the report he issued on September 19, 1962, stating
that the Soviets were unlikely to introduce strategic weapons into Cuba
– just one month before they were found to have done so.[19] His outlook
infects American intelligence agencies to this day.

The Iraq War (2003–) fits into the ideological framework described
by this book in two contrasting ways. When President George W. Bush
speaks on this subject, it is not hard to hear at least a distorted echo of
the voice of John Winthrop echoing down the centuries and telling us
that Massachusetts was to be a model for succeeding 'plantations', so

that men would say that the Lord had made them 'like that of New England'. Winthrop was, of course, thinking only of settlements in the New World, which were to be 'planted' by people like himself. It was Thomas Jefferson who widened the vision to include other nations, writing that the great American experiment would be extended to the rest of the world: 'to some parts sooner, to others later, but finally to all'.[20] However, this aspirational approach to international politics remained largely a matter of rhetoric until President Reagan turned the members of his Republican Party into Jeffersonian internationalists with a speech at the Palace of Westminster in London in 1982. George W. Bush's war put this point of view into practice.

On the other hand, the bungling execution of the war belonged strictly to the contemporary Cult of the (so-called) Expert. The Occupation of Japan in the 1940s and 1950s was a success; the Occupation of Iraq has (so far) been a failure. Why the difference? The answer lies in the quality of the planning and execution. The earlier event was characterized by brilliant decision-making undertaken by two great generals, Marshall and MacArthur. At a conference organized in Washington, DC in January 2005 and designed to teach soldiers and others lessons from this war, it was disclosed – amazingly – that no contingency planning had taken place in the Pentagon against the case that Saddam Hussein's regime would collapse when attacked.[21] All of which opens up another interesting area of speculation: would the Iraq War have taken place if proper decision-making procedures had been in place before it was initiated? It is probable that wiser counsels emanating from the State Department and its head, the good ex-soldier Powell, would have prevailed.

There is a strong resemblance between the recent secretary of defense, Donald Rumsfeld, and the occupant of that post during the Vietnam War, Robert McNamara. Both had 'boundless egos' and 'a taste for slicked back hair, rimless glasses and high tech warfare'.[22] Both were ex-business school professors whose approach was brutal, quantitative and 'top-down'. The younger man shared McNamara's obsession with statistics, which he demonstrated by declaring that 'we lack metrics to know if we are winning or losing the global war on terror. Are we capturing, killing or deterring and dissuading more terrorists every day than the madrasses and the radical clerics are recruiting, training and deploying against us?'[23] The awful shadow of McNamara's body count screams through.

On the very morning of September 11, 2001, by a supreme irony, even as terrorists were attacking the World Trade Center, newspapers carried an account of a speech by Rumsfeld calling for a massive campaign to cut costs at the Pentagon. 'I have never seen an organization which couldn't save 5 per cent of its budget', he said.[24] Half a century before, Henry Singleton – the brilliant founder and president of Teledyne Inc, a leading manufacturer of electronic instrumentation – said the last word on this subject in a sentence that should be engraved on the wall of every boardroom: 'any idiot can cut costs'. As a general rule, you can tell that a proposal to cut costs is arbitrary, and therefore foolish, if it is expressed as a multiple of 5 per cent, including 5 per cent. In his speech, Rumsfeld also proposed the 'out-sourcing' of cleaning and warehouse management, suggesting a lack of concern about security in the US defense establishment.

The Second Plum – Education and the (So-called) Experts

One can divide up the history of American education into at least three great phases. The first may be called the Age of the Common School and lasted for just over two centuries, from the introduction of compulsory education in Massachusetts in 1647 to, say, 1850. During this period, the Puritan inhabitants of the north-eastern colonies or states attained a high degree of literacy and numeracy. As already noted in Chapter 4, the quality of education offered in the common schools would greatly impress visitors from Europe, being considered by them a condition precedent for the emergence of the American System of Manufactures in the first half of the nineteenth century, which led directly to the Second (or American) Industrial Revolution in the second.

During the fifty years from 1850 to 1900, the existing school systems of the various states struggled hard to cope with the children of a new illiterate, innumerate working class, arriving from less-developed lands. By the end of the century, however, victory was in sight. As Raymond E. Callahan, Professor of Education at Washington University, St Louis, told us in his stimulating book, *Education and the Cult of Efficiency* (1966), and speaking now of the whole country:

> Any white American with ability and a willingness to work could get a good education and even professional training. The schools were far from perfect, of course: teachers were inadequately prepared, classrooms were overcrowded, school buildings and equipment were inadequate, and the education of Negroes had been neglected. But the basic institutional framework for a noble conception of education had been created. Free public schools, from the kindergarten through the university, had been established.[25]

Victory was achieved largely by tough Victorian schoolmarms teaching oversize classes and ruling them with supreme firmness. This complex phase may be referred to as the Age of Mass Migration. New immigrants were taught English – but they were also taught many other things; as late as 1910, half of all students in high schools learned Latin;[26] this subject in itself may or may not have been important or relevant to the needs of the pupils but the fact that it was taught at all indicates that *both their minds and their memories were being trained.* When education passes beyond the three Rs, its importance lies as much in the training of the mental faculties that results, as in what is being taught.

Victory, however, was turned to defeat in the succeeding decades under the influence of a new generation of educational administrators, who believed that schoolrooms were akin to factory floors. One of the earliest to write on this subject classified teachers as 'managers' and pupils as 'workmen'. His views, however, would be superseded by those of a certain Joseph Taylor (no relation of Frederick's), district superintendent of schools in New York City and one of the most influential people in the field of education before World War I. Believing that 'the teacher does not always understand the science of education',[27] this arrogant man reclassified the mostly male administrators like himself as 'managers' and the mostly female teaching body as 'workmen', the pupils presumably becoming 'work-in-progress' on an academic assembly line. A new 'profession' was born; the third phase, starting around 1900 and lasting to this day, may be called the Age of the Administrator.

There is a parallel between the advent of the 'professional' school administrators before World War I and of the new 'professional' corporate managers after World War II; both were expressions of the Cult of the (so-called) Expert. Like managing, teaching is best seen as a craft. The only proper way to learn it is 'on the job', under the supervision of an experienced practitioner, as teachers did in earlier times. While the subject matter that a high-school teacher conveys to his or her pupils (English, Latin, mathematics, physics and so on) can, and should, be formally acquired in a college, the *method of imparting it* is a different kettle of fish. Lowell doubted the value of 'any special training for general business' (see page 170); one can as easily doubt the value of 'any special training for general pedagogy'. Just as the new business schools put together a ragbag of courses of incidental interest to businessmen, so the new colleges of education put together one of incidental interest to the nation's future teachers and administrators, creating intellectually worthless paper qualifications of considerable commercial value, since they were the key to secure, reasonably well-paid employment accompanied (later) by free healthcare, with a taxpayer-supported pension at the end.

Significantly, Taylor-the-administrator referred to education as a 'science'; inevitably, the new class of men whom he sponsored and represented wanted the progress of pupils to be measured *quantitatively*. Elaborate questionnaires were drawn up to provide for the supposedly 'objective' evaluations. One has only to look at the documents in question, however, to realize that there was little objectivity in them. One form, drawn up for pupils to complete about themselves, offered, amongst others, the following credits: 5 per cent for enjoying school work; 2 per cent for sleeping with at least one window open; 3 per cent for attending and enjoying church; and (unaccountably) 2 per cent for 'loafing in the streets'.[28] This would have been funny if it had not been proposed in all seriousness by the reformers. Similar forms would be prepared for assessing the progress of teachers, janitors – and of administrators themselves. This absurd approach would spread beyond the high schools into all parts of American education, including the universities. College students would be awarded credits for attending courses, even if they slept through them. Professors would be rated according to the number of books published or articles contributed to specialist journals, even if no-one read them. Institutions would be rated according to the number of PhDs they employed, so long as the subject matter of their theses was broadly in the right area. As at General Motors (see page 143), the raw data – and, with it, the underlying reality – were being horribly manipulated.

The assault by the Scientific Managers on education would be renewed in the second half of the twentieth century, the factory once again providing the model. An influential article that appeared in *Fortune* in 1958, 'The low productivity of the education industry', told us that schools were no different from General Motors, since their job was 'to optimize the number of students and to minimize the in-put of man-hours and capital'. Whereas productivity per head had increased in the steel and other industries, it had fallen in education. The author did not seem to know what to do about this problem – so he proposed calling in management consultants![29]

The ultimate achievement of the quantifiers was SAT, which originally meant Scholastic Aptitude Test[30] but is now described simply as a 'brand name' for a controversial examination which, by the early 1960s, had become the standard hurdle for admission to the country's prime universities. SAT had been promoted by Henry Chauncey, a man who 'loved everything about testing' and frequently tested himself; the victim of an unhappy home life, he had even thought of testing couples statistically for compatibility in marriage. The motivation behind SAT may have been excellent: it was intended to provide a level playing field, opening up the universities to talent from all social classes and ethnic groups – but it ended up as the white middle class's best friend. As Richard Caldwell has told us, 'across big populations, SAT scores track income, exactly ...'. SAT is all about examination technique, not knowledge or intelligence; a better name for it would be Statistical Achievement Test. The long-gone Victorian schoolmarms would be horrified if they could see what the administrators have done to the great-grandchildren of their well-taught pupils.[31]

Flawed in concept, the system must work badly in practice. In 2002, one of the largest companies operating in this field, Pearson Educational Measurement, settled a major lawsuit over errors in scoring 8,000 tests, which prevented hundreds of high-school seniors from graduating; it then made significant scoring errors in Washington and Oregon, after which it assured the world that it had improved its methodology. In March 2006, however, there were another 4,000 significant scoring errors in Texas. According to Bruce J. Poch, dean of admissions at Pomona College in Claremont, California: 'It looks like they hired the people who used to do the books for Enron'.[32] The sad thing is that the errors turned up because of complaints by students; it is shocking and lamentable that, as Marilee Jones, dean of admissions of the Massachussets Institute of Technology has told us, there is no 'fail-safe' in the system to inform the examiners when something is going wrong.[33] One also wonders about the outcome for students who lack the self-confidence, or the social skills, required to question their results; are they to be numbered in hundreds or thousands or more? (In Britain, which has followed a similar path, 17,500 grades had to be revised in the summer of 2005 following protests from pupils – and there was a massive repeat performance in 2008.)[34]

Meanwhile, credentialism (the award of largely meaningless certificates – see page 134) became the order of the day in the world of education as well as in business and other walks of life. Here is a telling observation from Callahan's book, referring to the year 1966 when it was published: 'In too many instances standards for getting into and out of the institutions which prepare teachers (both public and private, graduate and undergraduate) are so low that it is possible for almost anyone to qualify to teach our children'.[35] In the subsequent forty years, there has been (if possible) a further deterioration. Some years ago, a teacher known to the authors sought promotion in a north-eastern state. She was required to take an evening course in order to secure an additional credit. When the course was complete, the class was invited by her teacher to play a well-known board game. When she protested, she was told that the teacher was obliged to test the class before issuing a credit. Since he was unable to think of any suitable way of doing so, he had proposed this stratagem. The candidate played the game, in both the literal and metaphorical sense, secured the necessary credential and was promoted. Her advancement had nothing to do with her undoubted merit. Another friend of the authors has two sons who performed miserably in a mathematics SAT paper. After eight two-hour sessions of intensive coaching, they were able to pass it with flying colors. As their father says, 'you have to fool the system'. Yet another friend failed to secure admittance to a leading business school on the basis of a similar kind of test; when he re-applied, accompanying his submission with an essay written with the help of a highly paid consultant, he was admitted.

Credentialism has been accompanied by 'grade inflation', which means that, in any one year, students receive better marks than they would have had in an earlier year for the same performance; consequently the qualification is progressively devalued. We are now speaking of the whole range of education. For example, in 2001 at Harvard, 'more than half the grades were A's, while 90% of the seniors graduated with honors' – far more, by way of contrast, than in the 1980s.[36] 'Grade inflation', by the way, can also be described as 'grade compression',[37] since nearly everyone is squeezed upwards into one category. This approach makes life much easier for the academics, who do not have to agonize over whether a student is an A, B, C or D; they can therefore give more time to research, which is more interesting, and to consultancy, which is more profitable. However, it makes life more difficult for future employers, for whom the examination results no longer serve as a useful signal. In 2002, the then-president of Harvard proposed a compromise with the creation of A+ and A++ grades.[38] One is reminded of the arbitrary way in which General Motors altered its 'pass mark' for cars from 60 to 100 so that none of its factories need lose face – see page 143. It would appear that anything less than an A grade is now considered to be insulting to a student, an attitude of mind that turns a B mark from a perfectly respectable result (which it was) into a mark of failure.

In addition to administrators, the Cult of the (so-called) Expert spawned another class of person in the world of pedagogy – academic authority figures known as educationalists, of whom the greatest by far in terms of influence was John Dewey (1859–1952), a man who promoted something called Progressive Education. Believing, bizarrely, that the need for literacy was declining as society became more advanced and that teaching children of six or seven years to read and write was dangerous because it 'cripples rather than furthers later intellectual development', Dewey added a fatal twist to the downward spiral in standards of American schooling:[39] he made 'dumbing down' respectable. According to Diane Ravitch, now the holder of the Brown Chair in Education Research at Brookings Institution, Dewey has, more than anyone else, been responsible for the anti-intellectual bias in contemporary American high schools. She also tells us that 'If we are to have a chance of reclaiming our schools as centers of learning, we must understand how they came to be the way they are';[40] this is a general approach with which the authors are in sympathy – indeed, it is one which has inspired the writing of *The Puritan Gift*. Deweyism has permeated and distorted the outlook of public school teachers throughout the English-speaking world. Increasingly, British private schools are turning away from the debased Anglo-American style of examination towards the tougher, international test offered in the English language by the International Baccalaureate Organization in Geneva.[41] More and more British families are sending their children to be educated in France. Significantly, almost one-third of teachers in New York City's public school system educate their children privately.[42]

At what point did the triumph of the administrators and educationalists reach a point where it was seriously damaging to the intellectual health of American society and therefore, indirectly, to business? Anecdotal evidence would point to some time in the 1970s. As late as the 1960s, for example, a poor boy named William Jefferson Clinton could receive a first-class education in a small town called Hope in the remote and impoverished state of Arkansas, which included instruction in Latin and mathematics and which enabled him to shoot right up through the ranks to become forty-second president of the United States.[43] It was in the next decade that the book *Summerhill* by the British author, A.S. Neil – one of the sacred texts of Progressive Education – became 'required reading' at hundreds of American universities, selling 200,000 copies. Charles Protzman III, grandson of one of our Three Wise Men, recalls standards being formally and deliberately lowered in his high school, Baltimore Polytechnic (not a tertiary educational institution like other bodies bearing that name) in the late 1970s to bring them into line with other local high schools – 'dumbing down' when an exercise in 'dumbing up' was needed.

By 1982, the deterioration had become so scandalous that a Republican administration set up a National Commission on Excellence in Education to take account of 'the widespread public perception that something is seriously remiss in our educational system'.[44] (At the risk of sounding pedantic, one is tempted to observe that this statement was self-proving; people may be remiss or negligent, not systems.) The federal government's National Assessment of Adult Literacy, conducted in 2003, showed that fewer than one-third of American college students were 'proficient' in terms of literacy, as defined by the ability to read and understand lengthy passages of prose; this figure compared with 40 per cent in 1992.[45] The root of the problem lay at the primary and secondary levels. An example will serve to illustrate the point: in its glory days almost a century ago, the Frederick Douglass High School in Baltimore was able to launch the grandson of a slave, Thurgood Marshall, on a career that ended on the bench of the Supreme Court. Today, according to the *Washington Post*, it is 'an educational disaster area' in which only 16 per cent of the students can pass an English proficiency test, while the corresponding pass rates for geometry and biology are 3 per cent and 1 per cent.[46] At the other end of the educational and social scale, according to Peter Beinart of the *New Republic,* graduates emerge from Harvard 'without the kind of core knowledge you would expect from a good high school student'.[47]

The collapse of standards in the public schools is one of the factors behind the 'home-schooling' movement, the other being Bible-based Christianity; home-schoolers wish their children to be well-educated in a healthy, spiritual environment. Something like 2 million American children – more than the entire school population of New Jersey – are now being educated at home, or in small groups, by their parents – one product being Jimmy Wales, the founder of the amazing open-source *Wikipedia*, which has eight times as many entries as the *Encyclopaedia Britannica*.[48] Acting collectively, some home-schooling families have also created the Patrick Henry College in Virginia, described by its director, Michael Farris, as 'a refuge from sex, drugs and rock 'n' roll. Well, at least sex and drugs'.[49] One of its courses teaches that, aside from the abomination of slavery, the society of early New England was 'nearly ideal'.[50]

The weaknesses in the entire system became obvious in the late 1980s when computer software firms in Silicon Valley firms found it impossible to recruit employees of the required standard. What did they do? They imported thousands of superbly educated and technically trained Asians; by July 25, 2001, 138,000 H1-B visas had been issued to Asians, more than half of them for entry into high-tech employment.[51] Such was the influx that a part of Sunnyvale in California became known as Gandhinagar – Gandhi Town. Once settled, the newcomers experienced little difficulty in outshining the native sons and daughters. In the last third of the twentieth century, over half the start-ups in the Valley were led or co-led by entrepreneurs born in India or China.

The co-founder of Sun Microsystems, Vinod Khosla, is a case in point; a graduate in electrical engineering from the Indian Institute of Technology, he is today a partner of Kleiner, Perkins, Caufield & Byers, one of Silicon Valley's leading firms of venture capitalists.[52] Most remarkable of all is the fact that one-third of NASA's employees are today of Indian origin[53] and that 'about 30 per cent of IBM's scientists and engineers come from Asia, mainly from India and China'.[54] Meantime, while thousands of foreigners throng to America's surviving, excellent 'polytechnics' (including, of course, the relevant departments of many universities), most young Americans neglect technology in favor of 'soft' subjects, such as management, the media, education and social sciences or 'hard' but non-productive subjects like the law. According to the Natural Science Foundation, only 6 per cent of twenty-four-year-old American graduates in 2002 had taken degrees in natural sciences or engineering, far fewer than in any other developed country except Switzerland. No wonder Scott McNealy, Khosla's partner at Sun Microsystems, has written that 'America's policy-makers would be well-advised to explore ways . . . to revive the US education system'.[55]

The Third Plum – Capital Expenditure and the (So-called) Experts

The Vietnam War led directly to massive inflation in the United States, which the Johnson and Nixon administrations blamed (wrongly) on rising capital spending by businessmen. The outcome was a campaign undertaken in the late 1960s and early 1970s by the White House and the US Treasury to force companies to spend less. This approach was unjustified by circumstances and to this day all Americans suffer from its consequences. This section tells the 'inside story' of these events, which has never appeared in print before; it will provide yet another illustration of the folly of misusing statistics – in this case through culpably misunderstanding them.

By the 1960s, American industrial equipment had grown very old. There was more than one reason for this state of affairs. During the depression years of the 1930s, the equipment had not been renewed – unsurprising, since there was massive over-capacity and, in any case, the cash flow required to fund new capital investment was simply not there. Then, during World War II, the extraordinary achievements of American manufacturers alluded to in Chapter 9 were accomplished largely by bringing disused equipment back into use. In any case, all of the nation's financial, human and material resources were required to fight the war, so none would have been available for renewing equipment, had anyone wanted to do so.

Immediately after World War II, there was heavy demand for everything that US manufacturers could produce, coming simultaneously from a home market starved of goods during the 1930s depression and the war years of the early 1940s, as well as from overseas countries whose economies had been wrecked by war. Just as important, there were no foreign imports to light a competitive fire under businessmen. It followed that there *seemed* to be no need to renew equipment. It was only when Japanese and German manufacturers started to penetrate the domestic market in the late 1950s that the truth came home to businessmen: their plants were thoroughly out-of-date. Obligingly, the Kennedy Administration enacted a 7 per cent investment tax credit in 1962. Thereafter, business capital expenditures rose at an accelerating rate to meet the competition. The great self-adjusting mechanism at the heart of American capitalist society was asserting itself.

It was then that President Johnson pulled a dirty trick. In a magazine article published in June 1966,[56] he blamed business capital expenditures for the loss in the value of the dollar, adding that he had instructed government departments to postpone making investments and asking businessmen to do likewise. This seed fell on stony ground; the need for new equipment in the corporate sector was too pressing for its leaders to heed his request. The Nixon administration (1969–1974) pursued the same objective. The new treasury secretary, David M. Kennedy, made a speech only a few weeks into his appointment that would be reported in the *New York Times* of March 15, 1969 under the headline:

BRAKING OF BOOM
IS PLEDGED BY U.S.
Treasury Chief, 'Disturbed'
By Plant Outlays, Calls the
Administration Resolute[57]

On April 6, another article in the same newspaper told us that President Kennedy's 7 per cent investment tax credit could be repealed or even replaced by a 10 per cent surcharge; and interest rates could be raised. 'If a business cannot borrow at all ...', the writer went on grimly, 'investment will be slowed'.[58]

On April 26, an article in *Business Week* quoted 'Washington economists' as saying that 'businessmen have all but thrown away the rule book when it comes to installing plants'. It also referred to a McGraw-Hill survey which showed that: 'companies plan to spend $72.4 billion for new plant and equipment this year – up 13% from 1968 outlays – and have made prelimnary plans to spend $75.5 billion in 1972'.[59] The administration now did, indeed, prove itself to be 'resolute'. President Kennedy's investment tax credit was repealed in the Tax Reform Act of 1969, to the accompaniment of a public relations fanfare that sent a ringing message to the corporate sector: capital investment was *bad*, so stop it. American business executives find it hard to resist for long a call to patriotic action (or inaction) by a Republican president, particularly when it is backed by a fierce fiscal deterrent. The ratio of business investment to gross domestic product dropped from 10.6 per cent in 1969 to 10.2 per cent in 1970 and 9.8 per cent in 1971; it would fall lower still by the middle of the decade. There was no commercial or economic justification for this reduction, which was achieved in spite of surging corporate cash flows, a situation that would not repeat itself for forty years.[60]

Statistics being produced by Washington's advisers purported to show that American plant and equipment was remarkably young. The idea that inflationary pressures caused by the war could be offset by reducing 'excessive' business capital expenditure without raising taxation proved irresistible to both Presidents Johnson and Nixon. However, it is unlikely that they would have behaved as they did, had they appreciated how old American industrial equipment really was. *They were, quite simply, misinformed by their economic advisers, who told them that the average age of industrial equipment was just over six years.* This figure was derived from Revenue Bulletin F, which contained the tables used for calculating depreciation allowances.[61] For 1965, the permitted annual write-off was 15 per cent – i.e., equipment was depreciated in just under seven years. The advisors had assumed that capital equipment was scrapped when depreciated to zero for tax purposes.

It is not as if America's industrial plant was buried in a deep vault in the Rockies; the Middle West was already turning into a rustbelt. Relying on unsystematic observations and conversations with managers of many different kinds of factory, Kenneth Hopper is prepared to guess that the average age of US industrial equipment at that time was twenty-five years – a view shared by Harold Barger, the outstandingly able Professor of Economics at Columbia. Inevitably, foreigners took their lead from the government's statisticians; in 1967, a report by the Organization for European Cooperation and Development, *Engineering Industries in North America, Europe and Japan*, stated that, in American metalworking industries, 'equipment is constantly renewed'. As a result, the US government's economists inflicted not one but two wounds on the domestic corporate sector. The misinformation that they generated led the Johnson and Nixon administrations to kybosh new capital investment at home; while, simultaneously, it encouraged manufacturers abroad to install the very latest equipment – becoming even more competitive with American manufacturers than they already were.

The belief that American equipment was new had been popularized in Jean-Jacques Servan-Schreiber's best-selling book, *The American Challenge*. First published in English in 1968, it told how America's manufacturing industry would soon dominate the entire world, to the extent of becoming a kind of second government in Europe. This idea had been derived from a speech delivered by Robert McNamara at Millsaps College in Jackson, Mississippi.[62] Both the talk and the book told the utter reverse of the truth; only three years later, America's international trade in manufactured goods would go into deficit for the first time since 1888; the US was losing the title of 'workshop of the world', which it had inherited from Britain a century before.

The slow turn of the intellectual tide began on July 27, 1970, when the knowledgeable editor of the *American Machinist*, Anderson Ashburn, published Special Report No. 644 by Kenneth Hopper entitled 'Can the U.S. Stay Competitive?'. It contained an analysis of the misunderstandings surrounding the Department of Commerce figures and included a comprehensive international comparison drawing attention to the excessive age of equipment in American industry; the low American investment ratio; the need to increase capital expenditure and savings; and the existence of investment incentives in other countries. It also questioned the validity of the industrial capacity/utilization statistics. Economists had argued that the move to a service economy relieved the US of the need to invest so much. The Hopper report warned that this was a dangerous argument, since the kind of service industry that did not need much investment would also not offer good paying jobs. For good measure, it questioned whether the kind of education offered by business schools had helped manufacturing and drew attention to the effective programs of technical training that were widespread in Europe. It suggested that an inadequately increasing gross national product threatened the standard of living of the rapidly growing pool of American workers, which would make it difficult to integrate disadvantaged minorities into the community. Everything that the document predicted would come to pass within a generation.[63] Kenneth Hopper circulated his report widely to leading economists and other figures in government and received many favorable responses. There was an almost immediate cessation in calls for a reduction in new investment by industry.

The general American press paid no attention to this report but the ever-alert Japanese seized hold of it. *Nikkei Business*, the Japanese equivalent of *BusinessWeek*, published a translation of the complete article.[64] The Japanese public was becoming better informed about the nature of US industrial problems than were the Americans themselves. In June 1971, however, the *American Machinist* returned to the subject by publishing several new articles on the same themes. This time the issue was noticed by the *Wall Street Journal*, which made it the central feature of a front-page news story under the dramatic headline: 'Dead Last and Losing Ground'. This was the first substantial article in a major US daily newspaper about the dire straits in which American manufacturing then found itself.[65] However, there would be no public confession of error by the US government. Then, on August 15, 1971, it managed to slip its trousers up without anyone noticing; on that day, buried among world-shaking economic proposals, for ever after known as the Nixon Shock (which finally abolished the Gold Standard), was the announcement of a new 10 per cent investment tax credit. It was barely two years since the earlier, more modest, measure had been repealed by the same administration.

It was too late. The back of the investment boom had already been well and truly broken. Businessmen had gone off on another tack: 'financial' – not mechanical – engineering became the order of the day. In 1975 an American Council for Capital Formation was formed but it also would make little impact. This may be because there were still Respectable Professors of the Dismal Science (the designation that Thomas Carlyle gave to economists) who suffered from the delusion that the nation's manufacturing equipment was new. As late as November 1977, Roger E. Brinner, senior economist at the highly regarded Data Resources, Inc., told the world in a document published by the US government that: 'it is often argued that the current capital stock is unusually old ... such claims are mistaken. The average age of the capital stock is currently quite low: 6.6 years.'[66] He went on to quote a Department of Commerce source to the effect that the average life of US manufacturing equipment (as opposed to infrastructure) had been only 4.6 years in 1965; the correct figure for 1977 was certainly in excess of thirty years.

It was only in 1979 that full national recognition was given to the problem of underinvestment. The annual report of the Council of Economic Advisors in that year sang a new song. There was a detailed discussion about the benefit that increased capital expenditures would bring to the nation and of how that worthy objective could be achieved. It included a table showing the decline in the ratio of investment to gross national product that had taken place in the early 1970s. In that same year the Joint Economic Committee of Congress issued a celebrated document that described the recent growth in productivity as 'dismal', compared the level of domestic capital investment unfavorably with levels abroad and called for a vast increase at home. It was the first time that the committee had issued an unanimous report. In the early 1980s American industry in general began to re-equip on a massive scale, a generation too late; the battle with foreign imports of high-quality goods had already been lost.

The Fourth Plum – Economic Policy and the (So-called) Experts

You will not find any references to neo-Taylorism in the published works of the late Milton Friedman, who was the prophet of monetarism, the doctrine that dominated national economic policy for twenty years from the early 1970s until the early 1990s – the period of economic decline that we will document in Chapter 15. Nevertheless, it is difficult to treat monetarism as anything but an application of Scientific Management to the field of economics. If this is so, we have to put Keynes' famous maxim about 'the ideas of economists and political philosophers' and 'practical men' into reverse (see page 132). Keynes assumed that ideas flowed in one direction only – from academics to 'practical men'. Although he lectured briefly at the B-School in the second decade of the last century, Taylor was unquestionably one of the 'practical men', Friedman a professor at the University of Chicago.

Before monetarism appeared on the scene, the prevailing philosophy had been Keynesian. Keynes had assumed that economies could and should be managed by political leaders. Indeed, the Keynesian economic state bore a distinct resemblance to the 'line-and-staff' structure of a US corporation of the Golden Age. The 'line manager' was the US Treasury, which funded the civil service (which in turn spent over 30 per cent of national income) and shaped the rest of the economy by fiscal measures. A 'staff' function was undertaken by the Federal Reserve System, which was responsible for monetary (or interest rate) policy and which, at least informally, reported to the Treasury – just as the 'staff' departments reported to the 'line' in a corporation. The weakness in the system was, as everyone knows, that it led to 'stop-go'; politicians seeking electoral advantage would over-expand the economy, to a point where the Federal Reserve System felt obliged to intervene by raising interest rates to minimize the consequent inflation. One of America's greatest central bankers, William Chesney Martin, Jr. had no doubt at all about his role; it was 'taking away the punchbowl just as the party is getting good'.[67]

Both 'go' and 'stop' were bad for business and for the economy. The expansionary periods resulting in excessive capital expenditure, which imposed a burden in rising interest costs and in other ways on companies and, through them, on consumers; while 'stop' caused widespread bankruptcies among incautious or unlucky businessmen. The in-built bias towards higher interest rates also led to a higher value for the dollar in the international exchanges than would otherwise have been necessary, which in turn damaged exporting industries. As Robert Chote has reminded us, countries with independent central banks have deeper recessions (although fewer in number) than countries which do not.[68] Central bank independence is justified on the grounds that the bankers are instinctively conservative and not subject to short-term political temptations.

Monetarism sought to provide a solution. It made its first appearance in Friedman's *Studies in the Quantity Theory of Money* in 1956 and was developed in a series of other books, particularly *Monetary History of the United States 1867–1960*, published in 1963, in which his co-author, Anna Schwartz, and he contended that the Great Depression of the 1930s was the result of the ill-conceived policies of the Federal Reserve. The publication of *Monetary History* was timely, if unfortunate. No-one apart from economic historians had been particularly interested in quantity of money theories in the inflation-free Eisenhower years (1953 to 1961). However, the severe inflation of the Johnson and Nixon presidencies (1963 to 1974) was just beginning when the book appeared.[69] The causes and control of inflation were about to move to the front of the political stage. Friedman emerged from the wings with his cure-all in hand – a so-called 'money supply' rule: if the Federal Reserve Board increased the supply of money at the same rate at which real gross national product increased, inflation would disappear – and, with it, the unemployment that resulted from conventional methods of attempting to correct it. Thus, while monetarism started off as a method of controlling inflation, it became *de facto* a method of ensuring the healthy growth of the whole economy.

In the purely monetarist model of the state, the responsibility for the control of the economy was entirely removed from the Treasury. Just as Taylor had lost confidence in the efficacy of the classical line-of-command in a manufacturing company, so the monetarists lacked confidence in the ability of politicians to manage the economy. 'Tinkering' and 'fine tuning' became terms of abuse hurled by them at Keynesian demand managers whose 'seat of the pants' approach was to be replaced by something allegedly more rigorous and 'scientific'. As good neo-Taylorites (although they did not know it), monetarists believed that the control of the economy should be left to apolitical experts, not to inexpert politicians.

To whom was this role assigned? Why, of course, to the very people who had exercised the above-mentioned 'staff' function, the central bankers. They became the equivalent of Taylor's eight 'functional foremen' and of the white-coated efficiency experts who still flitted around many factory floors, stop-watch in hand. Inevitably, the monetarists believed that control had to be exercised by a *quantitative* means. The numerator which they selected, equivalent to Taylor's work units (see page 75), General Motors' defects per 100 cars (see page

143) and McNamara's body count (see page 192), was to be nothing less than the old greenback itself, the amount of money in circulation. The monetarists were reviving old 'quantity of money' theories and applying them in a novel way.

The same difficulty arose with monetarism as with other versions of neo-Taylorism. It was never quite clear how the numerator was to be defined – was it to be M0, a narrow definition referring only to the total of all physical currency in circulation, plus accounts at the central bank which could be exchanged for physical currency; or a broader one like M1, M2, M3 or M4, which includes other items, like the balances in bank accounts?[70] And, not surprisingly, the same temptation to 'fudge' arose; the authorities would learn to massage statistics or even manipulate events so as to sidestep a discipline they had imposed upon themselves, just like the 'finance guys' at General Motors or the US army in Vietnam. As the economist, Marilyn Strathern, has told us, 'when a measure has become a target, it ceases to be a good measure' – which means, of course, that it ceases to be a good target, if it ever was. Professor Strathern was re-stating more generally Goodhart's Law, which tells us that 'any observed statistical regularity will tend to collapse once pressure is placed upon it for control purposes'. Very clever people (which does not include the authors of this book) will tell you that Strathern and Goodhart were offering us an analogue to Heisenberg's 'Uncertainly Principle' in quantum mechanics: 'measuring a system disturbs it'.[71] If measures are not to be treated as 'targets', how can statistics be put to fruitful use in economic policy-making? The answer is to treat them as an invaluable source of evidence, to be balanced against common sense, logic and also the all-important anecdotal knowledge, which is the primary source of information for all human beings about the world they live in.

The *World Economic Outlook* published by the International Monetary Fund in 1996 contained what the economic journalist, Anatole Kaletsky, called 'a spectacular recantation' of monetarism. As a theory, it had been weighed in the balance and found wanting. Like other expressions of neo-Taylorism, it had to fail in the United States because the richness and complexity of social, or even economic, behavior cannot be properly or totally captured in simplistic, quantitative terms. (In Kaletsky's view, monetarism is also responsible for Europe's recent current crisis of mass unemployment.)[72] John Kay has rightly satirized the more extreme members of Friedman's Chicago school of monetary economists by pointing out that, if they were true to the logic of their position, they 'would get married to derive economies of scale in household production and commit suicide when the net present value of future utility [became] non-positive . . .'[73]

Alan Greenspan was until early 2006 chairman of the Federal Reserve Board. An 'imperial', 'top-down', 'celebrity', 'chief executive' who uncollegiately wrote the minutes of meetings that he chaired before they started,[74] he was the archdruid of the Cult of the (so-called) Expert in its economic policy manifestation. By keeping 'real' interest rates (i.e. nominal rates, net of inflation) negative in his final three years of office (2003–2006), he encouraged citizens, corporations and government bodies to 'blow' their savings and go mindlessly into debt in a way that is both contrary to Puritan tradition and dangerous to society. One of the most mysterious as well as influential men of his day in American public life, his outlook also reflected his adherence to a second Cult – that of the novelist, Ayn Rand, who 'shaped him as a young man into a libertarian',[75] and whose best-known work, *Atlas Shrugged*, has been described as 'the second most influential book for Americans today', according to a joint survey by the Library of Congress and the Book of the Month Club.[76]

What is the nature of the book that has displaced Smiles' *Self-Help* and Alger's stories about Ragged Dick in the place of supreme honor at America's bedside? Rand's 'philosophy' is called Objectivism; it rejects not only religious belief but also altruism, which it defines as the claim that 'morality consists of living for others or for society'. John Galt, the hero of *Atlas Shrugged*, sums up his outlook in this way: 'I swear by my life and my love of it that I will never live for the sake of another man, nor ask another man to live for mine'.[77] The Objectivist rejects outright the third of our quartet of traditional American characteristics (a moral outlook that subordinated the interests of the individual to the group), envisaging man as a heroic but essentially solitary economic being, 'with his own happiness as the moral purpose of his life, with productive achievement as his noblest activity and reason as his only absolute'.[78] Greenspan admires above all else the *laissez-faire* capitalism of mid-nineteenth-century America before the launching of the US dollar as the national currency (1863); the enactment of anti-trust laws (1890); the establishment of the Federal Reserve as the central bank (1913) and of the Securities and Exchange Commission (1933); and the abandonment of the Gold Standard (in two stages, 1933 and 1971).

How did Greenspan justify holding the chairmanship of the Fed when, in his heart, he disapproved of its very being? According to an article in the *Wall Street Journal*:

> Mr Greenspan has a complicated way of reconciling his job with his economic theories. In an ideal world, he believes, there would be a gold standard and no central bank. But the end of the gold standard and creation of the Fed weakened market discipline. That created a

need for government intervention [which] the Fed chairman must do his best to fulfill.[79]

Weirdly, government intervention is required to offset itself. If Greenspan was not an altruist and had no wish to serve his fellow men, why did he accept the relatively low salary of a public servant? The former chairman's intellectual beliefs and practices were shot through with internal contradictions. The teachings of Ayn Rand amount to a total rejection of America's Puritan past.

Monetary irresponsibility is today matched by fiscal irresponsibility as one deficit is piled on another. If present trends continue, one can foresee – to quote Adam Posen, Senior Fellow at the Institute for International Economics in Washington, DC – 'the US economy following the path to extended decline of the British economy in the 1960s and 1970s and of Japan in the 1990s'.[80] Economic theory is today in such disarray that academics are unable to provide practitioners (that is to say, everyone else) with authoritative guidance on how to improve matters. As the late and very great economist, Robert L. Heilbroner and his colleague, William Milberg, once told us, economists have lost their concern for the social and political implications of their work, seeing themselves solely as sophisticated mathematicians or statistical analysts[81] – a pessimistic view shared even by an elderly and somewhat reformed Friedman, who told us that '[t]he use of quantity of money as a target has not been a success'.[82] However, there was no apology from him to the nation for the harm that a foolish policy had done. According to Paul de Grauwe, a professor at the University of London, the attempt to place economics on a 'scientific' basis means that many central bankers – by implication, most – live in 'a fairytale world'.[83]

The Fifth Plum: Medicine and the (So-called) Experts

Medicine has not escaped the influence of the Cult of the (so-called) Expert – indeed, it represents the single, most neo-Taylorized aspect of American society. The impact is most obvious in the organization and management of hospitals, a subject about which little of worth has yet been written by anyone.

To describe the well-managed 'blue-chip' American manufacturing companies of the mid-twentieth century, we coined the term, 'Great Engines of Growth and Prosperity'. An appropriate name for the equivalent institution in the field of medicine would be 'the Nightingale Hospital', so-called because it was organized along lines first laid down by the Lady with the Lamp in London a hundred years before. The backbone of these hospitals was a 'line-and-staff' system, the principal, largely male, line-of-command consisting of physicians and surgeons and headed by the registrar or senior physician. (Because titles varied from hospital to hospital in the US, we use the terminology with which the Lady was familiar.) These gentlemen were supported by two 'staff' departments, one largely female and headed by the matron, which was responsible for nursing care in the widest sense; and the other headed by the almoner or treasurer, which collected the income and paid the bills. Each of these departments contained its own, miniature line-of-command. The matron's line was simple; it led down to the ward sisters (the term 'sister' being borrowed from religious orders), each of whom managed, as the name implied, one or more hospital wards. In Toyota-speak, the wards were, collectively, the *gemba*, the real place, the place where value was created.

It was of the essence of the Nightingale system that every task was assigned to one person so that, if something went wrong, it was possible to pinpoint responsibility. As the Lady liked to say, someone had to be *in charge*. Conceptually simple but subtle in its *modus operandi*, the system would be imported wholesale into the American hospitals in the 1860s and 1870s, not long after the doctrine of line-and-staff had been formally promulgated by the mighty Pennsylvania Railroad (see page 71); management theorizing and its application were in fashion. The first American woman to receive a nursing diploma was Linda Richards, who graduated on October 1, 1873 from the New England Hospital for Women and Children. In 1877 she studied under Nightingale in England and Scotland. Today her diploma, nurse's cap and school pin can be viewed in the Smithsonian Institution in Washington, DC.[84]

In the Nightingale Hospital, the management of what is now called the 'core competences' was strictly in the hands of medically qualified men and women – both physicians and nurses. In the post-Nightingale world after 1970, however, responsibility would be increasingly entrusted to a new breed of medically *un*qualified, 'professional' managers remote from the ward floor and difficult to distinguish from the 'number-crunchers' who were beginning to occupy senior management positions in large companies. Today, the American College of Health Care Executives (always known, even by itself, as ACHE) lists 25,378 members who possess, between them, 21,885 masters' degrees – 69 per cent in 'hospital administration', or a similar non-subject, and 24 per cent in business administration.[85] Interestingly, it does not bother to record how many are medically qualified, which suggests that few (perhaps 5 per cent) are – although one or two well-known hospitals continue to appoint physicians as chief executives. It follows that important decisions of an essentially medical nature are being made by people not qualified to do so, i.e. without 'domain knowledge'. Our Eighteenth Principle underlying Good Managerial Practice (see page 286) has not just been violated, it is being raped. The messy business of actually treating the sick has been assigned to medically qualified specialists subordinate to 'professional' (i.e. financial) masters. It is not clear whether it is even appropriate to continue to talk about a line-and-staff structure.

At the same time, the relationships prevailing *among doctors* has changed. In the Nightingale Hospital, a senior doctor had been expected to share the benefit of his knowledge and experience with his subordinates. Under the new arrangements, based on the assumption that medicine is a 'marketplace', and that individuals – not institutions – are the 'players' in it, information represents a valuable asset to be hoarded, bought or sold. Consequently, senior doctors in many hospitals become reluctant to share their expensively acquired knowledge and experience with a younger generation of thrusting competitors. The principal victim of these developments is, inevitably, the patient. Previously, junior doctors had treated the simpler cases, while passing the more difficult ones up the line, so that the *best doctors treated the sickest patients*, while sharing their knowledge and experience with their subordinates. As a result of the replacement of the dynamics of the traditional medical hierarchy with those of the auction house, the *best doctors now treat the richest patients* – often for quite trivial complaints, that could have been as easily handled by junior colleagues. Meantime, the latter treat serious diseases in poorer patients, for which they are less well-equipped. The application of simplistic market theory to medical practice has resulted in a serious misallocation of resources. In line with this development, it is now deemed correct to refer to patients as 'clients', although 'customer' would be a better word, given that treatment is regarded as a commodity to be bought and sold.

The collapse of the physicians' hierarchy has been paralleled by that of the nurses. The matron had managed much of the Nightingale Hospital through the 'generalist' ward sisters, who supervised cleaning, catering and much else besides, in addition to carrying on their more obviously medical duties. As an implied but important part of their duties – and like the 'middle managers' in a Great Engine companies (see page 282) – the sisters also ensured that relevant information flowed easily upwards to the matron, and beyond her, to the senior physician and the Board of Trustees; downwards to the nurses and other employees; and sideways to others of equivalent rank. All of our

Twenty-five Principles (and not just the Eighteenth) of Good Management were being scrupulously observed. It was as if Nightingale had discovered these Principles for herself – which, in a sense, she had. For her, nursing meant a great deal more than sticking needles into people. Her nurses were responsible for ensuring that the whole person was taken care of: body, mind and spirit, cleanliness being next to godliness.

The ward sisters were an early casualty of neo-Taylorization; in the faddish theorizing of 1980s America, 'middle managers' were deemed to be superfluous because they were believed (absurdly) to constitute a barrier between top and bottom. The easy flow of information in all directions vanished. Principle Seven – 'one person, one boss' (see page 282) – could no longer be observed, there being no wise superior on whose shoulder the ward nurses could lean or cry. Matron, now renamed the director of nursing, was too remote for that purpose. From that time on, 'generalist' management disappeared from the hospital ward, no single person being responsible for supervising all activities carried on in it. Functions like cleaning and catering were 'out-sourced' to independent companies, where they could be monitored only loosely, if at all, by the hospital's non-medical executives.

A new generation of educators even taught that nurses were above performing certain undignified tasks that an earlier generation had taken for granted, like bottom-wiping. This development greatly offended one retired nurse, Alice C. Ream, who complained in 1982 about nurses who spent 'an inadequate time caring for patients'. Her scorn was also directed at academics who objected to nurses acting as:

> ... handmaidens to physicians. They are, for some unknown reason, ashamed of being nurses. Ashamed of bathing the sick? How else does one check for skin turgor, rashes and ulceration? Ashamed of handling excreta? How else does one arrive at first hand knowledge of ... intestinal bleeding? Not willing to carry a food tray? How does one assess the patient's appetite and potential need for supplemental nourishment? ... When some of those nurses who can't measure up in a hospital reach burnout, they return to college, get another degree and become professors of nursing. One can only shudder at the thought of what their students will face one day.[86]

One senses Nurse Ream's contempt for the creeping 'credentialism' – known as 'credentialing' in nursing circles – which was affecting hospital life – another sign that the Cult ruled. A malign combination of neo-Taylorism with feminism ensures that no-one performs the traditional womanly role of nurturing the sick in today's hospitals.

With the arrival of the 're-engineering' fad in the 1990s (see page 239), '[t]he operative phrase became "cost containment," and hospitals began to downsize, to merge, to substitute unlicensed assistive personnel for registered nurses, and to limit lengths of stay until legislation forced minimum stays for mothers and newborns and a 48-hour minimum postmastectomy'.[87] Poor pay resulted in a shortage of nurses, a problem that the American Medical Association tried to solve towards the end of the decade by replacing 'RNs' (registered nurses) with 'RCTs' ('registered care technologists'). Had it succeeded, the neo-Taylorite revolution would have been complete in that area; the requirement for 'domain knowledge' would have gone by the board. Fortunately, owing to opposition from the nursing profession, this proposal was abandoned but only after one pilot program had been put in place.[88]

A three-page article by Michael Berens, 'Nursing mistakes kill, injure thousands', in the *Chicago Tribune* of September 10, 2000 told all: 'Overwhelmed and inadequately trained nurses kill and injure thousands of patients every year as hospitals sacrifice safety for [higher profits]'. Berens went on to explain that traditional methods of control had been replaced by the use of statistical yardsticks – a ward was considered to be properly managed if the correct ratio was maintained between the numbers of nurses and patients. In some hospitals, this ratio was increased if patients were acutely ill; in others it was not. However, whether adjusted or not in this way, the ratios were not always observed in practice. (The use and misuse of yardsticks is always a sign that our so-called Experts are at work.)[89] A report in *Health Affairs* of May/June 2001 told us that 'reengineering has moved to reduce front-line leadership nurse roles', which seems to mean that the matron had herself been thrown to the wolves.[90] If this was so, it was not an event of much significance; deprived of the support of her ward sisters a decade before, she had long been impotent. The journal added that job satisfaction among nurses was much lower than among comparable groups of workers.

Nightingale's most famous dictum was that it is 'the very first requirement in a Hospital that it should do the sick no harm'.[91] Thanks to the impact of the Cult of the (so-called) Expert, the typical American hospital fails that test. (So, for that matter, does the typical British public-sector hospital, which also employs 'professional' managers, although of a somewhat different kind.) For the authors, the symbol of the new era has to be a half-eaten, dried-out meal sitting for hours by a hospital bed occupied by a semi-conscious patient. In an earlier and better-regulated age, a trained nurse would have felt obliged to feed the patient, if only to determine whether there was – in Ream's words – a 'potential need for supplemental nourishments'. This is a point on which Nightingale had strong views: 'to leave the patient's untasted food by his side . . . is simply to prevent him taking any food at all. Let the food come at the right time and be taken away, eaten or uneaten, at the right time.'[92]

It is not only in hospitals that medical services have deteriorated. In the last third of the twentieth century, the traditional family doctor also vanished. Many of these had charged fees to their richer patients while omitting to bill the others. Few regarded themselves as part of a 'market' in healthcare; business in general being held in low esteem in the 1930s and 1940s when they graduated, most considered, rather, that they had a kind of 'calling' – a secularized version of priesthood. They took it for granted that they should make 'home visits' at any hour of the day, night or weekend. Really conscientious ones would not go on vacation if one of their flock was seriously ill. Often serving successive generations of the same family, they were able to treat not just physical illnesses but the whole man, woman or child.

The old-fashioned family doctor was a 'generalist' manager of the health of his patients, just as Great Engine executives had been 'generalist' managers of companies or divisions. Like them, he has been replaced in a neo-Taylorized world by a mishmash of (so-called) Experts. At the one extreme stands the 'primary care professional', a sort of dumbed-down family doctor, whose job is to identify diseases and refer them to the right specialists. Then there are the 'patient advocates', retained by the sick to 'research medical options, make appointments [and] negotiate with insurance companies'; these can charge a $30,000 initiation fee and a $25,000 annual fee. (There are also non-profit advocacy centers.) Thirdly, health insurance companies have got into the act by employing 'disease management teams' to advise their clients.[93] Sick people suffering from more than one disease (not an uncommon phenomenon) are likely to find themselves advised by more than one of these teams — none of which is interested in the whole person or in the interaction between two or more diseases. (One is reminded of Taylor's attempt to replace the general foreman of the factory with a multiple of eight or more 'functional foremen or bosses' – see page 130.) A third medical hierarchy has collapsed.

Here as elsewhere in healthcare and medicine, to borrow Chandler's terminology (see page 96), the versatile 'visible hand' of 'administrative co-ordination' has been replaced by the clumsy 'invisible hand' of 'market co-ordination', the outcome being a critical loss of suppleness and efficiency. The greatest losers are the 45 million people who are uninsured: according to a report by the National Academies' Institute of Medicine published in 2002, they are 25 per cent more likely to die at any given age than their insured fellow citizens.[94] Since the bodies of the poor constitute the port of entry for diseases into the entire community, their illnesses should be of abiding concern to everyone, if only out of intelligent self-interest.

There are two other healthcare statistics that stick out like sore thumbs. The first is the American infant mortality rate, which is estimated at 6.43 per thousand in 2006. This compares with 5.08 in Britain, 3.24 in Japan and 2.76 in Sweden – and stands above even Cuba's dreadful 6.22 (itself by far the best in the Third World)! The CIA's website, which reports these figures, tells us that: 'This rate is often used as an indicator of the level of health in a country'.[95] If one can believe Dr. Irwin Redlener, associate dean at the Mailman School of Public Health at Columbia University and president of the Children's Health Fund, it is also getting worse; he tells us 'the rising rate of infant mortality is an early warning that we are headed in the wrong direction, with no relief in sight'. American women are 70 per cent more likely to die in childbirth than their European sisters.[96]

The second statistic is average height. According to Professor John Komlos of the University of Munich, military records show that in 1776 the average American male was two inches taller than his British counterpart. We can ourselves observe this differentiation in early nineteenth-century cartoons contrasting a squat and middle-aged John Bull with a long-limbed, slightly stooping and youthful Brother Jonathan, possessing elongated facial features. (The latter stereotype lingers today in occasional cartoons featuring a lean and stooping Uncle Sam.) At 6 feet 2 inches, George Washington would have been regarded as a giant if he had visited eighteenth-century London.[97] For over 200 years from the Declaration of Independence, America remained the tallest Western nation. After 1970, the average height of its citizens (disregarding those of Hispanic or Asian origins) shrank in relative terms as other Western nations grew taller – and there is even evidence to suggest that it shrank in absolute terms after 1995. In the course of a generation, America passed from being the tallest Western nation to being the shortest. Today your average American man is a half inch shorter than his British counterpart – and two inches shorter than the average Dutchman. Komlos tells us that the reason for this differentiation is 'a big mystery' but that it may be due to poor diet and inadequate medical care during childhood[98] – which brings one back to the high rate of infant mortality.

A recent, widely publicized, report tells us that Americans aged between 55 and 64 are much less healthy than Britons of the same age, being approximately twice as likely to suffer from diabetes or cancer and half again to suffer from heart disease.[99] It would be wrong to conclude, however, that the United States should copy the British National Health Service, at least in its present form. When it was formed after World War II, this service inherited the wonderful Nightingale hierarchies, only to abandon them in the 1970s on the advice of a neo-Taylorite 'scientific' manager, Brian Salmon, who went on to destroy the company which he chaired, J. Lyons, through excessive unhedged borrowing in foreign currencies.[100] Thanks to him, British hospitals are now run by 'professional' managers not noticeably more competent than their American counterparts. There is even a movement, largely sentimental, to 'bring back the matron'. In any case, the reason why the British enjoy better health today may have little to do with the quality of healthcare; Americans are suffering from two generations of obesity, their transatlantic cousins from only one – but the British are coming!

If America wants to repair its system of healthcare, it should look once again to the military. The Veterans Health Administration (VHA) offers a model of good practice for the whole community. How does it do it? The economist, Paul Krugman, tells us:

> The secret of its success is the fact that it's a universal, integrated system. Because it covers all veterans, the system doesn't need legions of administrative staff to check patients' coverage and demand payment from their insurance companies. Because it's integrated, providing all forms of medical care, it has been able to take the lead in electronic record-keeping and other innovations that reduce costs, ensure effective treatment and help prevent medical errors . . .

Krugman adds that the VHA also has an incentive to invest in prevention and disease management, pursuing quality systematically without threatening its own financial viability. And it can also bargain harder for, and pay far less for drugs, than the rest of us can.[101] Another reason why the system works well – and one which Krugman does not mention – is that the hierarchical structure of the Nightingale Hospital survives intact among both doctors and nurses, permitting the fast and accurate transmission of information upwards, downwards and sideways, but, above all, upwards. It is a structure that had its origins in a circular military tent in the Crimean peninsula a century and a half ago; the Lady with the Lamp liked her wards to be circular, so that she could stand in the middle and see what went on.

15

The Years that the Locust Ate
(1971–1995)

If the fifty years between 1920 and 1970 constituted a Golden Age of American Management, and the last twenty years of this period a Golden Age of American Society, how should one describe the succeeding period from 1971 until 1995, when the Great American Dream of ever-increasing prosperity for all citizens evaporated among adverse developments on many fronts? An appropriate Biblical name is the Years that the Locust Ate. It was as if many of the citizens – perhaps a majority – had been expelled, or threatened with expulsion, from their secularized version of Winthrop's 'Citty on a Hill'.

The baby-boomers of today look back with peculiar fondness on the decade of the Eisenhower and Kennedy presidencies (1953–1963). Post-war scarcities had all but disappeared. Inflation was low or non-existent. The economy was expanding. The nation was not engaged in a foreign war. It seemed for a time as if the dream of ever-increasing peace and prosperity had been definitively achieved. Surveys suggest that, on the whole, people were happy in their work – not subject to the kind of stress that would be endemic fifty years later. These benign tendencies continued until the end of the 1960s. As the *New York Times* columnist, Louis Uchitelle, has written:

> By most measures . . . the 60s expansion remains the gold standard for the American economy. Then, the economy grew more quickly, wages and family incomes rose by larger amounts each year. The poverty level and the unemployment rate fell more quickly and to lower levels. The gap between the wealthy and the poor was much smaller.[1]

Nearly everyone shared in the increase in prosperity.

The English poet, Percy Shelley, in his role as an early critic of industrial society, once observed that: 'the rich have become richer, and the poor have become poorer . . . Such are the effects that must ever flow from an unmitigated exercise of the calculating faculty' – his name for the market economy.[2] Karl Marx, an admirer of Shelley, took a less extreme view, observing that, under capitalism, the poor were getting *relatively* poorer – in other words, although both rich and poor were better off, the gap between them had widened.[3] Neither of these observations was borne out by economic developments in the United States in the century from 1870 to 1970, when the poor got richer in both absolute and relative terms. Capitalism, or more exactly industrialism, helped by public policy under Roosevelt's New Deal in the 1930s and 1940s, disproved both Shelleyism and Marxism.

After 1970, however, Shelleyism would come true. The absence of inflation under Eisenhower and Kennedy had been succeeded by the rapid price rises of the Johnson years (1963–1969) due to the Vietnam War, which were in turn followed by sharp rises in the numbers of unemployed. In the succeeding quarter century, not only did the gap between rich and poor open up but, according to the US government's own statistics, the wages of the average male worker adjusted for inflation actually fell in real terms – by a hefty 13.3 per cent.[4] Average family income fared a little better, but only because wives went out to work; since many working wives often employed a third adult part-time to perform housework, it is likely that true family income fell as well. Another way of looking at the same phenomenon is to compare movements in the average income of the top and bottom fifths of American society: according to the Bureau of the Census, the former rose by 18 per cent between 1973 and 1993 while the latter fell by 17 per cent.[5]

For the newly unemployed, the decline in income was precipitous. Simultaneously there was a loss of social mobility. A classic survey undertaken in 1978 found that among adult men whose fathers were in the bottom quartile of the population according to social and economic status, 23 per cent had made it into the top quartile; or, as Krugman, has pointed out in a *BusinessWeek* article, 'during the first thirty years or so after World War II, the American dream of upward mobility was a real experience for many people'. A new survey of adult men undertaken in 2003 found that the comparable figure was 10 per cent. Krugman's article, which reported on this development, was headed 'Waking up from the American Dream'.[6] In 2005, both the *Wall Street Journal* and the *New York Times* ran lengthy series of articles on this subject, both concluding that social mobility has failed to keep up with widening social divisions.[7]

Why did the earnings of ordinary people fail to increase over this lengthy period? Richard Lester, the director of the Industrial Performance Center at MIT, tells us unambiguously that the explanation lay in adverse developments in the field of labor productivity. In 1995 the United States had borne 'the dubious distinction of having had the lowest productivity growth of all the advanced industrial economies

... More than anything else it is this anemic productivity performance that accounts for the slow growth in the U.S. standard of living in recent years'.[8] Productivity, which had increased at an average annual rate of over 2.2 per cent between 1870 and 1970 and by 3 per cent in the decades immediately after World War II would average only 1.1 per cent in the Locust Years.[9] From 1973 to 1982, the more comprehensive index known as multifactor productivity (which measures the return to capital as well as to labor) actually declined from 87.8 to 86.2 (having been higher in between these dates).[10] The Morgan Stanley economists Joachim Fels and Manoj Pradhan have referred to the 'long-run decline in US productivity growth' over the period from the mid-1960s to the first half of the 1990s.[11] Labor productivity and average earnings go together like a horse and carriage, the first pulling the second along in its train. Higher productivity means higher profits for the employer, which is shared with the workforce, as employers compete for labor.

The rate of productivity increase or decrease also affects wealth creation in society as a whole. When productivity per man-hour expands on average at 2.4 per cent per annum, and assuming no great change in the number of hours worked, gross domestic product doubles roughly every thirty years – which it did in the century to 1970; at 1.1 per cent, doubling takes roughly sixty-five years. Furthermore, as Jeff Madrick has told us, '. . . the financial rewards of slow growth are not distributed as equally or as fairly as are the rewards of fast growth. Many get left behind and their confidence and ambition are undermined'; '. . . key services, notably education and healthcare, continue to rise in price faster than typical incomes in a slow-growing economy because they are not given to productivity gains. A rising number of Americans cannot afford them when the economy grows slowly.'[12]

No wonder Krugman has said, in a now famous phrase, that productivity may not be everything but it is almost everything. The reduction in the rate of growth in productivity was to some extent offset by an increase in hours worked; between 1979 and 1999, the average working year increased by 50 hours or 4 per cent.[13] Lester tells us that 'the causes of the productivity slowdown are still not well understood'.[14] *It is the principal thesis of this book that the slowdown was largely due to a decline in the quality of corporate and general management, which in turn resulted from the destructive impact of the Cult of the (so-called) Expert on the traditional culture of American business and government.*

What Lester has not pointed out, and perhaps should, is that what little growth in gross domestic product and productivity per man hour did occur after 1970 was largely due to the abandonment of the Puritan habit of thrift, so that income was spent instead of being saved; to old-fashioned credit-creation in the banking system, now carried to an extreme never experienced before; and to the increased purchasing power arising from the 'endowment effect' of higher share, bond and property prices – which the economist, Roger Bootle, has referred to as 'money for nothing'.[15] Everyone – the federal government, the state governments, the corporate sector, ordinary citizens with their credit cards – went deeply into debt and spent as if money was going out of fashion. The best comment on this form of borrowing from the future was made a century ago by the Austrian economist, Ludwig von Mises: 'It may sometimes be expedient for a man to heat the stove with his furniture. But he should not delude himself into believing that he has discovered a wonderful new method of heating his premises.'[16]

Credit is to the economy what steroids are to athletes; it enhances performance but, unless used in moderation, at a serious cost to the economic health of the nation. It follows that the modest degree of growth that America enjoyed in the Locust Years was due mostly to the economic equivalent of artificial stimulants. To the extent that this kind of growth is fostered, or at least not hindered, by the authorities, it can be described as 'privatized Keynesianism'[17] – in addition to stimulating the economy by borrowing and spending through the national budget, the authorities encourage the private sector to do it. The effect is much the same, except that the state cannot go literally bankrupt, whereas private citizens and corporations can and do. The result has been reckless over-borrowing, a subject on which Edward Chancellor wrote in May 2006 in the *Wall Street Journal*, a newspaper not known for its anti-capitalist views: 'What about scandalously incompetent borrowing?. . . Only when the [economic] cycle has turned down will the full extent of profligate lending be fully revealed'.[18]

The men who had run the Great Engine companies disliked borrowing because their planning was based on the worst assumptions: a debt-free company that encountered hard times – either on account of a general economic recession or because of some circumstances peculiar to itself or to the industry in which it operated – could survive by cutting the dividend on its common shares, restoring it when better times returned. In good times under the new regime, Boards of Directors would replace some dividend-bearing shares with fixed-interest debt, resulting in higher *reported* earnings per share, and a consequent increase in the value of the remaining shares. It followed that the shrewd beneficiaries of this quantitative trick grew richer, even as the value of their economic contribution to the community stood still or fell. (When all the transactions had been netted out, what actually occurred was an immediate *transfer* of wealth from those who did not borrow to those who did.) The downside was that the balance sheets of the debt-ridden companies lost their resilience, since interest had still to be to be paid and capital repaid. When hard times came, bankruptcy loomed.

The change in attitude was provided with a cloak of academic respectability by two economists, Franco Modigliani and Merton Miller, who launched something called 'Irrelevance Theory' in papers published in 1958 and 1963. The burden of their song was, amazingly, that share capital and debt were for practical purposes the same. It has been said that they 'set back for a generation the study by economists of corporate finance'.[19] Conceptually, 300 years of Puritan prudence were thrown out of the window. For this regrettable detraction from human wisdom, Modigliani and Miller were awarded Nobel Prizes. The best comment on their work is provided by Toyota's Financial Rule 1, which we quoted on page 98. For the world's most brilliantly successful company, an heir through the US Occupation of Japan to America's Great Engine companies, and through them to a long line of excellent managers reaching back to Col. Lee at the Springfield Armory, the difference between debt and ordinary share capital is by no means irrelevant. Modigliani and Miller must rank high in the ranks of our (so-called) Experts, remote from the world of practical men and women and not even good at theory.

The dangers inherent in over-borrowing have been enhanced by the neo-Taylorization of the lending process, i.e. the allocation to different parties of functions that should not be separated. Half a century ago, loans were made by banks which managed the procedure from beginning to end in the interests of both sides of the transaction; they undertook the investigation to determine whether the prospective recipient of funds was credit-worthy; offered the facilities; and 'monitored' the progress of the loan to ensure that interest payments and capital repayments were made, and other requirements met. If something went wrong, metaphorical red lights flashed and sirens sounded within the lending institutions, so that it could be put right. Their successors today, utilizing the so-called 'derivatives' market, may lay off the risk of non-payment of interest and non-repayment of capital to third parties like pension plans, which earn a fee for accepting the possibility of loss. Neither party performs an adequate credit analysis – the lenders because they do not need to, since they are no longer at risk; and the pension plans because they are not equipped to do so and, in any case, may not even know who the borrowers are. A mighty edifice is reared on feeble foundations. 'Moral hazard' is the technical name for this game, which means that institutions 'take on excessive risk because they are insured'; 'systemic risk' is the inevitable result – risk to the entire monetary system of the world.[20] There is an urgent need today to apply once again traditional 'generalist' management to the making of loans, as to everything else. Specialization of function may be desirable, or even necessary, in many walks of life but it always implies a need to bring the separate parts back together again at some level. Otherwise, as Nightingale would have said, no-one is *in charge*.

A pre-condition for the maturing of the Great Engine companies was the divorce of control from ownership that occurred in the 1920s. The Golden Age of American Management occurred *after* the founding shareholders had largely ceded control to non-family executives but *before* institutional investors would take it away again after 1970. In the intervening half-century, most shares would be owned by private individuals who were loosely, or not at all, organized and therefore incapable of exerting a decisive influence on corporate boards. This meant that, by default, everyone took a long-term view. This age would come to an end for a variety of reasons which we shall explore later in this book, one of which was the growing power, short-term outlook and herd-like behavior of the new financial masters, which was paralleled by a decline in the quality of corporate management as chief executives and their immediate subordinates became identified with the dominant new investor class. By the last quarter of the twentieth century, over half of the shares listed on the New York Stock Exchange would be in the hands of insurance companies, pension plans, mutual funds, banks and the like.[21] Today, significant family holdings remain in only one-third of the biggest listed US companies.[22] The paradox is that by *not* pursuing profitability to the exclusion of all else, the Great Engine companies in their Golden Age would achieve enormous increases in the value of their net assets, whereas, by single-mindedly pursuing profit on behalf of their new masters after 1970, these same companies and their successors actually created less genuine, lasting wealth; indeed, they would often destroy it.

The neo-Taylorization of money and capital markets led to 'group think' on a massive and dangerous scale, which in turn resulted in what was known as 'momentum buying' of shares. Instead of asking themselves what is good and what is bad, or what is undervalued or overvalued, in the traditional fashion, investing institutions tended to ask themselves 'what has been going up and is likely to continue to do so?' This approach resulted in self-fulfilling prophecies; if enough institutions decided that a share or other asset was going up in price, then it would do so by the iron law of supply and demand. Markets became 'one-way streets'. At some point, however, these one-way streets had to end in cul-de-sacs, when the irrationality of the pricing became obvious even to the dimmest of investors. At that point, the value of the asset in question would fall as early buyers bailed out. It was an elaborate game of 'pass the parcel', in which the last holder played the role of victim. This was based on the illusionary 'theory of the greater fool' – the belief that there would always be another buyer at the end of the chain of events.

It may seem strange at this point to introduce a reference to the book (and subsequent film) *The Wonderful Wizard of Oz* (1900) but there is good reason for doing so. We now think of it simply as a children's story but, like that other similar story, Swift's *Gulliver's Travels*, it started off, at least in part, as a political satire and morality tale for adults. Its author, L. Frank Baum, had been one of the opponents of the demonetization of silver. A 'bimetallist', he believed that relying on gold alone as currency, instead of on both gold and silver, would reduce the amount of money in circulation and lead to a deflation harmful to the population in general, although it would favor Wall Street and the political class.

The heroine of the book was a poor, six-year-old orphan girl called Dorothy, a juvenile descendant of our Puritan Brother Jonathan and an 'all-American girl from the heartland'. Like the hero of a much later novel but almost contemporary film, *Mr Smith Goes to Washington*, she would go to the nation's capital to sort out the country's woes, the capital being represented by Oz, a place ruled by the lure of gold, 'oz' equaling ounce. (Confusingly, Baum has also told us that he found the name by looking in a dictionary and finding the heading O–Z. One explanation does not exclude the other.) The Wizard was the president himself – an unkindly dig at all politicians who make promises and do not deliver. The Cowardly Lion was Williams Jennings Bryan, a Democratic candidate in the presidential election of 1896, famous for saying: 'You shall not press down upon the brow of labor this crown of thorns, you shall not crucify mankind upon a cross of gold' but mocked by Baum because he abandoned the good cause during the election campaign of 1900. The Tin Woodman and the Scarecrow represented, respectively, industrial and agricultural workers, unemployed in the recession brought on by the Stock Exchange Panic of 1893, while the Wicked Witch of the East represented Wall Street, allegedly the home of ruthless capitalists who exploited their fellow countrymen.[23]

When Baum wrote, the Great Engine companies of the mid-twentieth century, complete with their implied 'social contracts', had barely come into existence, with the magnificent exception of the

Pennsy. This was the period of the 'robber barons' who ruthlessly exploited their staff and their customers – like Jay Gould (1836–1892), the destroyer of McCallum's Erie. With the decline of the Great Engine companies after 1970, *The Wonderful Wizard of Oz* would once again become relevant as a morality tale. Bimetallism was no longer a political issue but greed and exploitation were reborn on a scale reminiscent of the earlier period. America would once again experience a pursuit of wealth by a tiny minority unconcerned about the public good or for the welfare of their employees. As the journalist, Geoffrey Colvin, has told us in an article published in *Fortune*:

> Thus began a managerial fashion that lives on: paying executives munificently despite lousy market performance . . . At some point in the late '70s – compensation experts disagree on the precise coordinates – an American CEO was paid more than $1.0 million. Every other CEO noticed. The dam was breached. The flood followed and has yet to subside.[24]

Twenty years on, in the 1990s, the *average* annual pay of chief executives came close to $1 million[25] and Roberto Goizueta, chief executive of Coca-Cola, became the first of his breed to take home $1 billion in one year (see page 153). In 1970, the typical chief executive of a large company had been paid twenty-five times the average wage – not far from the multiple of twenty that Pierpont Morgan, the New York financier, had recommended a hundred years before;[26] by 2006, this figure had risen to 475 (see page 108).[27] Meantime, there had been no obvious improvement in the contribution made by such people to the welfare of society or even of the companies that they ran – indeed, quite the contrary. In the 1880s and in their capacity as shareholders, the robber barons had stood outside the corporate tent, 'p—ing in' – to echo President Johnson's famously vulgar remark. In the 1990s, the new boys and girls (there were now girls, although it strains the metaphor) were right inside it, 'p—ing out'.

The economic decline that occurred in the Locust Years was accompanied by deterioration in the fabric of society. De Tocqueville had written of the young Republic of the 1830s:

> American of all ages, conditions and all dispositions constantly unite together. Not only do they have commercial and industrial associations to which all belong but also a thousand other kinds, religious, moral, serious, futile, very general and very specialized, large and small. Americans group together to hold fetes, found seminaries, build inns, construct churches, distribute books, dispatch missionaries to the antipodes . . . Where you see in France the government and

in England a noble lord at the head of a great new initiative, in the United States you can count on finding an association.[28]

He was particularly struck by the growth of temperance societies, a refinement of Puritanism that did not exist in colonial days.

In 2000, Robert Putnam, the Professor of Public Policy at Harvard University, would publish *Bowling Alone: The Collapse and Revival of American Community*. His thesis was that, in the last quarter of the twentieth century, there was a dissolution of the many and diverse bonds that bound citizens together, starting with, but not limited to, marriage. At the beginning of this period, Americans were still a clubbable people who liked to meet and play in groups – for example, in bowling alleys, whence the title of his book. Only a generation later, they lived lonelier lives cut off from their fellow citizens – metaphorically speaking, *bowling alone*:

> At midcentury young Americans (those we would come to label as the long civic generation) were happier and better adjusted than other people – less likely to take their own lives, for example. At century's end that same generation (now in retirement) remains distinctively well-adjusted psychologically and physiologically. On the other hand, at century's end, the children and grandchildren of the long civics (those we label boomers and X'ers) are much more distressed and more likely to take their own lives than their grandparents had been at their age.[29]

In Putnam's usage, 'boomers' are people born between 1955 and 1975 while 'X'ers' are those who first appeared between 1975 and 1995.

If the wide-open Levittowns had been the badge of the Golden Age of Society, the gated community – which first appeared in the 1980s and would soon be equipped with armed guards – became the symbol of the Locust Years. By 1997, eight out of every ten new urban projects were being gated.[30] There was a reason for the gates, guards and guns: aggressive begging, unknown in the immediate post-war years, had appeared on the streets. Today there are something approaching 3,000 'rough sleepers' to be found on a cold night in the streets of New York, ten times as many as in London, both cities having a population of around 7 million souls.[31]

Putnam quotes the example of the small town of Roseto, Pennsylvania, which had been the focus of study by sociologists for half a century. In the 1950s, Rosetans just did not die of heart attacks. The researchers looked for the usual explanations: diet, exercise, weight, smoking, genetic predisposition, and so forth, but none of these explanations fitted – indeed, by normal standards, Rosetans were actually more likely to exhibit these risk factors than their neighbors. So the researchers pondered the town's social dynamics. Founded by emigrants from one single Italian village in the previous century, its inhabitants had developed: '. . . a tight-knit community where conspicuous displays of wealth were scorned and family values and good behaviors reinforced. Rosetans learned to draw on one another for financial, emotional and other forms of support.' In the 1960s the researchers began to fear that changes in the nature of American society in general would destroy the Rosetans' inherited sense of solidarity. Sure enough, by the 1980s, the Rosetans suffered from an even higher rate of heart attack than the citizens of a nearby and comparable town.[32]

Putnam's thoughtful and well-documented book has to be taken seriously. He reports that, from the point of view of general health and well-being, getting married is the equivalent of quadrupling your income, and regularly attending the meeting of a club is the equivalent of doubling it. Communities with low social capital have lower educational performance and more teenage pregnancy, child suicide, low birth weight and prenatal mortality. 'Social capital', as it is called, is also a strong predictor of crime rates and other measures of the quality of life. In terms of risk to health, there is not much difference between being a smoker and belonging to no closely-knit social group.

While Putnam does not regard the fall in average earnings as the only, or even the principal, cause of the deterioration in the quality of life, he is convinced that there is a causal link, arguing that:

> . . . financial anxiety is associated not merely with less frequent moviegoing – perhaps the natural consequence of a thinner wallet – but also with less time spent with friends, less card playing, less home entertaining, less frequent attendance at church, less volunteering, and less interest in politics. Even social activities with little or no financial cost are inhibited by financial distress. In fact, the only leisure activity positively correlated with financial distress is watching TV.[33]

The 1990 Erika Rothenberg painting at the Museum of Contemporary Art in Chicago (see page 126) sums up what had happened to society – while still managing to convey through its humor the indomitable spirit of a nation.

Putnam's account of social decline is reinforced by other studies, including William Bennett's *The Index of Leading Cultural Indicators*. Beginning his analysis ten years earlier than Putnam, Bennett reported that, by 1997, there has been a 467 per cent increase in violent crime; a 463 per cent increase in federal and state prisoners; a 461 per cent increase of out-of-wedlock births; a more than 200 per cent increase in the number of children in single-parent homes; a more than doubling in the teenage suicide rate; a 150 per cent increase in the numbers living on welfare; an almost tenfold increase in cohabiting couples; a doubling of the divorce rate; and (see page 198) a drop of almost 60 points in SAT scores – all of which compares with an increase in the population of only 48 per cent.[34]

There are two important social indicators to which neither Putnam nor Bennett refers. The first is the decline, relative or otherwise, in the height of the average citizen, which we discussed in the previous chapter. The second is the rising birth rate. (Curiously, Putnam even refers to a *declining* birth rate at a time – 2000 – when it had been significantly increasing.)[35] It is a commonplace of demographics that there is an inverse correlation between shifts in the levels of prosperity and in the birth rate, except when there is an exogenous event. A 'total fertility rate' of 2.1 implies that a population replaces itself.[36] The fertility rate fell sharply in the United States during the prosperous 1920s and rose sharply again during the Great Depression of the 1930s. It fell again in the Golden Ages of Management and Society and their immediate aftermath from a peak of 3.8 (reflecting an exogenous event, the postwar baby boom) in 1957 to a trough of 1.7 in 1976. What did it do in the balance of the Years that the Locust Ate? Dutifully, it rose – all but reaching the 'magic' figure of 2.1 in the first half of the 1990s. The CIA website tells us that the estimated rate today is '2.09 children born/woman'.[37] Relying on conventional wisdom, one can say that it was the decline in the general standard of living during this period which encouraged the population of the United States almost to replace itself, something that no other developed nation was able to do. (The US National Center for Health Statistics presents a contrary view, arguing that the rise in the birth rate is a reflection of an increasing sense of financial security affecting all classes.[38]) Worldwide, there is today a visible inverse correlation between social deprivation and high birth rates.[39] The fertility rates for Britain, Canada and Germany at the end of the twentieth century were, respectively, 1.7, 1.6 and 1.4;[40] in all of these countries, reported productivity rose faster during the Years that the Locust Ate than in the United States. It is an ill wind that blows no-one any good.

One cannot disassociate the reported decline in the height of the American male, relative or not, and the increase in the fertility of the

American female from the stagnation that characterized the US economy between 1970 and 1995 – and it is also difficult to disassociate that stagnation from the triumph of the Cult of the (so-called) Expert. It is, therefore, likely that the business schools, as the principal temples and sponsors of the Cult and operating under the great Law of Unintended Consequences that governs much of what we are, think, say and do, carry some of the responsibility for both maintaining the size of the US population and reducing, at least in relative terms, its stature.

16

Dr. Deming Rides
to the Rescue – and Fails
(1980–1993)

It was then that Dr. W. Edwards Deming rode to the rescue of society and the national economy on television – specifically, by means of a fifteen-minute slot in a ninety-minute NBC documentary. called *If Japan Can, Why Can't We?*. His pitch was simple and seductive – the Japanese had achieved an Economic Miracle, and, in so doing, taken over a large part of certain US markets – for example, for television sets and automobiles – by instituting a managerial revolution that empha-sized the importance of quality in manufacture. By imitating Japan, America could not only resolve her current problems but also enjoy her own version of that miracle.[1]

The fall-out from *If Japan Can, Why Can't We?* was immediate and gratifying; the telephone in Deming's modest office rang more than ever before. One of the callers would be the Ford Motor Company; at this point it was hemorrhaging to death, thanks to the combined impact of foreign competition and 'decades of slavish devotion to short-term financial figures'.[2] In the three-year period beginning in 1980, it would lose another $3.5 billion. Ford – a company that had never quite made it to Great Engine status since it never properly devel-oped 'generalist', 'rounded' managers, as did, at least for a time, General Motors – was in trouble, big trouble.

The company's head of manufacturing, Bill Scollard, took home with him a video of Deming's television program, liked what he saw and sent a team of middle managers to visit the author in his basement office. *They* must have liked what they heard because Deming was invited to Motown, where he became a consultant to the company. By 1983, he had settled into a 'cozy routine' of monthly breakfast meet-ings with the president, Donald E. Petersen, during which they would discuss every aspect of the company's business.[3] Ford's reaction was mirrored throughout the business world and beyond. Quality became a mantra. Boards of Directors were proud to adopt 'quality programs' and special departments were created to put them into effect, not just in manufacturing but also in service companies like banking and insurance. Federal government departments and charities jumped on board. Societies were created that promoted Deming's ideas with a quasi-religious fervor reminiscent of the early days of Scientific Management. For the next thirteen years, until his death in 1993, Deming led a heroic campaign against the generation of 'number crunchers' and marketing men and women who had seized control of the commanding heights of American business and of much else besides. This chapter is about the man, his message – and how and why he lost.

Deming's life and career contained most of the elements of a Ragged Dick story (see page 67). He was born on October 14, 1900, in Sioux City, Iowa to a family that was 'often cold, hungry and in debt'.[4] When he was six years old, the family moved to a virgin plot in Wyoming that proved to be useless for agriculture or anything else. The first house that they constructed was a 'tar paper shack', affording little protection from the weather, being boiling hot in summer and freezing cold in winter. It was education that provided his escape route from poverty. He worked his way through high school, graduating with a degree in electrical engineering from the University of Wyoming in 1922. In 1925 he received an MSc from the University of Colorado and in 1928 a PhD from Yale – both graduate degrees being in mathematical physics. In a mere twenty-eight years, he had gone from near the bottom of the social pile to near its top. Thereafter he practiced for decades as a consulting statistician for government and industry, becoming well known in Japan after World War II for his lectures on Statistical Quality Control but otherwise living in a relative obscurity – that is to say, until June 20, 1980, the day of the broadcast.

If ever a man had a Puritan outlook, it was Deming, but his ways of thinking and acting related more to the western frontier than to the New England of his day, which by 1900 had settled into comfortable conformity. On the Atlantic coast, if there was no blacksmith in your village, you could count on finding one in the next; in Iowa or Wyoming in 1900, you were on your own. Childhood circumstances shaped the man. Frugal, diligent and unconcerned about the acquisition of wealth, he would live in the same modest house in Washington, DC from 1936 until his death in 1993. His office was in its basement, adjacent to a clothes washer and dryer. Hating ostentation as much as waste, he continued to drive his 1979 Lincoln Continental, and regularly took the bus or subway, until near the end of his life.

Deming was a devout and practicing high-church Episcopalian[5] of a peculiarly American kind, in that he rejected the concept of original sin in favor of a Universalist belief in the 'potential and essential goodness of most human beings'; 'What drove him was a messianic belief in the correctness of his vision'.[6] In previous ages, men of his ilk had led religious revivals. Like our Three Wise Men in Japan after World War II, Deming actually wanted to make the world a better place for people to live in. Married to the same woman for fifty-six years, he would be separated from her only by her death.

Life on any frontier demands a pragmatic outlook; this was one of his dominant personal characteristics. He had long been of the opinion that the 'Star-spangled Banner', although it possessed splendid words and an attractive melody, was deficient in one important respect: it called for a vocal range beyond most citizens. He therefore set out to provide a solution, composing a variation which would be premiered by the District of Columbia Orchestra in the year before his death. Is it fanciful to see here the same spirit that led John B. Jervis to substitute a truck for the front axle of the locomotive *Brother Jonathan* (see page 64) – in both cases, an existing artifact (defined by the dictionary as 'a product of human art and workmanship') was adapted to make it fit the needs of humanity better. He thought the effort worthwhile.

Deming distrusted deeply the concept of the mobile 'professional' manager that the business schools had introduced and which General Electric's chairman, Ralph Cordiner had sponsored (see page 146). 'Students of business are taught that there is profession of management . . .', he wrote, 'This is a cruel hoax. The MBA teaches managers how to take over companies, but not how to run them.'[7] Deming was attacking the erroneous belief, arising out of the Cult of the (so-called) Expert, that a person could somehow learn how to manage in the abstract and then apply that knowledge successfully in any walk of life, without possessing or acquiring a thorough understanding of the activity in question. What did Deming seek to put in its place? Stripped of its somewhat misleading rhetoric, his message was that America should revert to the pure milk of the gospel of good management that had characterized the middle years of the twentieth century. You have only to look at his famous Fourteen Points (see pages 242 and 243) to appreciate this truth. Designing quality into the product (Point 3) was part of the message that our Three Wise Men, as representatives of then contemporary American managerial culture, had brought to the Japanese in the late 1940s.[8] Moving 'towards a single supplier for any one item' (Point 4) was an inferior version of Procter & Gamble's 'preferred supplier policy' – in reality, a 'preferred suppliers policy', since it never relied on only one for any product. (See, for example, the company's presentation to the British Monopolies Commission in 1965.) Training on the job (Point 6) and encouraging people from research, design, sales and production to work together (Point 9) had long been normal practice in many companies. Instituting 'a vigorous program of education and self-improvement' (Point 13) is a phrase that could have been written by Given in 1949; it reminds us of the latter's observation: 'Self-education under guidance is one of the basic methods of bottom-up management'.[9] The instruction 'Remove barriers that rob the hourly worker of his right to pride of workmanship' (Point 12a) takes us even further back, reminding us of observations by seventeenth-century Puritan divine, John Cotton, quoted on page 6.

The fact that Deming felt obliged to re-assert these half-forgotten truths shows the extent to which American business had been penetrated by what we have described as the Business School Counter-Culture – a subset of the neo-Taylorite Cult of the (so-called) Expert. From this point of view, his Point 8 is particularly interesting. Deming wanted to: 'Drive out fear, so that every one may work for the company'. One is reminded of the injunction by the Puritan philosopher, Bacon, uttered over 400 years before in his essay, 'Of great place': 'Severity breedeth fear ... [and] roughness breedeth hate. Even reproofs from authority ought to be grave, and not taunting.'[10] The early Taylorism of the turn of the nineteenth century had used fear as a motivation on the factory floor but, by 1949, Given had been able to assume that human relations in business were based on trust, not fear.[11] In 1954, Drucker went so far as to say that: '[Fear] corrupts both him who uses [it] and him who fears. That we have got rid of fear as motivation to work is therefore a major achievement.'[12]

If Drucker in 1954 could believe that fear had been abolished as an incentive to work, why did Deming have to advocate its re-abolition? Both were highly intelligent men who knew what they were about, Drucker being as close to General Motors in the 1950s as Deming would be to Ford in the 1980s. The answer is, of course, that fear had been reintroduced as a motivation to work by the neo-Taylorite managers of the last third of the twentieth century. There was, however, to be an important innovation: at the turn of nineteenth century, fear had been used mostly to control the behavior of blue-collar workers; in the late twentieth century, it would be used to incentivize managers as well. Fear is the flipside of 'performance-related pay', which was an essential element in the newcomers' intellectual baggage; if your work pleases, you will be exceptionally well rewarded, over and above your salary; if it does not, watch out!

In the 1980s General Electric would initiate the practice of dismissing one-tenth of its employees each year ('the worst 10 percent'),[13] even if there was no dissatisfaction in absolute terms with the quality of their work. Known in the trade as 'rank and yank', this procedure was brutal and unethical. Imagine a department consisting of ten people, all hard-working, loyal and competent. One had to go; how did one pick him or her? In this way, more than careers were broken. Happily, under its new chief executive, Jeff Immelt, the company appears to be trying to discard or soften this procedure, not abolishing the ratings but asking its employees to make a greater use of 'common sense' in assigning them.[14]

A more sophisticated but equally pernicious form of 'rank and yank' is to be found at Microsoft, which uses a bell-curve to rate employees in each group, so that the number of over-achievers has to be statistically balanced by the number of under-achievers: 'Under the rating system, if a group works hard together to release a product, someone in the group has to be a low score for every high score that a manager dishes out'.[15] Both these approaches create a competitive spirit among employees and generate resentment in situations where teamwork is called for. One is reminded of the unfortunate British admiral John Byng, who was sent to the Mediterranean at the head of an ill-prepared and inadequate fleet to prevent the French from capturing the island of Minorca. Finding that they had already landed, he failed to attack them, was court-martialed for neglect of duty, found guilty and executed on March 14, 1757.[16] It was this event that led Voltaire to remark in his novel *Candide* that the English like to kill an admiral from time to time '*pour encourager les autres*'.

With the replacement of 'time (or work) study' with 'method study' (see page 77), performance-related pay for 'blue-collar' workers was being largely phased out in its impact on the factory floor in Great Engine companies by the 1950s, except in the case of highly repetitive businesses like knitwear. There was good reason for this development: in teamwork, normal on the factory floor, it was difficult to assign responsibility for success to individuals with any degree of precision and also easy to upset morale by rewarding the wrong person. As Deming never failed to point out, a person's success or failure in a job was to be attributed overwhelmingly to the excellence (or otherwise) of the system within which he operated and to the quality of the supervision. It followed that a quantitative procedure designed 'scientifically' to reward any single person was almost bound to miss the mark. Deming's view was that it was wasteful to: 'rank people, teams, salesmen, divisions, with reward at the top, punishment at the bottom', to which he added: 'Ranking . . . has led to the so-called annual appraisal of people. The result is conflict, demoralization, lower productivity, lower quality, suppression of innovation.'[17]

If performance-related pay had been softened in its impact on the factory floor by 1960, because it was too difficult to operate, was it wise even to contemplate applying it to managers, as was done increasingly after 1970, given the far greater complexity of the tasks that the latter were called upon to perform and the extreme degree of their mutual interdependence? If you attempt to do the impossible, you will create a mess – not a bad way of describing how executives would be rewarded under the new dispensation, which also provided an enormous opportunity for cheating and favoritism. Essentially, performance-related pay for managers is irrational. Men or women are selected to occupy senior positions on the assumption that they will perform well; and, for this, they are paid substantial salaries reflecting the extent of the responsibility that they carry. Why then pay them large bonuses for doing what they were supposed to do in the first place? Did the Boards who made the appointments not expect them to succeed? As a general principle, salaries should reflect responsibilities; bonuses should be limited to 10–20 per cent of salaries and, when due, spread across whole departments to promote teamwork and improve morale.

Deming failed to change Ford's basic managerial culture, in spite of having the attentive ear of the president. Much the same can be said of the impact of his Quality Movement on business and society as a whole. Why was his approach unsuccessful? It may be faulted on three grounds. First of all, he subsumed most of management theory and practice under the one rubric of Quality, usually capitalized; whilst this was undoubtedly good for public relations – who can be against Quality? – it meant that the essential message was skewed. Good managers have to take account of many other factors, including cost and safety, as well as Quality. This presentational weakness may have led to a second fault of a more basic nature: Deming understood processes and systems, but he had little understanding of the importance of managerial structure. While no fewer than five of our Principles of Good Practice (Three to Seven) deal with structure, not one of his Fourteen Points did so. He had, therefore, little or nothing of value to say on a whole range of critical subjects like delegation, multidivisional organizations, line-and-staff or the role of the middle manager. He seems instead to have veered towards a kind of structural nihilism, advocating the maximum dismantlement of barriers between departments, without realizing that, if you take down too many, you won't have any organization at all. Barriers exist for a purpose. Imagine trying to run a company of 400,000 employees as one large homogenized and seamless unit! From this point of view, engineers like Sarasohn, Protzman and Polkinghorn (see page 109), who taught the Japanese after World War II, were streets ahead of him; they laid emphasis on 'zones of management' and on the nature and purpose of delegation.

A final weakness lay in Deming's Doctrine of Profound Knowledge, which consisted of four elements: appreciation of the system; knowledge of variation; theory of knowledge; and knowledge of psychology.[18] It was the third of these that presented the greatest difficulty. He had learned it from his mentor, the statistician Shewhart, who had done so much to raise the levels of quality control in the manufacture of telephone equipment at the Hawthorne Works of Western Electric in the 1920s, even while Mayo's men were conducting their notorious Human Relations Experiment in the same place. Shewhart had in turn derived it from a book, *The Mind and World Order* by the distinguished Harvard philosopher, Clarence Irving Lewis.[19] One day in the 1930s, Deming told Shewhart that he had read Lewis' book seven times over without understanding a word. Shewhart told him to go back and read it an eighth time, adding that 'I read it fourteen times before it began to mean anything'.[20] This was the very subject, no doubt presented in a simplified form, which Deming sought to convey to senior, medium and junior management.

As a consultant and teacher, Deming would have done better to stick to his Fourteen Points and forget about Profound Knowledge. The probability is, however, that he would still have failed in his mission. His Points were not difficult to apply *given the right quality of management*; that was the rub. Deming taught that the creation of products of quality demanded a transformation in the outlook of all levels of managers and employees from the Board of Directors down. On the whole, however, Boards do not like having their outlook transformed. So, in most American companies, Quality Programs became a kind of 'optional extra', something that was enthusiastically adopted by the Board but affected only the lower orders. Assigning the task to separate Quality departments also suggested that responsibility did not lie even with 'line' managers; and if it did not lie with them, it was not going to happen. General MacArthur had faced a similar kind of problem in Japan after World War II, which he solved by firing all the top Japanese industrial managers, including the Boards, and by promoting men from the 'mezzanine' or middle level of management into senior positions. There was no General MacArthur to perform a similar trick on the whole of American industry in 1980 – for which, of course, we must be grateful for quite different reasons. Deming's mission was, therefore, probably doomed to fail before it had even begun. The resistance was too powerful.

The *coup de grace* for the Quality Movement came in an article written by a former MIT professor, Michael Hammer, for the *Harvard Business Review* of July–August 1990, called 'Re-engineering work: don't automate, obliterate'. Like Deming, the author believed there was something seriously wrong with US business. However, while Deming *de facto* advocated a return to at least some of the traditional American values and practices of the mid-twentieth century, Hammer blamed industry's problems on their persistence:

> We have institutionalized the ad hoc and enshrined the temporary ... Of the business processes that were designed, most took their present form in the 1950s. The goal then was to check overambitious growth – much as the typewriter was designed to slow typists who would otherwise jam the keys. It is no accident that organizations stifle innovation and creativity. That's what they were *designed* to do.[21]

These statements were quite simply untrue. As this book has sought to demonstrate, the 'business processes' in use in the 1950s were not developed during that decade – when there was very little procedural innovation, as factories sought to catch up on demand unsatisfied during World War II – but had come into existence in the course of the previous century and a half. The inventor, Christopher Sholes, may have created the 'QWERTY' keyboard with the object of slowing down the typist but that was with the object of speeding up her work by preventing the typewriter from jamming. Given offered a better illustration of the true attitude of mind prevailing at the mid-twentieth century when he wrote in *Bottom-up Management* (1949): 'The job of every manager [is] creative rather than merely administrative. He makes it his business to stimulate the organization to contribute ideas. And to apply imagination, ingenuity and resourcefulness to the solution of the daily problems of the business and to its long-range progress.'[22]

At the heart of Re-engineering, according to Hammer, was: 'The notion of discontinuous thinking – of recognizing and breaking away from the outdated rules and fundamental assumptions that underlie operations. Unless we change these rules, we are merely rearranging the deck chairs on the Titanic.'[23] This idea would be developed in detail in a book, *Reengineering the Corporation: A Manifesto for Business Revolution*, which Hammer wrote with James Champy in 1993, according to which:

> Fundamentally, reengineering is about reversing the industrial revolution. Reengineeering rejects the assumptions inherent in Adam Smith's industrial paradigm – the division of labor, economies of scale, hierarchical control and all the other appurtenances of an early stage developing economy. Reengineering is the search for new models of organizing work. Tradition counts for nothing. Reengineering is a new beginning.[24]

One has to question the sanity of the men who penned these words. They offered resonant phrases but begged scores of elementary questions. Did the United States really possess the characteristics of an 'early stage developing economy' in its Golden Age of Management, when it became the arsenal of democracy and successfully fought two world wars, one in each of the Pacific and Atlantic theaters? No-one denies that, from time to time, utterly original thoughts or spectacularly innovative actions may be required to resolve some problem or other but, by and large, most useful human progress takes place because of *continuous*, rather than discontinuous, thinking. Even apparently discontinuous thinking often reflects some deeper continuity with the past. Isaac Newton, the man who discovered gravity, calculus and the nature of light, expressed this point better than anyone else when he told us that 'If I have seen further it is because I have stood on the shoulders of giants'.[25]

Hammer and Champy were believers in the importance of the 'professional' manager who controlled a company primarily through the profit and loss account. Dishonestly, they tried to legitimate this approach by projecting it backwards onto Alfred Sloan, the great chairman of General Motors:

> In Sloan's view, corporate executives did not need specific expertise in engineering or manufacturing; specialists could oversee those functional areas. Instead, executives needed financial expertise. They had only to look at 'the numbers' – sales, profit and loss, inventory levels, market share, and so forth – generated by the company's various divisions to see if those divisions were performing well; if not, they could demand appropriate corrective action.[26]

They also argued that Sloan had applied 'Adam Smith's principle of the division of labor to management as Ford had applied it to labor'. Had he genuinely done so, Sloan would have been as disastrous a manager as Taylor was (see page 128).

It would seem that neither Hammer nor Champy had read *My Years with General Motors*; in a book of nearly 500 pages, Sloan devoted only thirty-two to financial controls. He was well aware of their limitations, telling us, for example, that 'rate of return', while being better than other financial principles, was not 'a magic wand for every occasion in business' and that, in divisional accounting, 'the figures did not give automatic answers to problems'.[27] According to Drucker, 'Sloan was "people-focused" to the point of being quixotic'[28] which does not suggest an obsession with the quantitative, the accounts being for him no more than a signaling system for use by the executive committee, on which the manufacturing divisions were well represented. His senior colleagues and he were engineers, not financial men, graduates of MIT and not of the B-School. They took an interest in *all* aspects of the company's business, including the accounts, and expected others to do the same. In his book, *Sloan Rules; Alfred P. Sloan and the Triumph of General Motors,* David Farber tells us that the statistical methods that Sloan and his colleagues devised to assist them in controlling their far-flung empire 'were not sufficient to ensure General Motors' success':[29] the company had to build cars that people wanted to buy. (By the way, not all of Sloan's innovations were good. He appears to have originated 'planned obsolescence', one of the several reasons why General Motors and its imitators were in the end to lose out to foreign competition.[30])

As explained on page 179, in 1991 the lawyers Easterhouse and Fischel had published *Economic Structure of Corporate Law*, which provided the doctrine of Stockholder Value with its intellectual and moral justification; *Reengineering the Corporation* became its operations manual. Henceforth, the order of the day would be to raise reported income by crudely cutting costs. As Gabor has told us: 'With its call for Tayloresque systems experts who would parachute into companies and cold-bloodedly root out waste regardless of the human cost, Hammer and Champy's book was the archetypal anti-Deming tract'.[31] Underlying and supporting the concept of Re-engineering was the basic business-school double fallacy described on page 168: that the skills of management could be acquired in an academic setting; and that, once acquired, they could be successfully applied in any industry, whether or not the manager possessed a thorough knowledge of it.

Reengineering the Corporation was one of the publishing sensations of the 1990s, selling 2.5 million copies and being translated into fourteen languages. Its impact is with us to this day. However, it was not long before Hammer's co-author began to have second thoughts. Only two years after its publication, Champy offered us a new book, *Reengineer-*

ing Management: The Mandate for New Leadership,[32] in which he would dramatically declare that Re-engineering was 'in trouble'; while some companies had benefited, other had not.[33] There was nothing wrong with the procedure in itself, said he; the trouble was that half a revolution could be worse than none all. And what was the other half revolution that Champy was calling for? It was a feebler version of the seventh of Deming's Fourteen Points: 'Institute leadership'. Champy's book was neither fish nor fowl; it left the reader in total confusion. Re-engineering remained (more or less) the order of the day.

For a complete disavowal, America had to wait until 2001, when Hammer would himself publish *Agenda: What Every Business Must Do to Dominate the Decade*. Whereas, in his *Harvard Business Review* article, he had told us that: 'Reengineering cannot be planned meticulously and accomplished in small and cautious steps',[34] he now advocated just that![35] His radicalism had flown out of the window. He also wanted businessmen to 'profit by the power of ambiguity', not an easy thing to do if you are trying to run a company, or anything. One is reminded of Nixon's reversing the abolition of Kennedy's investment tax credit; in neither case was an apology offered for the harm inflicted on the economy and society.

Deming was a kind of American Protestant Don Quixote, who broke the wooden lance of Quality on the heavily fortified windmill of Stockholder Value.

Deming's Famous 14 Points

1 Create constancy of purpose toward improvement of product and service, with the aim to become competitive and to stay in business, and to provide jobs.

2 Adopt the new philosophy. We are in a new economic age. Western management must awaken to the challenge, must learn their responsibilities, and take on leadership for change.

3 Cease dependence on inspection to achieve quality. Eliminate the need for inspection on a mass basis by building quality into the product in the first place.

4 End the practice of awarding business on the basis of price tag. Instead, minimize total cost. Move toward a single supplier for any one item, on a long-term relationship of loyalty and trust.

5 Improve constantly and forever the system of production and service, to improve quality and productivity, and thus constantly decrease costs.

6 Institute training on the job.

7 Institute leadership. The aim of supervision should be to help people and machines and gadgets to do a better job. Supervision of management is in need of overhaul as well as supervision of production workers.

8 Drive out fear, so that everyone may work effectively for the company.

9 Break down barriers between departments. People in research, design, sales, and production must work as a team, to foresee problems of production and in use that may be encountered with the product or service.

10 Eliminate slogans, exhortations, and targets for the workforce asking for zero defects and new levels of productivity. Such exhortations only create adversarial relationships, as the bulk of the causes of low quality and low productivity belong to the system and thus lie beyond the power of the workforce.

11 a Eliminate work standards (quotas) on the factory floor. Substitute leadership.

   b Eliminate management by objective. Eliminate management by numbers, numerical goals. Substitute leadership.

12 a Remove barriers that rob the hourly worker of his right to pride of workmanship. The responsibility of supervisors must be changed from sheer numbers to quality.

   b Remove barriers that rob people in management and in engineering of their right to pride of workmanship. This means, *inter alia*, abolishment of the annual merit rating and of management by objective.

13 Institute a vigorous program of education and self-improvement.

14 Put everybody in the company to work to accomplish the transformation. The transformation is everybody's job.[36]

17

The Third (or Sino-Japanese) Industrial Revolution

Since the Puritan Migrants landed at Salem in 1630, the world has experienced three industrial revolutions. If the first was primarily British and the second American, how should one describe the third? The best answer is Sino-Japanese, since it originated in Japan but will find its fullest expression in China. Its point of departure was the grounding which our Three Wise Men gave to the senior managers of the Japanese communications equipment industry in then contemporary American managerial methods, as described in Chapter 10.

We have already described how their pupils converted 'bottom-up' to 'middle-up' or *kacho* management; this is the first distinguishing mark of the emerging third revolution; the second was the systematic application of electronics to manufacturing. In the year after General MacArthur's men left Japan, John Diebold (HBS, 1951) published his book, *Automation: The Advent of the Automatic Factory*. As Richard Walters has told us: 'During the 1950s and 1960s, as electronic computing began to make its appearance in a wider area of human activity, Mr Diebold's was an influential voice in how the new technology would be applied'[1] However, American manufacturers – with full order books and no obvious need to change their ways – would be slow to apply the new procedures. The Japanese would take them up with a vengeance, being conscious of the need to compete in the post-war world. When America's business leaders finally awoke to the need to modernize in the late 1960s, presidents Johnson and Nixon kyboshed the additional capital expenditure that would have been required to achieve this end (see pages 203 to 207). It was not until the 1980s, and in part as a result of Dr. Deming's ill-fated Quality Movement, that American industry tried to modernize on a large scale, thirty years after the Japanese had set the example. It was too little and more than too late. The Japanese had taken over a substantial part of the world market.

There was a large element of chance in all these developments. If General MacArthur had decided that his command could function adequately using the resources of the Army Signal Corps, there would have been no Civil Communications Section to teach the Japanese good contemporary American manufacturing practice. If Congress had funded the supply of industrial equipment, which it could easily have done, given the amount of money it was pouring into Japan to feed and fuel the entire population, there would have been no need to rebuild the plants of the communications equipment manufacturers. If Sarasohn, Protzman and Polkinghorn had been more interested in taking an extended holiday at the expense of the American taxpayer – as thousands of their fellow countrymen did – than in performing their work of supererogation, there would have been no CCS Seminar or Manual. The luckiest break of all was that the one and only industry to be selected for modernization by the Americans was also the only one closely and inevitably linked to the emerging technology of electronics, namely communications. In all these ways, the cards fell in a fortunate manner for Japan and, ultimately, for the rest of East Asia. Otherwise, the Sino-Japanese Industrial Revolution would not have occurred – or, at least, not there and then. The blending of *kacho*-style management, as described in Chapter 10, with electronics lay at the heart of the new methodology.

In the early 1950s, and with a high sense of public mission, the communications equipment companies set out to teach this new approach to their opposite numbers in other Japanese industries – for example, automobile manufacturing. As Madrick has pointed out, the latter: '. . . learned how to make a wider variety of durable automobiles by linking new managerial methods with computerized information and inventory systems, as well as with computer-aided designing and manufacturing'.[2] He adds that '. . . analyses of the production methods of the period rarely mentioned information technology, although it played a central role'. By the mid-1960s the Third Industrial Revolution was well underway in Japan, the rest of the world becoming aware of the extent of the resultant prosperity at the Tokyo Olympic Games of 1964. By the mid-1980s, it would be making an impact on China. It was then that Inoue (see page 109) told Kenneth Hopper how anxious Sumitomo's customers from the mainland were to learn good managerial practices. The torch that America had handed to Japan was being passed on to another major country.

By the early sixteenth century, the Chinese had developed a technical, managerial and maritime culture that was far in advance of even that of the seventeenth-century English Puritans. They invented the ship's compass, apparently first using it in *feng shui* practices. (Bacon was of course wrong when he spoke of the recent 'invention' of the compass – see page 4; he should have referred to its recent *adoption* by Western mariners.) During the reign of the Ming Emperor Zhu (1402–1424), and under the command of his favorite admiral, the eunuch, Zheng, a great fleet made seven epic journeys to India, Malaysia, East Africa and possibly Australia. The largest of Zheng's ships sported nine masts, was over 400 feet long and would, therefore, have dwarfed Winthrop's *Arbella*.

The seven voyages had been sponsored by the powerful, forward-looking eunuch class, but opposed by the equally powerful, but backward-looking, Confucian court mandarins. The eunuchs (resembling our Puritans in at least some respects) believed in commerce and something like the Western concept of progress, while the Confucians (resembling our Anglicans in others) preferred agriculture and worshiped not so much the past as stability. The mandarins won, the ocean-going ships being broken up after Zhu's death. In intellectual, technical and practical terms, China fell asleep for almost 600 years, to be reawakened in the 1980s by a kiss of life from a new class of technocrats that Mao's otherwise appalling regime had placed in power. Behind the new technocracy lay, ultimately, the influence of France, as in the early nineteenth-century United States – but an influence that had penetrated far more deeply into the Chinese soul than into its American counterpart.

Weber has contrasted the differing impacts of Confucianism and Puritanism on economic behavior. For him, the Protestant ethic lay at the root of Western capitalism because it 'substituted rational law and agreement for tradition'. In China, on the other hand, 'the pervasive factors were tradition, local custom and the personal favour of the official', which worked in the opposite direction. Whereas Calvin and his followers appeared to welcome the profit motive (see page 11), Confucius distrusted it; in the collection of his teaching called *The Analects*, he is quoted as saying that 'if one is guided by profit in one's actions, one will incur much ill will'.[3] During the Years that the Locust Ate, when Americans in general became distressed by their own economic backwardness, they were inclined to attribute the success of the various Asian 'miracles' to the influence of Confucianism. In other words, Toyota was believed to function better than General Motors because the Japanese viewed the company – any company – as a kind of extended family ruled by a father figure, the chief executive, to whom the sons and daughters owed respect. There was probably some truth in this view; if so, one can say that a fusion of cultures derived from Confucius and Calvin contributed to the success of the Third Industrial Revolution.

The Third Industrial Revolution reached China through various channels, of which two stand out. The first is direct investment by leading Japanese companies, for example by Toyota, which has sunk $1.3 billion into twelve Chinese plants employing 5,800 local people. Toyota is the supreme model and exemplar of a Third Industrial Revolution company; like Shakespeare's Julius Caesar, it 'doth bestride the narrow world like a colossus'. We have already discussed its world-famous Production System. And Toyota is by no means alone; as Victor Mallet has told us, 'Today Japan is one of the biggest investors in China, with 32,000 Japanese companies accounting for more than 9m jobs'.[4] The second and even more important channel is Taiwan, which was a Japanese colony from 1895 to 1945. During that half century, large numbers of its middle and upper classes became both bilingual and bicultural. Bilingualism and biculturalism, on their own, however, would not have enabled Taiwan to act as an intermediary between the Chrysanthemum and Middle Kingdoms if the island had not also been industrialized by its colonial masters between the two World Wars. Even after the island became independent in 1945, close social and commercial links with Japan survived – many leading families still send their children to the universities of Tokyo or Kyoto – which made it easy for the islanders to absorb the new industrial methodology.

In the last two decades of the twentieth century, mainland China offered the Taiwanese a tantalizing prospect – 1 billion consumers, industrious, literate, numerate and willing to work for derisory wages. Around 1990, the floodgates opened as the islanders poured men and money onto the mainland. Today there are said to be about 600,000 Taiwanese businessmen and managers working there[5] – no-one seems to know the exact number – and the value of the island's accumulated investment, officially estimated at $50 billion, is probably two or three times as much.[6] Thirty per cent of Chinese exports are said to be manufactured by companies owned or controlled by Taiwanese citizens,[7] sometimes described, as 'the Jews' or even 'the Scots' of China. Intermediation is further facilitated by an odd form of 'arbitrage' between two labor markets: every weekend, thousands of ill-paid but highly competent senior Japanese executives fly up to Taiwan for lucrative exercises in 'moonlighting'. They convey their skills and (we are told) some of their companies' secrets to the island's manufacturers, whereupon both pass rapidly across the straits to the mainland. As a part of their remuneration, the 'moonlighters' are said to taste unpuritanical fruits in the island's many hot springs. Taiwanese investment in the mainland is motivated in part by sentiment. The island's second richest man, Terry Gou, has invested in a film studio and a coal liquefaction plant in Shanxi, one of the poorest regions of north-west China, from which his parents fled in 1949; we are told, credibly, that he wants to 'give something back'. The Formosa Group (Formosa, meaning beautiful, is the old Portuguese name for Taiwan) is now building hospitals and schools on the mainland, many of them for charity.[8]

The domestication of the Third Industrial Revolution in China could not have occurred if it had not been for the profound respect for education, and in particular for engineering, which has existed there since the nineteenth century. On the mainland, today, there is amongst educated classes a wider acceptance of the importance of technology and of the technologist than there has ever been in the United States. Quite remarkably, when the senior levels of government in China were reorganized in 2002, *all* the men appointed to the cabinet were engineers – President Hu being a specialist in hydropower, Premier Wen in geological structures.[9] This not only brought a genuinely scientific outlook – not the pseudo-scientific outlook of the Cult of the (so-called) Expert – into the highest level of government; it also set an example for society as a whole.

By way of contrast, only one member of each of George W. Bush's first and second cabinets can be called an engineer – Don Evans in the first, a 'roughneck' oilman who worked his way up from the bottom to the top of his profession to become secretary of commerce; and Samuel W. Bodman, the secretary for energy, in the second. (In December 2005, Evans would decline an invitation by Vladimir Putin to become the chairman of Rosneft, the Russian state-controlled oil company.) Most of the others had degrees in law or in 'soft' subjects like business or political science.[10] We are frequently offered statistics like 'each year, China turns out four times the number of engineers produced by the United States'. Such observations have to be treated with caution, since Chinese statisticians use a rather looser definition of 'engineer' than their American counterparts and the US figures include the large numbers of foreigners studying in the US. Evidence from employers would suggest, however, that there is a growing shortage of native-born engineers in the United States. American engineers as a class believe that their contribution to society is inadequately appreciated.[11] Robert Lawrence Kuhn has asked whether the difficulties experienced in relations between the United States and China today do not arise from the fact that the majority of American senators and congressmen were schooled as lawyers, while nearly all China's leaders are engineers. Lawyers are by nature pessimists, always preparing for the worst; engineers tend to be optimists, wanting to make the world better. If this is so, China's current leaders may adhere more closely to our traditional Puritan profile than do the inhabitants of Capitol Hill.[12]

The Third Industrial Revolution will prove to be far more comprehensive in its Chinese manifestation than it has been in Japan. The reforms imposed by the Occupation Authorities affected only a part of Japanese manufacturing, never extending to 'process' industries such as pharmaceuticals, to the service sector or to government agencies. Japan's economy became brilliantly but lopsidedly successful. Today, the Japanese possess a small number of world-beating companies in a small number of industries but the rest of their manufacturing and most of their service sector remains mired in the past. By way of contrast, the Third Industrial Revolution can be expected to transform the *entire* economy of China, the public as well as the private sector, 'process' industries as well as 'non-process', the service sector as well as manufacturing, the public as well as the private sector. This is because Mao's regime wiped out virtually the entire existing social structure, leaving a *tabula rasa* on which his heirs could design a new economy from the bottom up.

In China, medical and nuclear research are said to be highly sophisticated.[13] We are told, for example, that the Institute of Nuclear and New Energy Technology at Beijing's Tsinghua University operates a new style of 'pebble bed' reactor far ahead of most reactors in the West, in the sense that it cannot suffer from 'melt-down', and that spent fuel derived from it cannot be re-used in weaponry.[14] Apart from exceptions like these, however, today's Chinese technology is derivative from the West and, therefore, does not suffer too much from the survival of an autocratic political regime. In the future, politics (or, rather, its absence) could stifle innovation and cause the new managerial revolution to die an early death in its new home; in the long term, good industrial management can function well only in an open, democratic society. Another source of trouble lies in unrest due to land disputes, corruption and the widening gap between rich and poor in Chinese society – according to the security minister, Zhou Yongkang, 74,000 protests and riots, involving more than 3.7 million people, took place in 2004, compared with only 10,000 in 1994.[15]

The likelihood, however, is that simple patriotism together with a wish for a higher standard of living will propel the industrious, literate and numerate Chinese people, with the tacit support of their government, yet further along the democratic and capitalist road pioneered by America in the nineteenth century. Margaret Thatcher has pointed out, in a speech made in Beijing, that it does not matter whether you start off with political freedom or economic freedom – you will end up sooner or later with both. Or as Chris Patten, the last British governor of Hong Kong, has said, 'you cannot allow people a lengthening menu of economic choices, yet deny them political choices'.[16] If that happens, there will be, within a generation, a score of Chinese-owned Toyota-style companies dominating every major manufacturing industry in the world and, probably, many service industries as well.

Already, Galanz and Yue Yuen are the world's largest manufacturers of microwave ovens and branded footwear, while Meidi is the leader in electric fans and Pearl the second-largest producer of pianos – all Great Engine companies of the future. Coming fast down the 'pike are Lenovo (formerly Legend), a firm that had its origins in the Chinese Academy of Science, which has just acquired IBM's personal computer business, China Systems in computer software and Huawei Technologies in telecoms.[17] Haier, China's leading manufacturer of household appliances is, by the way, noted for its capacity for innovation – for example, it has recently devised a machine for washing vegetables.[18] It is quite wrong to attribute the success of these companies only to low labor costs; otherwise companies like Hochiki (fire-detectors) and Haier would not be successfully manufacturing in the United States, where they pay American-style wages.[19] And why should the Chinese leave it to Wall Street to cream off all the profits of the new age? Shanghai or Hong Kong will take over from New York as the financial capital of the world, just as New York took over from London in the past century. The international language will remain English – but Chinese will be heard everywhere.

How should the United States react to these prospects? Needless to say – with concern; no country, least of all a Great Power, likes to lose control of its destiny. There are, however, severe limitations on what it can do. The disparity in the size of the two populations may resolve itself to some extent in the USA's favor with the passage of time. In 1776, China's population was 100 times that of the United States; today the ratio is only four to one. On optimistic assumptions, if immigration to the United States continues at the present level; and if the fertility rate of American women remains high while that of Chinese women falls to the level prevailing today in Japan or Hong Kong, the US population could be half the size of China's by the twenty-second century.[20] However, that century is a long way off. In any case, why should immigration into the United States continue so high, if there are large competing prosperous societies elsewhere; and why will the US fertility rate not decline again to the levels of the mid-1970s if – as we hope – a new Golden Age of Society emerges? The population disparity is more likely to remain overwhelming.

Nor can America wave a magic wand and uncover vast new natural resources. However, she can at least attempt to emulate China's prospective success in qualitative terms – specifically, by taking measures to restore the persistently high rate of growth in productivity that she enjoyed from 1870 to 1970. To do so, the USA must *domesticate* the Third Industrial Revolution by de-throning its (so-called) Experts. Only in this way can the USA hope to remain in the 'big league' of economic and political powers alongside China, India, Russia, the European Union and Brazil.

What do we mean by 'domesticate' in this context? We defined the Sino-Japanese Industrial Revolution in terms of a combination of *kacho* (or middle-up) management with the most advanced use of electronics on the factory floor. However, we also said that traditional American-style 'bottom-up' management was superior to *kacho* management since it involved the whole workforce in the decision-making activity – even those below the rank of foreman. The Third Industrial Revolution in its American manifestation will almost certainly be 'bottom-up' in the manner described by Bill Given in 1949. A pre-condition is the preservation or (where necessary) re-creation within manufacturing of the traditional American mixed foreman force consisting partly of graduates at the outset of their careers and partly of non-graduates at the peak of theirs (see page 114). The use of advanced electronics can be taken for granted. In service industries, and in public administration, it will also be necessary to bring young graduates closer to the *gemba*. All of our Twenty-five Principles underlying Good Practice from the Golden Age of Management will have to be observed, with particular emphasis on efficient upwards communication.

So far we have argued that America should seek to restore its earlier rate of increase in productivity for external reasons. There are also compelling reasons of a domestic nature. Seventy-seven million of America's 'baby boomers' will start collecting their social security benefits in 2008 and their Medicare benefits in 2011; by the time they have all retired in 2030, the size of the elderly population will have doubled but the workforce will have increased by only 18 per cent. The implications of this demographic change for America's national finances were analyzed in detail in a monograph written in 2003 by the economists Jagadeesh Gokhale and Kent Smetters.[21] They compared the present value of all the revenues that the government could expect to collect in the future with the present value of all its projected expenditure, including debt service, and concluded that the shortfall was a staggering $44 trillion – nearly seven times the size of the federal debt outstanding. These liabilities were so large as to render the US government, *de facto*, bankrupt.[22]

Gokhale and Smetters argued that there are only two possible solutions to this problem: to effect a sharp cut in federal expenditure or a sharp increase in federal taxes – either course would be exceedingly unpopular with the electorate and difficult to enact. There is, however, a third way to bridge the gap – namely, sharply to increase productivity per man-hour and, therefore, taxable income. The rate of productivity increase is a bit like compound interest; the difference between a 1 per cent and a 2 per cent interest rate may seem, and indeed is, trivial in any one year but it is also the difference between a sum of money doubling itself every thirty-six instead of every seventy years. The US government assumes, in a figure buried deep in the social security statistics, that productivity per man-hour will rise by an average of only 1.6 per cent per year over the next three-quarters of a century, far beneath the 2.6 per cent achieved between 1870 and 1970 and identical to the rate achieved in the Years that the Locust Ate.[23] If that rate can be more or less doubled to the 3 per cent rate achieved in the 1950s, and, if it is accompanied by appropriate tax increases and expenditure curbs, a solution to the problem will be at hand.

Japanese companies like Toyota, with their high domestic wage costs, face exactly the same kinds of pressure from low-wage countries as do their American counterparts. However, their response has been more intelligent: when they export jobs, they ensure that all the essential skills and technologies remain embedded in the culture of the parent company. For Toyota, 'off-shoring' is a reversible process: repatriating manufacturing to Japan, if that ever becomes necessary or desirable, will be an exercise not essentially different from exporting it in the first place. It is by no means alone in this approach; Kenwood Yamagata, the Japanese maker of home and car electronic equipment, has recently repatriated the manufacture of portable minidisc players from lower-cost Malaysia, improving profitability through greater efficiency on the shop-floor. The answer for America on all levels must therefore be to 'make like Toyota' – and like Kenwood Yamagata as well.

PART V
REVIVAL

I absolutely loathe the notion of professional management.

Jeff Immelt, chief executive officer of General Electric,
in a speech at Massachusetts Institute of Technology (2004).[1]

Two American icons which have made picaresque journeys

(above) 13: The AT&T 'Golden Boy'. Statue placed atop AT&T's
new building at 195 Broadway in 1916.[2]
See pages 151 and 152.

(below) 14: The Newport News plaque. Plaque placed on the wall of
Newport News Shipyard, Newport News, Virginia in 1917.
See page 117 and 152.

18

The False Dawn
(1996–2000)

The final lustrum (1996–2000) of the twentieth century brought a false dawn to America – a belief that the trials and tribulation of the Years that the Locust Ate were a thing of the past. It seemed to some citizens that the nation had finally entered on a period of stability and rising prosperity, similar to the one that their parents had inhabited in the Eisenhower and Kennedy decade. The chairman of the Federal Reserve System, Alan Greenspan, even spoke of a new economy based on information technology. The stock market, which the financier Bernard Baruch once described as the 'total barometer of the nation', enjoyed the longest sustained rise in its history. The property and the bond markets were similarly affected, the rise in all three conferring enormous purchasing power on asset owners and appearing to confirm that Greenspan was right. Was the Puritans' 'Citty on a Hill' once again on the verge of being realized, if only in a material sense? The advent of the year 2000 even encouraged a few deeply religious people to think in millennialist terms.

This optimistic view was reinforced by statistics published by the federal government, purporting to show that productivity per man-hour had accelerated to a point where it exceeded the average for the 100 years from 1870 to 1970, falling only a little short of the rate experienced in the Golden Age of Society:

> 1870–1970: 2.2 %
> 1945–1970: 2.7%
> 1970–1995: 1.6%
> 1996–2000: 2.5%[1]

The mood in those parts of the nation that benefited was exuberant, being well caught by Jeff Madrick, economics correspondent of the *New York Times* when he wrote that it looked to some as if 'the nation had crossed the threshold to permanent prosperity again'.[2]

The trouble was that it did not all quite add up. First of all, for the greater part of the nation, there was no visible improvement. Prosperity was a strictly minority sport. The few who benefited enjoyed wealth beyond the dreams of avarice. For the majority, there was no reversal of the trend of the previous twenty-five years. Family incomes rose only slightly; before 1970, they had grown by roughly 25 per cent in each decade. Unemployment may have fallen in the 1990s but it had been lower before. Life would be particularly hard on fifty-year-old males at the end of the century, half of whom earned less in real terms than they had done twenty years before. Employment did not rise to the extent expected in an allegedly expanding economy.

All of which creates a bit of a conundrum. If the statistics point in one direction and the personal experience of tens of millions of citizens points in the other, whom do you trust? If the much-publicized Great Leap Forward of the late 1990s was an illusion, why did the federal government publish statistics for productivity per man-hour purporting to show the contrary? Before probing into this matter, let us remind ourselves just what the term means. Conceptually simple, it was calculated by dividing gross domestic product, or all of the wealth created by the nation in any one year, by the number of hours worked. If one of these figures was wrong, that would have been bad enough; regrettably, there is some reason to think that both were wrong – that the numerator (total wealth created) was overstated and the denominator (total hours worked) understated, each therefore exaggerating the published figure. Furthermore, there is also some reason for thinking that the former was being *increasingly* overstated. If all these assumptions are correct, the official figures were seriously misleading.

The principal problem with gross domestic product is, quite simply, that it is gross. That means that it takes no account of the depreciation in the value of the nation's assets during the period in question. Corporate accounts provide an analogy: a company investing $100 million in a new factory does not charge this item as an expense in its income statement in the year when the plant is being built. Instead, it 'capitalizes' the figure as an asset in its balance sheet and then 'writes it off' over the plant's useful life. If this is ten years, there will be an annual 'non-cash' charge to its income statement of $10 million. No money changes hands as a result of these charges, which is why they are called 'non-cash', but they represent a real loss of value to the shareholders. If companies did not record the depreciation of their assets in this way, they would totally mislead themselves and their shareholders. Yet that is what the government's statisticians do when they offer us gross domestic product as a guide to the increase in the nation's wealth; they seriously overstate it. An article in the *Economist* of April 10, 2004 was headed: 'Measuring America's economy: GROSSLY DISTORTED PRODUCT: Are official figures exaggerating America's growth?'.

At the same time, hours worked are likely to be *under*stated because the government's statisticians rely for them on employers' records. Fifty years ago, most professional people worked five days a week from 9.00 a.m. until 5.00 p.m. Today they often arrive early in their offices and stay late. The 6.30 p.m. news broadcasts of the Big Three television networks are losing viewers because of this tendency;[3] we are told that working plus commuting time is 'edging up to 11 hours daily'.[4] Many people take laptop computers home so that they can continue the day's activities into the evening or the weekend. Moreover, the existence of mobile phones and laptops means that traveling by train or plane is no longer 'downtime'. The truth is that, for people who are not hourly paid, it is no longer possible to calculate the actual hours worked with any degree of accuracy. As for the hourly paid who are in the legal workforce, employers may play down the number of hours worked, while the activities of illegal immigrants go largely unrecorded. (There are believed to be about 12 million unauthorized migrants,[5] including 5 million Mexicans[6] living in the USA, most of whom tend to be young and at work.) If you divide one seriously inaccurate figure by another, particularly when they are similarly biased, you pass through a statistical looking glass into the fantasy world of the (so-called) Experts.

Conceptually, there is also doubt whether hours worked is an appropriate denominator in the calculation of productivity. What about the unemployed and the millions who have, unwillingly, fallen right out of the labor force and are no longer so classified? Should their vanishing contribution be left out of the calculation, as it is at present? They are as much part of society as the employed. Under existing rules, national productivity actually rises when low-paid workers become unemployed, which is absurd. There is, therefore, a strong case for changing the formula, so that the denominator in the calculation becomes the number of adults in the population, a procedure recently promoted by Jan Hatzius and his fellow economists at the investment bank, Goldman Sachs; when that is done, a much more pessimistic picture emerges.

This problem is aggravated by the enormous amount of money now flowing into computer software. Because the useful life of this item is only one to two years, statisticians in Europe do not even bother to record it as an asset in their national balance sheets; they show it instead as a charge against income when the expenditure is incurred.

In the United States, by way of contrast, it is capitalized and never written off! Kay tells us that wrong accounting of this kind alone added between 0.4 and 0.5 per cent per annum to reported US productivity gains between 1996 and 2000. He adds that 'no private sector firm would be allowed to treat computer or software expenditures in the manner in which they are treated in the US national accounts'.[7] Other reputable economists have made similar estimates.[8] Another distortion occurs because capital expenditure by the American military is capitalized and not written off in the national accounts; consequently the construction of an battleship or nuclear missile shows up as an increase in the wealth of the nation; in the more conservative accounting of other countries, it is treated as a cost unless the item has a possible civilian use (for example, a military hospital).[9]

If these (and other) pessimistic arguments are correct, it seems likely that, far from being a period when the nation 'crossed the threshold to permanent prosperity once again', the years from 1995 to 2000 were simply an extension of the Locust Years – or, as Madrick has told us, the new era of 'unprecedented prosperity' was simply a myth.[10] Much the same can be said about the even more exaggerated figures that have been released by the government's statisticians since 2000. A paper published in October 2003 by Hatzius expressed the view that true productivity per adult member of the population had been rising by only 0.6 per cent per year since the turn of the century, a far cry from the Labor Department's estimate of 3.4 per cent and well below the assumed long-term trend of 2 per cent. This was reported in *CNN Money Magazine* under the heading, 'Productivity: Miracle or mirage?'[11] Similarly pessimistic views have been expressed by Stephen Roach, chief economist of the investment bank, Morgan Stanley:

> Have we finally found the key [to increasing productivity]? It's doubtful. Productivity growth is sustainable when driven by creativity, risk-taking, innovation and, yes, new technology. It is fleeting when driven simply by downsizing and longer hours. With cost cutting still the credo and workers starting to reach physical limits, America's so-called productivity renaissance may be over before Americans even have a chance to enjoy it.[12]

Why should the federal government's statisticians publish inaccurate economic data? The best and simplest answer to the question is that they engage in deceit by default. Their methodology was wrong in theory for years but did little harm when few services were imported; when military expenditure was small; and when most business assets had useful lives far in excess of one year – and therefore annual depreciation was relatively small. However, the growing importance to the economy of information technology, if nothing else, should have led to a revision of the methodology and did not. There is, of course, good reason for the deceit, whether by default or otherwise. When in power in Washington, DC, each of the two ruling parties has a vested interest in promoting the view that the economy has prospered on its watch; Bill Clinton won the presidency from George Bush Sr. in 1992 by using the slogan: 'It's the economy, stupid' to publicize and exploit a recent rise in unemployment; since World War II only one incumbent US president (Eisenhower) has been re-elected to office in a year in which unemployment has risen, and he succeeded because of his role in leading a nation at war.[13] It is not irrelevant that the US government first began to publicize annual increases in the size of the national economy in the 1940s as part of war-time propaganda.[14]

It would be helpful if, in future, whenever the Bureau of Labor Statistics published figures about the national economy, it also issued a commentary reflecting on the reliability of the information. This would enable the consumers of statistics to use them sensibly, being fully aware of their limitations; it would also direct attention to areas requiring additional resources for research.[15] Furthermore, to the extent that there was genuine growth in the Locust Years and after, the probability is that it was due to an increase in the size (but not the productivity) of the workforce or to a further extension of credit or to both. The household savings rate (i.e. savings as a percentage of income) fell to zero in June 2005, the lowest rate on record, except for one month in 2001 when it was actually negative;[16] this compares with 10.5 per cent in the United States as recently as the early 1980s[17] and around that same figure in the European Union today.[18] Borrowing against the future is not a sound basis for continuing prosperity since, one day, debts have to be repaid or written off.

If the true rate for growth in productivity that characterized earlier ages is to be resumed, it will be necessary, first, to restore the respect of technology and the technologist that existed in the United States until the onset of the Years that the Locust Ate. The change in the climate of opinion that occurred in the 1960s is illustrated by what happened to Dr. Myron Tribus, a former Xerox senior executive, when he became assistant secretary of commerce for science and technology in the Nixon administration. Having presided over some studies of hurricanes, Tribus concluded that, if the relevant clouds were seeded with ice crystals, it might be possible to alter the dynamics of the big winds so that they were directed away from centers of population. Before experiments of this kind could take place, however, a serious objection had to be overcome: any person suffering on this account would have a claim against the federal government. A proper method of compensation would, therefore, have to be developed but no precedent existed for it. Tribus abandoned his project when he discovered that no-one in the administration would support live experiments. Had these studies gone ahead, Hurricane Katrina might not have been so disastrous. Tribus resigned from the administration because it exhibited, as he says today, 'a complete lack of interest in the advancement of science and technology'. He became a very distinguished director of the Center for Advanced Engineering Study at MIT – and befriended the authors of this book, when he learned that it was being written.[19]

This general loss of respect for technology and the technologist would lead Larry Summers, then president of Harvard, to make a speech in October 2004 in which he lamented that, 'while it is socially unacceptable at an elite university to admit that you haven't read a Shakespeare play, no stigma at all attaches to not knowing the difference between a gene and a chromosome or the meaning of exponential growth. He wanted 'every student to live in science for a while and not just to do some sightseeing in a course designed to help you 'think like a biologist'.[20] In line with his beliefs, Summers also wanted to establish an engineering school at Harvard, 'while expanding initiatives in the biosciences and other cutting-edge fields'.[21] Neither Summers nor the authors propose that every senior position in American business or government be staffed by 'gearheads' on the model of China – although that might not be a bad idea – but rather that technology should be recognized as one of the pillars on which modern civilization rests and that men and women imbued with its outlook should be found at all levels of business and government. The (effective) dismissal of President Summers by a left-leaning faculty in February 2006 was a tragedy for the university and for the nation.

One is not dealing here simply with abstract ideas unconnected with the real world. We have already observed that ideas have legs and that they walk; sometimes they run away from us. An obvious consequence of the profound shift in American attitudes towards technology was the massive power failure that left 50 million people without electricity for several days in the north-eastern states, starting on August 14, 2003, inflicting an estimated $12 million of losses.[22] This disaster had three principal causes. First, there were serious technical weaknesses in the transmission system, as a result of thirty years of culpable neglect by the new style of financially oriented managers, whose focus was – and is – on maximizing the financial return on assets in the short term, at the cost of endangering the security of supply and the return on assets in the medium and long term. Anthony J. Alexander, president of First Energy, the company where the problem originated, has told us that the national system is 'not designed to do what it's being asked to do'[23] – or, in other words, it is thoroughly out-of-date. There is an urgent need to invest $150–200 billion in a series of regional grids, simultaneously converting from electro-mechanical to digital transmission.[24] A well-known Wall Street banker tells the authors that the present arrangements are 'a national disgrace'; he adds that between 4 and 5 per cent of power is lost in distribution, as compared with 2 per cent in the better European systems.

Secondly, there was a regulatory structure of unbelievable complexity:

> The National Electricity Reliability Council is an umbrella [body] for 10 regional reliability councils that contain 140 so-called control areas ... The control areas report back to 18 reliability co-ordinators, which are not necessarily neatly related to the reliability councils. [One co-ordinator] overlaps four reliability councils and covers 37 control areas.[25]

Nightingale would have damned it in four words: 'nobody was in charge'. Furthermore the element of deregulation that occurred in most states between 1990 and 1992 had an adverse impact on capital spending; previously the utilities had been guaranteed a minimum return on their assets, providing some incentive to invest; foolishly, that incentive has been removed.

The third cause of the problem, which has been highlighted by Jeff Immelt, the new chief executive of General Electric, is that 'in the US, the lack of a coherent energy policy has slowed the exploitation of new developments'.[26] He is of the opinion that European countries are far ahead of the United States in technological innovation, particularly with regard to clean power. They too suffer from electricity black-outs, but so far on a lesser scale. Since the 1970s, France has built fifty-eight nuclear power plants, which supply 78 per cent of its needs for electricity, whereas the United States has built only a handful, one of which has since been closed. Today 103 elderly nuclear power plants generate 20 per cent of American electricity.[27]

We are told that, if all the nuclear plants under construction or consideration in the United States in 1979 had been completed, coal consumption would have fallen sufficiently for the country to meet its putative obligations under the Kyoto Treaty.[28] Since the power failure in August 2003, the American electricity system has, if anything, deteriorated – quite simply, because the demands put on it are increasing, while no serious attempt has been made to remedy its failings. A report by the US–Canada Power System Outage Task Force told us in 2004 that that it was 'likely to be more vulnerable to cascading outages than it was in the past'.[29] America pays a terrible price for business's and society's loss of interest in technology. In July 2006, a blackout in Queens, New York, affected 100,000 people and lasted nine days; afterwards customers learned that the feeder cables bringing their electricity were between thirty and sixty years old.

America's physical infrastructure is quite literally falling to pieces – not just the power lines but also the roads that people drive on, the pipes that carry clean water and sewerage, flood defenses in Louisiana and much else besides. Most of it came into existence because of public works programs during the Great Depression or in the post World War II boom, for example, when President Eisenhower signed into law the Federal-Aid Highway Act of 1956. Today the highways are heavily congested, costing the nation an estimated $63.1 billion each year. This is not just a question of catching up on what has been neglected; global warming will create new problems that require to be anticipated. The billions spent thoughtlessly on so-called 'nation building' in Iraq should have been devoted to 'nation re-building' at home.

19

The First Light of the True Dawn? (2001–2006)

Earlier we said that there was a need for a mental counter-revolution to negate the impact of the Cult of the (so-called) Expert. This now appears to be underway. Once again, the US army was the pioneer. As explained in Chapter 14, the military had been Taylorized in the decade after World War II, initially with the legitimate object of improving the procurement, distribution and use of physical assets. Before long, however, the management of human beings was being neo-Taylorized as well, leading to the statistical abuses described so eloquently by Colin Powell in his autobiography. These became so extreme that a severe reaction set in after the end of the Vietnam War in 1974. As Powell has told us:

> Our senior officers knew the war was going badly. Yet they bowed to groupthink pressure and kept up pretenses [about] the phony measure of body counts, the comforting illusion of secure hamlets, the inflated progress reports. As a corporate entity, the military failed to talk straight to its political superiors or to itself . . . Many of my generation . . . vowed that when our turn came to call the shots, we would not quietly acquiesce in half-hearted warfare for half-baked reasons that the American people could not understand or support.[1]

When Powell was appointed to command V Corps in Germany in 1986, he made good on his vow, gathering his senior officers round him to make a speech that could have been lifted unaltered out of our Twenty-five Principles of Good Management. A believer in self-improvement, Powell had taken an MBA degree at George Washington University in 1971; he therefore had direct personal experience of the new enemy. 'I don't purchase the latest management fads', he said to his commanders, adding, in words that could have come from General Marshall's pen: 'bad news is not like wine – it does not improve with age'. Under President Reagan, Powell became, first, the twelfth chairman of the Joint Chiefs of Staff, and then, secretary of defense. As a result of efforts by him and like-minded officers, the army that went to fight the Gulf War in 1991 was one that Marshall could have recognized. The obscene doctrine of the 'body count', imposed from above in Vietnam, had been replaced with a genuine desire, not always achieved, to minimize casualties on both sides. 'Jarheads' (your typical Marines) had been encouraged to study non-military matters and go on to college after their years of service.[2] Having been among the first of the great American institutions to be neo-Taylorized, the US army became the first to proceed in the opposite direction.

The officers would have achieved little, however, without the support of Casper Weinberger, secretary of defense from 1981 to 1988, to whom Powell reported in various capacities. Like Governor Winthrop in 1630 (see page 6), 'Cap' (as he was always known) found himself in charge of a largely demoralized establishment. How he helped to restore both confidence and a sense of direction provides a model of good managerial practice. Like Charles Coffin, the founder chairman of General Electric, he was 'a man born to command, yet who rarely issued orders'.[3] Like Douglas MacArthur, he encouraged debate with and among his subordinates. Like George Marshall and Colin Powell, he expected his subordinates to bring him bad news promptly. Although not a military man, he understood the nature of armed conflict better than most civilians, arguing that the United States should go to war only if it possessed, and was willing to use, overwhelming force[4] – which means that he understood, and sought to apply, Clausewitz's First Principle of War. Tragically for up to 100,000 Iraqis and 2,500 US soldiers, his successor under George W. Bush, Donald Rumsfeld, would adopt an opposite approach, futilely attempting to win the Iraq War by the application of the *minimum* of force deemed necessary to achieve his object. Mindless cost-cutting is ever the banner and insignia of the (so-called) Expert. Rumsfeld has been the public sector's equivalent of the 'imperial' chief executive, a 'top-down', 'professional' manager who refused to listen to his senior military advisors.[5] He sinned a second time against well-established military doctrine by reinforcing failure; a good commander reinforces strength.

How has the army behaved during the current Iraq War? The answer has to be that, in spite of malign pressure from above, it has been able to maintain some at least of its re-found independence of spirit. Soldiers speak their minds, even when that is unpopular with their political masters: for example, General George W. Casey, Jr., the commander-in-chief of coalition forces in Iraq, has credited foreigners with a minimal role in the insurgency – 'in bold contrast to his [political] masters in Washington'.[6] In the successful assault on Tal Al in Northern Iraq in 2005, the US army's 3rd Armored Cavalry Regiment, led by Col. H.R. McMaster, was able to distinguish itself, in part because it was 'extremely conscious of the complex make-up of the area they were fighting to control'; this is how wars should be fought.[7] It was that same Col. McMaster who had published a book called *Dereliction of Duty: Lyndon Johnson, Robert McNamara, the Joint Chiefs of Staff, and the Lies that Led to Vietnam* in 1997, which analyzed why the Joint Chiefs of Staff seemed unable or unwilling to challenge civilian decisions during the war in Vietnam.[8] Today information flows easily upwards, aided by the novelty of 'embedding' journalists in the fighting units and by technical advances. When wrong information is imparted, it can be rapidly corrected. This development has, however, been offset by the absurd decision to 'out-source' important functions to civilian contractors; since the contractors' lines-of-command do not – and cannot – connect efficiently with their military equivalents, the upward flow of accurate information is impeded, which is one reason why there have been serious abuses in prisons.

Elsewhere in the public sector, there has been a favorable development at FEMA, the Federal Emergency Management Agency, where the unfortunate Michael D. Brown, a person with no previous experience of handling disasters and who was blamed for the ineptitude of Washington's response to Hurricane Katrina, has been replaced by his deputy director, R. David Paulison. Before joining FEMA, Paulison had spent his entire career in the Miami-Dade Fire Department in Florida, working his way up from firefighter to chief in the classic American fashion. His promotion appears to have occurred in part by default, because no-one else wanted the job; let us be grateful for small mercies. Paulison's new deputy, the former commander of the Coast Guard's Pacific Operations, is also experienced in handling emergencies.[9]

The de-Taylorization of the army and of FEMA is now being paralleled by similar developments in important parts of the corporate world. America may have acquired her very own Toyota in the form of a recently reborn Great Engine of Growth and Prosperity: General Electric. In Chapter 12, we explained how the Cult of the (so-called) Expert, and with it the Business School Counter-Culture, established itself in that company when Ralph Cordiner became its chairman in 1958. As the title of his book, *New Frontiers in Professional Management*, implied, Cordiner was a believer in the highly mobile 'professional' manager who could (allegedly) turn his hand to anything. He encouraged the company's famed research laboratory, the 'House of Magic', to wither away, being replaced by Crotonville, its 'in-house' business school, as the spiritual heart of the company.

General Electric's new chief executive, Jeff Immelt, conforms in all but one significant respect to the profile of a typical pre-Cordiner 1950s corporate president, as described by Newcomer (see page 94). A native-born American, he has spent almost his entire career in one company, reaching the top in 2001 at the age of forty-five, a few years younger than Newcomer's stereotype. (His engineering father had worked for thirty-six years in its jet engine division.) It is perhaps not totally surprising that, when he became chief executive, Immelt should have instituted a regime at General Electric that looked uncannily like the one that Cordiner had banished. As the journalist, Jerry Useem, has said:

> He is a throwback to GE's first leader, the low-profile Charles Coffin, who would write out customer proposals in longhand; he is a throwback to GE's second leader, Owen Young, who espoused the notion that managers were trustees of something they did not own; he is a throwback to GE's third leader, Charles Wilson, who in the 40s addressed rumors of Westinghouse's plan to catch up with GE [by saying] 'they should live so long.'[10]

Immelt loathes 'the notion of professional management' that the business schools have propagated, *loathe* being one of the most powerful words in the American language. On page 289, we quote a view expressed in Drucker's *The Practice of Management* to the effect that if 'the salary levels of the four or five men at the head of the ladder are all close together, then the performance and morale of the entire management group is likely to be high'. Immelt conforms; in 2005, he actually took home less pay than each of the four next most senior executives.[11]

The new buzzword in the company (and it is not just a buzzword) is 'domain knowledge': 'In other words, senior GE management should have deep knowledge and understanding of the industries they work in rather than – as so often in the past – being moved from business to business every few years'.[12] As Immelt says, probably thinking of his engineer father, 'the best engines are built by jet engine people'. He has put General Electric's money where its mouth is, more than tripling the number of engineers among the company's top officers. He has resuscitated the 'House of Magic', naming it the Global Research Center and plunging it deeply into a variety of projects in nanotechnology, photo-voltaics, hydrogen power, advanced propulsion and the like, where there can be no certainty about the timing or extent of the financial return. The company has also opened new research centers in Europe, China and India.[13] Immelt acknowledges that his company, in particular, and America, in general, must look to Europe for leadership in the area of controlling carbon emissions. As he says, 'America is the leading consumer of energy [but] we are not the technical leader. Europe today is the major force for environmental innovation.'[14]

Immelt has not abolished the company's 'in-house' business school but he has reversed its role – whereas previously its job was to turn engineers (and others) into 'professional' managers, it is now expected to encourage former 'professional' managers to focus on understanding the business in which each works. Today, General Electric's senior executives, like Toyota's, are expected to go to the *gemba*, work with the *gembutsu* and assemble the *genjitsu*. Furthermore, what we have called 'integrated decision-making' (see page 25) is once again the order of the day. When acquiring another company, we are told that: 'GE has learned to start planning the detailed integration of its quarry – even when it is still doing due diligence' – that is, *before* the decision to acquire is finally made.[15] Immelt also takes a view on the 'off-shoring' of manufacturing that resembles Toyota's. This brings us to the respect in which Immelt does not conform to the Newcomer stereotype: he is an alumnus of the B-School (HBS, 1982). There have always been a minority of alumni who questioned the value of the education that they received there – we have already quoted Marcus (HBS, 1926)[16] on page 167 in this respect – but until now most of the doubts have been expressed by senior professors.

Immelt is not alone in what he is trying to achieve. When asked whom he admired most in business today, he replied with the name of another B-School alumnus: A.G. Lafley (HBS, 1977), the present chief executive of Procter & Gamble and a non-executive director of General Electric: 'I like the way he works – making Procter & Gamble more innovative, more global. He does it in a great, understated way, never putting himself in front, just letting his actions speak.'[17] During the Years that the Locust Ate, Procter & Gamble, a company founded in 1837 by William Procter and James Gamble, who swept up scraps from the slaughterhouses of Cincinnati and rendered the fat to make soap and candles,[18] had become a 'lumbering soap and [diapers] giant'.[19] Meanwhile, Lafley, a man whose entire career had been spent in the company, was working his way quietly up from the bottom to the top, which he reached at the age of fifty-five in 2002, only three years older than the average for chief executives at the mid-twentieth century. His two immediate predecessors had been aggressive in manner and tended to intimidate their subordinates, one of them, Ed Artzt, becoming known, ominously, as the Prince of Darkness. 'Mr Lafley is, by contrast, affable and consensual in his approach. He speaks with a slightly nasal New England twang, and with a calm self-assurance.'[20] A listener rather than a talker, he is a person to whom it is easy for subordinates to give bad news – a characteristic shared with General Marshall (see page 194) and indeed, by definition, with all good managers. His stated ambition is 'to build into this organization … something that will last long after I'm gone'.[21] Lafley is a 'proctoid' with a difference: he *meditates*.[22] (Much as one admires the outlook now prevailing at Procter & Gamble, one must also regret the recent adoption of marketing practices such as sending products free of charge to 250,00 teenagers, who are encouraged to recommend them to their friends.)[23]

General Electric and Procter & Gamble are not the only large companies reverting to type; in Chapter 12 we recorded how Exxon Mobil – the successor company to Standard Oil of New Jersey and, according to Drucker, once the most collegiate of companies – appointed an 'imperial' chief executive in Lee Raymond, a man who has been described as 'arrogant and high-handed' and who excoriated journalists and others when they questioned his judgment. On January 1, 2006, Exxon Mobil redeemed itself by replacing him with Rex Tillerson, a man who matches Newcomer's profile to a T – he was fifty-three years old when he reached the top, against fifty-two for the professor's typical mid-twentieth-century figure. A 'company lifer', Tillerson is a good listener, noted for his diplomatic skills, as well as a superb organizer. Before his appointment, his greatest achievement had been to negotiate the legal rights to the company's massive Sakhalin-I natural gas project off the eastern coast of Russia and to bring it in on time and within 10 per cent of the budgeted cost. Raymond had 'poured scorn on the potential for renewable energy'; like Immelt, Tillerson believes that global warming is a real threat to the planet and must be addressed.[24] In spite of its recent aberration, the company that he chairs is imbued through and through with the ascetic and disciplined outlook imposed on it a century and a quarter ago by its earnest Baptist founder, John D. Rockefeller. There are no 'dress-down Fridays' at headquarters in Irving, Texas.

The fact that, at Exxon Mobil, General Electric and Procter & Gamble – respectively, the first, second and seventh largest companies by market capitalization in the United States in March, 2006[25] – an 'imperial' chief executive should have been replaced by one who is collegiate in outlook points to a growing realization that there was something deeply wrong with American corporate management in recent decades. Tillerson, Immelt and Lafley are important not just for what they do but also for what they are. They provide a model and pattern not only for the companies that they lead and serve but also for the rest of the corporate world and for society as a whole. They stand in the great tradition of Lee, McCallum, Carnegie, du Pont and Sloan – not to mention Winthrop, who started it all off as the principal architect of the Massachusetts Bay Company in the late 1620s, and his son, John Jr., who built the first factory on American soil in 1643.

The world watches with interest and sympathy to see how other former Great Engine companies afflicted by the Cult of the (so-called) Expert address their consequent weaknesses – for example IBM, Merck, Hewlett-Packard, Disney, Motorola and Boeing. The first of these lost its way in the 1980s to such an extent that, in 1990, the loquacious Bill Gates predicted its demise by 1996. Somehow, it survived the inanities of 'reengineering', heavy internal politics and the absence of a clearly formulated corporate strategy. Since then, under its new chairman, Sam Palmisano, there has been one adverse development offset by at least three favorable ones. The adverse event was the decision to commit vast human and material resources to the field of management consulting. This is an area in which there is huge competition from half a dozen leading firms, including the high-powered Gartner Group which employs over 1,000 research analysts and consultants in eighty locations worldwide and serves more than 10,000 clients. Another serious competitor is Accenture, whose advisory business is one third the size of IBM's but growing twice as fast.[26] It is difficult to see what 'competitive advantage' IBM will possess over them.

The three favorable developments have all been in the areas of research and development. First has come a revival of interest in 'pure' research. Nicholas M. Donofrio, who is the current head of technology, conforms to the template of the mid-twentieth-century senior executive. A second-generation Italian immigrant and a graduate in electrical engineering from the great Rensselaer Polytechnic Institute – see page 40 – he also is a 'company lifer', having worked there for nearly forty unbroken years. This means that he not only experienced IBM's fabled corporate culture in its years of greatness but also saw it deteriorate.[27] Donofrio argues that 'pure, untargeted research' has to take 20 to 30 per cent of the research budget if IBM is to remain a world leader; he is proud to tell us that this ratio applies once again.[28] Secondly, the company's design facilities have been reopened and are back in business; as Donofrio explains: 'When you are dying as a company, this is one of the first things you throw out'.[29] For him, design forms part of marketing, being the bridge between the scientist and the engineer.

Thirdly, IBM has begun to co-operate extensively with the vast community of 'geeks' that has grown up around the work of the Finnish immigrant, Linus Torvalds, the man who created the new, highly successful Linux computer operating system. Torvalds has not tried to patent his invention, which he makes available free of charge to all comers. The Linux community is, as its originator has told us, 'a huge spider web, or better still – multiple spider webs representing dozens of related open-source projects'. At its heart sits the Open Source Development Laboratories, of which Torvalds is an employee.[30]

One could be forgiven for thinking that, in Linux, we are dealing with an entirely new kind of social and business phenomenon – a vast confraternity motivated simply by a noble desire to create better software. The word 'confraternity' is, however, a give-away. When and where did we meet it before? The answer is: in Chapter 5. For Linus Torvalds, read Col. Roswell Lee; for the Open Source Development Laboratories, read the Springfield Armory; for 'the Linux community', read the 'confraternity of New England gunsmiths' who, almost two centuries ago, freely exchanged information about new technical developments. A century before that, Benjamin Franklin – now described as 'early open-source kind of guy' – had refused to patent any of his inventions, such as the lightning conductor, on the grounds that he wanted to promote their widest possible use for the benefit of humanity.[31] This attitude of mind would survive into the Golden Age of Management, when Great Engine companies would regularly exchange information on, for example, 'best practice'. It was our (so-called) Experts who brought the shutters down on such behavior after 1970. Today's Linux community more than exemplifies the third of our quartet of Puritan characteristics, namely a specific moral outlook that subordinates the interests of the individual to the group with respect to a particular undertaking or to society as a whole.

There are continuing models of good governance among a host of smaller long-established companies, which have never abandoned the approach characterizing the mid-twentieth century – for example, Nucor Corp and Emerson Electric. An operator of mini steel mills, Nucor has recently achieved such commercial success that it shipped no less than 20.7 million tons of steel in 2005, outperforming the more famous US Steel in this respect. It was run for over thirty years from the mid-1960s by a now legendary chief executive, F. Kenneth Iverson, on lines that would have qualified it to appear as an example of excellence in both Given's *Bottom-up Management* and Drucker's *The Practice of Management*. Responsibility was – and still is – thrown right down to the lowest level capable of accepting it. Remuneration is based on group effort. Today's chief executive, Daniel R. DiMicco, is paid only twenty-three times the salary of his average employee, which compares with the average of 475 for large listed companies.

In an otherwise accurate article about Nucor in *BusinessWeek*, Nanette Byrnes tells us that, if other companies are to emulate Nucor's success, they must 'abandon the command-and-control model that has dominated American business of this book for the better part of a century . . .'.[32] Readers who have carefully studied Chapter 9 will be able to fault her observation on two grounds. First, 'command-and-control' actually means the opposite of what she thinks; in its military context, it approximates to 'bottom-up', rather than 'top-down'. Secondly, and much more important, although much of US corporate management has operated in a 'top-down' manner since 1970, the opposite was true before. Iverson's achievement lay in perpetuating a culture absorbed from an earlier generation of managers, and in knowing how to pass it on to his heirs.

Emerson is based in St Louis and was founded 116 years ago. It is a specialist maker of electric motors and other power equipment including compressors for refrigerators. We know a lot about its approach to management because Charles Knight, who was its chief executive for twenty-seven years from 1973 to 2000, is the co-author of a recent book, *Performance without Compromise: How Emerson Consistently Achieves Winning Results.*[33] His successor, David Farr, is only the third person to hold that post in half a century. Like the classic boss of a mid-twentieth-century company, Farr worked in many different departments of the company on his way to the top. The emphasis at Emerson is on 'the technology that lies behind the products – rather than, say, their marketing and promotion'. The company spends $850 million a year on research and development. It avoids publicity; as Farr puts it, 'people may call us boring – but if we are, boring is OK'; almost alone among companies of its size, Emerson has no public relations department. Significantly, it recorded a 10.2 per cent increase in earnings in 2007 – continuing a near-unbroken run of earnings increases stretching back over fifty years. Good management of the traditional kind enhances profitability.

Even the railroads, that first great embodiment of early American capitalism, have begun to waken from their half-century of torpor. This has occurred for highly practical reasons: increasing congestion on the highways, a shortage of truck drivers and a sharp rise in the cost of gasoline have obliged manufacturers and distributors to turn back to rail. There are today four major systems, the largest being Union

Pacific, the company that first made transcontinental rail travel possible when it spanned the continent in 1869. The second largest carries a less romantic name, BNSF; according to its chief executive, Matthew Rose: 'higher fuel costs are a railroad's best friend up to the point at which it starts affecting the economy'.[34] Capital expenditures throughout the industry are rising with profits. One can hope that, before long, it will be possible to retire the man pathetically guiding traffic at the railroad crossroads of America with hand signals (see page 183). The nation deserves a twenty-first-century transport system.

The New York Stock Exchange, that traditional temple of capitalism, also seemed to be moving in the right direction when it appointed as its chief executive, John Thain, formerly president of the investment bank, Goldman Sachs. The contrast between him and his predecessor, Richard Grasso, is extreme. Whereas Grasso was a 'showman', Thain 'has his ego in check'. Whereas Grasso was 'autocratic', Thain is described as 'a good delegater' who welcomes the expression of dissenting opinions. Whereas Grasso's pay packet was enormous and highly controversial, Thain accepted a level of remuneration well below what he could have been paid elsewhere. A graduate in electrical engineering from MIT as well as an alumnus of the B-School (HBS, 1979),[35] Thain comfortably straddles two contrasting worlds and is ideally suited to effect a transition into a 'high-tech' world of electronic share dealing.[36]

It is away from the stock exchange, however, that one of the more interesting developments has occurred. We are referring the phenomenon known as 'private equity'. Private equity means, literally, shares not publicly listed on a stock exchange. More specifically, the term applies to the practice of de-listing the shares of a company, reorganizing it – and then re-listing the shares some years later, to benefit from the greater liquidity that characterizes the public market. This approach acknowledges the fact that it is today difficult – indeed, often impossible – to effect fundamental changes in a company while it is listed, the reason being that the institutional investors who own most such shares take a strictly short-term view and punish any company that fails to report higher earnings in every single quarter of every year. (All this is part of the 'Lake Wobegon syndrome', to which we referred on page 191.) As explained in Chapter 15, the typical shareholder of the Golden Age was a private investor who benefited the economy by taking a long-term view. Today's better practitioners of private equity restore sanity to the marketplace by taking at least a medium-term view, defined as extending to between five and nine years. Regrettably, many private equity companies also engage in the disastrous kind of 'financial engineering' that we deplored in the listed area on pages xx and 152.

The weaknesses in the listed markets were highlighted by Charles Koch, chief executive of Koch Industries, a highly diversified, manufacturing and trading company and the largest unlisted company in the United States, when he told the *Wall Street Journal*:

> No company could have achieved the profitability we have if we had been a public company. No investor would have been patient enough to allow us to build a firm oriented towards long-term growth and profits ... The short-term infatuation with quarterly earnings on Wall Street restricts the earnings potential of Fortune 500 publicly traded firms. Public firms are also feeding grounds for lawyers and lawsuits.[37]

Quarterly reporting by listed companies became the normal practice only in the 1960s, just before the Years that the Locust Ate.[38] By being privately held, Koch avoids the malign influence of institutional investors, with their herd instincts. The biggest problem facing large listed companies like General Electric today lies in the need to reconcile the insistent, short-term demands of shareholders with the long-term ones of the business. It is too big to go private and the innovatory approach of its new chief executive 'has not yet taken Wall Street by storm'.[39] American capitalism is sick because so many of its practitioners, and their advisors, have an inadequate grasp of the theory of markets. General Electric also carries with it a toxic legacy from its former chairman and chief executive, Jack Welch, namely its heavy involvement in derivatives, instruments which Warren Buffett once unerringly described as 'financial weapons of mass destruction'. (Also known as the 'Sage of Omaha', Buffett is, according to *Forbes*, the second richest man in the world, with net assets of $36 billion, after Bill Gates' $46 billion.)

What about education? Increasingly aware of the deficiencies of public school education, state boards have recently been looking to Asian countries for inspiration. Georgia 'plans to adopt Japanese math standards as part of its overhaul of secondary-school curricula'. Others favor Singapore as a model, in part because its citizens speak English as a first-equal language (alongside Chinese) and textbooks are, therefore, written in that language; as a result, the city-state's mathematical curriculum and textbooks have been appropriated by about 200 American schools.[40] One wonders, however, why Americans need to look to Asia for leadership when an excellent model is to be found to the north of the forty-ninth parallel of latitude. In an international survey of educational standards in mathematics among fifteen-year-olds conducted in 2004, Canada ranked third and the United States twenty-eighth.[41]

Meantime, there is an increasing awareness of the absurdity of the Scholastic Achievement Test (see pages 198 and 199); of the fifty top liberal arts colleges listed by the US News & World Report, twelve have recently made the test optional. Ken Himmelman, dean of admissions at Bennington College, tells us that 'whether you get 1300 or 1250 doesn't really tell you much about [a candidate] as a person or a student'. In his opinion, all the attention to numbers 'becomes so crazy, it is almost a distraction'. In the fall of 2007, Bennington will add its name to the naysayers.[42]

Has America become a more 'clubbable' society since Putnam made the observations recorded in *Bowling Alone*, as described in Chapter 15? The answer has to be a qualified 'yes'. A positive example is the sharp increase in the percentage of voters who took part in the 2003 presidential elections when George W. Bush's vote was 23 per cent larger than in 1999, John Kerry's was 16 per cent higher than Al Gore's had been and the smaller parties also did proportionately better.[43] Youth, particularly in universities, appears to have rediscovered an interest in politics. The probable cause is the tragic event known as '9/11', which bound the nation together, as World War II had done. This same event appears to have accelerated another trend that was already underway – the creation and expansion of 'pastoral mega-churches' – defined as those having average weekly attendances of at least 2,000. In 1960, there were fewer than ten of these; today there are estimated to be at least 2,200. In late 2002, Drucker would tell *Forbes* that: 'pastoral megachurches are surely the most important social phenomenon in American society in the past thirty years. This[,] to my mind, is the greatest, the most important, the most momentous event, and the turning point not just in churches, but perhaps in the human spirit altogether.'[44]

Drucker is, unquestionably, the greatest writer on management of the past hundred years. As readers will be aware (see page xii), he played a critical part in the series of events that led to the writing of this book; there are scores of references to him in our text. He favored the creation of the mega-churches, arguing that they offered three ingredients necessary for our troubled and fractionalized society: a heightened sense of communal solidarity; a sense of spiritual direction, which gives meaning to the vast amount of knowledge at humanity's disposal; and pastoral care. Drucker's views fit well with the theses of this book. The growth of the internet and the world-wide-web has also brought people together as never before, and in many different ways. Scattered families who used to communicate only by sending birthday and Christmas cards now exchange emails daily or weekly.

There is some hope even for architecture. On page 151, we recounted the sad tale of the desecration of the old Penn Station in New York, buried beneath the new Madison Square Garden by the new breed of 'professional' managers in the early 1960s. This event was especially regrettable because the station was one of a pair of facing and matching masterpieces designed by the architects McKim, Mead & White – the other being the James A Farley Building (or General Post Office), which sits on the opposite, western side of Eighth Avenue. Happily, there is now a proposal to improve upon the original concept by joining the two complexes to form what the *New York Times* has described as 'a truly breathtaking entrance' to the city.[45]

Has the management of the economy as a whole improved since the days when presidents Johnson and Nixon, misled by their generation of (so-called) Experts, broke the back of corporate capital spending in the early 1970s (see pages 203 to 207), with the disastrous consequences for all Americans described in Chapter 15? The answer is that there were marked improvements under presidents Reagan and Clinton. An important event was the 1993 Budget Act, introduced by Clinton's first secretary of the treasury, Lloyd Bentsen, a grandson of Danish immigrants and already famous for delivering 'one of the best put-downs in political history'. As the Democratic Party's vice-presidential candidate 1988, he took part in a television debate with the Republican, Dan Quayle, in which the latter compared himself with Jack Kennedy. Bentsen replied: 'Senator, I served with Jack Kennedy. I knew Jack Kennedy. Jack Kennedy was a friend of mine. Senator, you are no Jack Kennedy.'[46]

Regrettably, the electorate's puritanical sensitivity to sexual eccentricity destroyed the Clinton administration and opened the door to the absurdly profligate George W. Bush. Since then, cuts in taxes have reduced federal revenues to 16 per cent of gross domestic product, the lowest in half a century, while expenditure has soared.[47] According to the economist, Joseph Stiglitz, the Iraq War is likely to cost the nation something like $2,000 billion by the end of the day, or twenty times early estimates.[48] Meantime, the deficit on the nation's current account as a percentage of gross domestic product has risen to 7 per cent; as Michael Woolfolk, senior currency strategist of Hamilton's Bank of New York, has pointed out, this is twice the figure that led to the formal devaluation of the US dollar in 1985.[49] The national economy is now out of control. That is not just the opinion of the authors;

it is that of America's most distinguished financial statesman, Paul Volcker, who told us all in an article in the *Washington Post* in early 2005 that: 'Circumstances seem to be as dangerous and intractable as any I can remember, and I can remember quite a lot. What really concerns me is that there seems to be so little willingness or capacity to do much about it.'[50] Volcker had been the chairman of the Federal Reserve System from 1979 to 1987, when he was responsible for destroying the great inflation generated by the White House during the Vietnam War. The outlook that he now professes is bleak. However, in a curious and inverted way, it also provides a modicum of hope. This is because in America, as in most countries, basic reform usually occurs only after a serious shock to public opinion.

The last great shock of this kind occurred in the early 1980s when America woke up to the fact that its manufacturing industry was antediluvian. As explained in Chapter 16, Dr. Deming analyzed the malady and correctly prescribed at least a partial remedy in the form of a return to the values and practices prevailing at the mid-twentieth century. Regrettably, another generation of (so-called) Experts in the persons of the 'reengineers' (see page 239) broke the back of his beloved Quality Movement. As Warren Buffett has told us, ironically, when you combine ignorance with borrowing, you get 'some pretty interesting results'.[51] One day the nation's credit will run out, in both the literal and the metaphorical sense of this expression; when that happens, there may be a second, even more profound, shock to American self-confidence, which should with luck lead to a reassessment of priorities. The key problem to be addressed will be the same one that Deming identified: a failure of management at many significant levels of society.

The appointments of the academic economist, Ben Bernanke, as chairman of the Board of Governors of the Federal Reserve System and of the investment banker, Hank Paulson, as secretary of the treasury in early 2006, give grounds for renewed hope. Principle Twenty-three underlying Good Managerial Practice (see page 288) tells us that 'complementarity is one of the keys to making appointments'; few men could be more complementary in their outlooks than this pair, the first a superb theorist, the second a highly capable and successful practitioner. As Irwin Stelzer, director of economic policy studies at the Hudson Institute has told us, '[s]o now the economic policy of the nation is in the hands of grown-ups'.[52] Unlike his immediate predecessors, Paulson brings 'domain knowledge' of the world of both domestic and international finance to the task in hand.

Previously, Paulson chaired Goldman Sachs, a bank which appears to the authors to observe many of our Principles of Good Management; first observed by the authors on the factory floor, these are applicable with appropriate modifications in all contexts, whether in the corporate, the governmental or the charitable sector. Goldman's 'team approach to business, which plays down personalities and insists that everyone is replaceable',[53] reflects our Principle Five; the bank insists on 'forget[ting] "the star system" and 'minimizing the use of the first person singular'. The fact that its senior employees pass easily in and out of public service, where they often distinguish themselves, obliquely reflects Principle Fifteen. It 'rotate[s] high-potential workers through jobs . . . every few years', as required by Principle Twenty-one. Employees are taught to be 'long-term greedy', a curious phrase that seems to reflect both Principles Ten and Twenty-two. It is not surprising that, when Goldman Sachs needed someone to 'head its in-house executive development center', it should have hired an executive from General Electric.[54]

Like Immelt, Paulson is concerned about global warming *and* has done something about it; under his rule, Goldman Sachs invested $1 billion in developing sources and uses for renewable energy. Chairman of the Nature Conservancy, he favors the enforcement of the Kyoto Protocol to the United Nations Framework Convention on Climate Change and advocates the introduction of a greenhouse-gas-emissions trading system in America. Paulson's personal interest in nature is evidenced by an unusual hobby for a Wall Streeter: bird-watching.[55] A devout Christian Scientist who does not drink or smoke (although he is said to swear like a trooper) Paulson does not engage in vulgar personal display. He is pledged to give his enormous wealth (said to be at least $700 million) to charity. Other Goldman Sachs partners likely to make a major contribution to society as a whole include: Jon Corzine, the 'no-nonsense and seemingly fiscally responsible' current governor of New Jersey'[56] Reuben Jeffrey, the new chairman of the federal regulatory body, the Commodity Futures Trading Commission;[57] Roger Liddell, the new chief of Europe's largest clearing house for listed shares, LCH.Clearnet,[58] and Mario Draghi, the new governor of the much troubled Bank of Italy.

One assumption that will have to be called into question is the toleration of inflation at up to 2.0% per annum. Since World War II, central banks have been so concerned about the impact of price deflation on levels of employment that they did not discourage increases in prices from regularly attaining, and often exceeding, that level. Albert Einstein, once remarked that the greatest power on earth was the compounding of interest rates; he could have said something similar about the compounding of inflation rates: over sixty years, this trivial amount per annum represents more than a tripling of prices. The great housing bubble, which reaches back over decades, and whose acceleration triggered the current financial crisis, can be attributed to this laxity.

The academic theorist Bernanke and the banking practitioner Paulson should now join together to address the central problem of the American economy, namely Congress' failure to exercise control over national expenditure and to relate it to income. The best solution is the one proposed by Kay,[59] Blinder and others, namely: to create a Fiscal Policy Commission equivalent in status to the central bank, both entities operating under guidelines provided by the Treasury and routinely approved by Congress. By this means a clear federal line-of-command would be established, with a 'generalist' Treasury at its head and with both the central bank and the new commission playing supporting 'staff' roles of a traditional kind. There appears to be no other way of eliminating America's appalling fiscal deficit. There may also be a case for establishing a third new body: an independent Asset Valuation Committee – as John Calverley, chief economist of American Express, has suggested – to offer 'amber and red light warnings' when price bubbles threaten to develop in assets such as stocks, houses and commodities.[60] Charles Goodhart, a former member of the Bank of England's Monetary Policy Committee, has long argued that central banks should be concerned about price bubbles of all kinds;[61] an alternative would be to direct the central bank to take account of them. It is in ways like these that fiscal sanity can be restored, and economic policy de-neo-Taylorized, in the United States and other countries today.

Do all the diverse developments recorded in this chapter genuinely reflect the reversal of a mega trend, or are they merely deceptive straws blowing in a fanciful wind? Only time will tell. Taken together, they point to, at least, the possibility of restoring America's former rate of economic growth, which can be achieved only by returning to the pure milk of the doctrines and practices underlying the creation of the Great Engines of Growth and Prosperity. As the late Bunzaemon Inoue, chairman of Sumitomo Rubber, once remarked to Kenneth Hopper, 'good management is just good management, at any time and in any place'. For those who require some guidance on how to proceed, a first step will be to read and absorb the Twenty-five Principles which appear next; they provide all the theory that is needed – the rest will simply be hard grind.

APPENDIX

Twenty-five Principles Underlying Good Practice from the Golden Age of Management – all with Puritan Overtones

INTRODUCTION

In Chapter 10 we met Charles Protzman, one of the Three Wise Men who were responsible for teaching the Japanese how to manage manufacturing in the late 1940s and early 1950s. Half a century later, his grandson, Charles Protzman III, is a hands-on management consultant who attempts to re-teach Americans how to manage factory floors or their equivalent in other sectors of the economy. Having read a draft of this book, he has written to say how much he supports its conclusions and recommendations, adding:

> In most companies that I have visited, and some where I have worked, there are shop floor workers who have been around for twenty or thirty years, supervised by 'professional' managers, who have been there for eighteen months or less, some with MBAs and some without. When a new departmental head is appointed, he has no idea what the workers are doing – so the workers have to stop work to train him. They may try to explain to him the problems that they face but he is unlikely to do much about them because he does not want to upset his boss and endanger a future promotion. Then he will start implementing changes to respond to upper management's demands, in order to meet the month's or the quarter's financial projections.
>
> The 'professional' manager earns no respect from the workforce because he can't show them how to build a product or to meet their immediate concerns. The workers are frustrated because no one will listen to them. He typically ends up trying to make friends with them, in an attempt to persuade them to do his bidding. Most workers have no incentive to cooperate because they figure they can wear him out, or outlast him, or both. Our managerial culture is so far behind Toyota's that it's just not funny.[1]

The solution for all of us is to re-learn, and apply, the principles of good management which had turned the United States into a great industrial and political power by the mid-twentieth century. Our interpretation of these principles appears below. They have been derived in the first place from a study of the organization of manufacturing in the Golden Age of Management. However, they apply, with appropriate modifications, to decision-making in all walks of life – civil government, the military, service industries, charities, clubs, hospitals, even on some essential points in the family itself.

SYSTEMS AND ROUTINES

PRINCIPLE ONE

All successful organizations, however simple, consist of systems within a system (see page 56).

Comment

This is the Master Principle, on which all the others are a gloss. The organization itself is the Grand System. Once its objectives have been defined, the next task is to create, and to determine the objectives of, the sub-systems. The approach of any manager to his work has therefore to be *systemic*, a key word in any business vocabulary. (Henry Mintzberg appeared to be saying much the same when he told us that managerial roles collectively constitute a *gestalt* or integrated whole).[2]

PRINCIPLE TWO

All systems are nurtured by routines, which must be regularly reviewed and refreshed (see page 173).

Comment

When the principal sub-systems have been designed, the next task is to establish these routines and put them into effect. Routines *liberate*; when they are functioning smoothly, the manager can concentrate on those key activities that cannot be subjected to routine, like the design of new products or closing a complex deal with a customer or a supplier. If an organization fails to establish good systemic routines, its employees will suffer from burnout, since the same pedestrian problems will have to be solved afresh time after time. The work of the British cyberneticist, Anthony Stafford Beer (1926–2002), a professor at Manchester Business School, is particularly relevant to any study of systems.

STRUCTURES AND HIERARCHY

PRINCIPLE THREE

The most important sub-system in any organization is the managerial hierarchy, which is likely to be based on some form of line-and-staff (see pages 49 and 50).

Comment

Hierarchies permit the systematic delegation of functions, roles and tasks. Delegation is not as simple a concept as it might seem at first blush. When the American engineer Homer Sarasohn inquired into the weaknesses of Japanese manufacturing in the late 1940s, he observed that, when managers delegated a task to a subordinate, they thought that they had also delegated the responsibility for it. He taught that the delegater retains that responsibility, just as if he were performing the task himself. Around the same time, Given made a similar point in his folksy way: 'Always remember, your man's failure is your failure'.[3]

Hierarchy is sometimes attacked on the grounds that it inhibits the creation of cross-departmental teams designed to address problems that affect more than one area in a firm. Anyone who propounds this view has misunderstood the way in which such teams come into being and function. They do not simply materialize out of the thin air. Someone in authority has to appoint them and they are effective only if they report to a person whose position in the hierarchy is strong enough to ensure that their recommendations are put into effect.

PRINCIPLE FOUR

The best type of hierarchy is 'bottom-up' (see pages 102 to 106).

Comment

As we explained in Chapter 9, in Great Engine companies 'bottom-up' management went far beyond the simple delegation of tasks to appropriate levels that was (and is) a characteristic of all well-run hierarchies. It superimposed an additional, informal, structure which permitted *de facto* operational responsibility to be pushed down to the lowest level capable of accepting it – which in a manufacturing plant would be the foreman – while not abolishing the formal line-of-command as the ultimate channel of communication and control. In a crisis, or when a major change of direction was required, a senior manager could reassert control over a subordinate at the drop of a hat and without upsetting the relationship.

PRINCIPLE FIVE

Leadership should as far as possible be collective or 'collegiate' (see page 163).

Comment

This principle was laid down (although not in these words) by Drucker in *The Practice of Management*. He believed that by the mid-twentieth century the position of chief executive had become too burdensome for one man, which was why, in successful companies, it was being increasingly shared with others. There was usually still someone called a chief executive officer 'as there is at General Electric' but the job was in fact discharged by a team. This trend had been pushed furthest at Standard Oil of New Jersey, now known as Exxon Mobil. At the very top of the managerial ladder were usually to be found what the Japanese call 'two men in a box' (see page 95).[4]

PRINCIPLE SIX

The middle manager is the keystone of the managerial arch (see page 101).

Comment

In the Golden Age of Management, first-class middle managers were important to companies organized both on 'bottom-up' and on other lines. This was for several excellent reasons. Someone had to ensure that the first-level managers were behaving as they should, a task far beyond the physical capacity of senior managers – who had other things, such as policy questions, to concern them. Someone had to act as an intermediary in the exchange of information between top and bottom. Long-serving middle managers also acted as the organization's 'corporate memory', making it unnecessary to address problems that had been solved before. Finally, the middle managers as a whole constituted the reservoir of tested talent from which future senior executives could be drawn.

PRINCIPLE SEVEN

'One man, one boss' – which should now be re-stated as 'one person, one boss' (see page 101).

Comment

All Great Engine companies observed this rule. Only if each executive reported to one single person could information flow freely up and down the line-of-command. In fact, without 'one person, one boss', there was (and can be) no proper line-of-command. A similar idea is expressed in Henri Fayol's Principle 5: 'Unity of command: for any action whatsoever: an employee should receive orders from one superior only; otherwise authority, discipline, order and stability are threatened'.[5] However, he failed to stress the importance of upward-flowing information. An alternative to 'one person, one boss' is 'matrix management', whereby one person will report to two or more bosses – for example one within a regional and another within a functional structure. As the management writer, Sumantra Ghoshal has told us, an arrangement of this kind leads to 'conflict and confusion'.[6]

DECISION-MAKING

PRINCIPLE EIGHT
Meetings are 'the medium of management work'.

Comment
'Meetings – The medium of management work' is the title of a chapter from Andrew Grove's *High Output Management* (see page 102).[7] Once again, it would have seemed superfluous to make this point fifty years ago. However, Grove thought it was necessary to reassert it in 1985. There had been an assault by fashionable consultants on the very idea of meetings. Drucker had suggested (even Homer nods) that no more than 25 per cent of a manager's time should be devoted to them. Less distinguished writers proposed that they should be held standing up (to keep them short). Others suggested that managers who had an open-door policy (presumably to encourage communication in the form of impromptu meetings) should sit with their backs to the door (presumably to discourage communication). Meetings should be as long or as short as the agenda requires and are best conducted sitting down.

PRINCIPLE NINE
'Integrated decision making' leads to right conclusions (see page 25).

Comment
It is this trait that more than any other distinguished traditional American and European kinds of management from each other; in Chapter 2 we commented that it probably existed already in the Massachusetts Bay Company and went a long way to explaining why the initial colonization was such a success. So far as the authors are aware, it has never been described specifically in print before or even given a name. It meant, among other things, that: (a) the implications of any important policy were worked out in great detail *before* a decision was taken to proceed or not; (b) the same group of people was involved in all four phases of the managerial process: planning, decision-making, execution and follow-up, which were therefore to be viewed as a continuum; and (c) careful provision was made against the contingency that some of the original assumptions might be incorrect. It followed from this Principle, as the night follows the day, that the makers of a decision were recognized as being responsible for its success or failure.

PRINCIPLE TEN
 Planning should be for the short term (say, one to four years), the medium term (say, five to eight years) and the long term (say, nine years up) (see page 96).

Comment
Great Engine companies felt themselves obliged to plan for the long and medium, as well as the short, term because the building of a manufacturing plant obliged them to think at least a decade ahead. Success in achieving the objectives of the plan would not be measured simply in terms of the profit and loss account but by looking at a whole range of indicators, including rising cash balances and satisfying the customer.

PRINCIPLE ELEVEN
 You should make a careful study of the mistakes and successes of the pioneers in your field – and learn from them (see page 25).

Comment
This is what Governor Winthrop and his colleagues did before setting out for New England in 1630. Studying other people's successes and failures, assuming the information is readily available, is the cheapest form of research – indeed, it is better than research since we are dealing in actual full-scale 'pilot' projects financed and mounted at the expense of others. Great Engine companies paid particular attention to their competitors' mistakes as well as their own.

PRINCIPLE TWELVE
 Excellent internal communications in all directions – but above all upwards – are necessary in any successful organization (see page 101).

Comment
The good American company in the mid-twentieth century was noted for the high quality of its information flow – communicating upwards, sideways and downwards within the company. The upward flow was not only the most important; the entire structure of the Great Engine company was geared to it.

PRINCIPLE THIRTEEN
 The manager must be a leader in both a practical and a moral sense (see page 103).

Comment
In recent decades many writers have distinguished between the roles of manager and leader. Leaders are characterized as charismatic figures

who command loyalty and offer a vision – managers as dull, gray administrators. This is a false apposition – to be effective, a manager must be able to lead. It is possible to lead without fuss.

PRINCIPLE FOURTEEN
You should use consultants sparingly – and 'strategic' consultants never (see page 158).

Comment
There are proper uses for consultants – for example, to perform one-off tasks for which it is inappropriate to hire permanent staff or to teach a skill that new circumstances require and that is not available within the existing organization. However, a dangerous frontier is crossed when consultants are asked to determine, or even discuss, what the strategy of a company should be. If senior managers cannot perform that task for themselves, they should leave; that is why they were appointed.

PRINCIPLE FIFTEEN
A manager should be aware of his responsibilities to society as a whole, including to his company's employees as human beings (see page 116).

Comment
People are not commodities to be bought and sold like a pound of sugar – and even sugar should not to be bought and sold without serious regard for the people who produce and consume it. As Drucker, Given and many others have taught us, in everything they do, managers operate within a social context. A company guided by Principle Fifteen will be reluctant to hire large numbers of additional staff at the beginning of a boom if there is a likelihood that they will have to be laid off when the boom ends.

PRINCIPLE SIXTEEN
If it ain't broke, you should try to make it work better (see Deming's famous 14 Points on pages 242 and 243).

Comment
One of the commonest remarks in the English language is: 'if it ain't broke, don't fix it'. However, if the human race had followed this precept since its ancestors materialized on earth, we would still be living in caves, wrapped in animal skins. (There may be some doubt about the skins.) The huge rises in productivity that were a characteristic of the US economy from 1870 to 1970 were the product of a different out-

look, which is encapsulated in this Principle; it explains the reason for all the others. A passionate desire to do and make things better is one of the most abiding characteristics of American society. The Japanese have a name for it: *kaizen*, or continuous improvement.

FINANCE

PRINCIPLE SEVENTEEN

Avoid debt like the plague – or, if that is impossible, use it sparingly (see pages 97 and 98).

Comment

One of the greatest strengths of America's Great Engine companies in their Golden Age lay in their conservative (i.e. debt-free) balance sheets. This enabled them to 'roll with the punches', paying large dividends in good times and little or none in bad. The assumption was that an organization should be designed for survival and that bad times might be just around the corner. This habit of mind has been carried forward, and is brilliantly exemplified today, by Japanese companies such as Toyota Motor.

TRAINING

PRINCIPLE EIGHTEEN

A manager should possess or acquire what is now known as 'domain knowledge' (see page 266), i.e. a profound understanding of the technology and business of his company, which can normally be gained only through a long apprenticeship in that company or in the same industry.

Comment

The basic fallacy promoted by business schools is that management as a skill can be learned from a theoretical point of view in an academic setting and thereafter exercised in any kind of organization. The corollary, also a fallacy, is that a manager need not have a thorough understanding of his company's technology. One need hardly add that, in Great Engine companies, it was taken for granted that every manager possessed as thorough a knowledge as possible of the business in which he operated.

PRINCIPLE NINETEEN

The testing and training of managers should be pragmatic and continuous (see pages 101 and 102).

Comment

In recent decades an entire industry has come into being with the object of testing applicants for managerial positions, often through 'psychometric testing'; one of the objects is to identify 'high flyers' – that is to say, people who have the ability to move up fast through the managerial ranks. Psychometry is an exercise in talent spotting. There are two problems with this approach. First, all that the tests demonstrate is that the person in question is good at passing tests – or has been lucky in the choice of questions. Secondly, the high flyers selected in this way are likely to be promoted quickly into a senior position for which they have not been adequately prepared by a period of training in a lower position. There was no such concept as a 'high flyer' and little psychometric testing in the Great Engine companies of the Golden Age of Management.

PRINCIPLE TWENTY

Managers who wish to reach the top should start at or near the bottom (see page 95).

Comment

The Great Engine companies of the mid-twentieth century were profoundly meritocratic in their outlook. Blue-collar workers were encouraged to better themselves by taking evening classes and indeed one British visitor to the United States in the 1950s reported that some shop-floor workers whom he met had qualifications equal to a university degree. However, the true meritocracy existed among graduates. They were expected to start at the bottom, often as foremen mixing with the non-graduate foremen, and then work their way towards the top. Only in this way could they acquire the thorough familiarity with the business that was required if they were to occupy the highest positions.

PRINCIPLE TWENTY-ONE

Job rotation (sometimes known as intra-company mobility) is desirable to create the 'rounded' executive (see page 163).

Comment

This Principle is tied in closely with the previous one since, in order to acquire an acquaintance with all or most of the activities of his company, the rising executive had to pass through all or most of its departments. (The blinkered specialist had no place in the organization – at least not if he wanted to rise and perhaps even if he wanted to stay where he was.) That this was normal practice in Great Engine companies around 1950 is evidenced in Drucker's writings. Speaking of 'a large electrical manufacturer' (probably General Electric), he tells us that: 'Men in the promotable group will be rotated into special jobs in functions they are not familiar with, each job assignment to last six months to two years'.[8]

EMPLOYMENT

PRINCIPLE TWENTY-TWO
Employment should in general be for the long term – by which is meant, at least, eight and, if possible, ten years (see page 161).

Comment
One of the reasons why this was important is that it took a long time for a new manager to build up a sufficient knowledge of his company's business for him to be able to play a useful role. Another was that the expense of training could not be justified if he was expected to leave within a short period of time. Yet a third was that only in this way could the company have got to know an employee well enough to decide whether he was suitable for promotion.

PRINCIPLE TWENTY-THREE
Complementarity is one of the keys to making appointments (see page 25).

Comment
In some other world beyond our ken there may have been a class of perfectly 'rounded' super-managers, each sufficient unto himself for all the tasks he was called upon to undertake. In Great Engine companies of the mid-twentieth century, whilst every effort was made to create a fully 'rounded' executive by job rotation and other methods, the outcome would nearly always have been less than perfect. Each manager had his strengths and his weaknesses. Hence the doctrine of complementarity. This meant, among other things, building teams. Thus if a chief executive was strong on engineering but weak on finance, he would be expected to appoint a strong financial director – and if he did not, his Board might insist on one. Unless a manager acknowledged his weaknesses, nothing much could have been done about them.

PRINCIPLE TWENTY-FOUR
The remuneration system should promote and reward group effort (see page 237).

Comment

The management literature of the Golden Age was generally unhelpful on this subject. If you read parts of Sloan's *My Years with General Motors* or Drucker's *The Practice of Management* superficially, you will obtain the impression that their authors were as wedded to the idea of bonuses and stock option plans as any high-flying corporate executive of the 1990s. In fact, bonuses and stock options formed a relatively small percentage of total remuneration in most companies at that time. A better view of mid-twentieth-century habits is to be found in an opinion Drucker attributed to the research department of an unnamed bank:

> If the top executive in a company gets a salary several times as large as the salaries paid to the Number Two, Three and Four men, you can be pretty sure that the firm is badly managed. But if the salary levels of the four or five men at the head of the ladder are all close together, then the performance and morale of the entire management group is likely to be high. . .[9]

Incentive systems that over-reward senior executives have no place in any company that practices collegiate decision-making – and/or 'bottom-up' management; where much of real responsibility is passed down the line, so should much of the reward.

PRINCIPLE TWENTY-FIVE
Avoid ostentation like the plague (see page 98).

Comment

The good manager of the period was aware that any success he achieved was due to his entire team. He behaved unostentatiously, remembering that he was simply the first among equals. David Farr is chief executive of Emerson Electric, a company which has observed Golden Age principles right down to the present day; he tells us (see page 271) that 'people may call us boring – but if we are, boring is OK'.

Notes

Authors' Introduction to the Paperback Edition

1 Zweig, P.L., *Wriston: Walter Wriston, Citibank, and the Rise and Fall of American Financial Supremacy.* Crown Publishers, New York. 1996 (see in particular Chapter 26).
2 Dash, E. and Creswell, J., 'Citigroup saw no red flags even as it made bolder bets', *New York Times*, November 23, 2008.
3 Fisher, N.I., 'Homer Sarasohn and American involvement in the evolution of Quality Management in Japan, 1945–1950', *International Statistical Review*, Volume 77, to be published in 2009. Also Adams, Stephen B., and Miranti, Paul J., 'Global Knowledge Transfer and Telecommunications: The Bell System in Japan, 1945–1952', *Enterprise and Society*, September 20, 2007.

Prologue

1 Gimein, M., 'The skilling trap: He and Lay sacrificed the spirit of the law for the letter. They're not alone', *BusinessWeek*, June 12, 2006.

Part I

1 Walker, H.T., 'The evolution of the American locomotive', *Scientific American Supplement*, May 1, 1897 (part 2 of 3).

Chapter 1

1 The authors have derived several paragraphs of this chapter from *American Business and History*, American Heritage, New York, 1972.
2 Bacon, F., *Essays: Of Atheism*, 1625.
3 Bacon, F., *Novum Organum, Aphorism LXXIV*, 1620.
4 Ibid. *Aphorism CXXIX*.
5 Micklethwait, J., and Wooldridge, A., *The Company: A Short History of a Revolutionary Idea*, Phoenix, London, 2003, p. 27.
6 Verne, J., *De la Terre à la Lune*, Paris, first published 1865. 'Les Yankees, ces premiers mécaniciens du monde, sont ingénieurs, comme les Italiens sont musiciens et les Allemands métaphysiciens – de naissance.'
7 Tocqueville, A. de, *Democracy in America and Two Essays on America*, translated by G.E. Bevan, Penguin, London, 2003, p. 42.
8 Schiff, S., 'Poor Richard's redemption', *New York Times*, January 17, 2006.
9 http://www.hoboes.com/html/FireBlade/Politics/Texas/Superman.

10 'St Lawrence of Google', *Economist*, January 14, 2006.

11 Bremer, F.J., *John Winthrop: America's Forgotten Founding Father*, Oxford University Press, Oxford, 2003, p. 194.

12 Cotton, Rev. J., *A Briefe Exposition with Practicall Observations upon the Whole Book of Ecclesiastes*, n.p., Boston, 1657, pp. 22, 57 & 28 (original consulted in rare books department, New York Public Library).

13 Nichols, F.D., and Bear Jr., J.A., *Monticello*, Thomas Jefferson Memorial Foundation, Monticello, VA, 1967, p. 59.

14 Hawke, D.F., *Paine*, Harper & Row, New York, 1974.

15 London, S., 'The advantages of private equity eroded by its own success', *Financial Times*, February 15, 2006.

16 Bacon, F., *Essays: Of Friendship*, 1625.

17 Miller, P., *Errand into the Wilderness*, Harper Torch Books, New York, 1964, p. 143.

18 Ibid., p. 143.

19 Genesis, 1: 28. Our italics, not His.

20 Hofstadter, R., Aaron, D., and Miller, W., *The United States: History of a Republic*, Prentice-Hall, New York, 1967, p. 113.

21 Taylor, A., *American Colonies: The Penguin History of the United States*, Viking Penguin, New York, 2001, p. 186.

22 Einstein, A., 'Introduction', to De Villamil, R., *Newton: the Man*, G.D. Knox, London, 1931.

23 www.cslib.org/gov/winthropj.

24 Tawney, R.H., *Religion and the Rise of Capitalism*, Mentor, New York, 1954, p. 164 (first published 1926).

25 Herman, A., *How the Scots Invented the Modern World*, Crown, New York, 2001, pp. 199 & 200.

26 'How Anglo is America?', *Economist*, November 13, 2004 (quoting from James Webb's *Born Fighting*).

27 Taylor, A., op. cit., p. 178.

28 Tawney, op. cit., p. 93.

29 Wren, D., *The Evolution of Management Thought*, Wiley, New York, 1994, p. 24.

30 Coolidge, C., *Foundations of the Republic*, Scribner's, New York, 1926, p. 76.

31 Coolidge, C., *The Price of Freedom*, Scribner's, New York, 1924, p. 173.

32 http://www.calvin-coolidge.org/html/the_business_of_america_is_bus. html.

33 Quoted in Fischer, D.H., *Albion's Seed: Four British Folkways in America*, Oxford University Press, New York, 1989, p. 10.

34 Katutani, M., 'An identity crisis for Norman Rockwell's America', *New York Times*, May 28, 2004.

35 Glader, P., and Bellman, E., 'Mittal's Arcelor bid marks break with tradition', *Wall Street Journal*, July 10, 2006.

36 Trevor-Roper, H.R., *Religion, the Reformation and Social Change and Other Essays*, Macmillan, London, 1967, pp. 1–45.

37 MacCulloch, D., *Reformation: Europe's House Divided*, Penguin, London, 2004, p. 604.

38 Drinan, P., 'Opus Dei's legacy of liberal economics', *Financial Times*, May 17, 2006.

Chapter 2

1 Andrews, op. cit., pp. 98 & 100.
2 Amory, C., *Who Killed Society?*, Harper, New York, 1960, p. 44.
3 Elliott, J., 'Suffolk tombs hold key to US founding father', *Sunday Times*, June 12, 2005.
4 Taylor, A., op. cit., p. 131.
5 Warner, C.D., *Captain John Smith*, Kessinger, Whitefish, MT, 2004, p. 100 (first published 1881).
6 *Reasons to be Considered for Justifying the Undertakers of the Intended Plantation in New England, and for Encouraging such Whose Hearts God Shall Move to Join with Them in It,* written in the hand of Forth Winthrop, secretary to, and son of, Governor John Winthrop, c. 1628. See http://www.winthrop-society.org/doc_reasons.php.
7 Rowse, A.L., *The Elizabethans and America: The Trevelyan Lectures at Cambridge, 1959*, Harper & Row, New York, 1965, p. 67.
8 Ibid., pp. 81 & 82.
9 Gimen, op. cit.
10 Willison, G. F., *Saints and Strangers*, Reynal & Hitchcock, New York, 1945, pp. 242 & 314.
11 http://www.mayflowerhistory.com/History/voyage6.php.
12 Pomfret, J.E., *Founding the American Colonies: 1583–1660*, Harper, New York, 1970, p. 115.
13 Doherty, K., *William Bradford: Rock of Plymouth*, Twenty-First Century Books, Brookfield, CT, c. 1999, p. 42.
14 Willison, op. cit., pp. 147 & 148.
15 Ibid., p. 166.
16 Andrews, C.M., *The Colonial Period of American History*, Volume 1, Yale University Press, New Haven, CT, 1936, p. 395.
17 Ibid, p. 395.
18 Taylor, A., op. cit., pp. 168 & 169.
19 MacCulloch, D., *The Reformation: Europe's House Divided 1490–1700*, Penguin, London, 2004, p. 536 (first published 2003). Cf. http://www.bigelowsociety.com/rod/winthrop.htm.
20 Morison, S.E., *Builders of the Bay Colony*, Houghton Mifflin, Boston, 1964, p. 37.
21 Morison, op. cit., p. 70.
22 Ibid., p. 78.
23 Ibid., p. 80.
24 Taylor, A., op. cit., p. 170.
25 Morison, op. cit., p. 66.
26 Bremer, op. cit., p. 160.
27 Bacon, *Essays: Of Nobility*, 1625.
28 Morison, op. cit., p. 66.

29 Rodger, N.A.M., *The Command of the Ocean*, W.W. Norton, New York, 2005, p. 113.

30 Ibid., p. 122.

31 MacCulloch, op. cit., p. 536.

32 *Encyclopaedia Britannica*, 1994–2001.

33 Taylor, A., op. cit., p. 267.

34 Chernow, R., *Alexander Hamilton*, Penguin, New York, 2004, p. 87.

35 Ibid., p. 4.

36 Bacon, *Essays: Of Dispatch*, 1625.

37 Diamond, J., *Collapse: How Societies Choose to Fail or Survive*, Penguin Allen Lane, London, 2005, p. 398.

38 Williamson, J.G., *Real Wages and Relative Factor Prices in the Third World 1820–1940: Latin America*, discussion paper no. 1853, Harvard Institute of Economic Research, Cambridge, MA, 1998.

39 Mander, B., 'Mennonites find a place in modern Paraguay', *Financial Times*, August 8, 2006.

Chapter 3

1 Title taken from a poem 'On the prospects of planting arts and learning in America', by the Anglo-Irish bishop George Berkeley, who spent his last years living in Rhode Island, and after whom the university of that name in California would be called.

2 Francis, R., *Ann the Word: The Story of Ann Lee, Female Messiah, Mother of the Shakers, the Woman Clothed with the Sun*, Fourth Estate, London, 2001, p. 3.

3 http://www.geocities.com/Athens/Acropolis/1890/Brigham_Young. htm.

4 Francis, op. cit., p. 134.

5 Stein , S.J., *The Shaker Experience in America: A History of the United Society of Believers*, Yale, New Haven, CT, 1992, p. 303.

6 Ibid., pp. 273 & 274. Also email from Dr. Stein to William Hopper dated February 21, 2004.

7 Madrick, J., *Why Economies Grow: The Forces That Shape Prosperity and How We Can Get Them Working Again*, Basic Books, New York, 2002, p. 186.

8 Maurer, H. (ed.), 'Stormin' Mormons', *BusinessWeek*, August 21–8, 2006.

9 Hughes, J., *The Vital Few: American Economic Progress and its Protagonists*, Bantam, Boston, 1967, p. 102.

10 http://inventors.about.com/library/inventors/bl_Odometer.htm.

11 http://www.adherents.com/largecom/fam_lds_inv.html.

12 Hughes, op. cit., p. 89.

13 McLynn, F., *Wagons West: The Epic Story of America's Overland Trails*, Cape, London, 2002, passim.

14 Gorham, M., *The Real Book of Great American Journeys*, Garden City Books, New York, 1953, p. 98.

15 Ibid., p. 108.

16 Hughes, op. cit., p. 104.

17 Ibid., p. 109.

18 Shakespeare, W., *Twelfth Night*, act II, scene iii.

19 http://www.utahpriorities.net/briefs/rb8_crime.html.

20 'Methamphetamine: Instant pleasure, instant ageing', *Economist*, June 18, 2005.

Chapter 4

1 Judd, D.I., *Empire: The British Imperial Experience from 1765 to the Present*, Fontana, London, 1997, p. 25.
2 'A history lesson for Hoon', *Financial Times*, January 28, 2003.
3 Rodger, op. cit., p. 410.
4 Hounsell, D.A., *From the American System to Mass Production. 1800–1932*, Johns Hopkins University Press, Baltimore, MD, 1984, pp. 26 & 27.
5 Temin, P. (ed.), *Engines of Enterprise: An Economic History of New England*, Harvard University Press, Cambridge, MA, 2000, pp. 266 & 267.
6 *Encyclopaedia Britannica*, op. cit.
7 Long, F., 'Battle of Britain myth', *Evening Standard*, April 10, 1995.
8 Rowse, op. cit., p. 122. 123.
9 Gelb, Norman. 'Ferocious War of American Fratricide'. *Financial Times*, July 29, 2000.
10 Fischer, op. cit., p. 860.
11 Rowse, op. cit., pp. 122 & 123.
12 Hounshell, D.A., *From the American System to Mass Production, 1800–1932: The Development of Manufacturing Technology in the United States*, Johns Hopkins University Press, Baltimore, c. 1984, p. 25.
13 Rolt, L.T.C., *Tools for the Job: A Short History of Machine Tools*, B.T. Batsford, London, 1965, p. 140.
14 Pannabecker, J.R., 'Diderot, the mechanical arts, and the *Encyclopédie*: In search of the heritage of technology education', *Journal of Technology Education*, Vol. 6, No. 1, Fall, 1994.
15 We follow the usual practice of writing the family name in two words and the company's abbreviated name as one.
16 http://www.dupont.com/corp/gbl-company/hist1800.html.
17 Cobden, R., *England, Ireland and America*, Institute for the Study of Human Issues, Philadelphia, 1980, p. 94 (first published 1835).
18 Brooke Hindle, in conversation with K. Hopper, 1970.

Part II

1 Roe, J., *English and American Tool Builders*, McGraw-Hill, New York, 1916, reproduced in Rolt, op. cit., p. 150.
2 Reproduced in Wrege, C.D., and Greenwood, R.G., F*rederick W. Taylor: The Father of Scientific Management: Myth and Reality*, Business One Irwin, Homewood, IL, 1991, p. 210.

Chapter 5

1 Wren, op. cit., p. 73.

2 Drucker, P.F., 'The American CEO', *Wall Street Journal,* December 30, 2004.

3 Chandler, A.D., *The Visible Hand: The Managerial Revolution in American Business,* Harvard University Press, Cambridge, MA, 1997, p. 1 (first published 1977).

4 Tull, B. 'Draft Report to Department of Economics', presented to the History and Development Workshop, University of Massachusetts, n.d., p. 17.

5 Arndt, M., 'Creativity overflowing: After its initial efforts stumbled, Whirlpool is reaping big dividends from its push to jump-start innovation', *BusinessWeek,* May 8, 2006.

6 Kanigel, R., *The One Best Way: Frederick Winslow Taylor and the Enigma of Efficiency,* Viking, New York, 1997, p. 141.

7 http://www.rootsweb.com/~mahampde/christchurch/cc113.html.

8 Wren, op. cit., p. 74.

9 Ibid., p. 73.

10 Rosenberg, N., editor, *The American System of Manufactures,* Edinburgh University Press, Edinburgh, 1969, p. 47.

11 Ibid., p. 70, quoting Fitch, C., *Report on the Manufactures of Interchangeable Mechanism: Tenth Census of the U.S. 11,* 1880, pp. 13–19.

12 Hounshell, op. cit., quoted by Temin, P., *The Industrialization of New England 1830–1889, Engines of Enterprise: An Economic History of New England,* Harvard, Cambridge, MA, 2000, p. 120.

13 Rolt, op. cit., p. 151.

14 Owen, G., *From Empire to Europe: The Decline and Revival of British Industry Since the Second World War,* HarperCollins, London, 1999, p. 15.

15 Rosenberg, op. cit., p. 14.

16 Whitworth, J., *Mr. Whitworth's Special Report: Reports from Commissioners: New York Industrial Exhibition,* Volume 36, London, 1854, p. 42.

17 Rosenberg, op. cit., p. 15.

18 Smith, M.R., *Harper's Ferry Armory and the New Technology: The Challenge of Change,* Cornell University Press, Ithaca, NY, 1977, pp. 334–335.

19 Gibbs-Smith, C.H., *The Great Exhibition of 1851,* Her Majesty's Stationery Office, London, 1981, p. 23.

20 Cobden, op. cit., p. 89.

21 Chandler, A.D., *Scale and Scope: The Dynamics of Industrial Capitalism,* Harvard University Press, Cambridge, MA, 1990, p. 62.

22 Rolt, op. cit., p. 144.

23 http://www.vaes.vt.edu/steeles/mccormick/speech.html.

24 Kennedy, D.M., 'Whatever it is, I'm against it', review of Richard Norton Smith's *The Colonel: The Life and Legend of Robert R. McCormick, 1880–1955, New York Times Review of Books,* July 13, 1997.

25 *Encyclopaedia Britannica,* op. cit.

26 'Report of the Arbitrators to whom the Bramah Lock Controversy was referred', *Morning Chronicle,* September 8, 1851.

27 Telephone conversation between W. Hopper and Jeremy Bramah, July 9, 2002.

28 Rosenberg states it was on the same day. See Rosenberg, op. cit., Introduction, pp. 9 & 10.

29 http://uers.hol.gr/~dilos/prehis/prerm1.htm.

30 Rosenberg, op. cit., p. 57.

31 http://www/wbmt/tudelft.nl/pto/research/publications/Dissertation _Baartman/intro. . .07/02/2004.

32 Reproduced on page 47 with the permission of the National Portrait Gallery in Washington, DC.

33 Rolt, op. cit., p. 143.

34 Hart, J.D., *The Oxford Companion to American Literature*, Sixth Edition, Oxford University Press, Oxford, 1995, p. 91.

35 Morgan, W., *An American Icon: Brother Jonathan and American Identity*, Associated University Presses, London, 1988, p. 21.

36 Ibid., pp. 25 & 26.

37 Walker, H.T., *The Evolution of the American Locomotive*, Scientific American Supplement, May 1, 1897 (Part 2 of 3).

38 http:www.unicover.com/EA4PA2ZB.htm.

39 http://shipwrecks.ws/1865_BJ_Shipwreck.htm.

40 Tocqueville., op. cit., p. 744.

Chapter 6

1 Chandler, A.D., and Hikino, T., 'The large industrial enterprise', in Chandler, A.D., Amatori, F., and Hikino, T. (eds), *Big Business and the Wealth of Nations*, Cambridge University Press, Cambridge, 1997, p. 35.

2 http://www.horatioalger.com/junior.htm.

3 Chandler, *The Visible Hand*, op. cit., p. 98.

4 McCallum, D.C., *The Water Mill*, privately printed, 1870, p. 10.

5 http://clausewitz.com/CWZHOME/WhichTrans.html.

6 Wren, op. cit., p. 80.

7 Chandler, *The Visible Hand*, op. cit., p. 104.

8 Wren, op. cit., p. 81.

9 Chandler, *The Visible Hand*, op. cit., p. 176.

10 http://www.willamette.edu/~fthompso/MgmtCon/McCallum.htm.

11 Wren, op. cit., p. 85.

12 http://www.learner.org/biographyofamerica/prog14/transcript/page03.html.

13 'Pittsburgh pirate', *Economist*, February 1, 2003, quoting Krass, P., *Carnegie*, John Wiley, London, 2003.

Chapter 7

1 Wren, op. cit., pp. 105 & 106.

2 Kanigel, op. cit., p. 220.

3 Ibid., p. 412.

4 Taylor, F.W., *The Principles of Scientific Management*, Dover, New York, 1998, p. 28 (first published 1911).

5 Callahan, R.E., *Education and the Cult of Efficiency: A Study of the Social Forces that Have Shaped the Administration of the Public Schools*, University of Chicago Press, Chicago, 1962, p. 39.

6 http://countrystudies.us/united-states/history-83.htm.

7 Hunter-Tilney, L., 'Radical innocent', *FTmagazine*, July 1–2, 2004.

8 'Of meat, Mexicans and social mobility', *Economist*, June 17, 2006.

9 http://college.hmco.com/history/readerscomp/rcah/html/.

10 Gilbreth, F.B., and Carey, E.G., *Cheaper by the Dozen*, Thomas Y. Crewel, New York, 1948, pp. 2 & 3.

11 Mogensen, A.M., 'How it all started', in Graham, Jr., B.S., and Titus, P.S. (eds), *The Amazing Oversight: Total Participation for Productivity*, Amacom, New York, 1979.

12 Gelder, L. van, 'Millionaire and a mountain, forgotten', *New York Times*, November 8, 1996.

13 Kanigel, op. cit., p. 19.

Chapter 8

1 Chandler Jr., A.D. and Salsbury, S., *Pierre S. Du Pont and the Making of the Modern Corporation*, BeardBooks, Washington, DC, 1971, p. xxi.

2 http://www.henryfordestate.com/fordfamily.html.

3 Chandler and Salsbury, op. cit., p. 16.

4 'Science and profit', *Economist*, February 17, 2001.

5 Useem, J., 'Another boss, another revolution – Jeff Immelt is following a time-honored tradition: abandoning the most treasured ideas of his predecessor', *Fortune*, April 5, 2004.

6 Cane, A., 'Juggling genius of computing', *Financial Times*, March 15, 2001.

7 Goodheart, A., 'Ten days that changed history', *New York Times*, July 2, 2006.

8 'The fall of a corporate queen', *Economist*, February 3, 2005.

9 http://www.bbc.co.uk/print/radio4/reith2005/lecture3.shtml/print.

10 Galambos, L., 'Theodore N Vail and the role of innovation in the modern Bell system', *Business History Review*, Vol. 66, Spring 1992, p. 96.

Part III
Chapter 9

1 The business historian, Alfred Chandler, has used the phrase, 'the Golden Age of business', to refer to the decades immediately after World War II; the authors have extended the concept backwards, for reasons explained in this chapter.

2 London, S., 'Inside track: Who killed Arthur Andersen?', *Financial Times*, March 11, 2003.

3 Newcomer, M., *The Big Business Executive; the Factors that Made him, 1900–1950*, Columbia University Press, New York, 1955, p. 149.

4 Hopper, K., 'From foreman to company chief', *Financial Times*, February 21, 1969; 'Production men at the helm', *Financial Times*, January 23, 1969; 'Engineers take the controls', *Financial Times*, September 13, 1968; 'Creating Japan's new industrial management: The Americans as teachers', *Human Resource Management*, Summer/Fall 1982, pp. 13–34.

5 Whyte, W.H., *The Organization Man*, Simon & Schuster, New York, 1956, p. 1.

6 Chandler, *The Visible Hand*, op. cit., pp. 489 & 490.

7 Ibid., p. 10

8 Shakespeare, W., *Hamlet*, act I, scene iii.

9 'Dicing with debt: Budget deficits are fine in bad times – as long as they are cut in good times', *Economist*, August 21, 2003.

10 Hino S., *Inside the Mind of Toyota: Management Principles for Enduring Growth*, translated by Andrew Dillon, Productivity Press, New York, 2006, pp. 144 & 145.

11 Smiles, S., *Self-help; with Illustrations of Character and Conduct*, Harper, New York, 1860, p. 182.

12 Smith, L. 'Japan 2.0', *Fortune: Europe Edition*, July 24, 2006.

13 Putnam, R., *Bowling Alone: The Collapse and Revival of American Community*, Simon & Schuster, New York, 2000, p. 17.

14 Smockum, E., 'A sign of our times', *Financial Times*, February 19 & 20, 2005.

15 Crozier, M., 'A new rationale for American business,' *Daedalus: The Journal of the American Academy of Arts and Sciences*, Winter, 1969, p. 148.

16 Drucker, P.F., *The Practice of Management*, Harper Perennial, New York, 1986, p. x (first published 1954).

17 Chase, S., Ruttenberg, S.H., and Given, W.B., *The Social Responsibility of Management*, New York University Press, New York, 1950, p. xii.

18 See also Given, op. cit., p. 137.

19 Ibid., pp. 5 & 6.

20 Ibid., p. 4, emphasis added.

21 Grove, A., *High Output Management*, Vintage Random House, New York, 1985, p. 39.

22 Given, op. cit., p. viii.

23 Ibid. p. 22.

24 Drucker, *The Practice of Management*, op. cit., p. 142.

25 Ibid., pp. 140 & 141.

26 Ibid., p. 141.

27 Drucker, P.F., *The Concept of the Corporation*, Transaction Publishers, New Brunswick, NJ, and London, 1993, p. 51.

28 Ibid., p. 52.

29 Drucker, *The Practice of Management*, op. cit., p. 173.

30 Packard, D., *The HP Way: How Bill Hewlett and I Built Our Company,* Harperbusiness, New York, 1995. p. 72.

31 *Naval Command and Control*, Naval Doctrine Publication 6, chapter 1. Department of the Navy. Washington, D.C., 1995 (http://www.nwdc.navy.mil/Library/documents/NDPs/ndp6/ndp60002).

32 Nakamoto, M., 'Japan's electronics industry revived', *Financial Times*, August 5, 2004.

Chapter 10

1 Smith, L., 'Japan 2.0', *Fortune*, July 24, 2006.

2 Cohen, T., *Remaking Japan: The American Occupation as New Deal*, edited by H. Passin, Free Press, New York, 1987, p. 309.

3 Reischauer, E.O., *Japan: The Story of a Nation*, Knopf, New York, 1974.

4 Cohen, op. cit., p. 421.

5 Ibid., p. 199.

6 The communications engineer, W.S. McGill, who preceded them, also played an important role.

7 T. Kato, industrial consultant, in conversation with K. Hopper, on introduction of P.F. Drucker.

8 H. Sarasohn, in conversation with K. Hopper.

9 Kornicki, P.F., *Meiji Japan: Political, Economic and Social History*, Volume 2, Routledge, London, 1998, p. xxiv.

10 Smiles, S., *Self-help; with Illustrations of Character and Conduct*, Oxford University Press, Oxford, 2002, p. 1 (reprint of 1867 edition).

11 Ibid., p. 3

12 Col. Charles L. Kades, in telephone conversation with K. Hopper; Hopper, 'Creating Japan's new industrial management', op. cit., republished in Japanese in *Sengyo Kunren*, vols 338 and 339, Nikkeiren, the Japanese Federation of Employers' Associations, Tokyo, 1983.

13 H. Sarasohn, in conversation with K. Hopper.

14 B. Inoue, in correspondence with K. Hopper, 1979–1986.

15 Tsutsui, W.M., *Manufacturing Ideology: Scientific Management in Twentieth Century Japan*, Princeton University Press, Princeton, 1998, an unusually readable book on this subject. Tsutsui is director of the Confucian Institute at Kansas University. As a Korean, he can view Japanese affairs with objectivity but also with an understanding that is difficult for other nationalities to match. As a man at home in three languages – Korean, Japanese and English – he is able to convey his thoughts with clarity and precision.

16 Sarasohn, H.M., and Protzman, C.A., *The Fundamentals of Industrial Management: CCS Management Course*, Civil Communications Section, GHQ, SCAP, electronic edition, 1998, p. 160.

17 Gabor, A., *The Man Who Discovered Quality: How W. Edwards Deming Brought the Quality Revolution to America*, Times Books, New York, c. 1990, pp. 77–79.

18 Hopper, K., 'Graduates on the floor', *Management Today*, October 1966, pp. 74–7. Also Hopper, 'Creating Japan's new industrial mangement', op. cit.

19 S. Nagasaki, in telephone conversation with K. Hopper, 1980.

20 Keller, M., *Collision: GM, Toyota, Volkswagen and the Race to Own the Twentieth Century*, Doubleday, New York, 1993, p. 195.

21 Sarasohn and Protzman, op. cit., p. 148.

22 Ibid., p. 146.

23 Ibid., p. 149.
24 Ibid., p. 149.
25 Ibid., p. 150.
26 Morita, A., Reingold, E.M., and Shimomura, M., *Made in Japan*, Collins, London, 1987, p. 53.
27 Lyons, N. The Sony Vision, Crown, New York, 1975, p. 16.
28 Letter from Sarasohn to Akio Morita, April 20, 1990.
29 Hopper, 'Creating Japan's new industrial management', op. cit., p. 20.
30 Cringley, Robert X. *Accidental Empires,* Penguin, London, 1993, pp. 42 & 43 (first published 1992).
31 H. Sarasohn, in conversation with K. Hopper, 1982.
32 Drucker, *The Practice of Management*, op. cit., pp. x & xi.
33 'Woman dies in crash; two critically injured', *Morgantown News-Herald*, July 19, 1962.

Part IV
Chapter 11

1 Taylor, F.W., *The Principles of Scientific Management*, op. cit., p. iv.
2 Kanigel, op. cit., p. 418.
3 Ibid., p. 419.
4 Ibid., p. 354 (quoting from Copley, F.B., *Frederick W. Taylor: Father of Scientific Management*, Harper, New York, 1923, Vol. 2, p. 148).
5 Kanigel, op. cit., p. 396
6 Taylor, F.W., *On Shop Management,* Harper & Brothers, New York, 1911 (first published 1903).
7 'Roads could save $1,000,000 a day. Brandeis says Scientific Management could do it – calls rate increase unnecessary', *New York Times*, November 22, 1910.
8 Taylor, F.W., *The Principles of Scientific Management*, pp. 64 & 65.
9 Chandler, *The Visible Hand*, op. cit., p. 276.
10 Wren, op. cit. pp. 150–153.
11 Witzel, M., 'Dance teacher to the giants', *Financial Times*, August 11, 2003.
12 Hemp, P., 'Shake-up at the *Harvard Business Review*', *Boston Globe*, June 2, 1992. See also *USA Today*, May 29, 1992.
13 Keynes, J.M., *General Theory of Employment, Interest and Money*, Macmillan, London, 1936, Book VII, chapter 24.
14 Kohn, A., *Punished by Rewards: The Trouble with Gold Stars, Incentive Plans, A's, Praise, and Other Bribes*, Houghton Mifflin, Boston, 1993, p. 3.
15 Brittan, S., 'The flaw of education, education, education: The multiplication of paper credentials for employment contributes neither to true learning nor to the national economy', *Financial Times*, June 8, 2000.
16 'Cats' eyes in the dark?', *Economist*, March 19, 2005.
17 Alden. E., 'Bush aims to restore morale at CIA', *Financial Times*, March 4, 2005.
18 Boles, T., 'Journey to the red planet', *Financial Times*, July 31 & August 1, 2005.

19 'NASA's Mars-Moon initiative jeopardizes important science opportunities, according to American Physical Society report', APS Press Release, November 22, 2004.

20 Tomkins, R., 'No logos on the battlefield', *Financial Times*, March 19, 2003.

21 Edgecliffe-Johnson, A., 'Mr Stanley brought the gift of "shoppertainment" ', *Financial Times*, January 29, 2002.

22 Marcus, S., *The Viewpoints of Stanley Marcus: A Ten-year Perspective*, University of North Texas Press, Denton, TX, 1995, p. 114.

23 Cohn, L., 'A grocery war that's not about food', *BusinessWeek*, October 20, 2003.

24 Martin, P., 'The fall of the House of Marks', *Financial Times*, October 2, 2001.

25 'Intel: Not paranoid enough', *Economist*, May 27, 2006.

26 Tomkins, R., 'Goodbye to the golden age of global brands', *Financial Times*, June 6, 2003.

27 Birchall, J., 'The cultural maelstrom of international retailing', *Financial Times*, June 4 & 5, 2005.

28 Holmes, S., Kunii, I.M., and Ewing, J., 'For Starbucks, there's no place like home', *BusinessWeek*, June 9, 2003, p. 41.

29 Boyle, D., 'Brands are no substitute for the real thing', *Financial Times*, August 8, 2003.

30 Hakim, D., with Maynard, M., 'Top marketer quits Chrysler as car sales remain weak', *New York Times*, May 31, 2003.

31 Welch, D., 'The car guys take charge at GM', *BusinessWeek*, November 26, 2001.

32 Muller, J., 'Chrysler's wink-wink, nudge-nudge campaign: So far, its risqué new TV ads aren't adding up to car sales', *BusinessWeek*, December 17, 2001.

33 Liu, B., 'Kodak man to market Coca-Cola', *Financial Times*, June 6, 2003.

34 Drucker, *The Practice of Management,* op. cit., pp. 184 & 185.

35 Skapinker, M., 'A cost-effective way to lose control of your business', *Financial Times*, October 15, 2003.

36 O'Connell, D., 'Outsourcing giant casts off its "your mess for less" reputation', *Sunday Times*, May 15, 2005.

37 http://www.namesfacesplaces.com/html/view. Glover. T., 'EDS to cut 20,000 jobs as IT consultancy slumps', *The Business*, September 12 & 13, 2004.

38 Hamm, S., 'Is outsourcing on the outs?', *BusinessWeek*, October 4, 2004.

39 Holmes, S., 'The 787 encounters turbulence', *BusinessWeek*, June 19, 2006.

40 Jaggi, R., 'Hospitals to get bug-buster chiefs', *Financial Times*, July 12, 2004.

41 Skapinker, M., 'Outsourcing the essentials is bad for your health', *Financial Times*, January 26, 2005.

Chapter 12

1 Buckley, N., 'Procter's gamble on outside ideas has paid off', *Financial Times*, January 14, 2005.

2 'Pfizer's latest remedy', *Economist,* August 5, 2006.

3 Keller, M., *Rude Awakening: The Rise, Fall and Struggle for Recovery of GM,* Harper Perennial, New York, 1990, pp. 24 & 25, emphasis added (originally published 1989).

4 Ibid., pp. 29 & 30.

5 Chaffin, J., 'Myers portrays Ebbers as a hands-on boss', *Financial Times,* February 2, 2005.

6 http://www.sternstewart.com/content/evaluation/info/092002.pdf.

7 Keller, *Rude Awakening,* op. cit., p. 27.

8 Ibid., p. 264.

9 'General Motors: The lost years', *Economist,* June 11, 2005.

10 http://www.autointell.net/nao_companies/general_motors/gmpolm.

11 Keller, *Rude Awakening,* op. cit., p. 246.

12 Simon, B., 'Japanese gain top spots in US car league', *Financial Times,* March 2, 2006.

13 Shirouzu, N., 'Toyota runs low on expertise to power global push', *Asian Wall Street Journal,* July 13, 2005.

14 Chung, J. and Beales, R., 'Worst-kept secret takes market by surprise', *Financial Times,* May 7 & 8, 2005.

15 Simon, B., 'Chrysler's magic formula', *Financial Times,* March 21, 2005.

16 Murray, S., 'Expanded training centre for the best of General Electric', at http://www.ge.com/en/company/news/expanded_training.htm.

17 Useem, op. cit.

18 Lowe, J., *Welch, an American Icon,* Wiley, New York, 2001, p. 143.

19 Ibid., p. 19.

20 Plender, J., 'Rethinking strategy', *Financial Times,* February 6, 2006.

21 Wighton, D., and Roberts, D., 'GE's money machine is bucking the trend', *Financial Times,* July 22, 2005.

22 O'Boyle, T., *At Any Cost: Jack Welch, General Electric and the Pursuit of Profit,* Alfred A. Knopf, New York, 1998, p. 79.

23 Lowe, op. cit., p. 211.

24 Goldsworthy, C., 'GM: Look it up', *Fortune,* April 17, 2006.

25 Neave, H.R., *The Deming Dimension,* SPC Press, Knoxville, TN, 1990, pp. 76 & 77.

26 http://www.honeywell.com/about/page1_2_3.html.

27 Frietsch, D., *Statistical Quality Control: A Loss Minimization Approach,* World Scientific Publishing, Sinagport, 1999, p. 164.

28 Gabor, A., *The Capitalist Philosophers: The Geniuses of Modern Business – Their Lives, Times, and Ideas,* Crown Business, New York, 2000, p. 187.

29 Wheeler, D., 'The Six-Sigma zone' (see http://www.spc-press.com).

30 Witzel, M., 'The danger of mistaking the science of measuring as divine', *Financial Times,* August 3, 2005.

31 http://www.3sigma.com.

32 Cane, A., 'Bland image of a latter-day business saint', Financial Times, August 9, 2006.

33 Drucker, *The Practice of Management,* op. cit., pp. 38 & 39.

34 Temin, P., with Galambos, L., *The Fall of the Bell System,* Cambridge University Press, Cambridge, 1987, p. 320.

35 Gore, A., and Blood, D., 'It is essential that investors look to the long term', *Financial Times*, July 7, 2005.

36 http://members.tripod.com/~ntgen/bw/vail_ntbl.html.

37 http://www.thecityreview.com/sonyatt.html.

38 Politi, J., and Kirchgaessner, S., 'Independent board plan for Bell Labs', *Financial Times*, March 27, 2006.

39 Ward, A., and Gregan, P., 'Coke settles SEC probe into Japanese unit', *Financial Times*, April 19, 2005.

40 Foust, D., 'Gone flat', *BusinessWeek*, December 20, 2004.

41 http://www.goizueta.emory.edu/aboutgoizueta/goizueta_legacy.html.

42 Ward, A., 'Pepsi's market value tops Coke', *Financial Times*, December 13, 2005.

43 Brooker, K., 'The Pepsi machine', *Fortune*, February 6, 2006.

44 Ward, A., 'Buffett backs Coke Scheme', *Financial Times*, April 7, 2006.

45 Ward, A., 'Coke to buy back 13% of shares', *Financial Times*, July 21, 2006.

46 Cringely, R.X., *Accidental Empires: How the Boys from Silicon Valley Make their Millions, Battle Foreign Competition and Still Can't Get a Date*, Penguin, London, 1992, p. 134.

47 London, S., 'Is Big Blue fading again? Costs are being cut but new profit areas are hard to find', *Financial Times*, May 9, 2005.

48 Drucker, *The Practice of Management*, op. cit., p. 260.

49 Donofrio, N., 'The value of innovation', 2004 Hinton Lecture, *Ingenia*, issue 22, London, March 2005.

50 http://www.reasearch.ibm.com/resources/awards.shtml.

51 http://money.cnn.com/magazines/fortune/fortune_archive/2005/.

52 'J. Collins: Built to last', *Economist*, July 24, 2004.

53 Collins, J.C., and Porras, J.I., *Built to Last: Successful Habits of Visionary Companies*, Random House, New York, 2000, p. 83 (first published 1994).

54 Skapinker, M., 'Why I was wrong about Airbus's new super-large jet', *Financial Times*, May 4, 2005; O'Connell, C., 'Boeing bounces back in air wars', *Sunday Times*, June 12, 2005.

55 Spiegel, P., 'America's Eagle is brought down to earth with a bump', *Financial Times*, August 6, 2004.

56 Samuelson, R.J., 'How Airbus eclipsed Boeing', *Washington Post*, June 26, 2003.

57 Done, K., 'Airbus in a spin as investors punish delays', *Financial Times*, June 15, 2006.

58 Collins, J., *Good to Great: Why Some Companies Make the Leap . . . and Others Don't*, Random House, New York, 2001, pp. 110 & 112.

59 Norris, F., 'Tangled balance sheets? Fannie Mae can rebound', *International Herald Tribune*, December 18 & 19, 2004.

60 http://www.treas.gov/press/releases/js4065.htm.

61 Bowe, C., 'The big defence challenge', *Financial Times*, April 21, 2005.

62 Bowe, C., 'Criminal investigation hits Merck', *Financial Times*, November 9, 2004.

63 Simons, J., and Stipp, D., 'Will Merck survive Vioxx?', *Fortune*, November 1, 2004.

64 Bowe. C., 'The man who has to shake up Merck', *Financial Times*, March 27, 2006.

65 http://www.indsp.org/MMispep/php.

66 Stern, S., 'How consultancies grabbed management's ear', *Financial Times*, June 21, 2006.

67 Byrne, J.A., 'White knights and grey areas', *The Business*, July 21 & 23, 2002; 'Ahold out', *Economist*, March 1, 2003.

68 'Judge sets date for Enron trial', *Financial Times*, February 25, 2005; 'The rogues checklist', *Evening Standard*, March 4, 2005.

69 Parker, A., 'Andersen settles with Worldcom investors', *Financial Times*, April 26, 2005.

70 London, S., and Bradshaw, D., 'Shredded credibility? The MBA industry may be facing a shakeout', *Financial Times*, April 29, 2005.

71 Keller, *Rude Awakening*, op. cit., p. 181.

72 Drucker, *The Practice of Management*, op. cit., p. 274.

73 Chaikin, A., *A Man on the Moon: The Voyages of the Apollo Astronauts*, Penguin, London, 1998, p. 58.

74 http://history.msfc.nasa.gov/vonbraun/bio.html.

75 http://history.msfc.nasa.gov/milestones/chpt7.pdf.

76 http://www.medaloffreedom.com/JamesWebb.htm.

77 Griffith, V., and Cookson, C., 'Troubled Hubble reveals tensions', *Financial Times*, July 30, 2004.

78 The Presidential Commission on the Space Shuttle Challenger Accident Report, June 6, 1986, pp. 40 & 70–81.

79 Gibson, J.P., 'Software engineering and ethics: When code goes bad', Department of Computer Science, NUI, Maynooth, February, 2003.

80 'Safely into harbour', *Economist,* October 25, 2001.

81 'NASA, back into the frying pan', *New York Times*, February 27, 1994.

82 Wong, E., 'Supervisor at shuttle plant cites pressure over repairs', *New York Times*, March 4, 2003.

83 Leary, W.E., 'NASA chief disputes idea that space shuttle was hopeless', *New York Times*, March 1, 2003.

84 Keough, D., 'Ten commandments for losing', letter to W. Hopper from Coca-Cola, October 25, 1993.

85 http://www.nasa.gov/about/highlights/griffin_bio.html.

86 Leary, W.E., 'In opposing launching, 2 NASA officials feared shuttle's loss, not crew safety', *New York Times*, June 22, 2006.

87 Nightingale, F., *Notes on Nursing: What it Is and What it Is Not*, D. Appleton & Co., New York, 1860, p. 18.

Chapter 13

1 Drucker, *The Practice of Management*, op. cit., p. 10.

2 http://www.hbs.edu/about/htmltimeline.html.

3 http//dallas.bizjournals.com/dallas/stories/2002/01/21/daily30.html.

4 Edgecliffe-Johnson, op. cit.

5 http://www.clemmer.net/excerpts/three_basic.shtml.

6 Marcus, op. cit., p. 64.

7   *Fortune*. April 5, 1993.

8   'MBA programmes: Back to business school', *Economist*, October 27, 2001; *Which MBA?*, Economist Intelligence Unit, London, 2001.

9   Maslow, A.H., *The Psychology of Science, a Reconnaissance,* Harper & Row, New York, 1966.

10 See http://www.gemba.com/glossary.htm.

11 Marcus, op. cit., pp. 57 & 58.

12 Muggeridge, G., 'Energising with e-business', *Financial Times*, May 23, 2001.

13 'An interview with Henry Mintzberg', *Economist*, November 2, 2001.

14 Skapinker, M., 'An MBA in the wrong hands can be a lethal weapon', *Financial Times*, March 31, 2004.

15 London, S. and Bradshaw, D., 'Shredded credibility? The MBA industry may be facing a shakeout', *Financial Times*, April 29, 2005.

16 Hubbard, G., 'Do not undervalue the impact of business education', *Financial Times*, June 29, 2006.

17 http://www.rediff.com/money/2000/sep/29suman.htm.

18 Ghoshal, S., 'Business schools share the blame for Enron', *Financial Times*, July 17, 2003.

19 Skapinker, M., 'It is time to knock shareholder value off its pedestal', *Financial Times*, February 23, 2005.

20 'Business Schools: Bad for business?', *Economist*, February 19, 2005.

21 Mintzberg, H., *Managers not MBAs: A Hard Look at the Soft Practice of Managing and Management Development*, FT-Prentice Hall, London, 2004, p. xii.

22 Skapinker, M. 'Inside track: A split sense of purpose', *Financial Times*, September 18, 2002.

23 Copeland, M.T., *And Mark an Era: The Story of the Harvard Business School*, Little, Brown, Boston, 1958, pp. 6 & 7.

24 'But can you teach it?', *Economist*, Special Report: Business Schools, May 20, 2004.

25 http://www.cgu.edu/pages/281.asp.

26 Cruikshank, J.L., *A Delicate Experiment: The Harvard Business School 1908–1945*, HBS Press, Boston, 1987, p. 34 (see also Copeland, op. cit., p. 7).

27 Cruikshank, op. cit., pp. 37 & 38.

28 Schlesinger, A., *A Life in the Twentieth Century*, Houghton Mifflin, Boston, 2000, p. 221. (In this book, Schlesinger reminds us of the observation made by the philosopher G.E. Moore on reading Wittgenstein's *Tractatus Logico-Philosophicus*: 'This is a work of genius but otherwise it satisfies the requirements of a Ph.D.').

29 Copeland, op. cit., p. 148, emphasis added.

30 Cruikshank, op. cit., p. 40.

31 Wren, op. cit., p. 119.

32 Copeland, op. cit., p. 80.

33 Ibid., p. 78.

34 The authors are indebted to Bob Miesonczek for drawing their attention to an unpublished manuscript by Dr. James Lee and to published work by Greenwood and Wrege on this subject (see note 3 on page 294.

35 Copeland, op. cit., p. 242.

36 Gillespie, R., *Manufacturing Knowledge: A History of the Hawthorne Experiments*, Cambridge University Press, Cambridge, 1993 , p. 63 (first published 1991).

37 Lee, J., unpublished manuscript, p. 132.

38 C.W. Protzman, in telephone conversation with Kenneth Hopper.

39 Gillespie, op. cit., p. 198.

40 Drucker, *The Practice of Management*, op. cit., p. 279.

41 Arthur Spinanger, in telephone conversation with K. Hopper in 1980.

42 Gabor, *The Capitalist Philosophers*, op. cit., p. 87.

43 Bradshaw, D., 'A textbook relaunch', *Financial Times*, September 23, 1996.

44 http: //www.netmba.com/strategy/matrix/bcg/.

45 Kay, J., 'A message from Macbeth, and Adam Smith', *Financial Times*, September 25, 2003.

46 'Beyond shareholder value: Survey of capitalism and democracy', *Economist*, June 28, 2003.

47 London, S., 'An uprising against stock arguments', *Financial Times*, August 20, 2002.

48 Mintzberg, H., Simons, R., and Basu, K., 'Beyond selfishness', *MIT Management Review*, Vol. 44, No. 1, Fall 2002.

49 Ghoshal, S., 'Business schools share the blame for Enron', *Financial Times*, July 17, 2003.

50 Stout, L., 'Shareholders should not always come first', *Financial Times*, March 28, 2005.

51 Roberts D., Parkes, C., and Grant, J., 'Bottled up: US transport infrastructure feels the strain of growing global trade', *Financial Times*, November 16, 2004.

52 Wright, R., 'Eurostar seeks a speedy transformation', *Financial Times*, September 25, 2003.

53 Although from a terminal that is inconveniently far from the city center.

54 Dunne, M.J., 'In China, it's hurry up and wait', *International Herald Tribune*, December 17, 2004.

55 Dickie, M., 'China paves way for first foreign-owned rail track', *Financial Times*, June 15, 2005.

56 Sobell, R., *When Giants Stumble*, Prentice Hall, New York, 1999, p. 204.

57 http://www.buyandhold.com/bh/en/education/history/2001/the_collapse_of_penn_central.

58 http://www.trainweb.org/pt/pc.html.

59 Grant, J., 'Ageing US rail network is stuck in one-track world', *Financial Times*, September 13, 2004.

60 Ward, A., 'US freight customers rail against delays from outdated tracks', *Financial Times*, May 10, 2006.

61 Chandler, A.D., *Inventing the Electronic Century*, Harvard University Press, Cambridge, MA, 2001, p. xii.

62 Skapinker, M., 'Inside track: A split sense of purpose', *Financial Times*, September 18, 2002.

63 Larson, M.J., 'Practically academic: Forming British business schools in the 1960s', Business History Conference, 2004, http://www.thebhc.org.

64 Nakamoto, M., 'Hitachi faces turbine claims', *Financial Times*, August 3, 2006. See also Nakamoto, M., 'Battery trouble hinders Sony's bid for brand supremacy', *Financial Times*, August 26–27, 2006.

65 Knight, R., 'New Harvard Business School dean to focus on globalisation', *Financial Times*, April 25, 2006.

66 London, S., and Bradshaw, D., 'Shredded credibility? The MBA industry may be facing a shakeout', *Financial Times*, April 29, 2005.

67 Merritt, J., 'MBA applicants are MIA', *BusinessWeek*, April 18, 2005.

Chapter 14

1 Powell, C., with Persico, J.E., *My American Journey*, Ballantine, New York, 1995. p. 213.

2 Ibid., p. 141.

3 Servan-Schreiber, J.-J., *The American Challenge*, Athenaeum, New York, 1968, p. 75.

4 Powell with Persico, op. cit., p. 142.

5 Ibid., p. 100.

6 Scheffer, D., 'Timely insights into the arrogance of power', *Financial Times*, October 13, 2004.

7 Harding, J., 'Reporters who get Iraq story from inside and outside', *Financial Times*, May 18, 2004.

8 Powell with Persico, op. cit., p. 141.

9 Ibid., p. 100.

10 'General William Westmoreland. Obituary', *Economist*, July 30, 2005.

11 Powell with Persico, op. cit., pp. 139 & 141.

12 Halberstam, D., *The Best and the Brightest*, Ballantine, New York, 1992, p. 622 (first published 1969).

13 'American military intervention: Sanctified swords', *Economist*, June 24, 2006, quoting from Preston, A., *The War Council: McGeorge Bundy, the NSC, and Vietnam*, Harvard University Press, Cambridge, MA, 2006.

14 Conversation between the authors and a former senior World Bank official who wishes to remain anonymous, 2005.

15 Mallaby, S., *The World's Banker: A Story of Failed States, Financial Crises and the Wealth and Poverty of Nations*, Yale University Press, London, 2005, p. 36.

16 Johnson, B.T., 'The World Bank and economic growth: 50 years of failure', *The Heritage Foundation*, May 16, 1996.

17 http://www.quoteworld.org.

18 Brooks, D., 'The art of intelligence', *New York Times*, April 2, 2005.

19 Kamarck, E., 'Use probes of Sept. 11 to learn, not blame', *Newsday*, August 26, 2002.

20 Ignatieff, M., 'Who are Americans to think that freedom is theirs to spread?', *New York Times*, June 26, 2005.

21 Dinmore, G., 'Catalogue of errors bedevilled period of occupation', *Financial Times*, January 29 & 30, 2005.

22 'The not-so-quiet American', *Economist*, March 29, 2003, p. 55.

23 http://slate.msn.com/id/2090250/.

24 Wolfle, R., 'Rumsfeld to wage war on Pentagon red tape', *Financial Times*, September 11, 2001.

25 Callahan, op. cit., p. 1.

26 Shlaes, A., 'When progressiveness leads to backwardness', *Financial Times*, October 24, 2000.

27 Callahan, op. cit., p. 103.

28 Ibid., p. 109.

29 Ibid., pp. 256 & 257.

30 http://www.collegeboard.com/student/testing/sat/about/about-FAQ.html.

31 Green, H., 'How the SATs changed America', *BusinessWeek*, October 25, 1999. See also Caldwell, R., 'The stupidity lies in the test', *Financial Times*, September 3, 2006.

32 Arenson, K.W., 'SAT problems even larger than reported', *New York Times*, March 23, 2006.

33 Arenson, K.W., and Henriques, D.B., 'Company's errors on SAT scores raise new qualms about testing', *New York Times*, March 10, 2006.

34 Hayes, D., 'Thousands were given the wrong grades in exams', *Evening Standard*, May 10, 2006.

35 Callahan, op. cit., p. 261.

36 Symonds, W.C., and Miller, R., 'Harvard: Larry Summers has an ambitious agenda to remake the nation's leading university. Can he do it?', *Business-Week*, February 18, 2002.

37 'Economics focus: An eye for an A', *Economist*, March 9, 2002, p. 92.

38 'Grade expectations', *Economist*, March 20, 2004.

39 Ravitch, D., *Left Back: A Century of Failed School Reforms*, Simon & Schuster, New York, 2000, pp. 357 & 358.

40 Ibid., p. 17.

41 Cunningham, A., 'Baccalauréate begins to gain momentum', *Financial Times*, February 27 & 28, 2005.

42 'Graduating Harpo', *Economist*, February 19, 2005.

43 'Good ingredients, badly cooked', *Economist*, June 26, 2004.

44 Wolf. A., *Does Education Matter? Myths about Education and Economic Growth*, Penguin, London, 2002, p. 139.

45 'Proof of learning at college', *New York Times*, February 26, 2006.

46 'Baltimore's disgrace: Its public schools are an educational disaster area', *Washington Post*, April 10, 2006.

47 Lloyd, J., 'Danger, iconoclast at work', *FTmagazine*, March 11–12, 2006.

48 Taylor, C., 'It's a Wiki, Wiki world', *Time*, July 18, 2005.

49 'A university for homeschoolers', *Economist*, February 26, 2004.

50 Kirkpatrick, D.D., 'School rules, from VH1 to hand-holding', *New York Times*, March 8, 2004.

51 Hamilton, J.O., 'A shadow in the valley', *BusinessWeek*, October 29, 2001.

52 'Any colour, provided it's purple', *The Business*, September 21 & 22, 2003.

53 Luce, E., 'A tiger trapped by its pride', *Financial Times*, February 5 & 6, 2005.

54 Cookson, C., 'The invention house in the east', *Financial Times*, June 12, 2005.

55 McNealy, S., 'The advantages of the global village', *Financial Times*, June 8, 2006.

56 Johnson, L.B., article in *Management Review*, American Management Association, June 1966, pp. 4–8.

57 Shanahan, E., 'Braking of boom is pledged by U.S. Treasury Chief "disturbed" by plant outlays – calls the administration resolute', *New York Times*, March 15, 1969.

58 Dale, E.L. 'How investment fuels the inflation', *New York Times*, April 6, 1969.

59 'Why Nixon wants to wield the ax', *BusinessWeek*, April 26, 1969.

60 Symonds, W.C. et al., 'Corporate coffers are stuffed with dough', *BusinessWeek*, July 19, 2004.

61 'Survey of current business' US Department of Commerce, November 1962, p. 18. See also K. Hopper, 'Can the U.S. stay competitive?', *American Machinist Special Report*, No. 644, July 27, 1970, p. 70.

62 Servan-Schreiber, op. cit., p. 76.

63 In Britain, two Oxford academic economists, Roger Bacon and Walter Eltis published a book called *Britain's Economic Problem: Too Few Producers*, Macmillan, London, 1976, and four subsequent articles in the London *Sunday Times* that duplicated much of Ken Hopper's earlier research.

64 *Nikkei Business*, October 5, 1970.

65 'Dead last and losing ground', *Wall Street Journal*, December 28, 1971.

66 Brinner, R.E., 'The future of productivity', National Conference for Productivity and Quality of Working Life, Winter 1977, US Govt. Printing Office, p. 56.

67 'A fragile superpower', *Economist*, August 4, 2001.

68 Chote, R., 'An expensive lunch: The political economy of Britain's new monetary framework', *Social Market Foundation*, June, 1997, p. 1.

69 http://www.econlib.org/library/Enc/bios/Friedman.html.

70 On March 23, 2006, the Federal Reserve ceased publishing M3 data.

71 http://www.atm.damtp.cam.ac.uk/people/mem/papers/LHCE/goodhart.html.

72 Kaletsky, A., 'IMF delivers a spectacular recantation of monetarism', *The Times*, September 27, 1996.

73 Kay, J., 'Everyday economics makes for good fun at parties', *Financial Times*, May 2, 2006.

74 Miller, R., 'In Greenspan's shadow', *BusinessWeek*, July 19, 2004.

75 Uchitelle, L., 'After the Fed, exuberance', *New York Times*, March 10, 2006.

76 Rand, A., *Atlas Shrugged*, Random House, New York, 1957, p. 71.

77 http://www.atlasshrugged.tv/book.htm.

78 http://www.aynrand.org/site/PageServer.

79 Ip, G., 'U.S. Fed chief's record is marked by opposition to market regulation', *Wall Street Journal*, November 20 & 21, 2004.

80 Posen, A., 'The economics of a second term', *Financial Times*, November 9, 2004.

81 Noble, H.B., 'Robert Heilbroner, Writer and Economist, Dies at 85', *New York Times*, January 12, 2005.

82 Stern, S., 'It's time for managers to put the cult of the new behind them', *Financial Times*, May 9, 2006.

83 Grauwe, P. de, 'A central banking model for neither gods nor monkeys', *Financial Times*, July 26, 2006.

84 Parsons, C., and Whalen, K., *Eleven Awesome Vermont Women*, SerVermont, Huntington, VT, 2004, p. 49.

85 http://www.ache.org/PUBS/research/demographics.cfm.

86 Donahue, M.P., *Nursing: The Finest Art: An Illustrated History*, Mosby, St. Louis, c. 1996, pp. 456 & 457.

87 Schorr, T.M. with Kennedy, M.S., *100 Years of American Nursing*, Lippincott, New York, 1999, p. 179.

88 Ibid., p. 156.

89 Berens, B.J., 'Nursing mistakes kill, injure thousands: Cost-cutting exacts toll on patients, hospital staffs', *Chicago Tribune*, September 10, 2000.

90 'Cross-national comparisons', *Health Affairs*, Vol. 20, No. 3, May/June, 2001.

91 Nightingale, F., *Notes on Hospitals*, third edition, Longman, Green, London, 1863, p. iii.

92 Nightingale, *Notes on Nursing: What it Is, What it Is Not*, op. cit.

93 Hoffman, J., 'Patients turn to advocates, support groups and e-mail, too', *New York Times*, August 14, 2005.

94 Hamman, H., 'Tennessee healthcare costs catch a cold', *Financial Times*, August 4, 2005.

95 www.cia.gov/cia/publications/factbook/fields/2091.html.

96 Kristof, N.D., 'Health care? Ask Cuba', *New York Times*, January 12, 2005.

97 McCrystal, C., 'Order without restraint', *FTmagazine*, March 12, 2005.

98 Komlos, Dr. J., *Today*, BBC Radio4, 8.15 a.m., June 21, 2005. http://news.bbc.co.uk/1/hi/health/3625031.stm.

99 'Health in America and Britain: Transatlantic rivals', *Economist*, May 6, 2006. The study in question, by Dr. Michael Marmot, refers only to England but the figures for the whole of Britain would not be very different.

100 Cameron, S., 'Lyons pioneer and iconoclast', *Financial Times*, June 2, 2001.

101 Krugman, P., 'Health care confidential', *New York Times*, January 27, 2006.

Chapter 15

1 Uchitelle, L., '107 months and counting', *New York Times*, January 30, 2000.

2 Shelley, P.B., *A Defence of Poetry etc.* Porcupine, London, 1948, p. 50 (originally published 1821).

3 Marx, K., *Das Kapital*, Chapter XXV, 'The general law of capitalist accumulation', London, n.p., 1867 onwards.

4 Lester, R.K., *The Productive Edge: How U.S. Industries are Pointing the Way to a New Era of Economic Growth*, Norton, New York, 1998, p. 41.

5 'Proof of learning at college', *New York Times*, February 26, 2006.

6 Krugman, P., 'The death of Horatio Alger', *The Nation*, January 5, 2004.

7 'Lexington: Minding about the gap', *Economist*, June 11, 2005.

8 Lester, op. cit., p. 36.

9 Ibid., p. 35.

10 http://data.bls.gov/servlet/SurveyOutputServlet. Bureau of Labor Statistics. Major Sector Multifactor Productivity Index.

11 Fels, J., and Pradhan, M., 'Why natural interest rates should not be overlooked', *Financial Times*, February 23, 2006.

12 Madrick, J., *Why Economies Grow: The Forces That Shape Prosperity and How We Can Get Them Working Again*, Basic Books, New York, 2002, p. 29.

13 Ferguson, N., 'The atheist sloth ethic, or why Europeans don't believe in work', *Telegraph*, August 7, 2004.

14 Lester, op. cit., p. 36.

15 'The dragon and the eagle', *Economist*, October 2, 2004.

16 'The burning issue facing America', *Economist*, quoted in *The Week*, January 31, 2006.

17 Pirie, M., 'How the politicians have privatised Keynesianism', *The Business*, August 8 & 9, 2004.

18 Chancellor, E., 'Scandals seem bad now? Just wait', *Wall Street Journal*, May 27 & 28, 2006.

19 'Beyond irrelevance: Why companies' financial structure matters after all', *Economist*, February 11, 2006.

20 Partnoy, F., and Skeel, D., 'Credit derivatives play a dangerous game', *Financial Times*, July 17, 2006.

21 *Shareownership 2000*, Special Report, New York Stock Exchange, New York, 2000.

22 Gapper, J., 'Keeping it in the family is good for the business', *Financial Times*, September 30, 2003.

23 Ritter, G., *Goldbugs and Greenbacks: The Antimonopoly Tradition and the Politics of Finance in America*, Cambridge University Press, New York, 1997, p. 9.

24 Colvin, G., 'A concise history of management hooey', *Fortune*, June 28, 2004.

25 Skapinker, M., 'The skill of designing a pay-off', *Financial Times*, July 30, 2004.

26 'In praise of the unspeakable', *Economist*, July 20, 2002.

27 Skapinker, M., 'CEO: (n) greedy liar with personality disorder', *Financial Times*, July 2, 2003; Partnoy, F., 'Investing in fantasy land', *Financial Times*, December 28, 2005.

28 Tocqueville, op. cit., p. 596.

29 Putnam, op. cit., p. 263.

30 'Fortress suburbia', *The Business*, October 13, 2001.

31 'Where have all the homeless gone?', *Economist*, August 14, 2004.

32 Putnam, op. cit., p. 329.

33 Ibid., p. 193.

34 Bennett, W.J., *The Index of Leading Cultural Indicators: American Society at the End of the 20th Century*, Broadway, New York, 1999, p. 4.

35 Putnam, op. cit., p. 188.

36 Orange, R., 'The world needs more people', *The Business*, February 6 & 7, 2005.

37 See also 'Total fertility rates and birth rates, by age of mother and rate: United States 1940–99', National Center for Health Statistics, p. 1, http://www.cdc.gov/nchs/data/statab/t991x07.pdf.

38 http://www.cbsnews.com/stories/2002/02/12/health/main329154 .shtml.

39 'Centrifugal forces', *Economist*, July 16, 2005.

40 http://www.npg.org.popfacts/htm.

Chapter 16

 1 Dobyns, L., and Crawford-Mason, C., *Quality or Else: The Revolution in World Business*, Houghton Mifflin, Boston, 1991, *passim*. Hall, A., 'A champion for quality', *Kybiz.com*, April, 1999.

 2 Gabor, *The Capitalist Philosophers*, op. cit., p. 193.

 3 Ibid., p. 194.

 4 http://www.deming.org/theman/biography/html.

 5 Email dated June 9, 2003 from Dr. Deming's son-in-law, Bill Radcliffe, to W. Hopper.

 6 Gabor, *The Capitalist Philosophers*, op. cit.

 7 Neave, op. cit., p. 53.

 8 Sarasohn, H., 'CCS – an agency for change', paper delivered to a seminar at Embassy of Japan in London. December 13, 1995, p. 13.

 9 Given, op. cit., p. 112.

10 Bacon, *Essays: Of Great Place*.

11 Given, op. cit., p. 23.

12 Drucker, *The Practice of Management*, op. cit., p. 264.

13 http://www.workindex.com/editorial/whar/whar02023-02.asp. See also Kellaway, L., 'Don't try this at home', *Financial Times*, September 24, 2001.

14 McGregor, J., 'The struggle to measure performance', *BusinessWeek*, January 9, 2006.

15 Greene, J., 'Troubling exits at Microsoft', *BusinessWeek*, September 26, 2005.

16 *Who's Who in British History*, Collins & Brown, London, 2000, p. 132.

17 Deming, W.E., 'Foreword', to Sherkenbach, W.W., *Deming's Road to Continual Improvement*, SPC Press, Knoxville, TN, 1991, p. vii.

18 Gabor, *The Capitalist Philosophers*, op. cit., p. 199.

19 Lewis, C.I., *The Mind and the World Order: Outline of a Theory of Knowledge*, Dover, New York, 1929.

20 Kilian, C.S., *The World of W. Edwards Deming*, Second Edition, SPC Press, Knoxville, TN, 1992, p. 90.

21 Hammer, M., 'Reengineering work: Don't automate, obliterate', *Harvard Business Review*, July–August, 1990.

22 Given, op. cit., p. 33.

23 Hammer, op. cit., p. 4.

24 Hammer, H., and Champy, J., *Reengineering the Corporation: A Manifesto for Business Revolution*, Nicolas Brealey, London, 2001, p. 52 (first published in 1993 by HarperBusiness, New York).

25 Newton, I., letter to Robert Hooke, 1676. www.historyguide.org.

26 Hammer, *Reengineering the Corporation*, op. cit., p. 17.

27 Sloan, Jr., A.P., *My Years with General Motors*, edited by John McDonald with Catherine Stevens, Currency Doubleday, New York, 1990, pp. 140 & 142 (first published 1963).

28 Sloan, op. cit., p. ix.

29 Farber, D., *Sloan Rules: Alfred P. Sloan and the Triumph of General Motors*, University of Chicago Press, Chicago, 2002, p. 58.

30 Sloan, op. cit., p. xix.

31 Gabor, *The Capitalist Philosophers*, op. cit., p. 187.

32 Champy, J., *Reengineering Management: The Mandate for New Leadership*, HarperBusiness, New York, 1995, p. 1.

33 Byrne, J., 'Reengineering: What happened?', *BusinessWeek*, January 30, 1995.

34 Hammer, 'Reengineering work: Don't automate, obliterate', op. cit., p. 2.

35 Hammer, M., *The Agenda: What Every Business Must Do to Dominate the Decade*, Crown, New York, 2001, p. 15.

36 Deming, W.E., *Out of the Crisis*, MIT Center for Advanced Engineering Study, Cambridge, MA, 1986.

Chapter 17

1 Waters, R., 'Computing pioneer with a wide influence', *Financial Times*, December 24, 2005.

2 Madrick, op. cit., pp. 101 & 102.

3 'Confucianism: New fashion for old wisdom', *Economist*, January 21, 1993.

4 Mallet, V., 'Japan's best chance to strike a deal with China', *Financial Times*, September 27, 2006.

5 'Taiwan's missing links', *Financial Times*, March 28, 2006.

6 Hille, K., 'Taiwan "kills a monkey" but this could force others to flee', *Financial Times*, January 11, 2006.

7 Email from Sinolinks to Will Hopper dated February 25, 2006.

8 Hille, K., 'Taiwan tycoon puts his money where his home is', *Financial Times*, August 3, 2006.

9 Pan, P.P., and Pomfret, J., 'Vice President Hu ascends to top post in sweeping transfer of power', *Washington Post*, November 15, 2002.

10 http://www.commerce.gov/bios/evans_bio.html.

11 Engardio, P., 'Engineering: Is the U.S. really falling?', *BusinessWeek*, December 27, 2005.

12 Kuhn, R.L., 'A problem of perception: Why China and the U.S. aren't on the same page', *BusinessWeek*, April 24, 2006.

13 Jonquieres, G. de, 'The myth behind China as a high-tech colossus', *Financial Times*, January 25, 2005.

14 Dickie, M., 'China poised to make breakthrough in generating "meltdown-proof" N-power', *Financial Times*, February 8, 2005.

15 'China sets up anti-terror squads as riots spread', *Reuters*, August 17, 2005.

16 Patten, C., 'Saddled with the worst of both worlds', *Financial Times*, June 12, 2006.

17 Redding, G., 'China: Rough but ready for outsiders', *Financial Times*, August 26, 2003.

18 Sull, D., 'Emerging markets give flight to new industry champions', *Financial Times*, August 5, 2005.

19 'Spreading their wings: While all eyes are on foreign investments in China, the country's companies are busily buying up assets overseas', *Economist*, September 6, 2003; and Nakamoto, M., 'How to turn the tables on outsourcing', *Financial Times*, January 6, 2005.

20 Wolf, M., 'Though precedents are ominous, China's rise to greatness need not bring conflict', *Financial Times*, September 15, 2005.

21 Gokhale, J., and Smetters, K., *Fiscal and Generational Imbalances: New Budget Measures for New Budget Priorities*, AEI Press, Washington, DC, 2003; Tyson, L.D., 'The White House is no place for voodoo accounting', *BusinessWeek*, September 23, 2002.

22 Ferguson, N., and Kotlikoff, L., 'The fiscal overstretch that will undermine an empire', *Financial Times*, July 15, 2003.

23 Mandel, M.J., 'Is America broke?', *BusinessWeek*, August 30, 2004.

Part V

1 Useem, op. cit.

2 The authors have written to the chairman of the new AT&T and to the Mayor of New York suggesting that the statue be restored to its former place of honor atop 195 Broadway as part of the the reconstruction of the area in which the World Trade Center was located.

Chapter 18

1 http://data.bls.gov/servlet/SurveyOutputServlet. Arithmetic average of annual figures for 1948 to 1969, 1970 to 1995 and 1996 to 2000, downloaded from US Bureau of Labor Statistics on June 30, 2003.

2 Madrick, op. cit., p. 115. Much of the data in this chapter has been drawn from this book.

3 'ABC News anchor is badly injured by bomb in Iraq', *New York Times*, January 30, 2006.

4 Sennett, R., 'Middle-aged, middle-class, stranded by the "new economy" ', *Financial Times*, March 7, 2006.

5 'Increase in illegal immigrants to US', *Financial Times*, March 8, 2006.

6 Thomson, A., 'Tension over migrants puts walls around US democracy', *Financial Times*, February 11 & 12, 2006.

7 Kay, J., *National Accounting for the New Economy*, www.johnkay.com, London, 2001, p. 23. See also: 'The new "new economy"', *Economist*, September 11, 2003.

8 Wensink, S., 'Setting the record straight on European Growth', *BusinessWeek*, March 24, 2003.

9 Giles, C., 'In pursuit of the wealth of nations', *Financial Times*, January 25, 2006.

10 Madrick, op. cit., p. 144.

11 Gongloff, M., 'Productivity: Miracle or mirage?', *CNN Money Magazine*, October 13, 2003.

12 Roach, S., 'The productivity paradox', *New York Times*, November 30, 2003.

13 Beattie, A., 'Seeking employment: Why economic recovery without creating jobs spells electoral danger for George W. Bush', *Financial Times*, July 29, 2003.

14 'Incredible shrinking countries', *Economist*, January 7, 2006.

15 Weale, M., 'Statistics users also need reliability data', *Financial Times*, October 8, 2004.

16 Swann, C., 'Americans cut back on saving to spend', *Financial Times*, August 3, 2005.

17 Balls, A., 'Current account deficit "poses risk to US economy" ', *Financial Times*, October 7, 2004.

18 'Scares ahead: Can the world economy sustain its stunning pace of growth?', *Economist*, October 2, 2004.

19 M. Tribus, email to W. Hopper, September 25, 2005.

20 Shlaes, A., 'It's OK to say that women are from Venus', *Financial Times*, January 24, 2005; Traub, J., 'Harvard radical', *New York Times*, August 24, 2003.

21 Symonds, W., with Bernstein, A., 'No longer most likely to succeed: Larry Summers' bold reform plan for Harvard could be derailed', *BusinessWeek*, March 7, 2005.

22 Kulish, N., 'Things fall apart: Fixing America's crumbling infrastructure', *New York Times*, August 23, 2006.

23 Pérez-Peña, R., and Wald, M.L., 'Blackout report blames Ohio utility', *New York Times*, November 20, 2003.

24 Conversation between W. Hopper and a former senior executive of a leading electric utility company who wishes to remain anonymous.

25 Beales, R., and Roberts, D., 'Little light on tangle of electricity grid', *Financial Times*, August 13, 2004.

26 Immelt, J., 'Business demands a consistent approach to energy', *Financial Times*, June 29, 2005.

27 Sterlicchi, J., 'BNFL in pole position for US nuclear revival', *Evening Standard*, April 28, 2005.

28 Shlaes, A., 'America must exorcise its nuclear demons', *Financial Times*, April 25, 2005.

29 Smith, R., 'Faults still plague electric system', *Dow Jones Newswires*, April 13, 2004.

Chapter 19

1 Powell with Persico, op. cit., pp. 144 & 145.

2 Fowler, D., 'Operation poetry', *FTmagazine*, May 21, 2005.

3 http://ge.com.

4 Webb, J., 'Caspar Willard Weinberger', *Wall Street Journal*, March 31, 2006.

5 Sevastopulo, D., 'Military calls intensify for Rumsfeld to go', *Financial Times*, April 13, 2006.

6   'When deadly force bumps into hearts and minds', *Economist*, January 1, 2005.

7   Collins, T., 'Iraq on the slide: Is there time to save it?', *Sunday Telegraph*, September 18, 2005.

8   McMaster, H.R., *Dereliction of Duty: Lyndon Johnson, Robert McNamara, the Joint Chiefs of Staff, and the Lies that Led to Vietnam*, HarperCollins, New York, c. 1997. See also Shanker, T., and Schmitt, E., 'Young officers join the debate over Rumsfeld', *New York Times*, April 23, 2006.

9   Lipton, E., 'Nominations made for top post at FEMA and three other slots', *New York Times*, April 7, 2006.

10 Useem, op. cit.

11 Robert, D., 'General Electric: Immelt waives bonus in favour of shares', *Financial Times*, March 4 & 5, 2006.

12 Durman, P., 'Brit is the catalyst for growth at GE', *Sunday Times*, April 17, 2005.

13 Roberts, D., and Harney, A., 'GE acquires IDX for $1.2bn', *Financial Times*, September 30, 2005.

14 'Feeling the heat', *Economist*, May 14, 2005.

15 'Learn as you churn', *Economist*, April 8, 2006.

16 Former Nieman Marcus exec Stanley Marcus dies', *Dallas Business Journal*, January 23, 2002.

17 'AG Lafley: Procter & Gamble', *Fortune*, August 9, 2004.

18 Lloyd, J.S., 'How can I help you?', *FTmagazine*, February 4 & 5, 2006.

19 'Mr Lafley's makeover', *Economist*, March 20, 2003.

20 Buckley, N.A.G., 'Lafley: The calm reinventor', *Financial Times*, January 30 & 31 2005.

21 Brooker, K., 'Procter & Gamble: The Un-CEO', *Fortune*, September 3, 2002.

22 'A post-modern proctoid: A.G. Lafley has made Procter & Gamble great again. But commodity hell is never far from his mind', *Economist*, April 15, 2006.

23 Richards, B., and Yacob, F., 'Marketers' stealth on the web will not pay for long', *Financial Times*, May 26, 2006.

24 Catan, T., 'A subtler force at the top of Exxon Mobil', *Financial Times*, April 24, 2006.

25 'Biggest companies', *Fortune*, April 17, 2006.

26 Kirkpatrick, D., 'IBM shares its secrets', *Fortune*, September 5, 2005.

27 Donofrio, Hinton Lecture, op. cit., p. 25. http://www.raeng. org.uk/news/publications/ingenia/issue22/Donofrio.pdf.

28 Cane, A., 'The chips are up at IBM', *Financial Times*, January 21, 2005.

29 Kirkpatrick, D., 'The 9-in-1 wonder chip', *Fortune*, September 5, 2005.

30 Hamm, S., 'LINUXINC', *BusinessWeek*, January 31, 2005.

31 Guthrie, J., 'The Franklin way to start a business', *Financial Times*, January 18, 2006.

32 Byrnes, N., 'The art of motivation', *BusinessWeek*, May 1, 2006.

33 Knight, C.F., with Dyer, D., *Performance without Compromise: How Emerson Consistently Achieves Winning Results*, Harvard Business School Press, Boston, MA, c. 2005. See also Marsh, P., 'Growth strategy: When boring beats buccaneering', *Financial Times*, June 7, 2006.

34 Ward, A., 'Profits soar on freight volumes', *Financial Times*, April 27, 2006.
35 http://www.sec.gov/spotlight/soxcomp/bios/biojthain.pdf.
36 Wighton, D., Wells, D. and Postelnicu, A., 'Wall Street's cool hand', *Financial Times*, April 30, 2005.
37 Moore, S., 'The *Journal* interview with Charles Koch: Private Enterprise', *Wall Street Journal*, May 8, 2006.
38 Miller, P.W.B., 'Quarterly reports', *Fortune*, May 15, 2006.
39 Guerrera, F., 'GE plays it straight to a tough audience', *Financial Times*, July 31, 2006.
40 Prystay, C., 'In math-strapped U.S., Singapore's curriculum multiplies in popularity', *Asian Wall Street Journal*, December 13, 2004.
41 Colvin, G., 'The 97-pound weakling', *Fortune*, Vol. 152, No. 3, Europe Edition, August 8, 2005.
42 Bruno, L., 'More universities are going SAT-optional', *U.S. News & World Report*, April 6, 2006.
43 'The glue of society', *Economist*, July 16, 2005.
44 http://www.wesleymission.org.au/ministry/sermons/21church.asp.
45 'A grand entrance to New York', *New York Times*, May 29, 2006.
46 Martin, J., 'Democrat responsible for one of the best put-downs in political history', *Financial Times*, May 24, 2006.
47 Ratner, S., 'America's demands outstrip its willingness to pay up', *Financial Times*, October 7, 2005.
48 Sydhoff, B., 'A time of redress for torture victims', *Financial Times*, January 28 & 29, 2006.
49 Johnson, S., 'Size of US deficit hurts dollar', *Financial Times*, March 15, 2006.
50 'World economy: A call to action', *Economist*, April 14, 2005.
51 Plender, J., 'The foreign perspective on US guns and butter', *Financial Times*, October 3, 2005.
52 Stelzer, I., 'Bush selects a winning team for the US economy', *Sunday Times*, June 4, 2006.
53 'Wall Street's Mr Big', *Economist*, June 3, 2006.
54 Weber, J., 'The leadership factory', *BusinessWeek*, June 12, 2006.
55 White, B., and Kliment, A., 'Hank Paulson: Titan in the treasury', *Financial Times*, June 2, 2006.
56 'New Jersey: All bets are off', *Economist*, July 8, 2006.
57 Grant, J., 'Futures regulator fosters closer links abroad', *Financial Times*, July 19, 2006.
58 Cohen, N., 'Ex-Goldman man chosen as LCH Clearnet chief', *Financial Times*, July 21, 2006.
59 Kay, J., 'Take the politics out of fiscal policy', *Financial Times*, February 27, 2003.
60 Coggan, P., 'No sign of an apocalypse now', *Financial Times*, October 17, 2004.
61 'Economics focus: Steering by a faulty compass', *Economist*, February 26, 2005.

Appendix

1 Email from C. Protzman III to W. Hopper, August 26, 2006.
2 Minzberg, H., *The Nature of Managerial Work*, HarperCollins, New York, 1973, p. 96.
3 Given, op. cit., p. 151.
4 Drucker, *The Practice of Management*, op. cit., p. 173.
5 Harwood, F.M. (ed.), *Classics in Management*, American Management Association, New York, 1960, p. 222.
6 'Good management: The heart of the business', *Economist*, June 11, 2005.
7 Grove, op. cit., p. 71.
8 Drucker, *The Practice of Management*, op. cit., p. 186.
9 Ibid., p. 174 (the quotation in question was taken by Drucker from an article in the April 1954 issue of *Harper's Bazaar*).

Bibliography

Amory, C., *Who Killed Society?*, Harper, New York, 1960.

Andrews, C.M., *The Colonial Period of American History*, Volume 1, Yale University Press, New Haven, CT, 1936.

Bacon, F., *Essays*, first published 1625.

Bacon, F., *The New Organon*, first published 1620.

Bennett, W.J., *The Index of Leading Cultural Indicators: American Society at the End of the 20th Century*, Broadway, New York, 1999.

Bremer, F.J., *John Winthrop: America's Founding Father*, Oxford University Press, Oxford, 2003.

Callahan, R.E., *Education and the Cult of Efficiency: A Study of the Social Forces that have shaped the Administration of the Public Schools*, University of Chicago Press, Chicago, 1962.

Chaikin, A., *A Man on the Moon: The Voyages of the Apollo Astronauts*, Penguin, London, 1998.

Champy, J., *Reengineering Management: The Mandate for New Leadership*, HarperBusiness, New York, 1995.

Chandler, A.D., *The Visible Hand: The Managerial Revolution in American Business,* Harvard University Press, Cambridge, MA, 1997 (first published 1977).

Chandler, A.D., *Scale and Scope. The Dynamics of Industrial Capitalism*, Harvard University Press, Harvard, 1990.

Chandler, A.D., and Hikino, T., 'The Large Industrial Enterprise', in Chandler, A.D., Amatori, F., and Hokino, T. (eds), *Big Business and the Wealth of Nations*, Cambridge, Cambridge University Press, 1997.

Chandler Jr., A.D. and Salsbury, S., *Pierre S. Du Pont and the Making of the Modern Corporation*, BeardBooks, Washington, 2000.

Chase, S., Ruttenberg, S.H., and Given, W.B., *The Social Responsibility of Management*, New York University, New York, 1950.

Chernow, R., *Alexander Hamilton*, Penguin Press, New York, 2004.

Cobden, R., *England, Ireland and America*, Institute for the Study of Human Issues, Philadelphia, 1980 (first published 1835).

Collins, J., *Good to Great: Why Some Companies Make the Leap . . . and Others Don't*, Random House, New York, 2001.

Collins, J.C., and Porras, J.I., *Built to Last: Successful Habits of Visionary Companies*, Random House, New York, 2000 (first published 1994).

Copeland, M.T., *And Mark an Era: The Story of the Harvard Business School*, Little, Brown, Boston, 1958.

Cringely, R.X., *Accidental Empires: How the Boys from Silicon Valley Make Their Millions, Battle Foreign Competition and Still Can't Get a Date*, Penguin, London, 1992.

Crozier, M., 'A new rationale for American business', *Daedalus (The Journal of the American Academy of Arts and Sciences)*, Winter, 1969.

Deming, W.E., 'Foreword' to Sherkenbach, William W., *Deming's Road to Continual Improvement*, SPC Press, Knoxville, TN, 1991.

Diamond, J., *Collapse: How Societies Choose to Fail or Survive*, Penguin/Allen Lane, London, 2005.

Donahue, M.D., *Nursing: The Finest Art*, Mosby, St Louis, 1996.

Drucker, P.F., *The Practice of Management*, Harper Perennial, New York, 1986 (first published 1954).

Drucker, P.F., *The Concept of the Corporation*, Transaction Publishers, New Brunswick, NJ, and London, 1993.

Drucker, P.F., *The Effective Executive*, HarperBusiness, New York, 1993 (first published 1954).

Farber, D., *Sloan Rules: Alfred P. Sloan and the Triumph of General Motors*, University of Chicago Press, Chicago, 2002.

Fischer, D.H., *Albion's Seed: Four British Folkways in America*, Oxford University Press, Oxford, 1989.

Francis, R., *Ann The Word: The Story of Ann Lee, Female Messiah, Mother of the Shakers, the Woman Clothed with the Sun*, Fourth Estate, London, 2001.

Gabor, A., *The Capitalist Philosophers: The Geniuses of Modern Business – Their Lives, Times, and Ideas*, Crown, New York, 2000.

Gibbs-Smith, C.H., *The Great Exhibition of 1851*, Her Majesty's Stationery Office, London, 1981.

Gilbreth, F.B., and Carey E.G., *Cheaper by the Dozen*, Thomas Y. Crewel, New York, 1948.

Gillespie. R., *Manufacturing Knowledge: A History of the Hawthorne Experiment*, Cambridge University Press, Cambridge, 1993 (first published 1991).

Given, W.B., *Bottom-Up Management: People Working Together*, Harper, New York, 1949.

Gokhale, G., and Smetters, K., *Fiscal and Generational Imbalances: New Budget Measures for New Budget Priorities*, AEI Press, Washington, DC, 2003.

Gorham, M., *The Real Book of Great American Journeys*, Garden City Books, New York, 1953.

Green, W., *Famous Fighters of the Second World War*, Hanover House, New York, 1958.

Grove, A., *High Output Management*, Vintage Random House, New York, 1985.

Halberstam, D., *The Best and the Brightest*, Ballantine, New York, 1992 (first published 1969).

Hammer, H., and Champy, J., *Reengineering the Corporation: A Manifesto for Business Revolution*, Nicolas Brealey, London, 2001 (first published in 1993 by HarperBusiness, New York).

Hammer, M., *The Agenda: What Every Business Must Do to Dominate the Decade*, Crown, New York, 2001.

Hart, H.D., *The Oxford Companion to American Literature*, Sixth Edition, Oxford University Press, Oxford, 1995.

Herman, A., *How the Scots invented the Modern World*, Crown, New York, 2001.

Hughes, J., *The Vital Few: American Economic Progress and its Protagonists*, Bantam, Boston, 1967.

Judd, D.I., *Empire: The British Imperial Experience from 1765 to the Present*, Fontana Press, London, 1997.

Kanigel, R., *The One Best Way*, Viking, New York, 1997.

Keller, M., *Rude Awakening: The Rise, Fall and Struggle for Recovery of GM*, Harper Perennial, New York, 1990 (first published 1989).

Keller, M., *Collision: GM, Toyota, Volkswagen and the Race to Own the Twentieth Century*, Doubleday, New York, 1993.

Kilian, C.S., *The World of W. Edwards Deming*, Second Edition, SPC Press, Knoxville, TN, 1992.

Leapman, M., *The World for a Shilling: How the Great Exhibition of 1851 Shaped a Nation*, Headline, London, 2001.

Lester, R.K., *The Productive Edge: How U.S. Industries are Pointing the Way to a New Era of Economic Growth*, Norton, New York, 1998.

Lewis, C.I., *The Mind and the World Order: Outline of a Theory of Knowledge*, Dover, New York, 1929.

Lyons, N., *The Sony Vision*, Crown, New York, 1975.

MacCulloch, D., *Reformation: Europe's House Divided 1490–1700*, Penguin, London, 2004 (first published 2003).

McLynn, F., *Wagons West: The Epic Story of America's Overland Trails*, Cape, London, 2002.

Madrick, J., *Why Economies Grow: The Forces That Shape Prosperity and How We Can Get Them Working Again*, Basic Books, New York, 2002.

Mallaby, S., *The World's Banker: A Story of Failed States, Financial Crises and the Wealth and Poverty of Nations*, Yale University Press, New Haven, CT, 2005.

Marcus, S., *The Viewpoints of Stanley Marcus: A Ten-Year Perspective*, University of North Texas, Denton, TX, 1995.

Marx, K., *The General Law of Capitalist Accumulation*, Part VII: *The Accumulation of Capital*, n.p. London, 1867 onwards.

Micklethwait, J., and Wooldridge, A., *The Company*, Phoenix, London, 2003.

Miller, P., *Errand into the Wilderness*, Harper Jorch Books, New York, 1964.

Mintzberg, H., *The Nature of Managerial Work*, HarperCollins, New York, 1973.

Mintzberg, H., *Managers not MBAs: A Hard Look at the Soft Practice of Managing and Management Development,* FT-Prentice Hall, London, 2004.

Mogensen, A.M., 'How it all started', in Graham, Jr., B.S., and Titus, P.S. (eds), *The Amazing Oversight: Total Participation for Productivity,* Amacom, New York, 1979.

Morgan, W., *An American Icon: Brother Jonathan and American Identity,* Associated University Presses, London, 1988.

Morison, S.E., *Builders of the Bay Colony,* Houghton Mifflin, Boston, 1964.

Morita, A., Reingold, E.M., and Shimomura, M., *Made in Japan,* London, Collins, 1986.

Neave, H.R., *The Deming Dimension,* SPC Press, Knoxville, TN, 1990.

Newcomer, M., *The Big Business Executive,* Columbia University Press, New York, 1955.

Nightingale, F., *Notes on Nursing: What it Is and What it Is Not,* D. Appleton & Co., New York, 1860.

Owen, G., *From Empire to Europe: The Decline and Revival of British Industry Since the Second World War,* HarperCollins, London, 1999.

Packard, D., *The HP Way: How Bill Hewlett and I Built our Company,* HarperBusiness, New York, 1995.

Powell, C., with Persico, J.E., *My American Journey,* Ballantine, New York, 1995.

Putnam, R., *Bowling Alone: The Collapse and Revival of American Community,* Simon & Schuster, New York, 2000.

Ravitch, D., *Left Back: A Century of Failed School Reforms,* Simon & Schuster, New York, 2000.

Ritter, G., *Goldbugs and Greenbacks: The Antimonopoly Tradition and the Politics of Finance in America,* Cambridge University Press, New York, 1997.

Rodger, N.A.M., *The Command of the Ocean,* W.W. Norton, New York, 2005.

Rolt, L.T.C., *Tools for the Job: A Short History of Machine Tools,* B.T. Batsford, London, 1965.

Rosenberg, N., *The American System of Manufactures,* Edinburgh University Press, Edinburgh, 1969.

Rowse, A.L., *The Elizabethans and America: The Trevelyan Lectures at Cambridge, 1959,* Harper & Row, New York, 1965.

Sarasohn, H.M., and Protzman, C.A., *The Fundamentals of Industrial Management: CCS Management Course,* Electronic Edition, Civil Communications Section, GHQ, SCAP, 1993.

Schlesinger, A.M., *A Life in the Twentieth Century,* Houghton Mifflin, New York, 2000.

Schorr, T.M., and Kennedy, S.K., *100 Years of American Nursing,* Lippincott, New York, 1999.

Servan-Schreiber, J.-J., *The American Challenge,* Athenaeum, New York, 1968.

Shelley, P.B., *A Defence of Poetry etc.* Porcupine, London, 1948.

Sloan, Jr., A.P., *My Years with General Motors,* edited by John McDonald with Catherine Stevens, introduction by Peter Drucker, Currency Doubleday, New York, 1990 (first published 1963).

Smith, Merritt Roe, *Harper's Ferry Armory and the New Technology: The Challenge of Change,* Ithaca, NY, Cornell University Press, 1977.

Sobell, R., *When Giants Stumble,* Prentice Hall, New York, 1999.

Stein, S.J., *The Shaker Experience in America: A History of the United Society of Believers,* Yale University Press, New Haven, CT, 1992.

Tawney, R.H., *Religion and the Rise of Capitalism,* Mentor, New York, 1954 (first published 1926).

Taylor, A., *American Colonies: The Penguin History of the United States,* Viking Penguin, New York, 2001.

Taylor, F.W., *The Principles of Scientific Management,* Dover, New York 1998 (first published 1911).

Temin, P., with Galambos, L., *The Fall of the Bell System,* Harvard University Press, Cambridge, MA, 2000.

Temin, P. (ed.), *Engines of Enterprise: An Economic History of New England,* Harvard University Press, Cambridge, MA, 2000.

Tocqueville, A. de, *Democracy in America and Two Essays on America,* translated by G.E. Bevan, Penguin, London, 2003.

Trevor-Roper, H., *Religion, the Reformation and Social Change,* Macmillan, London, 1967.

Walker, H.T., *The Evolution of the American Locomotive, Scientific American* Supplement, May 1, 1897 (Part 2 of 3).

Welch, W., and Byrne, J.A., *Jack: Straight From the Gut,* Headline, London, 2001.

Willison, G. F., *Saints and Strangers,* Reynal & Hitchcock, New York, 1945.

Wolf, A., *Does Education Matter? Myths about Education and Economic Growth,* Penguin, London, 2002.

Wren, D., *The Evolution of Management Thought,* Wiley, New York, 1994.

Selected articles by Kenneth Hopper on the themes of this book, all of which are available at www.puritangift.com.

'Relationships in organizations', *Management* (Journal of the Irish Management Association), October 1960.

'The hosiery and knitwear industry', *Economic Survey of Irish Industry,* December 1962, Committee on Industrial Organization (jointly with E.R. O'Neill and L.B. Leonard).

'Graduate foremen', *Executive Letter,* Harvard Business School, September 1966.

'The growing use of college graduates as foremen', *Management of Personnel Quarterly,* University of Michigan, Summer/Fall 1966, pp. 2–12. (Described as 'of outstanding value' by Dale S. Beach in *Managing People at Work,* (Rensselaer Polytechnic Institute), Macmillan, 1971.

'Graduates on the floor', *Management Today,* October, 1966, pp 74–77.

'The new look in supervision: The trend is toward college men', *Executive's Bulletin*, June 15, 1967.

'Are college graduates better foremen?', *Factory Magazine*, September 1967.

'Engineers take the controls', *Financial Times*, September 13, 1968.

'Production men at the helm', *Financial Times*, January 23, 1969.

'From foreman to company chief', *Financial Times*, February 21, 1969.

'Foremen in the boardroom', *Observer*, March 2, 1969.

'The nature of American management', *Moor Gate and Wall Street*, Fall 1969, pp. 34–51.

'Can the U.S. stay competitive?', *American Machinist Special Report,* no. 644, July 27, 1970 (republished in Japanese, *Nikkei Business*, October 5, 1970).

'Has America turned its back on the factory?', *Innovation*, March 1971, pp. 24–31.

'Tall ships guide: The operating technology of schooners, brigs, barks, barkentines', *Newsday* Weekend Magazine, Bicentennial Edition, June 27, 1976.

'America wakens to productivity', *Nikkei Business,* November 5, 1979, pp. 77–82.

'Sharing Japan's new management', *Japan Times*, December 9, 1979.

'Creating Japan's new industrial management: The Americans as teachers', *Human Resource Management*, University of Michigan, Summer/Fall 1982, pp. 13–34 (republished in Japanese in *Sengyo Kunren*, volumes 338 and 339, 1983 by Nikkeiren, the Japanese Federation of Employers' Associations).

'Quality, Japan, and the U.S.: The first chapter', *Quality Progress*, September 1985, pp. 34–41.

'Fear on the Kanto plain – Thoughts on Japan's industrial miracle', *Shire Trust Newsletter*, Winter 1988/89 pp. 3–4.

Index of Names

Subject Index